THE HISTORY OF LANGUAGE LEARNING AND TEACHING
VOLUME III
ACROSS CULTURES

LEGENDA

LEGENDA is the Modern Humanities Research Association's book imprint for new research in the Humanities. Founded in 1995 by Malcolm Bowie and others within the University of Oxford, Legenda has always been a collaborative publishing enterprise, directly governed by scholars. The Modern Humanities Research Association (MHRA) joined this collaboration in 1998, became half-owner in 2004, in partnership with Maney Publishing and then Routledge, and has since 2016 been sole owner. Titles range from medieval texts to contemporary cinema and form a widely comparative view of the modern humanities, including works on Arabic, Catalan, English, French, German, Greek, Italian, Portuguese, Russian, Spanish, and Yiddish literature. Editorial boards and committees of more than 60 leading academic specialists work in collaboration with bodies such as the Society for French Studies, the British Comparative Literature Association and the Association of Hispanists of Great Britain & Ireland.

The MHRA encourages and promotes advanced study and research in the field of the modern humanities, especially modern European languages and literature, including English, and also cinema. It aims to break down the barriers between scholars working in different disciplines and to maintain the unity of humanistic scholarship. The Association fulfils this purpose through the publication of journals, bibliographies, monographs, critical editions, and the MHRA Style Guide, and by making grants in support of research. Membership is open to all who work in the Humanities, whether independent or in a University post, and the participation of younger colleagues entering the field is especially welcomed.

EDITORIAL BOARD

The History of Language Learning and Teaching

VOLUME III

Across Cultures

❖

EDITED BY

NICOLA MCLELLAND AND RICHARD SMITH

l

LEGENDA

Modern Humanities Research Association

2018

Published by Legenda
an imprint of the Modern Humanities Research Association
Salisbury House, Station Road, Cambridge CB1 2LA

ISBN 978-1-78188-700-4 (HB)
ISBN 978-1-78188-375-4 (PB)

First published 2018

Copy-Editor: Richard Correll

CONTENTS

❖

ACKNOWLEDGMENTS

❖

Every chapter in this collection has been submitted to blind (i.e. anonymized) peer-review by at least two readers. We sincerely thank all those who read and commented on earlier drafts of chapters for their very helpful comments. We also acknowledge gratefully the generous support of the A. S. Hornby Educational Trust and, above all, the support of the Arts and Humanities Research Council network grant that led to the production of these three volumes [AH/J012475/1]. We owe a special debt of gratitude to Louis Cotgrove, our editorial assistant on this project. Finally, we thank the editors at Legenda, in particular Graham Nelson, and our contributors for their commitment and forbearance during the complex process of bringing this three-volume collection to publication.

CHAPTER 1

❖

Comparing Cultural Content in English-Language Textbooks for Germans in the Eighteenth and Nineteenth Centuries

Friederike Klippel

This chapter offers an overview of historical developments in English-language textbooks in Germany with regard to their cultural content from about 1700 to 1900. The analysis of a number of successful textbooks from both centuries shows that culture-general and target-culture-specific contents were common throughout the period under consideration, albeit with varying emphases. However, with the introduction of English as a subject taught at secondary schools in the nineteenth century and the onset of the Reform Movement, information about England and the USA was integrated to a much larger extent.

Introduction

When we look at the historical roots of foreign-language teaching with regard to the cultural content of materials and lessons, we need to consider which kinds of sources are helpful for such a study. Today we might consult articles in academic or pedagogical journals, read monographs on the topic, or we might look at teaching materials. Three hundred years ago not all of those sources were available. Treatises on language teaching were relatively rare — Seidelmann (1724) is an early example — even if the language textbooks of that time quite often contained extensive prefaces in which the authors outlined their ideas on language learning and teaching. Journals dealing with educational matters only began to be published in the late eighteenth century, e.g. in Germany. But textbooks — i.e. grammar books, collections of dialogues and anthologies with texts for reading — have been in use for many centuries (cf. Hüllen 2005: 47–62). They are the historian's most valuable source.

Historical research in the field of language learning and teaching so far has looked at textbooks largely with the intention of analysing the status of language description in them (e.g. Turner 1978) or of discovering their ideas on how to teach language (e.g. Niederländer 1981; Klippel 1994). Some studies give a close description of individual textbooks (e.g. Driedger 1907; Waentig 2002; Hüllen 2005: 47–62); a few authors have studied certain categories of textbooks, e.g. collections of dialogues (cf. Radtke 1994; Franz 2005).

This chapter looks at textbooks of English from the eighteenth and nineteenth centuries from a particular angle, namely that of cultural content, i.e. information and opinions on cultural matters in a wide sense. These may refer to national (culture-specific, i.e. English or American in the case of English-language textbooks) or universal or encyclopaedic aspects. As will be outlined below, cultural content can be found both in texts explicitly dealing with cultural matters as well as in sample sentences illustrating points of language structure. A corpus of over thirty textbooks of English for the two hundred years under consideration was examined for the present chapter. Of this number, roughly one quarter originate in the eighteenth and three quarters in the nineteenth century. This is not a large number considering that according to Konrad Schröder's bibliography (Schröder 1975) more than two thousand textbooks of English (including multiple revised editions, however) were published in Germany before 1900. As is to be expected, not all of those two thousand textbooks are still accessible. Textbooks were, and are, not seen as valuable publications which are carefully kept in libraries and preserved for posterity. Rather, textbooks are intended for practical purposes, useful for a time and after that often discarded. Once replaced by newer and supposedly better textbooks, the old ones are no longer of any interest for the teacher or learner, only for the historian. Therefore not all of the textbooks we know of are still to be found.

Between 1700 and 1900, English became established as a major foreign language in Germany and was made compulsory in *Realschulen* in Prussia in 1859 (Klippel 1994: 288) and in grammar schools throughout Germany in 1900 (Lehberger 2003: 611). These two centuries therefore represent the rise of English, reflected in the growing interest in books, journals and goods from England as well as in travel to England and in the increasing number of people wanting to learn the language, which led to ever more grammar books, text anthologies, manuals for conversation and many other instructional materials being published.

Two Language Teaching Traditions

Tom McArthur's (1991: 12-13) distinction between two different traditions of language learning is compelling for the analysis of cultural content in English textbooks in Germany. He speaks of a 'marketplace tradition' and a 'monastery tradition'. The 'marketplace tradition' refers to traders and travellers learning as much of a foreign language as they need to conduct their business. Their aim is to be able to converse and interact — in modern terminology, they want to communicate successfully. From the Middle Ages onwards the 'monastery tradition' can be seen in the monastic schools and grammar schools, where the classical languages were taught so that the store of knowledge laid down in Latin and Greek writing could be unlocked. Here, the foreign language provides access to learning of a more theoretical, intellectual or religious kind, so that the classical authors and Church Fathers may be understood and translated. With regard to cultural content, the two traditions have different objectives. Traders and travellers, on the one hand, need to know relevant facts (*realia*) about the country or region whose language they are acquiring — information on units of currency, weights, and such matters. They need to be informed about local customs and acceptable forms of social and linguistic behaviour — in short, everyday culture. Their interest in cultural matters is pragmatic rather than theoretical and firmly linked to their communicative objectives. In terms of language, their goals are to achieve comprehensible pronunciation, a sufficiently large subject-specific vocabulary, and pragmatic skills in interaction. Within the monastery tradition, on the other hand, an interest in culture is connected to literature and learned texts in the foreign language and thus to a literary, philosophical or intellectual tradition in which the language learners want to partake. It becomes obvious that the learners' perspective as regards cultural content is quite different in the two traditions.

Cultural Content

When one considers the teaching of culture in language classrooms or in individual tutoring in the past from the teacher's perspective rather than the learners', further aspects become relevant. Teachers and textbook writers make assumptions as to what may be useful or appropriate for learners to know. And these assumptions are based on their own knowledge of the world, of the target culture(s) and the learner's background and goals, as well as on the current thinking of their time. What is considered self-evident and 'normal' in a particular period does not need to be spelled out. Before the last decades of the nineteenth century there was little theoretical reflection on these matters. According to Risager (2007), theoretical debate and reflection on the cultural dimension of language learning and teaching only began in the late nineteenth century within the Reform Movement; from then on one might talk about 'theoretical culture pedagogy' (Risager 2007: 2). However, '[l]anguage teaching has admittedly always had a cultural dimension in terms of content, either universal/encyclopedic or national' (Risager 2007: 4). Yet, it is somewhat difficult to talk about national cultural content for some languages before their nation states had established themselves, e.g. the German-speaking areas before the nineteenth century. Still, the distinction between target culture-specific and culture-general content is an important one.

So far the term 'cultural content' has been used rather loosely. What does 'content' comprise? Risager distinguishes three dimensions for the cultural focus of language teaching: the content dimension, the context dimension, and the poetic dimension (cf. Risager 2007: 8). The first dimension refers to the thematic content of language teaching or materials; the second to information for appropriate language use; and the third to literature as a means for cultural learning. Each of these dimensions may be realized in a more universal or more culture-specific manner. All three dimensions have been relevant to language teaching and learning to different degrees at different times.

Sampling and Questions for Analysis

This investigation concentrates on the two hundred years between 1700 and 1900. As can be seen from Schröder's (1975) bibliography of English-language textbooks in Germany before 1900, many more books were published in the second half, rather than the first half, of the eighteenth century and more again in the nineteenth rather than the eighteenth century. Not all of the textbooks examined can be presented in detail here. A selection needs to be made, to allow both a chronological survey showing a development and a comparison of major features in the textbooks of the eighteenth and nineteenth centuries. I have therefore selected very popular and prototypical as well as a few less common but noteworthy textbooks from the first and the second half of each century for closer analysis. Textbooks not containing any references to cultural matters are disregarded, since it is not my aim to undertake a quantitative survey, but rather to analyse more thoroughly works which carry cultural information.

The analysis focuses on two questions:

(1). Which parts of a textbook carry cultural content and how much is there?

(2). What kinds of cultural content — culture-specific or universal/encyclopaedic — can be distinguished?

The first question may sound simple. However, things are not as straightforward as they seem at first sight. Cultural content can be explicit and in that case easy to discover; but it may also be implicit. Explicit information on the foreign culture may be given in texts or lists, in the preface or in illustrations, i.e. in sections of the textbook which the author has selected or formulated with the express intention of teaching about culture. It should be noted that illustrations only became a feature of language textbooks from the late nineteenth century onwards, starting with the Reform Movement (although Comenius and the educationalists of the Enlightenment had used them, too (cf. Reinfried 1992)). Many authors of the eighteenth century set out their goals and explain the composition of their textbook in a preface; and these prefaces sometimes contain explicit statements as to cultural content, thus presenting the instructor's perspective. Texts may be included in a textbook because they are part of the target culture, as in the case of literature; or because they provide information about, or insights into, the foreign language culture; or, finally, because they are part of a general culture of educated citizens at the time and therefore familiar to the learners, as is the case with Aesop's Fables or the Bible, for example. This last focus is not pursued further here, however. Lists and other factual genres inform the learner of certain circumstances, usages or customs in England. It is also interesting to note which kinds of texts are included, and whether they are original texts, have been adapted, or specially written for the textbook. In order to find explicit cultural information, an analysis of textbooks must therefore include the preface, all texts, lists and illustrations. Explicit cultural content in language textbooks may cover all three domains distinguished by Risager (2007: 8): cultural topics (content); appropriate language use (context); and literary texts from the target culture (poetic).

A NEW
ENGLISH GRAMMAR,
OR A SHORT,
BUT
CLEAR AND SURE
DIRECTION
FOR THE TRUE
PRONUNCIATION, ACCENTUATION
AND
COMPLEAT ACQUISITION
OF THE ENGLISH TONGUE.

Together with

1. The chiefest English Idioms
2. The English Coin, Weight and Measure
3. Several familiar Dialogues.
4. The exquisitest English Proverbs
5. Some elegant and very curious Letters.
6. A short Collection of the Titles, and
7. A Vocabulary of the most needful Words,
In an Alphabetical Order.

BY
THEODORE ARNOULD.

Of joyned Letters Syllables, of Syllables Voices,
Of joyned Voices Sentences and sense.

HANOVER
Printed for NICHOLAS FÖRSTER.
Bookseller of the Court. 1718.

Neue Englische
GRAMMATICA,
Oder kurtzgefaßte,
Jedoch deutliche und sichere
Anweisung
Zur richtigen
Pronunciation, Accentuation und
völligen Begreiffung
der Englischen Sprache.

Nebst

1. Denen vornehmsten Englischen *Idiotismis.*
2. Der Englischen Müntze, Gewicht und Maaß.
3. Allerhand gemeinen Gesprächen.
4. Denen auserlesensten Englischen *Proverbiis.*
5. Einigen zierlichen und sehr *curieusen* Briefen.
6. Einem kurtzen Auszug derer Tituln und Auffschrifften.
7. Und einem Wörter-Buch derer nöthigsten *Partium Orationis,* in einer Alphabetischen Ordnung.

Durch
THEODORUM ARNOLD.

Ex conjunctis Litteris Syllabæ, ex Syllabis Voces,
Ex Vocibus conjunctis sententiæ & sensus.

HANNOVER
Verlegts Nicolaus Förster, Bibl. Aulic.
1718.

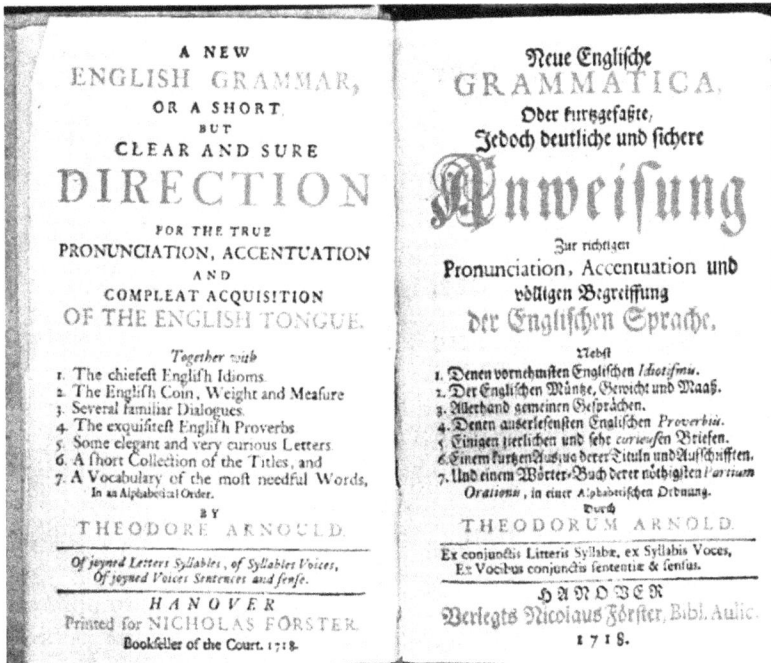

FIG. 1.1. Title page of Arnold (1718)

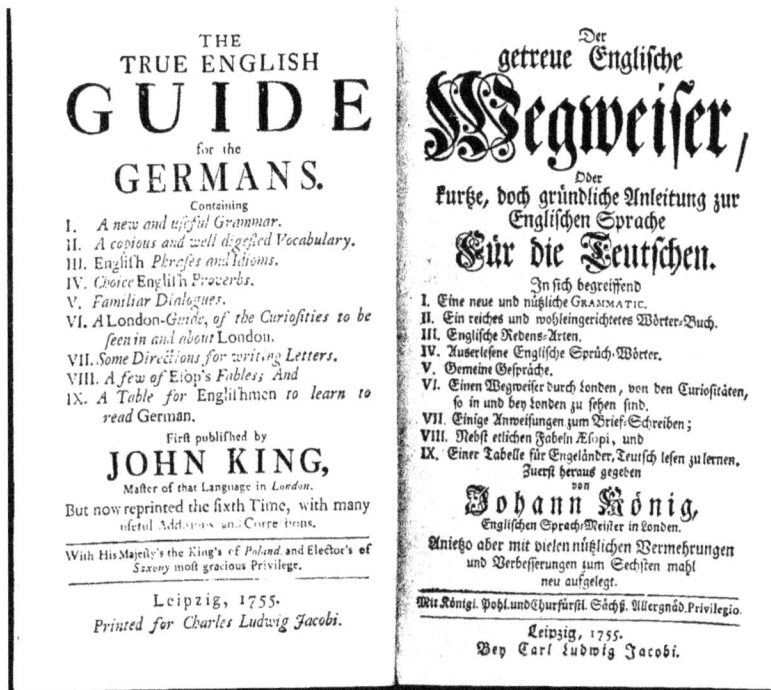

THE
TRUE ENGLISH
GUIDE
for the
GERMANS.

Containing

I. A new and useful Grammar.
II. A copious and well digested Vocabulary.
III. English Phrases and Idioms.
IV. Choice English Proverbs.
V. Familiar Dialogues.
VI. A London-Guide, of the Curiosities to be seen in and about London.
VII. Some Directions for writing Letters.
VIII. A few of Esop's Fables; And
IX. A Table for Englishmen to learn to read German.

First published by
JOHN KING,
Master of that Language in London.

But now reprinted the sixth Time, with many useful Additions and Corrections.

With His Majesty's the King's of Poland and Elector's of Saxony most gracious Privilege.

Leipzig, 1755.
Printed for Charles Ludwig Jacobi.

Der
getreue Englische
Wegweiser,
Oder
kurtze, doch gründliche Anleitung zur
Englischen Sprache
Für die Teutschen.

In sich begreiffend

I. Eine neue und nützliche GRAMMATIC.
II. Ein reiches und wohleingerichtetes Wörter-Buch.
III. Englische Redens-Arten.
IV. Auserlesene Englische Sprüch-Wörter.
V. Gemeine Gespräche.
VI. Einen Wegweiser durch London, von den Curiositäten, so in und bey London zu sehen sind.
VII. Einige Anweisungen zum Brief-Schreiben;
VIII. Nebst etlichen Fabeln Æsopi, und
IX. Einer Tabelle für Engeländer, Teutsch lesen zu lernen.

Zuerst heraus gegeben
von
Johann König,
Englischen Sprach-Meister in London.

Anietzo aber mit vielen nützlichen Vermehrungen und Verbesserungen zum Sechsten mahl neu aufgelegt.

Mit Königl. Pohl. und Churfürstl. Sächß. Allergnäd. Privilegio.

Leipzig, 1755.
Bey Carl Ludwig Jacobi.

FIG. 1.2. Title page of König ([6]1755)

It is much more difficult to find and interpret implicit cultural content, which may be hidden in unexpected places and phrased in ways no longer current today, such as in example sentences given in grammatical sections or translation exercises. A close analysis of all the books surveyed for this chapter for implicit cultural content would, however, be beyond its scope. Below I do, however, examine some examples from the nineteenth century, once textbooks begin to include translation exercises which might carry some implicit cultural content.[1]

Eighteenth-Century Textbooks for Adult Learners

For the first half of the eighteenth century the textbooks of English for German speakers by Theodor Arnold (published 1718; see Fig. 1.1) and Johann König (first edition 1705, here: sixth edn 1755; see Fig. 1.2) may serve as typical examples.

As can be seen in Figures 1.1 and 1.2, it was common at the time to list the contents of the books on the title pages. Both König's and Arnold's books were undoubtedly the most successful English-language textbooks of the whole century; both saw at least ten editions before 1800 (see Schröder 1975: 19 and 147); and I have therefore chosen them for closer analysis over other plausible candidates such as the works by Lediard (1725) or Ludwig (1717), which were also published at the beginning of the eighteenth century but which were much less successful and widespread.

As Table 1 shows, there is a high degree of overlap in the contents of both textbooks. Explicit cultural content can be seen in the 'London-guide' of König; in the facts about currency, weights and measures given in Arnold; and in the lists of titles and forms of address provided in both textbooks. Phrases and idioms, proverbs, dialogues, letters and texts for reading may contain explicit or implicit cultural content.

The most explicit cultural content is to be found in König's 'A London-Guide, of the Curiosities to be seen in and about London' (König 1755: 353-92). Johann König was a German and a master of languages who lived in London. His text contains six bilingual dialogues, each about five pages long, which take the reader to a great number of London sights and offer him basic facts about England, Wales, Scotland and Ireland ('How many fine cities have you in England? — Five and Twenty; and Six Hundred and Forty One great Market-Towns, and Nine Thousand Seven Hundred and Twenty Five Parishes' (König 1755: 353)); these dialogues inform the reader of transport routes and prices, describe the postal service, the calendar, and particular feast days.

The intention underlying König's London dialogues is clearly to be practically informative, as is the case with Arnold's lists of titles, weights etc. However, König also wants the reader to understand something of the character of the English, for he stresses how they dealt with the aftermath of the Great Fire (1666) in building up the city of London once again. His description of the Fire is both emotional and factual. Throughout his London dialogues the voice of the person explaining and describing the city and the country is a positive one; the listener's reactions are a mixture of emotional or general comments and interested questions. König

Textbook components	Arnold 1718 (606 pp.)	König [6]1755 ([1]1705) (425 pp.)
grammar	336 pages	225 pages
dictionary	93 pages (alphabetical)	25 pages (onomasiological, i.e. by topic)
phrases and idioms	37 pages	16 pages
proverbs	25 pages (alphabetical)	31 pages (alphabetical) plus titles of relevant books
dialogues	61 pages	53 pages
London-Guide	–	39 pages
letters	39 pages	10 pages
reading texts	–	15 pages (Aesop's Fables)
lists: weights, measures, coins	6 pages	(included in London-Guide, VI. Dialogue, 5 pages)
titles, forms of addressing letters	3 pages	3 pages
pronunciation rules for German	–	3 pages

TABLE 1. Arnold's (1718) and König's ([6]1755) textbooks compared

(1755) thus succeeds in dressing a lot of information in a very attractive format. Unfortunately we do not know what the learners of English who used König's *Guide* as their textbook made of this text. Maybe it was instrumental in stirring some *Wanderlust* in some of them and making them travel to London.

Less explicit cultural content can be found in the 'Familiar Dialogues' (König 1755: 299-352), as well as in König's collections of proverbs and idioms. In these sections König adds specific information about England in some places: for instance, when to address someone as *Mr.* or *Sir.* Some of the dialogues carry implicit cultural evaluations and judgments. Thus, a dinner conversation contains statements like 'You have very good Meat in England' (König 1755: 323); or a dialogue with a shopkeeper selling cloth lets us catch a glimpse of how the English see themselves in relation to the French:

What's this a Yard?	Wie theuer die Elle ? (Yard)
Twenty Shillings.	Zwantzig Schilling.
How? Twenty Shillings?	Wie? Zwantzig Schilling?
you take me for a stranger, I see.	ihr sehet mich für einen Fremden an, wie ich mercke.
No Sir, we are not in *France*.	Nein, mein Herr, wir sind nicht in Franckreich.
We sell no dearer to a Stranger in this Country than to an Englishman.	Wir verkauffen hierzulande einem Fremden nicht theurer als einem Engelländer.

(König 1755: 327)

But König's textbook, while very popular, is an exception in the early eighteenth century with its cultural specificity and its explicit and positive bias towards London and England, possibly due to its author's first-hand experience of living there. By comparison, the explicit cultural content in the more typical Arnold (1718) is mainly factual and restricted to information on currency, measures and titles, i.e. information which could be obtained from relevant books or informants and which does not require personal knowledge. In fact, we do not know if Theodor Arnold ever set foot in England. Similarly, Arnold's dialogues are of a more general nature than those of König (1755) and make no reference to England or the English as such, but cover the topics found in most dialogue collections of that time: greetings, rising in the morning, eating, going to bed, taking a walk. As was common at the time, these dialogic texts are seen as a collection of contextualized expressions and vocabulary rather than a depiction of authentic exchanges in the real world.

In the second half of the eighteenth century Johann Elias Greiffenhahn (1778) seems to have taken his inspiration from König's *Guide*, because he includes a section called 'An addition of some profitable Discourses upon several remarkable Things of England' (Greiffenhahn 1778: 258-334), running to some seventy pages. These discourses are written as continuous text, even though the sentences are meant to be read as utterances of different speakers. The topics of the discourses start with the English weather, culminating in the rather clichéd statement: 'Thus from the Premises we may draw this general conclusion, that the Air of England is gross and thick, that the Weather here is commonly overcast, gloomy and melancholy, subject to Rain and Fogs, in Winter especially' (Greiffenhahn 1778: 259). The topics of the other discourses show a broad spectrum of cultural matters and information on England, mostly concerned with everyday life, as can be seen from the list of contents:

> The First Discourse: Of the Air of England and its Influences
> The Second Discourse: Of the Buildings and Fewel [i.e. fuel] of England
> The Third Discourse: Of the English Food
> The Fourth Discourse: Of the Use of Brandy, Coffee, Tea, Chocolate and
>   Tobacco
> The Fifth Discourse: Of Coffee-Houses and of the Uses a Stranger may make
>   of them
> The Sixth Discourse: Of Clubbs and of the English Custom for every one to
>   pay his Clubb
> The Seventh Discourse: Of the English Mony
> The Eighth Discourse: Of London and the Way to it from Paris through
>   Calais
> The Ninth Discourse: Of the principal Curiosities of London
> The Tenth Discourse: Of the Post-Days at London; Of the Peny-Post; Of the
>   English Calendar and Style
> The Eleventh Discourse: Of some particular Days, observed in England
> The Twelfth Discourse: Concerning the Laws of England
>   (Greiffenhahn, 1778: 258-334)

In the sections on London Greiffenhahn borrowed heavily from König, a practice which was by no means uncommon in the eighteenth century — and in those times, before there was awareness of what constitutes intellectual property, this kind of borrowing was not seen as plagiarism. In his 'Ninth Discourse. Of the principal Curiosities of London' (Greiffenhahn 1778: 303–27) Greiffenhahn uses König's text (König 1755: 354–73) nearly verbatim except for the fact that he dispenses with the German translation and makes small modifications in the language but not the content, as the example in Table 2 shows.

König 1755: 354-55	Greiffenhahn 1778: 303
If you intend to see the Curiosities of this Place and about it, I freely offer you my Company. That I would desire of you. So we may begin at White Hall, the Royal Palace. In our Way thither you will see at *Charing-Cross* a Brazen Horse, which is reckoned a very good Piece. There you shall see sitting on Horseback, the Statue of King *Charles I.* who was beheaded before this Palace, January 30, 1648 by a rebellious Faction. From thence we shall come to *White-Hall*, being but a few Paces asunder.	If you intend, to see the Curiosities of this Place and about it, I freely offer you my Company. That I did expect from you. So we may begin at White-Hall, the Royal Palace. In our Way thither you will see at Charing-Cross a brazen Horse, which is a good Piece. There you shall see sitting on Horse-Back the Statue of King Charles I. who was beheaded before this Palace, January 30, 1648 by a rebellious Faction. From thence to White-Hall 'tis but two Steps.

TABLE 2. Borrowing of Greiffenhahn (1778) from König (1755)

Greiffenhahn's textbook (1778) also includes the dialogues on everyday matters that were common in textbooks of the time, and we find implicit cultural information of a kind is given in one such conversation between an Englishman and a German. The Englishman is full of praise for Germany ('Tis the Finest Country in the World' (Greiffenhahn 1778: 251)); and he also comments on its inhabitants: 'Have we not here handsome Ladies? They are handsome, as Angels'. The dialogue continues:

Have a care yourself, Sir!	Der Herr hüte sich!
Of what, Sir?	Wovor, mein Herr?
Of falling into their chains.	In ihre Ketten (Netze) zu fallen.
I desire no better.	Ich wills nicht besser haben.
You shall not break them when you will.	Sie werden sie nicht zerreissen wenn sie wollen.
Sir, if I fall in them, I will die in them.	Mein Herr, wenn ich hineinfalle, will ich drinnen sterben.
I thank you for the Esteem you have for our German Women.	Ich danke ihnen vor die Hochachtung, so sie vor unser deutsches Frauenzimmer haben.
I speak the Truth.	Ich sage die Wahrheit.

(Greiffenhahn 1778: 251-52)

It is not quite clear if this exchange written by a German textbook author reflects his true attitude towards (German) women and his attempt to praise them in the light of possible misconceptions abroad; if it shows his concept of polite conversation; or if it is to be read as an ironic comment on the wily ways of women as seductresses.

Anthologies

In the last decades of the eighteenth century a new type of textbook began to appear: the text anthology. According to the context in which these text collections were to be used, they could take quite different formats. Two striking and very different examples are the *English Miscellanies* (in two volumes) by John Tompson (1766)[2] and Christoph Daniel Ebeling's *Vermischte Aufsätze in englischer Prose [Assorted Essays in English Prose* (1784)]. Both are intended to be used by learners of English, albeit at different kinds of institutions. John Tompson, who taught as a professor of English at the University of Göttingen, chose his texts, one may assume, for the educated young adult at university who was looking for reading matter in English. His title page lists some of the fields and authors he has included with excerpts — divinity, philosophy, morals, politics and history. As authors from whose works he gives extracts, he lists Locke, Milton, Addison, Thomson, Dryden, Cowley, Pope and others mainly from the seventeenth and early eighteenth century. He selected authors who are well known and respected as poets and dramatists (John Milton, Abraham Cowley, John Dryden, James Thomson, Alexander Pope), as philosophers (John Locke) or essayists (Joseph Addison) and who were in some way representative for their time, like Addison and Steele, who founded important journals like *Tatler* and *The Spectator* at the beginning of the eighteenth century. The text genres range from sermons to plays, from essays to poems, from historical writing to moral maxims.

In contrast to Tompson's *Miscellanies*, Ebeling's collection was intended to be used by quite a different class of learners, those who wanted to acquire English for the business world. Therefore Ebeling selected texts on topics which he considered relevant for his pupils. Ebeling worked as a teacher both at the *Handlungsakademie* (school for future merchants; i.e. young male adults) and the grammar school in Hamburg. In his preface he emphasizes that his goal is to teach practical English — 'Zum Gebrauche des gemeinen Lebens, zum Sprechen und zu bürgerlichen Geschäften' [For use in everyday life, for speaking and for business] (Ebeling 1787: v). He criticizes Tompson's earlier *Miscellanies* for two reasons. Firstly, the books could only be used with academically educated people and, secondly, one could not acquire colloquial English through the texts in the *Miscellanies*. As for his own anthology, he would have liked to include examples of business correspondence, which he, unfortunately, had not been able to find (Ebeling 1787: vii).[3] Ebeling also states that he deliberately chose both entertaining and instructional texts in order to sweeten the labours of language learning and to prepare his learners for the business world (Ebeling 1787: vi). His selection of texts is wider-ranging than Tompson's; however, they show a clear bias towards encyclopaedic topics like world geography, world history, natural history, trade and literature, and thus address a much wider field.

Ebeling (1787), König (1755), Arnold (1718) and Greiffenhahn (1778) are all firmly rooted in the marketplace tradition of language learning. In their textbooks, explicit cultural content is intended to help those acquiring English to use it in direct written or oral interaction with speakers of English and who need to know how to behave correctly and appropriately in England. A second function of the cultural content is to provide information about London (as in König), England more generally (as in Greiffenhahn) or the world at large (as in Ebeling). A great number of reading texts and most of the dialogues in these textbooks, however, have a more cosmopolitan bent and are not situated in England. They serve, by and large, the two dimensions of 'content' and 'context' distinguished by Risager (2007: 8). In contrast, Tompson's *Miscellanies* (1766) seem to be more in line with the monastery tradition and the poetic dimension of cultural learning, giving access to at least some major writers in English literature and to more philosophical thinking. This may reflect the fact that Tompson, as professor at the University of Göttingen, used his book with university students acquiring English in a more academic setting than, for example, Ebeling.

Nineteenth-Century Textbooks of English for Schools

Throughout the nineteenth century, English-language textbooks continued to provide a basis for private tutoring and autonomous language learning, as had been the case in the eighteenth century, but at the same time they began to be used far more widely in language classes at secondary schools. In Germany, English became the second compulsory modern language after French at *Realschulen* in Prussia in 1859, because its value was slowly being recognized; English had been an optional subject at a number of schools before then, but could only be offered if a teacher was available who was willing and able to teach it (Klippel 1994: 277-86). *Realschulen* were secondary schools where — in contrast to the traditional grammar schools with their emphasis on a classical education based on Latin and Greek — natural sciences, mathematics and modern languages played a greater role.

As soon as textbooks are used as course books in a school system, they have to be adapted to the requirements of the system. Whereas language tutors teaching individuals may pick and choose language and content best suited to the capabilities, interests and goals of their learners, school teachers are forced to proceed with more conformity and in a more systematic way in order to comply with the demands of a structured school system, which leads in stages to some kind of final standard of achievement. Language textbooks, therefore, first of all need to have a clear progressive structure, so that elementary contents are taught before complex ones and teachers know what to teach first. Everything needs to be graded in sequence to make lessons at a certain stage similar across the range of schools. Thus school-leaving standards can be assured. It is obvious that König's *Guide* (1755) and Arnold's *Grammar* (1718) would not have been suitable for English-language teaching at schools, because they were not compiled according to the progressive course principle which makes it necessary that a course book is worked through from beginning to end. As can be seen from the tables of contents of König (1755) and Arnold (1718) in Figures 1.1 and 1.2, individual sections which a learner would consult at the same time (e.g. grammar and lexicon) are arranged one after the other. The structure of their grammar sections follows the Latin model of word classes and begins with the article. It is obvious that these books are not course books.

Rather, they are comprehensive collections of different kinds of linguistic and factual information and sample texts, which are not graded by difficulty in any way.

In the nineteenth century, the principle of grading was widely adopted for language textbooks for schools, because different grades needed different input. The idea of organizing language teaching into two different progressive stages was first developed by Seidenstücker (1795 and 1811/1813), who stipulated that beginners should start with reading easy texts and only later deal with the most important points of grammar. Intensive grammar work and translation activities should follow at a second stage, when there is some language knowledge to make grammar work more effective (see also Klippel 1994: 137). Later in the nineteenth century a typical course design involved three major stages. First, there was an elementary book containing basic grammar with accompanying exercises and perhaps simple texts illustrating grammar points. The second stage involved a more comprehensive grammar book and a reading book or an anthology of texts. Original fictional or factual texts were normally tackled only at the third stage, after completing two or three years of learning English with a textbook, while some grammar work would have continued. This textbook structure can be seen in the course books by Plate (1850) or Gesenius (1874), but it was adopted quite widely and many more textbooks could be used as examples.

The second innovation which characterizes school textbooks from about 1800 onwards are exercises for translation and other practice activities. In the eighteenth century textbook authors left it to teachers and learners to practise language in whatever manner they chose. When Meidinger (1783) invented translation exercises in the form of word lists or sentences attached to individual grammar chapters, his innovation was quickly taken up by other textbook authors and became a staple element of language textbooks; and many books claimed to be following Meidinger's method (Fick 1793 was an early example).

There was a great variety of different types of textbooks within this general framework of graded books. Although textbook authors realized that translation and other exercises were necessary so that new structures could be practised, the ways in which texts were included differed widely. This is pertinent here, because texts are the main carriers of cultural information. Whereas in the eighteenth century texts in textbooks and anthologies were largely direct and unaltered extracts from English publications — literary or other — the need for texts suitable for a particular level in schools led to adaptations of original texts, as well as to the authoring of specially written texts for the new textbooks.

The Interlinear Method

Within the general framework outlined above, there were so many different kinds of textbooks in the nineteenth century that it is impossible to present one prototype for the whole century. Below I therefore present a few textbooks whose treatment of culture is noteworthy in some way.

My first two examples are English language textbooks following Hamilton's interlinear method (Klippel 1994: 221-47). This method is based on reading texts given in the original with a verbatim translation in the learner's language in between the lines, hence the name 'interlinear method'. Leonhard Tafel (1835), my first example, argues in the extensive preface of his textbook that school curricula ought to be revised and more room given to subjects like History and Geography. Not surprisingly, then, his textbook, which starts off with forty-eight lengthy dialogues on the usual everyday topics, contains a very long text on the history of England beginning with Roman rule. According to Tafel (1835: xxxvi), it is important in the foreign-language class to read those kinds of texts which forge a connection to other school subjects, in this case History. Thus, the pupils being taught English with his book receive a comprehensive course in English history at the same time. However, Tafel provides no information on the provenance of his texts.

A second textbook also following the Hamiltonian method was written by J. F. W. Zimmer, a teacher of English from Heidelberg (Zimmer 1844). Zimmer stresses in the preface that he has graded his texts, progressing from easy ones to complex ones. In his book we find an extensive table on English forms of address, both in speaking and writing. The main part of his textbook is made up of interlinear renderings of dialogues, short narratives, and extracts from the works of both contemporary authors like Walter Scott and older ones like Joseph Addison, for example. He also includes individual scenes from plays, letters and short extracts from historical works on the discovery of America, Queen Elizabeth and Mary Stuart, and from Gibbon's *Decline and Fall of the Roman Empire* (Gibbon 1776-88), a very popular multi-volume history. The common denominator between both interlinear textbooks is English history, which is given modest space in Zimmer (1844) and a good deal of space in Tafel (1835).

Carl Munde and his Textbooks

The interlinear method never caught the interest of language teachers throughout Germany but retained its followers mostly in the south-west. After its demise, different types of language textbooks became popular. The textbooks by Carl Munde ([1]1843, [10]1856 for *Erster Unterricht im Englischen*; [1]1846, [4]1863 for *Zweiter Unterricht im Englischen*) illustrate nicely how textbooks changed from the middle of the nineteenth century onwards, insofar as they now assumed the guiding hand of a teacher and could no longer really be used for self-study. The elementary book destined for beginners now does not contain original texts, even in extracts. Rather, the typical texts at beginner's level are random sentences which are constructed to illustrate a grammar point or to provide some sort of context for new vocabulary. As a consequence, it seems obvious that at least for elementary books and thus the first two years of learning English, culture becomes largely irrelevant. Of course, one can find implicit cultural content in some of these sentences, but there is no attempt to integrate information on the target culture(s) in any systematic way. For example, Carl Munde's textbook contains a few relevant sentences in his 'Catechism or questions and answers on some of the most necessary things to be known' (Munde 1856: 139–62):

Q. What are the capitals of England, Scotland and Ireland?
London, Edinburgh, and Dublin.
Q. What are the inhabitants of those kingdoms called?
English, Scotch, and Irish.
Q. What do England and Scotland form?
They form Great-Britain, and with Ireland are called the British Isles. [...]
Q. Is there no other country annexed to the above named three kingdoms
that form Great Britain?
Yes, Wales.
Q. What is Wales?
[...]
Q. What is the capital of Prussia?
Berlin. [etc.] (Munde 1856: 151–52)

Carl Munde was forced to emigrate to the United States after the revolution of 1848 in which he had taken part in Dresden. When the second edition of his book *Zweiter Unterricht im Englischen* was published, Munde added an appendix which was no doubt influenced by his years of living abroad: 'A few Rules on the Usages of Society and on English and American Etiquette' (Munde 1863: 309-43). Here the learners are told how to behave properly in social situations such as dinner parties, visits, dances, while smoking and generally interacting with women. This advice is clearly relevant to adult male learners. It is interesting to note that in this textbook the organization and the arrangement of its contents are based on a grammatical progression suited to language classes for adolescent boys on the one hand, but that on the other hand the intercultural advice they are given is firmly focused on their later lives as adults, perhaps in an English-speaking country.

Pre-Reform and Reform

The final decades of the nineteenth century again showed a great increase in textbook production, because English was taught to more pupils in more and different types of schools (Klippel 1994: 429–37). We can observe two parallel processes in textbook development. First of all, up to the start of the Reform Movement grammar was introduced and practised in increasingly similar ways. For this purpose, contrived and invented sample sentences (or short texts in which the grammar point is highlighted by bold print or italics) became the generally accepted norm. The example in Figure 1.3 is taken from the most successful textbook of English in the nineteenth century, by Heinrich Plate. His books reached more than fifty editions in the thirty years between 1850 and 1882; and his elementary book achieved its ninety-fifth edition in the 1920s (Schröder 1975: 208).

Sampling these sentence collections suggests that authors focused clearly on the grammar points in question and gave little thought to finding particularly informative content. It was only the Reform Movement which led to a significant change, when textbook authors began to replace sentences or texts carrying German or unspecified cultural content by texts giving information on, and insight into, English and American culture (cf. Klippel, 1994: 416–18).

Zur Anschauung.

One and two are three. Four times five are twenty. Six times seven are forty two. Eight times nine are seventy two. Ten times ten are a hundred, and ten times a hundred are a thousand. A year has twelve months, a month has thirty or thirty one days, a day has twenty four hours, and an hour has sixty minutes. The Bible has been translated into more than 140 languages. About 2000 stars are visible to the naked eye. The empire of Austria contains 11,575 square miles with 38 million inhabitants. The capital is Vienna; it is the largest town in all Germany and has at present 470,000 inhabitants. The kingdom of Prussia contains 5100 square miles, and the capital, Berlin, has 440,000 inhabitants. Hamburg, the most important commercial town in Germany, has 200,000 inhabitants. — 6666 men composed a legion with the Romans. In order to write Chinese, the common man must know 80,000 letters or characters, but the learned must know 160,000. Since the birth of Christ, 1859 years have elapsed. Our clergyman's income amounts to 250 pounds a year. I have just received my tailor's bill, which amounts to 12 pounds 16 shillings and 6 pence (£ 12. 16. 6). What is the price of this cloth? It costs 15 (shillings) and 9 pence. Let me have 5 ells of it. How much do I owe you? £ 3. 18. 9. (Three pounds eighteen shillings and 9 pence) if you please.

FIG. 1.3. Sentences for grammar practice in Plate (1863: 83), here focusing on numerals

A second development in the late nineteenth century is one of diversification. The eighteenth century offered basically two types of textbook: comprehensive textbooks containing grammar, vocabulary, texts, dialogues and various lists; and anthologies. In the second half of the nineteenth century a new range of different textbook formats emerges. These books are either intended for different levels of the course, i.e. elementary books for beginners or grammars for advanced learners; or for different types of learners, e.g. boys, girls, emigrants, business people, or those wanting to teach themselves; or for different kinds of schools and for different skill areas and goals in learning. In addition to the traditional books with selected reading texts, which continued to be published, annotated readers with original or adapted texts appeared in great numbers in the famous Tauchnitz *Collection of British Authors* (1842-1955),[4] for example. Works by English (and later American) authors were published by Tauchnitz in Leipzig in cheap paperbound editions, which were frequently used as readers in secondary schools. In addition, there were books with exercises for practising translating (e.g. Herrig 1844), guides for essay writing (e.g. Boyle 1875) and letter writing (e.g. Gantter 1856), and collections of conversations (e.g. Fick 1813; Haas 1855) for different levels and types of students.

If the Reform Movement was not entirely successful in establishing a new language-teaching methodology in schools, it was certainly instrumental in putting cultural content in terms of *realia* into all kinds of textbooks (cf. Risager 2007). The English-speaking world was well represented in most books. Although England remained the main focus, from both a historical and a contemporary perspective,

Einleitung.

England	i·ŋglʰnd	shawl	ŝɔ̃l
John Bull	dẑɔñ bul	strike	strǎǐk
lord	lɔ̃rd	Newcastle	nᵛûkɑ̃·sl	4
lady	lŝ·dᵊ	Southampton	sâuÞæ·mptn
gentleman	dẑeˑntlmʰn	Connaught	kɔˑnɔ̃t
roast beef	rôᵘˑstbîf	Lloyd	lɔ̃d
plum-pudding	plʊm pudᵊŋ	Mary	mŝrᵊ	8
clown	klǎⁿñ	Stuart	stjaᵛrt
speech	spîŝ	America	ǎmᵉˑrᵏkᵊ
tramway	træ·mẉŝᵊ	Yankee	jæŋkᵊ
waterproof	ẉɔ̃ˑtᵊrprûf	humbug	hʊˑmbɔ̃ĝ	12

Do you speak English? du ju spᵏk iˑŋglïŝ.

English spoken here iˑŋglïŝ spᵒᵘkn hᵛʳ

Die Aussprache obiger Wörter, verglichen mit ihrer Schreibung, lehrt,
daß im Englischen mehr noch als im Deutschen ein und derselbe Buch- 16
stabe zur Bezeichnung verschiedener Laute dient;

daß die englische Sprache mehrere Laute hat, die im Deutschen fehlen;

daß trotz einer gewissen Ähnlichkeit mehrerer Laute in beiden Sprachen
es im Englischen kaum einen Laut giebt, der völlig mit einem 20
deutschen Laute übereinstimmte;

daß die Aussprachebezeichnung allein nicht ausreicht, Wesen und Klang
des fremden Lautes völlig klar zu machen.

Diese Verschiedenheit der Laute beruht wesentlich auf der Verschie- 24
denheit der Zungenlage, der Stellung des Unterkiefers und der Lippen-
bewegung in beiden Sprachen.

The English Student.   1

FIG. 1.4. Hausknecht (1898: 1)

the United States and even Australia and other English-speaking parts of the
world found their way into the textbooks. Hausknecht's *The English Student* (1898)
carries the subtitle *Lehrbuch zur Einführung in die englische Sprache und Landeskunde*,
i.e. *Introduction to English Language and Culture*, if one may translate *Landeskunde* as
'culture', literally, 'knowledge of the country'. The vocabulary used in the very first
lesson intended to introduce English pronunciation is a good example (see Figure 1.4).

Current political matters are also included in the form of a text on Queen
Victoria's jubilee (Hausknecht 1898: 112-13). There is another innovation to the
textbooks of the very late nineteenth century. Cultural information is no longer
given solely in texts, but also in the illustrations — maps, drawings, etchings
or photographs — that were beginning to be used to a much greater extent.
Hausknecht's *English Student* contains pictures of the flags of Britain and America
plus a map of New York and various illustrations accompanying the texts.

In the other types of textbooks mentioned — in conversation manuals, guides
for essay or letter writing — cultural content is ubiquitous. The books containing
reading texts largely concentrate on those topics related to England, or represent
English literature. As one textbook author puts it:

> Bei der Bearbeitung dieses Lesebuches habe ich zunächst mein Augenmerk
> darauf gerichtet, einen ebenso anziehenden als würdigen Stoff für die englische

Lektüre zusammenzutragen. Erschien es sodann geboten, bei der Auswahl der Lesestücke eine möglichste Mannigfaltigkeit anzustreben, um die Sprache in verschiedenen Anschauungs- und Wissenskreisen zu Wort kommen zu lassen und so zugleich eine Anlehnung an die verschiedenen Unterrichts-Sparten zu ermöglichen, so wird es andererseits kaum der Rechtfertigung bedürfen, wenn die Stücke, welche die britische Nation, ihre Geschichte und Sprache, ihr Land, ihre Sitten und Eigenthümlichkeiten zum Gegenstande haben, in besonders reichem Masse vertreten sind. England und die Engländer — das wird doch wohl in einem englischen Lesebuch das Hauptthema sein müssen. (Steuerwald 1886: iii)

To paraphrase this quotation, Steuerwald states that he has tried to select both interesting and worthy material for reading. He wants to achieve a great variety so that many domains are represented and links may be found to other school subjects. The main focus lies on texts which deal with the British nation, its history and language, its country, customs and special characteristics. For him it is quite clear that England and the English ought to be the main focus in an English reading book.

By the end of the nineteenth century a prototypical English language textbook for secondary schools in Germany delivered factual information on contemporary Britain and other English-speaking countries in texts and pictures, gave an insight into English history and customs, contained some extracts from English literature and used an English-culture backdrop taken from the everyday life of children and adolescents in England, quite often even in contrived texts and exercises which were intended to introduce and practise grammar. It is obvious from this that the foundations for the way English-speaking cultures are represented in today's English language textbooks in Germany were laid in the late nineteenth century.

Everyday culture, to use this phrase in analogy to the German *Alltagskultur*, was present in the textbooks of the eighteenth century in dialogues and letters. It was replaced for a while in the nineteenth century by literary and historical texts, by 'culture with a capital C', as we would term it today, while sample sentences for modelling grammar points were taken from any cultural background. While high culture and literature were prevalent in English-language anthologies and readers from the late eighteenth to the late nineteenth century (one need only think of Herrig's famous anthology *The British Classical Authors*, first published in 1849 and reprinted into the second half of the twentieth century (Klippel 2010)), this focus changed again with the Reform Movement, which advocated that colloquial language and everyday matters should be given more weight. The reformers also laid a great deal of emphasis on *realia*, the basis for factual knowledge of the target culture; they propagated what in Germany was called *Realienkunde* — information about history, geography, politics and facts of life in the target culture. Advanced learners continued to read texts from the broad literary tradition (Klippel 2005), with Shakespeare as the author who was considered indispensable.

Conclusion

This chapter gives an overview of some salient developments in the cultural bias of English language textbooks in Germany over a time span of two hundred years, with a few glimpses of what some popular and successful textbooks from those centuries contain. My original expectation that cultural content in those books from the eighteenth century which were aimed at educated adult learners would be quite different from cultural content in schoolbooks of the nineteenth century has been both disproved and confirmed. There are continuities between the dialogues and the factual information given on England in the eighteenth-century books, for instance in König's *Guide* (1755), and this kind of information in late nineteenth-century schoolbooks. Everyday life plays a certain role in the eighteenth century and towards the end of the nineteenth century. The marketplace tradition is present in both centuries.

And yet there are differences as well, which stem from the fact that the learners of English in the eighteenth century were educated adults who knew something of the world. These learners used English also as a means of access to those writings which interested them. Their need to be informed about English history and to be educated in cultural matters was far smaller than that of the adolescent boys being taught English in the second half of the nineteenth century. English-language textbooks used as schoolbooks needed to comply with pedagogical goals as well as those of efficient and comprehensive language instruction. And, being schoolbooks, they were subject to the regulations for curricula issued by the state. These regulations were not very explicit in the late nineteenth century in Germany, which explains why there is such great variation between textbooks.

It is very difficult to sum up the developments, because the variety of textbooks in the two hundred years under scrutiny is just too great. Any attempt to generalize may be criticized for leaving out certain works or putting too much emphasis on those selected. This chapter could only take very few books into consideration. However, in a previous large-scale study I looked at roughly three hundred textbooks from this period (Klippel 1994), so the summary in Table 3 is based on more background knowledge and a much wider analysis of sources than could be reported here. Taking Risager's (2007) three dimensions and distinguishing two kinds of cultural content — universal / encyclopaedic content and culture-specific content referring to England (and other English-speaking cultures) — we can chart the development for three periods: the eighteenth century, the nineteenth century and the Reform Movement at the end of the nineteenth century. As we have seen, the Reform Movement must be seen as a new phase, because at this time the content of language teaching was firmly focused on the target cultures, more than ever before.

Given the wealth of textbooks, and seeing how much they can reveal to us of language teaching and learning in bygone times, historical research must continue to use them as sources. These textbooks are windows into the multi-dimensional past of language teaching, which remains uncharted in many ways. We should venture to look more closely through those windows and discover many more facets of a rich and varied history.

Dimension:	universal / encyclopaedic	culture-specific
Content		
eighteenth century	texts in anthologies (e.g. Ebeling 1787), texts in grammars	a few texts (e.g. König 1755), lists and facts (e.g. weights)
nineteenth century	sample sentences illustrating and practising grammar points	a few texts and sentences
Reform Movement	not much	many texts, *realia*, pictures
Context		
eighteenth century	dialogues	rare; some dialogues forms of address
nineteenth century	a few dialogues	rare; some direct advice (e.g. Munde 1863)
Reform Movement	–	in texts, dialogues
Poetic		
eighteenth century	classical texts, e.g. Aesop's Fables	texts in literary anthologies (e.g. Tompson 1766)
nineteenth century	rare	literary anthologies and reading books (e.g. Herrig 1849)
Reform Movement	–	literary anthologies and reading books; original texts

TABLE 3. Overview of Cultural Dimensions in English-Language Textbooks 1700 to 1900

Bibliography

ARNOLD, THEODOR. 1718. *Neue Englische Grammatica, Oder kurtzgefaßte, Jedoch deutliche und sichere Anweisung zur richtigen Pronunciation, Accentuation und völligen Begreiffung der Englischen Sprache* (Hanover: Nikolaus Förster)

BACHMAIR, JOHN JAMES. 1771. *A Complete German Grammar*, 3rd edn (London: G. Keith)

BOYLE, GEORGE. 1875. *Englische Aufsätze. Nebst einer theoretischen Anleitung und 170 Dispositionen zum Anfertigen derselben für die oberen Klassen der höheren Lehranstalten* (Wiesbaden: Gestewitz)

DRIEDGER, OTTO. 1907. 'Johann Königs (John King's) deutsch-englische Grammatiken und ihre späteren Bearbeitungen (1706-1802)' (unpublished doctoral thesis, University of Marburg)

EBELING, CHRISTOPH DANIEL. 1787. *Vermischte Aufsätze in englischer Prose hauptsächlich zum Besten derer welche diese Sprache in Rücksicht auf bürgerliche Geschäfte lernen woolen*, 4th edn (Hamburg: Herold) [1st ed. 1784]

FICK, JOHANN CHRISTIAN. 1793. *Theoretisch-praktische Anweisung zur leichtern Erlernung der Englischen Sprache. Erster Theil: Praktische Sprachlehre für Deutsche beiderlei Geschlechts. Nach der in Meidingers französischen Grammatik befolgten Methode* (Erlangen: Palm und Enke)

———. 1813. *English Dialogues upon the Most Common Subjects of Life, with an English-German Vocabulary for Schools and Private Use* (Erlangen: Heyder)

FINKENSTAEDT, THOMAS .1992. 'Auf der Suche nach dem Göttinger Ordinarius des Englischen, John Thompson (1697-1768)', in *Fremdsprachenunterricht 1500–1800*, ed. by Konrad Schröder (Wiesbaden: Harrassowitz), pp. 57-74

FRANZ, JAN. 2005. *Englischlernen für Amerika: Sprachführer für deutsche Auswanderer im 19. Jahrhundert* (München: Langenscheidt)

GANTTER, LUDWIG. 1856. *Collection of English Letters. Mustersammlung Englischer Originalbriefe als Stylübungen für den Schul- und Privatgebrauch* (Stuttgart: Metzler)

GESENIUS, FRIEDRICH WILHELM. 1874. *Lehrbuch der englischen Sprache. Teil: 1. Elementarbuch der englischen Sprache nebst Lese- und Übungsstücken, Teil 2: Grammatik der englischen Sprache nebst Übungsstücken* (Halle: Gesenius)

GIBBON, EDWARD. 1776-88. *The History of the Decline and the Fall of the Roman Empire*, 6 vols (London: Cadell)

GREIFFENHAHN, JOHANN ELIAS. 1778. *Englische Sprachlehre*, 4th edn (Jena: Crökers Witwe)

HAAS, CAROLINE. 1855. *Deutsch-Französisch-Englische Kinder-Gespräche zunächst für Mädchen von 8 bis 14 Jahren* (Darmstadt)

HAUSKNECHT, EMIL. 1898. *The English Student. Lehrbuch zur Einführung in die englische Sprache und Landeskunde*, 3rd edn (Berlin: Wiegandt & Grieben)

HERRIG, LUDWIG. 1844. *Aufgaben zum Übersetzen aus dem Deutschen ins Englische für obere Klassen. Nebst einer Anleitung zu freien schriftlichen Arbeiten* (Elberfeld: Baedeker)

——. 1849. *The British Classical Authors: Handbuch der englischen Nationalliteratur von G. Chaucer auf die jetzige Zeit* (Brunswick: Westermann)

HÜLLEN, WERNER. 2005. *Kleine Geschichte des Fremdsprachenlernens* (Berlin: Schmidt)

KLIPPEL, FRIEDERIKE. 1994. *Englischlernen im 18. und 19. Jahrhundert: Die Geschichte der Lehrbücher und Unterrichtsmethoden* (Münster: Nodus)

——. 2005. 'Englische Literatur im Englischunterricht des 19. Jahrhunderts', in *Sprachen der Bildung — Bildung durch Sprachen im Deutschland des 18. und 19. Jahrhunderts*, ed. by Friederike Klippel and Werner Hüllen (Wiesbaden: Harrassowitz), pp. 185-209

——. 2010. 'Sprache, Literatur, Lehrerbildung: die Leistungen von Ludwig Herrig und Hermann Breymann im Prozess der Professionalisierung im 19. Jahrhundert', *Fremdsprachen Lehren und Lernen*, 39: pp. 40-52

KÖNIG, JOHANN. 1755. *Der getreue Englische Wegweiser*, 6th edn (Leipzig: Jacobi)

LEDIARD, THOMAS. 1725. *Grammatica Anglicana Critica oder Versuch zu einer vollkommenen Grammatik der englischen Sprache* (Hamburg: The Author)

LEHBERGER, REINER. 2003. 'Geschichte des Fremdsprachenunterrichts bis 1945', in *Handbuch Fremdsprachenunterricht*, ed. by Karl-Richard Bausch, Herbert Christ and Hans-Jürgen Krumm, 4th edn (Tübingen: Francke), pp. 609-14

LUDWIG, CHRISTIAN. 1717. *Gründliche Anleitung zur Englischen Sprache* (Leipzig: Fritschen)

MCARTHUR, TOM. 1991. *A Foundation Course for Language Teachers* (Cambridge: Cambridge University Press)

MEIDINGER, JOHANN VALENTIN. 1783. *Practische Französische Grammatik wodurch man diese Sprache auf eine ganz neue und sehr leichte Art in kurzer Zeit gründlich erlernen kann* (Frankfurt am Main: The Author)

MUNDE, CARL. 1856. *Erster Unterricht im Englischen*, 10th edn (Leipzig: Arnold)

——. 1863. *Zweiter Unterricht im Englischen*, 4th edn (Leipzig: Arnold)

NIEDERLÄNDER, HELMUT. 1981. *Französische Schulgrammatiken und schulgrammatisches Denken in Deutschland von 1850 bis 1950* (Frankfurt am Main: Lang)

PLATE, HEINRICH. 1850. *Methodisch geordneter Lehrgang der englischen Sprache in zwei Teilen.* (Hanover: Ehlermann)

——. 1863. *Vollständiger Lehrgang zur leichten, schnellen und gründlichen Erlernung der Englischen Sprache. Elementarstufe*, 2nd edn (Dresden: Ehlermann)

RADTKE, EDGAR. 1994. *Gesprochenes Französisch und Sprachgeschichte: Zur Rekonstruktion der Gesprächskonstitution in Dialogen französischer Sprachlehrbücher des 17. Jahrhunderts unter besonderer Berücksichtigung der italienischen Adaptationen* (Tübingen: Niemeyer)

REINFRIED, MARKUS. 1992. *Das Bild im Fremdsprachenunterricht: Eine Geschichte der visuellen Medien am Beispiel des Französischunterrichts* (Tübingen: Narr)

RISAGER, KAREN. 2007. *Language and Culture Pedagogy: From a National to a Transnational Paradigm* (Clevedon: Multilingual Matters)

SCHRÖDER, KONRAD. 1975. *Lehrwerke für den Englischunterricht im deutschsprachigen Raum, 1665–1900* (Darmstadt: Wissenschaftliche Buchgesellschaft)

SEIDELMANN, CHRISTIAN FRIEDRICH. 1984 [1724]. *Tractatus Philosophico-Philologicus de Methodo Recte Tractandi Linguas Exoticas Speciatim Gallicam, Italicam et Anglicam*, facsimile and translation by Franz-Josef Zapp and Konrad Schröder (Augsburg: Universität Augsburg)

SEIDENSTÜCKER, JOHANN HEINRICH PHILIPP. 1795. 'Lateinische Stilübungen auf Schulen', in *Aufsätze pädagogischen und philologischen Inhalts*, ed. by Johann Heinrich Philipp Seidenstücker (Helmstedt: Fleckeisen), pp. 1-37

——. 1811. *Elementarbuch zur Erlernung der Französischen Sprache. Erste Abtheilung* (Dortmund and Leipzig)

——. 1813. *Elementarbuch zur Erlernung der Französischen Sprache. Zweite Abtheilung* (Dortmund and Leipzig)

STEUERWALD, WILHELM. 1886. *Englisches Lesebuch für höhere Lehranstalten* (München: Stahl)

TAFEL, LEONHARD. 1835. *Lehrbuch der englischen Sprache nach Hamiltonischen Grundsätzen* (Stuttgart: Cotta)

TOMPSON, JOHN. 1766. *English Miscellanies*, 4th edn, 2 vols (Göttingen: Vandenhoek)

TURNER, JOHN FRANK. 1978. 'German Pedagogic Grammars of English, 1665-1750' (unpublished doctoral thesis, University of Braunschweig)

WAENTIG, PETER W. 2002. 'Die venezianische Ausgabe der *Colloquia et Dictionariolum Octo Linguarum* von 1656: Editionsgeschichte, Werkstruktur, Sprachkultur', in *Heilige und profane Sprachen: Holy and Profane Languages*, ed. by Werner Hüllen and Friederike Klippel (Wiesbaden: Harrassowitz), pp. 175-97

ZIMMER, J. F. W. 1844. *Lehrbuch der Englischen Sprache nach Hamilton'schen Grundsätzen*, 3rd edn (Heidelberg: Mohr)

Website

Tauchnitz Editions <http://www.tauchnitzeditions.com/> [accessed 21 September 2015]

Notes to Chapter 1

1. In the eighteenth-century grammars, I have in general disregarded the section on grammar, particularly since the early textbooks use Latin grammar as their basis and deal with each word class one after the other with the rules generally given in German and the few examples in a bilingual format.

2. For a biographical sketch of Tompson see Finkenstaedt 1992.

3. An example of such a letter is given in Bachmair 1771: 288-89.

4. See <http://www.tauchnitzeditions.com/> [accessed 21 September 2015] for a history of Tauchnitz and his publishing work.

CHAPTER 2

❖

Internationalism and Education in the 1920s and the Case of Foreign Language Teaching Policy in Britain

Michael Byram

After the nationalisms of World War I, there was a return in some political quarters to the internationalism which had begun to appear in the nineteenth century; this was particularly evident in the work of the League of Nations. Yet the tension with nationalisms continued in many social policies. This chapter traces those tensions in education policies — and foreign language policies in Britain in particular — in the post-war years through the analysis of the observations of two contemporaneous American scholars in Europe. The effects of internationalism turned out to be relatively short-lived in education generally. A more internationally oriented policy for foreign language teaching might be expected, but an analysis of the Leathes Report in Britain reveals a surprising lack of attention to internationalism in its arguments for language teaching in the post-war years.

Introduction

The purpose of this chapter is to analyse the tensions between nationalism and internationalism in the post-1918 decade and to what extent this had an impact on language teaching policy in Britain.

Given that the First World War was heavily influenced by nationalist aspirations, it is perhaps not surprising that the incipient influence of internationalism from the nineteenth century seemed to have disappeared under the jingoism of the recruitment of the first non-professional armies. However, as a result of the experience of a new kind of war, first described to the general public by Henri Barbusse's *Le Feu* (1916), one might expect internationalism to re-appear as a reaction to the 'horror'; and Barbusse and others tried to make this happen. Furthermore, with the development of the League of Nations and its internationalist ambitions, and the influence of intellectual movements such as the one led by Barbusse, one might expect to find traces of internationalism in education policy and practice. One might expect this as a reaction to the nationalism of education systems which had been part of the run-up to the war, well documented by historians such as Hobsbawm (1992) and Gellner (1987). At the same time there was what, in retrospect, is easily recognized as a nationalist reaction to the war and its costs — both human and economic — starting with the Treaty of Versailles and ending with the Second World War.

The history of internationalism, as Kuehl (2009) points out, has not been given as much attention as the history of nationalism, and yet it is an important phenomenon both historically and in contemporary times. In this chapter I shall focus on internationalism in the 1920s, reviewing to what extent internationalism played an important role in those turbulent post-'Great War' times. The analysis of foreign language education policy reveals one of the locations of the tensions between nationalism and internationalism.

So what might one expect of Foreign Language Teaching? The phenomenon of *Kulturkunde* in foreign-language teaching in Germany and the submission of language teaching to nationalism are well known in the history of language teaching (Risager 2007). Here is an extract from a text for teaching English in Germany where an Englishman is being quoted:

> We in Great Britain are now intensely jealous about Germany [...] because in the last hundred years, while we have fed on platitudes and vanity, they have had the energy and humility to develop a splendid system of national education, to toil on science, art and literature, [...] to clamber above us in the scale of civilisation. (Lincke 1927: 56)

Theory on intergroup relations argues that the glorification of an in-group by denigration of an out-group — in this case through a reverse perspective of the out-group denigrating itself — leads to increased self-esteem for members of the in-group (e.g. Tajfel 1981; Ellemers 2012). The nationalist intention here is clearly that the German learners of English would feel their self-esteem rising as they read that their civilization was better than the one they were learning about. Was there no contrary attempt to use foreign language teaching for internationalist purposes? I shall address this question by analysing in this chapter the position in Britain; the same question could also be considered for other countries.

The Historiography and Definition of Internationalism

To take up again Kuehl's (2009) point that there is little research on internationalism either as a concept or as a historical phenomenon, we need to note that this has led to a lack of clarity in definitions. Kuehl's own approach to definition is to trace the use of the concept by historians, but Holbraad (2003) makes his own historical analysis and uses it as a basis for positing three types of internationalism, which provides a good start to resolving the problem.

First, Holbraad identifies 'liberal internationalism', which is linked with 'confidence in the rational and moral qualities of human beings' and 'faith in progress towards more orderly social relations' (2003: 39). Holbraad argues that 'liberal internationalism' is a phrase, often employed without definition, that is associated with both pre-and post-1914 to 1918 periods and was associated with peace movements before the War and peace settlement after it. This is therefore what will interest us most, but it needs to be contextualized by reference to other kinds of internationalism.

Holbraad's second type is 'socialist internationalism', within which he distinguishes two sub-types: 'reformist' and 'revolutionary'. The distinction between the two is a matter of different responses to nationalism. Where reformist socialism, like most other types of internationalism, accepts nationalism as an inevitability, revolutionary internationalism posits a basis in a non-nationalist solidarity of the proletariat, believing that class affinities are stronger than national allegiances.[1]

A third type, 'conservative internationalism', is older than the others, and Holbraad argues that these have more explicit and recognizable ideologies which conservative internationalism lacks. One form of conservative internationalism can be seen in the 'awareness of a shared interest in security and a common interest in survival' (Holbraad 2003: 12) among states resisting dominance by powers such as Napoleonic France. Another form is that of 'solidarity' among states, manifest in alliances and leagues at moments of critical challenge to their existence, such as the Holy Alliance against revolution after the French Revolution. This kind of internationalism is above all political, although it may be linked with a moral stance, for example in the battle with Bolshevism after 1917.[2]

Another concept is proposed by Halliday (1988: 193), who argues that liberal internationalism has been challenged by 'hegemonic internationalism': 'the belief that the integration of the world is taking place on asymmetrical, unequal terms, and that this is the only possible and indeed desirable way for such an integration to take place'. The obvious manifestation of this has been colonialism, but it is also present in contemporary international relations dominated by a very few states and symbolized in the dominance of the English language.

The complexity of the different analytical types of internationalism and its connotations, which change over time, are, as Halliday says (1988: 188), best caught in the notion of the 'cluster concept' where there is no single, core meaning. On the other hand one common feature is the need to define internationalism in contrast to nationalism, and this brings us to the 1920s.

Internationalism Defined through Nationalism[3]

A first indication of how internationalism in the 1920s was defined in contrast to nationalism can be seen in Barbusse's statement on the aims of the 'Clarté' group (1920: 9). In his analysis of the contemporary world he argues as follows: 'Le capitalisme déclenche le nationalisme, et le nationalisme s'appuie sur la guerre comme la paix sur la justice'. The alternative is: 'L'infaillible raison nous commande de substituer l'idéal humain à l'idéal patriotique et l'internationalisme au nationalisme'. The Clarté movement, established by Barbusse, took its political doctrine from the Third International (Barbusse 1920: 133) and the socialist movement.

At about the same time, and in stark contrast, John Maynard Keynes in *The*

Economic Consequences of the Peace (1920) described the nationalist atmosphere and the characters of the negotiators in Paris:

> The future life of Europe was not their concern; its means of livelihood was not their anxiety. Their preoccupations, good and bad alike, related to frontiers and nationalities, to the balance of power, to imperial aggrandizements, to the future enfeeblement of a strong and dangerous enemy, to revenge, and to the shifting by the victors of their unbearable financial burdens on to the shoulders of the defeated. (Chapter 4: p. 56)

Keynes is clear that the people in power, and especially Clemenceau, were fixated on national concerns. Internationalism was certainly not on the agenda of these powerful individuals. On the other hand, the idea of a League of Nations struggled into being in parallel with the Versailles process; and McCarthy (2011) describes the League of Nations as a manifestation of 'liberal internationalism'.[4]

The League of Nations and Internationalism in Education

Those who supported the League of Nations, whatever their country, saw education systems as crucial sources of support and development; and as far as Britain is concerned, it is the League of Nations Union (LNU) which was most important in education. The LNU was formed in 1918 to support acceptance of the League of Nations itself; and its Reconstruction Committee recommended 'organizing research and discussion on matters of international concern and influencing education in schools and universities so as to increase public relations and promote a just appreciation of the principles and spirit of the League' (Elliott 1977: 131). Elliott's account of a League of Nations approach to the teaching of history in the 1920s charts considerable success in schools, with support from intellectuals such as Bertrand Russell, who argued that 'history should be taught in the same way in all countries of the world' using a textbook produced by the League of Nations (Russell 1932: 82). There was also support from government, not immediately but eventually. Yet opposition gained strength in the 1930s, with accusations of the League being 'international, pacifist, anti-patriotic and anti-empire', a combination of adjectives from a Conservative Member of Parliament (Cobb 1927: 8). Towards the end of the 1930s, the strength of the work of the LNU was failing fast, and Elliott (1977: 140) concludes his analysis with these words:

> The mistaken assumption of those distinguished British educationalists and classroom teachers who subscribed to the Union's ideas, was to imagine that a newly-formed pressure group, with such fundamentally reformist objectives, could hope to influence the deep-rooted conservatism of English educational institutions.

Elliott uses here the term 'reformist' and a few lines later refers to the Union's '"internationalist" emphasis which it stressed was wholly benign', a combination of terms — including the scare quotation marks — which echoes Holbraad's categorizations of 'reformist' and 'revolutionary' socialist internationalism mentioned above.

What we see in Britain is part of a wider international effort. Fuchs (2007) describes in some detail the networks which the League of Nations supported, both the informal networks whose complexity needs to be analysed by mathematical modelling; and the formal networks which are his main focus. In the 1920s, he says, there were four networks relevant to education and apparent in institutional structures and educational discourses. One of these related to child welfare; a second to peace and moral education; a third to university relations; and a fourth to the teaching profession (Fuchs 2007: 200). Fuchs does not, however, analyse the ideas in circulation, only the mechanisms, which led, for example, to attempts to introduce an international textbook for history, an idea developed by representatives of the New Education Movement and supported by Bertrand Russell, as mentioned above. This ultimately failed, although there was some success in the 1930s in the adoption of an international declaration on history teaching in 1937, but this, too, as a consequence of the Second World War, was never implemented (Elliott 1977).

On the other hand, there was educational success in one concrete realization of League of Nations principles in the founding in 1924 in Geneva of the first international school for the children of employees of the League. This was 'in response to a view that one of the reasons that the world is so divided is because of nationalism and that an effective way of combating this reality would be through international education' (Cambridge and Thompson 2004: 170).

Contemporaneous Views on Internationalism in Schools

The interesting question is now what was actually happening in schools, whether directly founded by internationalists or influenced by internationalist thinking. There were two researchers at the time who were asking themselves similar questions. They were both from the USA: Jonathan French Scott and Daniel Prescott.[5]

Jonathan French Scott's *The Menace of Nationalism in Education* was published in 1926 and republished in 2012. He was an 'instructor in history at the University of Michigan',[6] and his book analyses textbooks in England, France and Germany. He attracted the attention of *The Spectator* and a review in 1926 provides a good overview of his work:

> His conclusions may be summarized: Chauvinism and vituperation of Germany are sharpest in French histories of to-day; but if there is less vituperation against France in German manuals there is a deeper nationalism and more glorification of the past; the British mind is quicker to forget, as is shown in the treatment of the American Revolution, but school books reveal too complacent a desire to 'take up the white man's burden' and dispense light to surrounding nations. (*The Spectator*, 23 April 1926: 26)

This is a fair and accurate summary, although rather than using the term 'chauvinism', Scott himself refers to the:

> patriotic purpose of French education and the way in which, as a reaction to French defeat in 1870, the 'école laique' is now devoted to nationalism in the way it was once used to foster 'piety and loyalty to the Roman Catholic church'. (Scott 1926: 22)

Not surprisingly, Scott focuses on the teaching of history in the three countries, both its contribution to educating the patriotic citizen and how it represents the other two countries. The relationship of nationalism and internationalism is a theme he pursues in some detail without clarifying his understanding of internationalism. In France, he says, the teacher unions asked the Minister of Public Instruction to eliminate textbooks which incite hatred among nations and to request help from the League of Nations in developing international school programmes or curricula with an emphasis on the teaching of peace. When he turns to Germany, in phrases such as 'a moment of clear vision', we catch a glimpse of his own ideals in his account of the revolutionary movements immediately after the cessation of war:

> Revolutions are born in moods of spiritual exaltation. Enslaved humanity, bursting its chains, seeks for the quick realisation of Utopia. Idealism seemed to triumph [...]. In a moment of clear vision the Germans saw the abyss into which national hatreds were plunging unhappy Europe. In their revolution of 1918 they had repudiated that government which had been so largely responsible for their own blind cult of self-centred nationalism. And from the bondage of such self-centred nationalism, with its unhappy consequences, they would fain free their children. Henceforth 'moral education, civic sentiment, and personal and professional service in the spirit of German patriotism and international reconciliation' were to be inculcated in all German schools. (Scott 1926: 95)

Scott gives examples, from Brunswick and Prussia, of government circulars forbidding the teaching of revenge and encouraging the teaching of solidarity with 'the Little and the Great Fatherland, of the state and the human community'. These are quotations from immediate post-war years and include a veto on opposition to the revolution:

> whereas previously historical instruction, together with other branches of learning, was misused to stir up hatred of peoples, this sort of thing in future is to be absolutely barred, to give place rather to a reasonable social-historical type of instruction. All tendentious and false teachings in regard to the world war and its causes are to be avoided. All books which glorify the war as such are to be removed from the school libraries. In no branches of instruction are the teachers to express unfavourable and false opinions in regard to the causes and results of the revolution, nor in regard to the present government. (Scott 1926: 96, quoting his translation of the *Zentralblatt für die Gesamte Unterrichts-Verwaltung in Preussen*, 1918: 708)

This was soon succeeded by reaction and right-wing governments, for example in Prussia, where the Ministry of Education decreed in 1923 that:

> all schools have a duty of fulfilling their tasks as German schools, while in suitable fashion they work for the intensification of German culture: to inspire youth with enthusiasm for German speech, the German race under German greatness of spirit is the more earnest task than ever before [...] today, more strongly than ever, the old demand holds, that every lesson shall be a German lesson. (Scott 1926: 102, quoting his translation of the *Zentralblatt für die Gesamte Unterrichts-Verwaltung in Preussen*, 1923: 199)

In other provinces such as Baden, Scott finds a more conciliatory tone in the ministerial documents which suggest that patriotism and international relations can be combined; and he also finds some counter influences in the *Jugendbewegung*[7] and an organization of German pacifist teachers — the *Bund Entschiedener Schulreformer* — who have their own review, *Die neue Erziehung*,[8] which criticizes government documents for their narrow patriotism. Scott is, however, not optimistic about the strength of influence of such a body.

When he comes to England and its textbooks, Scott finds a similar emphasis on patriotism even if it is not enforced or openly encouraged by the state: 'If there is no state cult, however, there is a very real emphasis on patriotism in British education' (Scott 1926: 145). This anticipates the analysis of later historians of the effects of the League of Nation Union in England, as we saw above.

The second empirical researcher of the time is Daniel Prescott.[9] Prescott was a Professor of Education and a psychologist who in his early career carried out a comparative education research project, as a young Harvard graduate, entitled 'International Problems and Policies in Relation to Educational Aims. Methods and Materials'. He published a book from this project in 1930 with Harvard University Press entitled *Education and International Relations: The Study of the Social Forces That Determine the Influence of Education*. The book opens in a way reminiscent of Barbusse's account of the war in the trenches in *Le Feu*:

> Twelve years ago today I was in Europe, along the Chemin des Dames. I had felt the call to 'make the world safe for democracy'. A native of Wilson's own state, I had a holy idealism for democracy, and having read broadly, among historical novels, I felt the glory of the war crusade. I was nineteen years of age then. Six months later I was twenty-nine. That much time at the front had taught me something about warfare besides its glory (Prescott 1930: 1).[10]

He goes on to explain that he began to consider the factors which might have created a condition in warring countries which would lead to 'the orgy of killing'. Later, he turned to the experiences which might lead children 'to distrust other peoples, to feel that war is glorious, to believe that ours is the greatest nation on earth, to feel that we have a Destiny and that other nations threaten that Destiny' (1930: 2). His conclusion is that 'such conditioning influences can readily be discerned' (1930: 2).

His ambition was considerable:

> I wish to describe the different factors that, by their interplay, condition large masses of the world's population to this or that attitude. I wish to show why none of the nations visited is now homogeneous in outlook and feeling, to point out the directions in which the greatest changes of attitude are taking place, and to account for these in terms of the earlier experiences of the groups. (1930: 3)

Prescott did his fieldwork from 1926 to 1927 in several European countries: Britain, Switzerland, Austria, Germany, Czechoslovakia and France. He also planned a trip to Russia but had to abandon it for lack of funds. He used a variety of techniques to gather information — document analysis, interviews, visits to schools — and his list of interviewees is impressive both in quantity and in terms of the key people he managed to meet. This can be seen from one of his monthly reports to his mentor at Harvard (22 November 1926), where he described his interviewees in Britain and mentioned, *inter alia*, Lord Eustace Percy, President of the Board of Education; Mr Richards, H. M. Chief Inspector; H. A. L. Fisher, who had 'procured the passage of the famous Education Acts of 1918' (UMCP); Sir Michael Sadler; and Professor Arnold Toynbee. Prescott also devised a 'Test of attitudes about international problems' which he tried to have administered in schools. He was not always successful, particularly in France, where he found a wariness of psychological testing and a more general anti-American feeling because of American policy on debt. This material does not appear in his ensuing book and I assume he had to abandon it for lack of cooperation.

In the book from 1930, in contrast to Scott's investigation of textbooks and curriculum, Prescott focused on social psychology, 'for, as it turned out, it is the "spirit" of the schools that matters most': 'I found places where the subject-matter in the courses of study appeared very "internationally-minded" but where the instruction or the atmosphere of the school influenced the children to very different sentiments' (Prescott 1930: 3). On the basis of his analysis of the spirit of the schools, Prescott's conclusions with respect to nationalism and internationalism are as follows:

> The attitudes that the schools tend to encourage in their pupils vary between two extremes according to the weight of the social forces that determine the policies of these schools. On the one extreme is the selfish national individualism and international anarchy of 1914 and at the other is an almost fanatical worship of a 'new world' ideal based upon brotherly love. The situation most often found is that the interplay of forces causes the schools to create a consciousness of the undesirability of selfish national individualism and hope for a 'new world' without giving any very definite suggestions as to how this 'new world' can be realised. (Prescott 1930: 121)

The accuracy of Prescott's criticism of a lack of clarity and definition among the opponents of nationalism is an issue which cannot be pursued here, but it may well be a factor in the failure of internationalism to overcome what Elliott, quoted earlier and referring to England, described as 'the deep-rooted conservatism of English educational institutions' (Elliott 1977: 140). The next step here will therefore be to look more closely at the British situation and to focus on language teaching policy.

Foreign Language Teaching Policy in Britain

The Leathes Report — properly entitled *Report of the committee appointed by the Prime Minister to enquire into the position of Modern Languages in the Educational System of Great Britain* — is well named. It is evident that Leathes himself was the main author when one compares the style, and some of the content, of the Report with Leathes' own writings, especially his book *What is Education?* (1913). Leathes was at the time of the report the First Commissioner of the Civil Service and, before moving to the Civil Service, had been a lecturer in History at Trinity College Cambridge, where he was closely involved in planning and writing the *Cambridge Modern History* (Dampier, revised Matthew 2004).

The Leathes Committee was one of four subcommittees dealing with the modernization of education under a general Reconstruction Committee. This had been formed in response to calls for a review of education which had become particularly strong by 1916. As Bayley (1991) shows, education was being blamed for lack of success in the war; and in particular the focus on classical studies was criticized in the light of a lack of expertise in modern languages:

> The Diplomatic Service and Foreign Office required linguists to deal with inter-allied relations and enemy propaganda. The Army needed interpreters and translators to accompany Britain's various armies in the field. A British naval blockade of neutral countries, Scandinavia, The Netherlands, and Spain, required the appointment of consuls and consular agents. (Bayley 1991: 12)

Nonetheless, the committee's terms of reference were broader than the concern with the war, even though they made explicit the importance of languages in public service and commerce. The committee were charged to enquire into 'Modern Languages' in secondary schools and universities, 'regard being had to the requirements of a liberal education and appreciation of the history, literature and civilisation of other countries, and to the interest of commerce and public service' (Leathes Report 1918: 1).

The first thing to say about the Leathes Report is that it introduced the concept of 'Modern Studies' as an alternative to, but largely modelled on, 'Classical Studies'; and there is much in the Report which fulfils the requirement to consider how language study can be a contribution to the individual's 'liberal education and appreciation of history, literature and civilisation of other countries', whilst acknowledging the country's need for people who know other languages and other countries. Perhaps the most striking statement of values in the whole document is the following:

> We have devoted four sub-sections to the practical ends of Modern Studies, and we owe no apology for putting practical ends first. Knowledge and training have a clear value in the struggle for existence; and in order to live well it is first of all necessary to live. Practical education is the only foundation on which idealistic achievements can be raised; to neglect the practical ends of education is foolishness; but to recognise no other is to degrade humanity. (Leathes Report 1918: 16)

It is then suggested that the Arts, history and philosophy also motivate. Although they have no 'survival value' — with echoes of a Darwinist language here — nonetheless 'men [sic] will work for the joy of comprehension, for the joy in beauty, for the joy of creative construction' (ibid.). Furthermore, since Modern Studies is 'the study of man in all his higher activities', it may have special moral value, and is 'an instrument of culture', i.e., the 'training which tends to develop the higher faculties, the imagination, the sense of beauty, and the intellectual comprehension' (ibid.).

Bayley (1991: 16) considers that the Leathes Report is elitist, reflecting the views of the Board of Education and its civil servants who were of Oxbridge and independent (i.e. private) school background; it is not, she says, 'epoch-making'. The assertion that the consequences of education cannot be enjoyed 'in their fullness' by all might support this interpretation, but the related assertion that they may be shared 'in some measure' by all who desire them is not a statement that a liberal curriculum is suitable only for some people. This must also be placed in the wider context of educational reform in the final years of the war. In 1918, the Minister for Education, H. A. L. Fisher, introduced a substantial new Education Act and in so doing focused on the importance of widening access to education in the same way as there was growing recognition of the need to extend the franchise:

> [T]hat same logic which leads us to desire an extension of the franchise wants also an extension of education. There is a growing sense, not only in England but through Europe, and I must say especially in France, that the industrial workers of the country are entitled to be considered primarily as citizens and as fit subjects for any form of education from which they are capable of profiting. (*Hansard*, 10 August 1917, cited in Maclure 1965: 173)

Fisher says that workers want education not only to earn higher wages, or to rise out of their own class, but also to have 'a source of pure enjoyment and refuge from the necessary hardships of a life spent in the midst of clanging machinery in our hideous cities of toil' (cited in Maclure 1965: 173).

Turning now to our main focus on internationalism, it is certainly true that in this respect the Leathes Report is not epoch-making. The focus is on other languages and countries of Europe and on understanding the 'national life' of 'modern peoples' (p. 1), based on the notion that languages are a key to the 'national psychology' of countries. The discussion centres on which languages are needed by whom and for what reasons (Byram 2015), ultimately leading to the establishment of a hierarchy of languages.

As we look for signs of internationalism, it is noteworthy that the report also has a special section on 'artificial languages', particularly Esperanto, although the rivalry with Ido is noted. The text discusses the advantages of ease of learning — and the possible speed with which it is also forgotten if there is no opportunity for practice. The potential for communication in 'commerce between nations' and for making scientific publications 'intelligible to all peoples' (p. 22) is prized; and it is suggested that there should be further investigation into the possible practical advantages. It is stated as obvious that artificial languages cannot serve the other, liberal education purposes of language teaching:

> Of course, no artificial language can have the individuality, the associations, the inherent charm of a natural language; it is therefore unlikely that any artificial language can ever have much literary value. But these things are not needed for commerce or for science, for which certainty, precision, and elaboration are the principal requirements. (ibid.)

There is thus no attention paid to the ideology behind Esperanto, which in the view of its inventor, L. L. Zamenhof, had an 'inner idea' which was not incompatible with patriotism, but which went beyond loyalty to country. Zamenhof refers to 'Esperantists', to 'Esperantism' and even to 'Esperanto-land' as a metaphor for the utopian notion of 'human brotherhood' (Forster 1982: 98). The relationship of language, people and place in this string of concepts is analogous to the relationship of language, country and people at national level. In 1905 Zamenhof spoke to the annual congress of the Esperanto movement about how Esperanto would allow people to communicate 'not as foreigners, not as competitors, but as brothers who, not inflicting their own language on one another, understand one another [...] shake each other's hand not hypocritically as one national to another, but sincerely as man to man' (Forster 1982: 83–84). None of this is present in the Leathes Report but it anticipates the references to brotherhood which Prescott found in his investigations two decades later.

In short, we can conclude that the internationalism which had been present in European thought and action until 1914 and which re-appeared in the 1920s was not present in the thoughts of the Leathes Committee.[11] It might be argued that this was not surprising in a document written at the height of the war years, when victory for either side seemed unlikely and patriotism was a necessary foundation for continuing support of the war effort.[12]

On the other hand, there were others in British society who were taking a different view. In the same year as the publication of the Leathes Report, the League of Nations Union (LNU) was established, as noted earlier, under the presidency of the former British Foreign Secretary, Lord Grey (Elliott 1977: 131). This was a fusion of existing bodies supporting the League of Nations concept; and indicates an internationalist thread of ideas contemporaneous with the workings of the Leathes Committee, even though the Report reveals no awareness of this, for example in the list of witnesses it examined. As mentioned earlier, the LNU, through its Education Committee, had some success in persuading educationists to teach the principles of 'internationalism'. Just as the internationalism of the League of Nations itself was evolving in parallel with the nationalism of the Treaty of Versailles at a supra-national level, we can see the parallelism of the League of Nations Union and the Leathes Report, although without the jingoism of the Versailles negotiations described by Keynes.

Another indication of support for an internationalist curriculum is a report for the British Association for the Advancement of Science (BAAS) on 'training for citizenship', with no date of publication but described by Scott (1926: 145) as appearing soon after the war. Here strong recommendations are made for curricula which promote 'International Brotherhood', with support for teaching about the League of Nations, recommended too by the Association of Assistant Masters. Contrary to Prescott's pessimistic view of the vagueness of calls for international brotherhood, Scott was optimistic about England providing the right environment for the flourishing of 'the international ideal' (1926: 154):

> Take it all in all, there are probably few more fertile fields for the germination and growth of the international ideal than England. In the first place, that ideal will flourish best in an atmosphere of freedom and frankness, such as prevails in that country. There one may stand up fearlessly for any creed. In the next place, England is a 'satiated State'. She has no thirst for colonies, as Germany had before the Great War, no stinging sense of loss as Germany has today. Her territorial ambitions gratified, she wants no disturbance of international peace.

In the third place, her isolation makes for the growth of sentiment for peace. She is far less subject than the Great Powers of the Continent to the nationalist alarms and fears that make for war — though, of course, the development of aviation may, in time, work havoc with that isolation. Finally, her economic interests, more than those of any other country, demanded the comity of nations.

Nonetheless, rather astutely Prescott picks out one important negative factor:

> [T]here is however one important force militating against the success of internationalism in British education: the Briton's belief in the essential rightness of the British Empire, his tendency to identify the welfare of the Empire with the welfare of humanity. [...] It is this belief that leads the British Association for the Advancement of Science to speak of the Empire as 'the greatest human institution under heaven, the greatest secular organisation for good'. (ibid.)

The obvious major difference between the internationalism of the report for the BAAS, however high its status, and the absence of internationalism in the Leathes Report is the official status of the latter and the wide-ranging inquiry on which it was based. The concerns with national need, practical applications and 'liberal education' remained dominant.

Conclusion

The presence of internationalism in education in the 1920s is limited but not without its importance as a counterbalance to the weight of nationalism. We might have expected a greater presence in the policy on teaching of foreign languages, since this is one area of the curriculum which turns learners' attention outwards beyond national boundaries. The 1918 Leathes Report certainly expresses admiration for the achievements of countries outside the national borders — and does so in the name of liberal education — but does not conceptualize this admiration in anything but national and nationalist terms. Scott (1930) and Prescott (1930) saw attempts to move education systems in the direction of internationalism but these remained short-lived. Nationalism and the economic consequences of punitive international sanctions created the patriotism which, as Keynes foresaw, ultimately led to another war.[13]

Bibliography

BARBUSSE, HENRI. 1916. *Le Feu: journal d'une escouade* (Paris: Flammarion)

——. 1920. *La Lueur dans l'âme: ce que veut le groupe Clarté* (Paris: Clarté)

BAYLEY, SUSAN. 1991. 'Modern Languages: An "Ideal of Humane Learning": The Leathes Report of 1918', *Journal of Educational Administration and History*, 23.2: 11–24

BYRAM, MICHAEL. 2015. 'Languages and Other Priorities in the Leathes Report to the British Government (1918)', in *Français, anglais et allemand: trois langues rivales entre 1850 et 1945 — French, English and German: three languages in competition between 1850 and 1945. Actes du colloque international tenu à Essen le 13–15 septembre 2012*, ed. by M. Reinfried (= *Documents pour l'Histoire du Français Langue Etrangère ou Seconde*, 53) (Paris: SIHFLES)

CAMBRIDGE, JAMES, and JEFFREY THOMPSON. 2004. 'Internationalism and Globalisation as Contexts for International Education', *Compare*, 34: 161–75

COBB, CYRIL S. 1927. 'The League and the Schools', *The Times*, 16 July 1927, online at *The Times Digital Archive* [accessed 8 February 2018]

DAMPIER, WILLIAM CECIL. 2004. 'Leathes, Sir Stanley Mordaunt (1861–1938)' (rev. by Henry Colin Gray Matthew), *Oxford Dictionary of National Biography* (Oxford: Oxford University Press) <http://www.oxforddnb.com/view/article/34458> [accessed 27 Sept 2012]

ELLEMERS, NAOMI. 2012. 'The Group Self', *Science*, 336: 848–52

ELLIOTT, BRIAN J. 1977. 'The League of Nations Union and History Teaching in England: A Study in Benevolent Bias', *History of Education: Journal of the History of Education Society*, 6: 131–41

The Education of the Adolescent (The Hadow Report). 1926. (London: HM Stationery Office)

FORSTER, PETER G. 1982. *The Esperanto Movement* (The Hague: Mouton)

FUCHS, ECKHARDT. 2007. 'The Creation of New Networks in Education: The League of Nations and Educational Organizations in the 1920s', *Paedagogica Historica*, 43: 199–209

GELLNER, ERNST. 1987. *Culture, Identity and Politics* (Cambridge: Cambridge University Press)

HALLIDAY, FRED. 1988. 'Three Concepts of Internationalism', *International Affairs*, 64: 187–98

HOBSBAWM, ERIC J. 1988. 'Working Class Internationalism', in *Internationalism in the Labour Movement, 1830–1940*, ed. by Frits van Holthoon and Marcel van der Linden, 2 vols (Leiden: Brill), I, 3–16

——. 1992. *Nations and Nationalism since 1780* (Cambridge: Cambridge University Press)

HOLBRAAD, CARSTEN. 2003. *Internationalism and Nationalism in European Political Thought* (Basingstoke: Palgrave)

KEYNES, JOHN MAYNARD.1920. *The Economic Consequences of the Peace* (London: Macmillan) <http://oll.libertyfund.org/titles/303> [accessed 9 June 2015]

KUEHL, WARREN F. 2009. 'Concepts of internationalism in history', *Peace and Change*, 11.2: 1–10

LADEMACHER, HEINRICH. 1988. 'Kosmopolitanismus, Solidarität und Nation: Einige Bemerkungen zum Wandel von Begriff und Wirklichkeit im internationalem Sozialismus', in *Internationalism in the Labour Movement. 1830–1940*, ed. by Frits van Holthoon and Marcel van der Linden, 2 vols (Leiden: Brill), II, 371–91

[LEATHES REPORT]. 1918. *Report of the committee appointed by the Prime Minister to enquire into the position of Modern Languages in the Educational System of Great Britain* (London: HMSO)

LEATHES, STANLEY MORDAUNT. 1913. *What is Education?* (London: Bell)

——. 1915–23. *The People of England: A Social History for Schools*, 3 vols (London: Heinemann), I (1915): *The People in the Making*

LEONE, BRUNO. 1986. *Internationalism: Opposing Viewpoints* (Saint Paul, MN: Greenhaven)

LINCKE, KURT 1927. *Lehrbuch der englischen Sprache: für höhere Lehranstalten* (Frankfurt am Main: Diesterweg)

MACLURE, J. STUART. (ed.). 1965. *Educational Documents: England and Wales 1816 to the Present Day* (London: Methuen)

McCARTHY, HELEN. 2011. *The British People and the League of Nations: Democracy, Citizenship and Internationalism* (Manchester: Manchester University Press)

PRESCOTT, DANIEL. 1916. *Patriots in the Making: What America Can Learn from France and Germany* (New York: Appleton)

——. 1930. *Education and International Relations: A Study of the Social Forces that Determine the Influence of Education* (Cambridge, MA: Harvard University Press) <http://babel. hathitrust.org/cgi/pt?id=mdp.39015020212646;page=root;seq=17;view=1up;size=100;orient=0;num=1> [accessed 8 February 2018]

REISNER, EDWARD H. 1922. *Nationalism and Education since 1789: A Social and Political History of Modern Education* (New York: Macmillan)

RISAGER, KAREN. 2007. *Language and Culture Pedagogy* (Clevedon: Multilingual Matters)

RUSSELL, B. 1932. *Education and the Social Order* (London: Allen and Unwin)

SCOTT, JONATHAN F. 1926. *The Menace of Nationalism in Education* (London: Allen and Unwin) <http://babel.hathitrust.org/cgi/pt?id=uc1.$b264620;view=1up;seq=1> [accessed 8 February 2018]

TAJFEL, HENRI. 1981. *Human Groups and Social Categories: Studies in Social Psychology* (Cambridge: Cambridge University Press)

WILLIAMS, RAYMOND. 1977. *Marxism and Literature* (Oxford: Oxford University Press)

Archive material

UMCP HBK Maryland Room Library, University Record ARCV 81–10

Notes to Chapter 2

1. It is often argued that class affinities did not withstand the demands of nationalism at the beginning of the 1914-18 war and undermined this non-national type of internationalism (e.g. Lademacher 1988). Hobsbawm (1988) would, however, contest this view as missing at least two important points. First, he argues that theorists of the working-class movement, beginning with Marx and Engels, had in common with theorists of bourgeois Liberalism an evolutionary view, in which there would be a development from smaller social entities to larger ones and ultimately to a global society, but passing through the necessary stage of the nation-state: '[T]he world of nations is an intermediate stage on man's progress from localised to global existence, for Marx and Engels as well as numerous non-socialist thinkers of their time' (Hobsbawm1988: 6). Second, Hobsbawm points out that in fact workers at the beginning and during the 1914-18 war did not suffer the same traumatic sense of conflict between international movement and national identification as did their leaders. He gives the example of Welsh miners who followed syndicalist leaders in striking during 1915 in the coalfields but were also 'pouring into the army in 1914 as volunteers' (ibid.: 11).

2. An example of the rejection of internationalism because it is associated with Bolshevism is to be found in the speech of Henry Cabot Lodge in the American Senate in 1919 against the idea of the United States joining the League of Nations: 'I must think of the United States first, and when I think of the United States first in an arrangement like this I am thinking of what is best for the world, for if the United States fails, the best hopes of mankind fail with it. I have never had but one allegiance — I cannot divide it now. I have loved but one flag and I cannot share that devotion and give affection to the mongrel banner invented for a league. Internationalism, illustrated by the Bolshevik and by the men to whom all countries are alike provided they can make money out of them, is to me repulsive' (Quoted in Leone 1986: 26). Cabot Lodge was, however, arguing for American isolationism i.e. nationalism without internationalism — whether Bolshevik or liberal.

3. The theoretical basis for the analysis which follows is Williams's concept 'structure of feeling' of the times, those 'formally held and systematic beliefs' and the 'meanings and values as they are actively lived and felt' (Williams 1977: 132).

4. McCarthy in fact offers no definition of what she means by this phrase but we can take it that she is using it much as Kuehl and Halliday do, as cited above.

5. These two authors contrast, in their interest in internationalism, with another American author, Edward H. Reisner, who in his 1922 book has no reference to internationalism and only a passing reference to the international thought of the eighteenth century, which, he implies, was replaced by the nationalism of the nineteenth century.

6. As indicated on his previous book *Patriots in the Making: What America can Learn from France and Germany* (1916). Available online at: <http://ia600502.us.archive.org/22/items/patriotsinthemak014269mbp/patriotsinthemak014269mbp.pdf> [accessed 25 July 2015].

7. The *Jugendbewegung* [Youth Movement] began in the late nineteenth century with a turning away from the life of the industrialized modern city and a Romanticism-inspired search for life in the country. The first realization was in the *Wandervogel* movement of young people spending time in the countryside, re-discovering traditional folk-songs and 'wandering' through the countryside.

8. The international networks which grew in the 1920s linked these organizations in Germany with the New Education Fellowship in Britain, especially through the presence of Elisabeth Rotten (for a biography see: <http://paed.com/rotten/> [accessed 25 July 2015]). Their commitment to 'internationalism' was, however, limited and the main focus was on improving pedagogy and methods of teaching and learning.

9. Prescott's archives are held at the University of Maryland, and I am grateful for the help of the library in providing access to them.

10. Prescott does not need to give a source for the quotation except indirectly in his reference to Woodrow Wilson because Wilson's call to 'make the world safe for democracy' in his justification of the entry of the USA into the war was well known.

11. It is possible to speculate on the strength of Leathes' influence here. He was certainly much concerned with national life, as is evident from the preface to the first of his three volumes of a history of England: 'I hold the view — which some may consider fanciful — that there is a people of England with a national life of its own. It is at any time composed of all the men, women, and children of England, just as I am composed of the innumerable cells that make up my body. But it has a personal life, just as I have a personal life. And that personal life has been continuous at least since the time of Alfred' (Leathes 1915: ix). The similarities in style and content between the Report and Leathes' own writings are striking but cannot be pursued here.

12. A later report on secondary education in general, the Hadow Report (1926), does have one indication that foreign language teaching might be linked to an international perspective with the use of the phrase 'citizen of the world': 'A MODERN FOREIGN LANGUAGE. *We may begin by summarising our reasons for suggesting the inclusion of a modern foreign language in the courses of study for post-primary schools.* In the first place a foreign language is an excellent educational subject, since it brings into play and stimulates the mental activities of the pupils and widens their outlook and interests as citizens of the world. From another aspect, it affords a good means to literary culture, through the study of works of great literature, and thus to a truly liberal education. Further, it may be of practical use in certain industries and occupations, and helps to equip the pupils for the work of earning their livelihood. It has thus at once a disciplinary, a literary and a practical value' (*The Education of the Adolescent*, 1926: 211-12) (emphasis in original).

13. On the day I write this, I read a *Guardian* newspaper article tracing the increase in patriotism in Russia caused by European economic sanctions: Amelia Gentleman: 'Patriotism, propaganda and parmesan: what do Muscovites really think?' (*Guardian*, 9 June 2015 < https://www.theguardian.com/cities/2015/jun/09/patriotism-propaganda-parmesan-what-do-muscovites-really-think>).

CHAPTER 3

❖

Creating an International Penfriend Network at the End of the Nineteenth Century: The Scholars' International Correspondence (1896-1914)

Marlis Schleich

Language proficiency and peace among nations — expectations were flying high in 1896 when Paul Mieille (1859-1933), an English teacher in the South of France, turned to the English journalist, publisher and peace activist William T. Stead (1849-1912) to set up an international correspondence scheme between French and British pupils, henceforward referred to as the Scholars' International Correspondence. In March 1897, Germany joined in, when the teacher of modern languages Martin Hartmann (1854-1926) founded the German Central Office for International Correspondence (*Deutsche Zentralstelle für internationalen Briefwechsel*) in Leipzig. In 1898, the French teacher Edward Hicks Magill (1825-1907) introduced the Scholars' International Correspondence at Swarthmore College, Pennsylvania. Thus an international penfriend network was established which worked primarily on a European, but also on a transatlantic scale. This chapter first recalls the aspects of the historical context at the end of the nineteenth century which constituted the requisite pre-conditions for the development of the Scholars' International Correspondence. It then outlines how the Scholars' International Correspondence was established and organized with the help of journals and magazines (France, Great Britain) or central offices and committees (Germany, the US). Finally, it looks into the practicalities of the Scholars' International Correspondence.

'It may appear to be a very small thing, this of writing a letter regularly in a foreign language to an unknown correspondent, but from such small things great ones may arise.'[1]

Introduction

Facilitating intercultural encounters in face-to-face or virtual settings is nowadays an integral part of teaching foreign languages. This chapter aims to uncover the historical roots of the current situation by investigating the first attempts to organize a systematic exchange of letters between pupils of secondary schools in different countries at the end of the nineteenth century, the Scholars' International Correspondence. These attempts can be seen as the precursors of present-day programmes like those offered by the European Union for the school sector (such as Erasmus+ and eTwinning).[2]

The international penfriend network,[3] which was initially established in the course of the year 1897 by two foreign-language teachers (Paul Mieille in France and Martin Hartmann in Germany) and one journalist, publisher and peace activist (William T. Stead in London), has been noted by historians of foreign-language education such as Monique Mombert (2001: 176), Sébastien Rival (2012: 61, 66), Volker Raddatz (1977: 24-25) and Sabine Doff (2002: 434-35). However, the only contribution I am aware of with a clear focus on the international correspondence scheme as introduced above is an article by Hermann Josef Ody (1957). Since then a comprehensive account of the Scholars' International Correspondence has remained a desideratum, addressed in my doctoral dissertation (Schleich 2013, 2015). The purpose of this chapter is to introduce the topic to an English-speaking readership.

The Historical Background

Following a 'contextual approach' (Bevir 2011: 11; see Schleich 2015: 23-35), the aspects of the historical context which are most relevant for the development of the Scholars' International Correspondence are discussed below.

The Transportation and Communication Revolution

For society as a whole, the Industrial Revolution had proceeded with tremendous technological progress in the fields of transportation and communication. Between 1830 and 1900 the length of the railway system in Great Britain expanded from 138 kilometres to over thirty thousand kilometres and that in France from thirty-two kilometres to over thirty-eight thousand kilometres (Roth 2009: 33). Travelling by rail became not only more and more convenient thanks to an ever more closely knit transportation network, but also became faster and faster (Gall 1999: 57; Görtemaker 1987: 140). This was also true of steam shipping, which was important for the exchange of letters with America. A journey from, say, Liverpool to New York took fifteen days in 1840, but only five-and-a-half days in 1900 (Fried 1905: 37).

The progress in transportation also impacted on communication, namely the postal system, in which rail increasingly replaced stage coaches (Bernold 2002: 74). The nineteenth century saw postal reforms, such as those in Great Britain closely associated with Rowland Hill (1795–1879) and the introduction of the Penny Post in 1840 (Daunton 1985). On a global scale, the foundation of the World Postal Union in the year 1874 marked a watershed (Cotreau 1975: 3) when one of the first big international organizations harmonized and reduced postage charges (Moser 1974: 25; Fried 1905: 39).

These developments led to an ever stronger internationalization of trade and finance, politics and science, as well as in the private lives of more and more people, an occurrence which has been referred to as the 'first globalization' (e.g. Nonn 2009: 78–79). However, the revolution in transportation and communication provided not only the infrastructure, but also the mind-set, to make the development of the Scholars' International Correspondence possible and probable. This can be seen in the increased use of the word *international* and its derivatives.

Internationality, Internationalism, and International Correspondence

William T. Stead, one of the founding fathers of the Scholars' International Correspondence, and his secretary E. Annie Lawrence wrote in 1906: 'TRULY this may be called the age of Internationality, prepared for by the triple inventions of printing, steam, and electricity, and, as is usual, the impulse once given, progress is extremely rapid' ([Stead and Lawrence] 1906: 540).[4] They use the word *internationality* for what we would nowadays refer to as internationalization or globalization.[5] In a similar vein, Martin Hartmann, founder of the Central Office for International Correspondence in Germany, pointed out the absolute 'necessity' of the term *international*, which had become a buzz word in the second half of the nineteenth century.[6] According to William T. Stead, this was also true for the word *internationalism*:[7] 'Internationalism promises to be the watchword of the New Century' (Stead 1901: 4). Of the different types of internationalism as outlined by Michael Byram in this volume, following Holbraad (2003), Stead's internationalism can clearly be classified as Holbraad's first type, i.e. 'liberal internationalism', which was linked to the peace movements of the time. William T. Stead was also very active in the international peace movement and involved in the organization and journalistic coverage of The Hague Peace Conferences in 1899 and 1907 (Whyte 1925: 122-66, 287-91). Accordingly, internationalism, as defined by Stead and Lawrence, was 'the promotion of good feeling between the peoples' ([Stead and Lawrence] 1900b: 585). One way of promoting internationalism — 'the most pressing duty which lies before us in the new century' ([Stead and Lawrence] 1900b: 585) — was to help set up the Scholars' International Correspondence. Stead expressed the high hopes which he attached to the establishment of an international penfriend network as follows:

> If we could imagine such a thing as the existence, let us say, of a standing army of schoolboys and schoolgirls one hundred thousand strong and corresponding once a month with each other in the two countries, explaining to each other how they live and what they are interested in, correcting each other's mistakes, and, in short, throwing out any number of mental tendrils round each other, it is easy to appreciate the immense force that this would give to an improvement of the international relations between the British Empire and the French Republic. If even out of the one hundred thousand scholars only ten thousand really become friends with their correspondents, that in itself would be a great force making for peace and for good understanding between two great nations. ([Stead] 1897: 77)

The mere numbers Stead evokes here ('If even out of the one hundred thousand scholars only ten thousand really become friends') show to what extent he was a visionary when it came to pacifist ideas.[8] To him, as to many others promoting the penfriend scheme (see for example Mieille 1901: 33), the 'mechanism' was as easy as it was convincing: exchanging letters with a correspondent from another country would help to overcome national prejudice by widening the correspondents' horizons and by creating personal bonds. In Stead and Lawrence's words:

> It is an open secret that one of the great uses of the International Correspondence is, that it tends to remove unfounded prejudices and to discover to people of one nation that natives of another country may have like aims, ideals, and wishes. ([Stead and Lawrence] 1900a: 302)

In an earlier contribution they wrote in a similar vein:

> [W]hatever the result may be in the acquisition of a language, the putting into correspondence of so many hundreds of the ingenuous youth of both nations cannot fail but widen the horizon and deepen the sympathies of all who take part in this scheme. ([Stead and Lawrence] 1897b: 397)

For Stead and Lawrence, language learning through letter-writing was important but the first and foremost aim of international correspondence was to work towards world peace. However, the roots of the scheme are not to be found in the peace movements, but in modern language teaching.

Modern Language Teaching and the Reform Movement

The teaching of modern languages was also taking place in an increasingly international context. For example, in the year 1900 two international congresses were held in Paris, the *Congrès international de l'enseignement secondaire* for secondary education in general and the *Congrès international des langues vivantes* for teachers of modern languages. Both congresses supported the Scholars' International Correspondence by passing resolutions in its favour, thus giving new impetus to the movement (Mieille 1900: 5).[9] It was also here in Paris in the year 1900 that the three main protagonists of the Scholars' International Correspondence — Paul Mieille, William T. Stead and Martin Hartmann — actually met in person.

The Reform Movement in teaching modern languages was also an international undertaking: 'The Movement was international and felt in Germany, France, Holland, Belgium, Scandinavia, Russia and the United States, as well as in England' (Bayley 1998: 43). Its onset is commonly associated with Viëtor's pamphlet *Der Sprachunterricht muss umkehren!* from 1882. Its title was translated as *Language teaching must start afresh!* by Howatt (1984: 340) and as *Language Teaching Must Change Direction!* by Howatt and Smith (2002: xi). Both translations refer to the emancipatory shift away from teaching modern languages as if they were classical ones.

Especially in Germany, an explicit connection was drawn between the Reform Movement and the Scholars' International Correspondence. Martin Hartmann referred to himself as being 'im Lager der Reform' [in the camp of the reformers] (Hartmann, quoted in Gassmeyer, 1899: 349–50). Block — a teacher of modern languages who participated in the International Correspondence, too — called it 'eine der jüngsten Früchte der Reform' [one of the most recent fruits of the reform] (Block 1899: 617). The proponents of the scheme considered it a near-perfect way of putting the Reform into practice: exchanging letters with a correspondent of the target-language country met the designated aim of the Reform to teach modern languages in order actually to use them. This aim had also led to a growing interest in direct and personal contacts with the target-language countries, which can be seen in the increasing number of holiday courses and travel grants for the teachers of modern languages.[10]

Against the backdrop of this historical context, which made internationalization a matter of fact and practical language skills a necessity, the development of a scheme like the Scholars' International Correspondence seems all too natural. However, it was only the interplay of this context and a handful of individual protagonists which brought the new project into being.

The Development of the Scholars' International Correspondence

The historical context provided fertile soil for the idea of providing foreign-language learners with a possibility to exchange letters with partners abroad. In fact, this idea popped up in different places, notably in France and in Germany, beginning around 1893. It was 'in der Luft' [in the air], as one contemporary put it (Kretzschmar 1897: 307; see also Hartmann 1897: 273 and 1899: 54). However, the 'founding duo' consisted of France and Great Britain.

France and Great Britain

There is one person to whom the merit of being the actual founder of the Scholars' International Correspondence is generally ascribed (Massoul 1898: 87). In the sources, Paul Mieille is referred to as a 'Pioniere' [pioneer] (Hartmann 1901: 55), as the person who 'created' the Scholars' International Correspondence (Ehrenthal 1903: 4) and as the 'der eigentliche Begründer' [real founding father] (Grote 1915: 731), because it was Mieille who launched an international exchange of letters systematically and on a large scale.

Paul Mieille (1859-1933)[11] was a teacher of English in the South of France. The never-ending translation exercises, which he refers to as 'monotone et ardu' [monotonous and arduous] (Mieille 1897: 1), frustrated him and his pupils alike, so he started to assign translations in the form of letters. In a next step, he encouraged his pupils to write letters to each other as well as to himself in English. From there, it was only what he calls 'la conclusion logique' [the logical conclusion] (Mieille 1896: 44) to put his learners in contact with English pupils in order to exchange real letters. He was able to do so because he had friends in London who sent him the addresses of young people willing to correspond. In this way, he created a privately based international correspondence scheme which lasted from 1892 to 1896. Mieille was more than happy with the result, because he considered his hopes to make his English classes livelier and more interesting more than fulfilled (Mieille 1896: 44; 1897: 3; 1900: 7-8; Hartmann 1901: 55). His correspondence scheme was so successful that, at some point, demand exceeded supply, and he was no longer able to provide the necessary number of English addresses through personal acquaintances. It was then, in the year 1896, that he turned to the French educational journal *Revue Universitaire* and wrote to William T. Stead, journalist, peace activist and publisher of the political monthly magazine *Review of Reviews*, who was internationally noted for his social involvement and interest in foreign-language learning.[12]

After the details of the cooperation had been worked out, it was in January 1897 that the Scholars' International Correspondence was launched. On 15 January, Paul Mieille's article 'Essai d'organisation d'une Correspondance scolaire internationale' (1897) appeared in the *Revue Universitaire* and, at the same time, the *Review of Reviews* published the article 'How to Learn a Language by Letter-writing: A French Teacher's Brilliant Idea' ([Stead] 1897). The scheme was set up as follows: French teachers were to send lists with details of the name, age and school of pupils who wished to correspond to the *Revue Universitaire*. British teachers were asked to do the same and to send their respective lists to the *Review of Reviews*. The French lists were then sent to the *Review of Reviews*, where Stead's secretary, Miss Lawrence, did the pairing and sent the paired lists back to Paris, where they were published in the *Revue Universitaire*. These lists contained the names of the French pupils on the left and the names of the designated British partners on the right. As copies of the *Revue Universitaire* were generally available at schools in France, the French teachers could then pass on the British addresses to their pupils, who were to open the correspondence by writing the first letter ('Aux professeurs de langues vivantes' 1897; [Stead and Lawrence] 1897a: 293; Mieille 1901: 32). In this way, the first list of correspondents appeared in the February edition of the *Revue Universitaire* in 1897. It listed two hundred French and English boys and girls ('Correspondance anglo-française. Première liste' 1897).

Germany

In Germany, Martin Hartmann (1854-1926), a teacher of English and French at a grammar school (*Gymnasium*) in Leipzig, had got wind of the new scheme. He was a proponent of the Reform Movement and very active in the Society of Modern Philology in Saxony (*Sächsischer Neuphilologenverband*). This Society of Modern Philology launched many innovations in the field of modern-language teaching at the time. In addition to the international correspondence, the scheme of international recitations (*fremdsprachliche Rezitationen*) was the best-known and most widespread (Schleich 2015). The idea here was to invite native speakers to schools to perform professional readings of French or English literature in order to create an opportunity for language learners to be exposed to 'real' language and especially to 'authentic' pronunciation.

It was under the auspices of this Society of Modern Philology in Saxony that Martin Hartmann instigated the creation of the 'German Central Bureau for International Correspondence' (*Deutsche Zentralstelle für internationalen Briefwechsel*), which was officially founded on 20 March 1897 (Hartmann 1898: 265–67), only two months after the first list of correspondents had appeared in the *Revue Universitaire*.

In order to make the new institution known to the world, Hartmann made contact with William T. Stead in London. He published articles in journals and newspapers and, last but not least, he sent circular letters to hundreds of schools in France and Great Britain. Again, the idea fell on fertile soil, and thus, by 4 July of the same year (1897), he had registered 1347 applications.

In Germany, the organization was realized not through the help of journals, but through the Central Bureau — in the very person of Martin Hartmann — which did all the work, from what we now would call public relations or marketing to the actual pairing of candidates and distribution of addresses. However, in Germany, too, one journal played an important role for the International Scholars' Correspondence, namely *Die neueren Sprachen*, which, by 1893, had evolved from the journal *Phonetische Studien*, which had been founded by Willhelm Viëtor in 1888 (see also the contribution by Linn in Volume II). The new journal, *Die neueren Sprachen*, was the designated mouthpiece of the Reform Movement in Germany. It was here that Martin Hartmann published his annual reports of the Central Bureau of International Correspondence, which are very important sources and provide details of the numbers of registrations for each year (see Hartmann 1902 and 1915 for the first and last of these reports in *Die neueren Sprachen*). Soon enough, the movement spread over the ocean to America.

The United States

In the United States, Edward Hicks Magill (1825-1907), a professor of French at Swarthmore College, Pennsylvania, introduced the international correspondence scheme in 1898 (Magill 1899a: 49).[13] Like William T. Stead, Magill was committed to the peace movement and saw letter-writing as a means of improving practical language skills and, equally importantly, as a means of working towards peace and understanding among nations:

> While introduced primarily to simplify and advance the study of the various languages, it [a system of international correspondence] is ultimately likely to accomplish an important work in drawing nearer together in bonds of sympathy and love the various nations of the world, thus tending toward the establishment of universal peace. (Magill 1901a: 161)

As the International Correspondence gained more and more ground in the USA, not only at the college level but also in schools, the Modern Language Association of America established an International Correspondence Committee in December 1898 and Magill was appointed chairman of this committee (Magill 1902b: 82). One year later, at the annual meeting of the Modern Language Association of America, where the committee presented a — as Magill puts it — 'very satisfactory report' (Magill 1902a: 227), the Committee was officially turned into the 'American Bureau of International Correspondence' (Magill 1901b: xxxii). As with the German Central Bureau, its main tasks were to make the correspondence scheme known and to organize it by collecting and distributing addresses. In order to achieve these aims, Magill worked together with Paul Mieille in France and Martin Hartmann in Germany (Magill 1901b: xxxiii).

However, Magill and his co-workers resigned in 1904, and the American Bureau was closed. Reasons given were disagreements with Germany over the questions of fees, the fact that neither Germany nor France was able to supply the number of addresses demanded in the USA, and the enormous work load (Magill 1904: viii). Despite the fact that no new central bureau was founded in America thereafter, the correspondence between Germany and America continued to flourish because Martin Hartmann took over much of the organization and American teachers sent lists with addresses directly to the Central Bureau in Leipzig (Hartmann 1905: 365; 1907: 352).

An International Correspondence Network

What we have seen so far — the organization of the Scholars' International Correspondence in Great Britain, France, Germany and the USA — are the main pillars in an ever-growing network of international correspondence. Many other countries joined in: for example, Italy, Belgium, Sweden, Russia and Canada. Some letters went as far as Australia, Africa and India (e.g. Lupati 1902; [Stead and Lawrence] 1898: 191). Interestingly, both Mieille and Stead used nature metaphors to convey the proliferation of the International Correspondence. Mieille wrote: 'Il en est de certaines idées comme de ces arbres vigoureux qui poussent constamment des branches nouvelles' [Some ideas are like these vigorous trees which constantly grow new branches] (Mieille 1900: 25). Stead and Lawrence noted: 'the scholars' scheme [...] is as a stream widening on its way, and continually reinforced by countless small rivulets' ([Stead and Lawrence] 1899: 93). The latter metaphor is actually even more fitting because the growth of rivers is more associated with the influx of 'small rivulets'. It builds up, rather than being generated only from within itself. This image corresponds to the finding that more and more initiatives (also on a private basis, for example, when correspondents imparted their friends' addresses, avoiding the official organization) and journals participated in the International Correspondence, so that the emerging network cannot be traced to its smallest 'ramifications'. But what was the scale of this widespread international network?

In 1900 Paul Mieille published a book on the International Correspondence scheme in which he provided numbers for each branch of the French correspondence until then. The French–British correspondence (eleven thousand pupils) and the French–American (one thousand) as well as the French–Italian (one thousand) together total thirteen thousand pupils (Mieille 1900: 13–14). Martin Hartmann counts 44,329 registrations between 1897 and 1914 (Hartmann 1915: 649). This makes a grand total of over fifty-seven thousand correspondents, without counting private initiatives or the development of the correspondence between France and Great Britain or America after 1900, so that the grand total must have easily been over sixty thousand correspondents.

But how did the scheme work in the daily lives of all these correspondents? Having presented the Scholars' International Correspondence from an organizational perspective, we shall now look into its practicalities.

The Scholars' International Correspondence in Practice

The organizers had some rules in mind for the practical implementation of the scheme. These rules were very much based on Paul Mieille's first attempts and then taken up and modified, especially by the German Central Bureau. The rules were issued in French, English and German and made available for teachers as well as students.

Rules for the Management of the Scholars' International Correspondence

The following extracts (all from Stead et al. 1902: 85) show how the international correspondence was to be put into practice according to the rules:

- Supervision
  'The exchange of letters is always and everywhere under the supervision of the foreign language teacher. All foreign letters and other postal communications are under his control.'
- Frequency
  '[L]etters must be exchanged once a month, a bi-monthly arrangement is the rule.'
- Use of one's own and the foreign language
  'The rule is that the scholar should write alternately in his own and the foreign language, but the first letter should always be in his own tongue and written with great care as a satisfactory development depends largely on the first impression received.'
- Language learning
  'It is advisable that letters received in the foreign tongue should be entered in a note-book; at any rate, all unknown or idiomatic expressions should be thus noted.'
  'The mistakes in English of the foreign writers must be carefully corrected by the partner, in English, and returned with his answer.'
- Form and content
  'As the letters in the mother tongue are intended as models for the partner, they must be written with care and must be grammatically correct. The scholar should endeavour to find something of interest to tell his friend. Questions should be asked and answered, and a helpful bond of union thus be formed. Courtesy and sympathy are imperative.'

The rules show that the Scholars' International Correspondence originated in the foreign-language classrooms with a clear focus on using the letters to improve practical language skills. Language learning was supposed to take place through imitating the native speaker as a model and through receiving corrective feedback (see also, for instance, Markscheffel 1903: 30). It is interesting to note that learners were asked to pay special attention to idiomatic expressions in order to sound as 'natural' as possible: 'As the vocabulary employed by the foreigner will almost always be that of ordinary intercourse, the foreign letters furnish an abundance of those genuine colloquial phrases, the memorizing and repetition of which are so valuable and so highly recommended' (Magill 1899b: xvi).[14] Here the aim of learning to use the kind of language which would enable learners to communicate in real encounters underlines the close link to the ideas of the Reform Movement. Nevertheless, the pacifist discourse also shines through ('helpful bond of union', 'courtesy', 'sympathy').[15]

It has to be noted, though, that, even if the organizers and, above all, Martin Hartmann tried to enforce the 'rules', the question of whether teachers and pupils who took part in the international correspondence actually abided by these rules has to be answered by 'yes' and 'no'. There were indeed teachers, for instance, who deliberately chose a minimum degree of control. Among them, there was even Paul Mieille, whose advice appears in the *Review of Reviews* in English: 'As I wanted to make that letter-writing a pleasure to the boys, I made a point not to interfere in the sending or the receiving of them' (Mieille quoted in [Stead] 1897: 78). But how about the actual letters?

The Learners' Letters

In Germany, quite a few letters were published by teachers who took part in the Scholars' International Correspondence with their pupils. These appeared mostly in the yearbooks of their schools. The two largest collections are from a modern-language teacher named Heinrich Ehrenthal, who published a collection of thirty letters written by twenty-two French pupils in 1903 (Ehrenthal 1903) and a collection of twenty-two English letters written by three English, one Scottish and seven American boys (Ehrenthal 1905). The sample letters in the appendix below are also taken from Ehrenthal (1905). Looking at these letters, we must bear in mind that they were not published as facsimiles, but that they might have been subject to changes, even though Ehrenthal claims not to have made any modifications except for the correspondents' names (Ehrenthal 1903: 6). Furthermore, the letters had obviously been selected for publication, thus representing a certain choice, possibly to convey a positive impression of the scheme. Unfortunately, Ehrenthal only published letters written in the respective correspondents' own languages.

The first question one might ask is what the correspondents actually wrote about. Haertel, another teacher involved, answers as follows:

> The principal subjects discussed are, in the order of their popularity: the person of the writer — his occupation and special interests; the school — description of the buildings, grounds, and the daily routine of work; the home town; games; interesting localities near the home of the writer. (Haertel 1904: 95)

Or, as Magill puts it in more general terms: 'As in ordinary letter writing, let the daily lives of the writers, and their surroundings be the ever fruitful theme. Thus, too, will they learn the more rapidly the ordinary spoken language of everyday life' (Magill 1899a: 50). To a large extent, the statements by these two teachers are confirmed in the letters published by Ehrenthal, for instance in George Andrew's opening letter (Fig. 3.1). George excuses himself for not having been able to write earlier due to examinations — a very common excuse. Then the correspondence itself is addressed and the hope that it might prove 'beneficial to both of us'. George

1.   Grammar School.   Farnham, May 26th, 1902.
                                      Surrey.

Dear Charles,

I am sorry I have not been able to answer your letter before now, but I have been very busy just lately, so you must please excuse me. I am preparing for an Examination to be held on the 5th, 6th, 7th of June, so I do not get much spare time. I was not aware that I was to be put into correspondence with a German boy, so your letter arrived quite unexpected. I was very pleased to receive your letter and I hope our little correspondence will be beneficial to both of us. But now I will tell you a little about myself. I am the only boy in the family. I have one sister who studies at the Girls' Grammar School, Farnham.

I had the good fortune to win a scholarship at the Grammar School; that is the reason why I am studying there.

It is a curious fact that you and I were both born in the same year 1886 within about a month of one another, your birthday being on the 6th of December 1886 and mine being on the 14th of October 1886. Are you still at school in Breslau? and have you passed any examinations?

I think in your letter you asked me whether you should write to me in Latin letters. I do not mind at all, but write to me in the way that is most convenient to you. I am writing this letter as you see all in English, but if you wish I will correspond with you half in German and half in English.

I will now try to tell you a little about Farnham (Surrey). It is a very pretty little town and surrounded by some of the finest scenery in England. It has a very ancient castle which has been and is the residence of the Bishops of Winchester. Do you collect postage-stamps? If so I will put some different kinds on to each letter. I collect them, so perhaps you will do the same for me. Do not put on stamps above the value of the letter, but put on different kinds at different times and I will do the same to you if you wish. Do you take photographs? I do and will send you some over some time.

I must close now,
with kind regards,
George Andrews.

3

FIG. 3.1. Sample Letter 1. Source: Ehrenthal 1905: 7

10.

Warwick House, New St., May 1st 1903.
B'ham.

Dear Friend,

Should have written to you before, but I have been ill for a week, and was confined to my room for four days. I have now completely recovered. In your last letter you asked me to explain the difference between "to have" and "to get". "To have" a thing, is to have it at the present time (now). "To get" a thing is "to win" it, or obtain it at some future time. "I have a book" is the same as "I have got a book".

The words "in" and "at" mean the same. "in" means the { interior / inside }, "at" means either inside or outside a place.

If you cannot understand this, I will try to explain more fully in my next { writing / letter }.

To-morrow I shall cycle to Worcester in order to see my relations and friends. I bought a new cycle last week which I think is very nice, it is called the "Rover". I hope you have had a { nice / good } time lately.

Next Saturday I am going to Stratford-on-Avon, the birthplace of the great poet Shakespeare.

I have no space or time to write any more. I will write sooner next time. Kind regards to Herr S. and yourself

I remain

Your very sincere friend,

Thomas Gray.

FIG. 3.2. Sample Letter 2. Source: Ehrenthal 1905: 13

goes on to introduce himself. He is the only boy in the family; he has one sister. He writes about his school, a grammar school, which he is only able to attend because he received a scholarship. He also writes his birth date, which is 14 October 1886 and — what a coincidence — only two months away from that of his correspondent. In the third paragraph he turns to the modalities of the correspondence, the German script[16] being an issue as well as the language. The fourth paragraph starts with a description of Farnham, George's home town. He then moves on to talk about stamps and photographs.

All in all, the range of topics covered by George in this first letter can be regarded as typical (apart only from the fact that this boy apparently did not know that he was going to have a German correspondent). Especially descriptions of towns and places come up frequently, but this is probably also due to the fact that these descriptions were very popular with the teachers who published the letters. It was the kind of

16.

High Bank, Palmerston Road.

Southsea, Dec. 15 th, 03.

Dear Friend,

Many thanks for your nice post-card. My reason for not writing before is — I no longer live with my Parents, but am living at Southsea, a portion of Portsmouth¹), a naval port on the south coast of England.

My brother has gone to Kent, a county south-east of England, a distance 200 miles from home.

Southsea is a very fashionable sea-side resort and is most healthy. The population of Portsmouth is about 180000. There are stationed here many battle-ships. I was fortunate enough to see the King of Italy when he visited England two weeks ago, I should very much like to see your Emperor. Now I will wish you good-bye.

I remain

Your very sincere friend,

Thomas Gray.

---

1) Portsmouth really consits of four towns, Portsmouth proper, Portsea, Landport, and Southsea. Southsea is a pleasant watering-place. (Geographical Readers. England and Wales, Cassell, London.)

FIG. 3.3. Sample Letter 3. Source: Ehrenthal 1905: 16

knowledge that was important to them because they wanted the letters to convey as much information on the geography, life and institutions of the foreign country as possible (*Realienkunde*).[17] Preußner, for example, states that letters 'die Kenntnisse der Realien fördert' [foster the knowledge of realia] (Preußner 1904: 460).

Furthermore, with regard to the goal of language learning through the letters, the sample letters show that some teachers had instilled in their pupils an understanding of the correspondence to serve this aim. So the letters reveal that language–switching and mutual correction actually did take place — if not to the extent envisaged by the organizers in their rules. In his second letter, George Andrew writes: 'I have corrected your English letter for you. It is not very full of mistakes and I only hope I shall write my German part as well as you have written your English part' (letter of 12 June 1902, quoted in Ehrenthal 1905: 8). In other letters, correspondents ask each other questions on language–related issues and give explanations. An example of this phenomenon is a letter written by Thomas Gray on 1 May 1903 (Fig. 3.2), whose German correspondent had asked him about the difference between *to have* and *to get* and about the difference between the prepositions *in* and *at*. In addition, he provided synonyms for his partner in curly brackets to help expand his vocabulary.

Conclusion

To conclude, connecting correspondents from different countries and cultures through letter-writing meant, first, learning and using the other's language; second, gaining knowledge about the other's country and culture; and, third, perhaps, turning the partner into a friend. Admittedly, not all the correspondents reached that level; some gave it up rather soon and never progressed beyond the stage of exchanging more or less impersonal — sometimes superficial — pieces of information. Others, however, kept up the correspondence, even after they had left school. This was the case with Thomas Gray, which can be seen in his tenth and last letter in the sequence published by Ehrenthal (Fig. 3.1). Thomas has in the meantime left school and started work. In this letter he tells his German friend that he has moved out from his parents' home and is now living in Southsea. Comparing this letter to the previous one (Fig. 3.2), we realize that, in this earlier letter by the same writer, language learning — in the form of explanations given and synonyms provided — played a dominant role. The correspondence was meant to be useful. The second letter by Thomas Gray (Fig 3.3) is short. There is also 'useful' information about Southsea, but the focus has shifted somewhat. Thomas's main purpose in this letter seems to be to keep the German friend updated about the changes in his life. It is a matter of keeping in touch because he wants to keep in touch, not because a teacher tells him to do so. A friendship seems to be developing. This was what the organizers of the Scholars' International Correspondence had hoped for: that mutual understanding and sympathy might arise from knowing each other's language, manners and customs. Doniat, an American teacher, wrote:

> But more important even than the linguistic advantage is the element of culture involved in this friendly intercourse. The student gains a fund of information about the manners and customs of the foreign nation, and as he grows to respect and even love his partner, he realizes that foreign modes of life, while they may be different, are not, on that account, inferior to his own. (Doniat 1904: 77)

The fact that the protagonists of the Scholars' International Correspondence, Paul Mielle, William T. Stead, E. Annie Lawrence, Martin Hartmann and Edward Hicks Magill, systematically facilitated this kind of 'friendly intercourse' for young people on a large scale is an impressive and important achievement in the history of modern-language teaching.

Bibliography

Primary sources

'Aux professeurs de langues vivantes'. 1897. *Revue Universitaire*, 6: 5–6
BÉRENGER, HENRY. 1900. 'Le Congrès international de l'Enseignement secondaire à l'Exposition universelle de 1900', *Revue Universitaire*, 9: 230–58
BLOCK, J. 1899. 'Die internationale Schülerkorrespondenz', *Die neueren Sprachen*, 6: 617–26
BREBNER, MARY. 1909 [1898]. *The Method of Teaching Modern Languages in Germany*, 4th edn (Cambridge: Cambridge University Press)
BREYMANN, HERMANN, and GEORG STEINMÜLLER. 1905. *Neusprachliche Reform-Literatur*

(Drittes Heft): Eine bibliographisch-kritische Übersicht bearbeitet von Prof. Dr. Steinmüller (Leipzig: Deichert)

'Correspondance anglo-française. Première liste'. 1897. *Revue Universitaire*, 6: 124–27

DENIKER, J. (ed.). 1901. *Congrès international de l'enseignement des langues vivantes tenu à Paris du 24 au 28 juillet 1900: rapports, mémoires, liste des membres, etc.* (Paris: Société pour la propagation des langues étrangères en France)

DONIAT, JOSEPHINE C. 1904. 'International Correspondence of Pupils: Its History, Purpose, and Management', *The School Review*, 12: 70–77

EHRENTHAL, HEINRICH. 1903. *Lettres de la correspondance scolaire internationale: Beilage zum Programm der städtischen katholischen Realschule zu Breslau* (Breslau [Wrocłow]: Grass, Barth & Comp. (W. Friedrich)).

———. 1905. *English Letters of the Scholars' International Correspondence: Beilage zum Programm der städtischen katholischen Realschule zu Breslau* (Breslau [Wrocłow]: Grass, Barth & Comp. (W. Friedrich))

FRIED, ALFRED HERMANN. 1905. *Handbuch der Friedensbewegung* (Leipzig: Reichenbach)

GASSMEYER, M. 1899. 'Bericht über die dritte Hauptversammlung des Sächsischen Neuphilologen-Verbandes (S.-N.-V.), abgehalten am 2. Juli 1899 zu Döbeln', *Die neueren Sprachen*, 7: 348–71

GROTE, W. 1915. 'Schülerkorrespondenz, internationale', in *Lexikon der Pädagogik*, ed. by Ernst M. Roloff (Freiburg i. Br.: Herder), pp. 731–33

HAERTEL, MARTIN H. 1904. 'International Correspondence of Pupils: Its Present Status in English-Speaking Countries', *The School Review*, 12: 89–96

HARTMANN, MARTIN K. A. 1897. 'Der internationale Schülerbriefwechsel', *Pädagogisches Wochenblatt*, 6: 273–75

———. 1898. 'Die erste Hauptversammlung des Sächsischen Neuphilologen-Verbandes, abgehalten Sonntag den 4. Juli 1897 zu Chemnitz', *Die neueren Sprachen*, 5: 257–77

———. 1899. 'Ueber Wesen und Stand der internationalen Schülerbriefwechsel', *Blätter für höheres Schulwesen*, 16: 54–58

———. 1901. 'Rückblick auf die Entwickelung des internationalen Schülerbriefwechsels', in *Comrades All. Annuaire de la Correspondance Interscolaire. Internationaler Schülerbriefwechsel*, ed. by William T. Stead, Paul Mieille, Martin K. A. Hartmann (London: 'Review of Reviews' Office), pp. 55–57

———. 1902. 'Jahresbericht der deutschen Zentralstelle für internationalen Briefwechsel (1. Juli 1901 bis 30. Juni 1902)', *Die neueren Sprachen*, 10: 342–53

———. 1905. 'Jahresbericht der deutschen Zentralstelle für internationalen Briefwechsel. 1904-1905', *Die neueren Sprachen*, 13: 365–76

———. 1907. 'Jahresbericht der deutschen Zentralstelle für internationalen Briefwechsel. 1906-1907', *Die neueren Sprachen*, 15: 351–63

———. 1915. 'Jahresbericht der deutschen Zentralstelle für internationalen Briefwechsel 1913-14', *Die neueren Sprachen*, 22: 648–67

'Hommage à Paul Mieille, promoteur de la correspondance scolaire internationale'. 1934. *Revue Universitaire*, 43: 72–74

KABISCH, OTTO. 1896. 'Die neusprachlichen Ferienkurse für Lehrer höherer Lehranstalten Preussens', *Die neueren Sprachen*, 3: 449–61

KRETZSCHMAR, [F.]. 1897. 'Zur Vor- und Nebengeschichte des internationalen Schülerbriefwechsels', *Deutsche Zeitschrift für Ausländisches Unterrichtswesen*, 2: 305–07

LOEV, E. VON. 1901. 'Internationaler Kongress für fremdsprachlichen Unterricht zu Paris. 24.–28. Juli 1900', *Die neueren Sprachen*, 9: 337–58

LUPATI, CESARINA. 1902. 'La Corrispondenza Internazionale. Italiá', in *Comrades All. Annuaire de la Correspondance Interscolaire. Internationaler Schülerbriefwechsel*, ed. by William T. Stead et al. (London: 'Review of Reviews' Office), p. 36

MAGILL, EDWARD H. 1899A. 'The International Correspondence', *Modern Language Notes*, 14: 48–51

——. 1899B. 'International Correspondence. Proceedings 1899', *Publications of the Modern Language Association*, 14 (Appendix I and II): xiv–xx

——. 1901A. 'The Best Methods to Prevent the Growth of the Military Spirit', *Advocate of Peace*, 63: 160–62

——. 1901B. 'International Correspondence. Proceedings 1901', *Publications of the Modern Language Association*, 16 (Appendix I and II): xxxii–xxxiv

——. 1902A. 'History of the International Correspondence in the United States of America', *Modern Language Notes*, 17: 227–29

——. 1902B. 'History of the International Correspondence in the United States of America', in *Comrades All. Annuaire de la Correspondance Interscolaire. Internationaler Schülerbriefwechsel*, ed. by William T. Stead et al. (London: 'Review of Reviews' Office), pp. 81–82

——. 1904. 'Report of the Committee on International Correspondence. Proceedings of the Twenty-Second Annual Meeting of the Modern Language Association of America 1904', *Publications of the Modern Language Association*, 19 (Appendix): viii–ix

——. 1907. *Sixty-five Years in the Life of a Teacher, 1841–1906* (Boston and New York: Houghton, Mifflin)

MARKSCHEFFEL, KARL. 1903. *Der Internationale Schülerbriefwechsel: Seine Geschichte, Bedeutung, Einrichtung und sein gegenwärtiger Stand (Fremde und eigene Erfahrungen). Beilage zum Jahresbericht des Grossherzogl. Realgymnasiums zu Weimar* (Weimar: Hof-Buchdruckerei)

MASSOUL, HENRY. 1898. 'Versuch eines internationalen Schülerbriefwechsels', *Die neueren Sprachen*, 5: 87–88

MIEILLE, PAUL. 1896. 'Les Professeurs de langues vivantes et l'Alliance française', *Revue Universitaire*, 5: 43–44

——. 1897. 'Essai d'organisation d'une correspondance scolaire internationale', *Revue Universitaire*, 6: 1–4

——. 1900. *La Correspondance inter-scolaire et les correspondances internationals: les bureaux d'échanges inter-scolaires* (Tarbes: Lescamela)

——. 1901. 'Comment fut fondée. [*sic*] La Correspondance Scolaire Internationale', in *Comrades All. Annuaire de la Correspondance Interscolaire. Internationaler Schülerbriefwechsel*, ed. by William T. Stead, Paul Mieille, Martin K. A. Hartmann (London: 'Review of Reviews' Office), pp. 31–33

PETRI, ALBERT. 1898. 'Über die mit der *Correspondance interscolaire* gemachten Erfahrungen', *Die neueren Sprachen*, 6: 511–15

PREUSSNER, OSKAR. 1904. 'Programmabhandlungen. 1903', *Monatschrift für höhere Schulen*, 3: 450–60

REICHEL, GEORG. 1900. 'Congrès international des langues vivantes', *Die neueren Sprachen*, 7: 724–25

ROSSMANN, PHILIPP. 1897. 'Ein Studienaufenfhalt in Paris', *Die neueren Sprachen*, 4: 257–95

SCOTT, M. 1900. 'Congrès internationale de l'enseignement secondaire de 1900. Rapports préparatoires. De la correspondance interscolaire internationale', *Revue Universitaire*, 9: 131–37

[STEAD, WILLIAM T.]. 1892A. 'How to Learn a Language in Six Months; or, a Royal Road to Foreign Tongues', *Review of Reviews*, 5: 511–17

——. 1892B. '"How to Learn a Language in Six Months:. A Report of Progress', *Review of Reviews*, 6: 286–87

——. 1893. 'A Royal Road to Learn Languages: The Result of Six Months' Experiment', *Review of Reviews*, 7: 70–75

——. 1897. 'How to Learn a Language by Letter-writing: A French Teacher's Brilliant Idea', *Review of Reviews*, 15: 77–78

——. 1901. 'Introduction', in *Comrades All. Annuaire de la Correspondance Interscolaire. Internationaler Schülerbriefwechsel*, ed. by William T. Stead, Paul Mieille, Martin K. A. Hartmann (London: 'Review of Reviews' Office), pp. 3–7

——, PAUL MIELLE, MARTIN HARTMANN and E. HICKS MAGILL (eds). 1902. *Comrades All. Annuaire de la Correspondence Interscolaire. Internationaler Schülerbriefwechsel* (London: 'Review of Reviews' Office, Mowbray House)

——, [AND E. A. LAWRENCE]. 1897A. 'Learning Language by Letter-writing', *Review of Reviews*, 15: 293–94

——, [AND E. A. LAWRENCE]. 1897B. 'Learning a Language by Letter-writing: A Gratifying Report of Success', *Review of Reviews*, 15: 397–98

——, [AND E. A. LAWRENCE]. 1898. 'Learning Languages by Letter-writing', *Review of Reviews*, 17: 191

——, [AND E. A. LAWRENCE]. 1899. 'Learning Languages by Letter-writing', *Review of Reviews*, 19: 93

——, [AND E. A. LAWRENCE]. 1900A. 'Learning Languages by Letter-writing', *Review of Reviews*, 22: 302

——, [AND E. A. LAWRENCE]. 1900B. 'Learning Languages by Letter-writing', *Review of Reviews*, 22: 585

——, [AND E. A. LAWRENCE]. 1906. 'Languages and Letter-writing', *Review of Review*, 33: 540

QUOUSQUE TANDEM [VIËTOR, WILHELM]. 1882. *Der Sprachunterricht muss umkehren! Ein Beitrag zur Überbürdungsfrage* (Heilbronn: Henninger)

Secondary literature

BAYLEY, SUSAN N. 1998. 'The Direct Method and Modern Language Teaching in England 1880-1918', *History of Education*, 27: 39–57

BERNOLD, JOHANNES. 2002. *Trari, Trara, die Post ist da: Vom Cursus publicus zur Flugpost* (Asparn an der Zaya: Zeitgeschichtliches Dokumentations-Archiv)

BEVIR, MARK. 2011. 'The Contextual Approach', in *The Oxford Handbook of the History of Political Philosophy*, ed. by George Klosko (Oxford and New York: Oxford University Press), pp. 11–23

BUTTJES, DIETER. 1991. 'Culture in German Foreign Language Teaching: Making Use of an Ambiguous Past', in *Mediating Languages and Cultures: Towards an Intercultural Theory of Foreign Language Education*, ed. by Dieter Buttjes and Michael Byram (Clevedon: Multilingual Matters), pp. 47–62

COTREAU, JAMES D. 1975. *Historical Development of the Universal Postal Union and the Question of Membership* (Boston: [no pub.])

DAUNTON, MARTIN J. 1985. 'Rowland Hill & The Penny Post', *History Today*, 35.8: 31–37

DOFF, SABINE. 2002. *Englischlernen zwischen Tradition und Innovation: Fremdsprachenunterricht für Mädchen im 19. Jahrhundert* (Munich: Langenscheidt-Longman)

FORSTER, PETER G. 1982. *The Esperanto Movement* (The Hague and New York: Mouton)

GALL, LOTHAR. 1999. 'Eisenbahn in Deutschland: Von den Anfängen bis zum Ersten Weltkrieg', in *Die Eisenbahn in Deutschland: Von den Anfängen bis zur Gegenwart*, ed. by Lothar Gall and Manfred Pohl (Munich: Beck), pp. 13–70

GÖRTEMAKER, MANFRED. 1987. *Deutschland im 19. Jahrhundert: Entwicklungslinien*, 3rd edn (Bonn: Bundeszentrale für politische Bildung)

HOLBRAAD, CARSTEN. 2003. *Internationalism and Nationalism in European Political Thought* (New York: Palgrave Macmillan)

HOWATT, ANTHONY P. R. 1984. *A History of English Language Teaching* (Oxford and New York: Oxford University Press)

——, and RICHARD SMITH. 2002. *Modern Language Teaching: The Reform Movement*, 4 vols (London and New York: Routledge)

McGREW, ANTHONY. G. 1992. 'Conceptualizing Global Politics', in *Global Politics: Globalization and the Nation-State*, ed. by A. G. McGrew and P. G. Lewis (Cambridge and Oxford: Polity Press and Blackwell), pp. 1–28

McLELLAND, NICOLA. 2015. *German through English Eyes: A History of Language Teaching and Learning in Britain, 1500–2000* (Wiesbaden: Harrassowitz)

MOMBERT, MONIQUE. 2001. *L'Enseignement de l'allemand en France, 1880–1918: entre 'odèle allemand' et 'langue de l'ennemi'* (Strasbourg: Presses universitaires de Strasbourg)

MOSER, MARC. 1974. '100 Jahre Weltpostverein. I. Teil', *Archiv für deutsche Postgeschichte*, I: 3–26

NONN, CHRISTOPH. 2009 [2007]. *Das 19. und 20. Jahrhundert*, 2nd edn (Paderborn etc.: Schöningh)

ODY, HERMANN JOSEPH. 1957. 'Aus der Frühzeit der internationalen Schülerkorrespondenz', *Bildung und Erziehung*, 10: 170–71

RADDATZ, VOLKER. 1977. *Englandkunde im Wandel deutscher Erziehungsziele, 1886–1945* (Kronberg/Taunus: Scriptor)

RIVAL, SÉBASTIEN. 2012. *L'Échange des assistants de langue vivante entre la France et l'Allemagne avant la Seconde Guerre mondiale: les 'directeurs de conversation' et la 'langue de l'ennemi'* <http://docnum.univ-lorraine.fr/public/DDOC_T_2012_0366_RIVAL.pdf> [accessed 6 November 2015]

ROTH, RALF. 2009. 'Die Entwicklung der Kommunikationsnetze und ihre Beziehung zur europäischen Städtelandschaft', in *Städte im europäischen Raum: Verkehr, Kommunikation und Urbanität im 19. und 20. Jahrhundert*, ed. by Ralf Roth (Stuttgart: Steiner), pp. 23–62

SCHLEICH, MARLIS. 2013. 'Die Anfänge des internationalen Schülerbriefwechsels', in *Schulsprachenpolitik und fremdsprachliche Unterrichtspraxis: Historische Schlaglichter zwischen 1800 und 1989*, ed. by Friederike Klippel, Elisabeth Kolb and Felicitas Sharp (Münster: Waxmann), pp. 139–51

——. 2015. *Geschichte des internationalen Schülerbriefwechsels: Entstehung und Entwicklung im historischen Kontext von den Anfängen bis zum Ersten Weltkrieg* (Münster: Waxmann)

——. 2016. 'Die Reformbewegung in der Praxis: Fremdsprachliche Rezitationen im Rahmen des neusprachlichen Unterrichts um 1900', *Teaching languages — Sprachen lehren*, ed. by Friederike Klippel (Münster and New York: Waxmann), pp. 295–316

SCHRIEWER, JÜRGEN. 2000. 'World System and Interrelationship Networks: The Internationalization of Education and the Role of Comparative Inquiry', in *Educational Knowledge: Changing Relationships between the State, Civil Society, and the Educational Community*, ed. by Thomas S. Popkewitz (Albany, NY: State University of New York Press), pp. 305–43

WHYTE, FREDERIC. 1925. *The Life of W. T. Stead*, 2 vols (London, New York and Boston: Jonathan Cape and Houghton Mifflin), II

Notes to Chapter 3

1. Stead 1901: 3.

2. See <http://ec.europa.eu/programmes/erasmus-plus/index_en.htm>, <https://www.etwinning.net/en/pub/index.htm> [both accessed 6 November 2015].

3. The expression *penfried*, which is common today, is used for reasons of reader-friendliness and stylistic variation. In the sources, contemporaries refer to correspondents, correspondence or letter-writing.

4. Square brackets indicate that the authorship is not clearly marked in the source, even though the authors' names can be identified from the content or intertextual context.

5. See Schriewer: '*Internationalization* originated as a term of international law. [...] Since the nineteenth century, it has been used to denote limitations of the sovereignty of a State over all or parts of its national territory (such as cities, waterways, or harbors) in favor of other States or the international community as a whole. Only after 1945 did the term take on a more general meaning. At present, *internationalization* — like its more recent twin term *globalization* — is used to describe tendencies toward the intensification of global relations of interaction and exchange, the worldwide interweaving of fields of social communication, and the transnational harmonization of social models and structures (cf., for example, McGrew, 1992). Internationalization and globalization refer to a social reality that increasingly extends into the everyday experiences of individuals as well' (Schriewer 2000: 305, referencing McGrew 1992).

6. 'Noch leben wir erst am anfange der weltgeschichtlichen periode, die durch die verwendung des dampfes und der elektrizität eingeleitet worden ist, aber schon jetzt stehen die völker materiell wie geistig in einem verhältnisse gegenseitiger bedingtheit und abhängigkeit, wie es in keiner früheren zeit stattgefunden hat. Mit naturnotwendigkeit fast hat sich in der zweiten hälfte des 19. jahrhunderts der begriff "international" entwickelt. Er konnte noch nicht in der ersten hälfte unseres jahrhunderts entstehen, wo es zwar schon nationen im vollen sinne des wortes gab, aber noch keinen reich entwickelten, die grenzen der länder überbrückenden verkehr. Erst unsere zeit, die im zeichen des verkehrs steht, konnte den begriff schaffen, und sie musste ihn schaffen' [We are just now witnessing the beginning of the era in world history which was heralded by the use of steam and electricity, but at this moment already peoples are connected and depend on each other both materially and intellectually like never before. It seems that the term "international" had to emerge with absolute necessity in the second half of the nineteenth century. It couldn't develop as early as in the first half of our century, when, admittedly, there were nations in the true sense of the word, but not the highly developed means of transportation that bridge borders between countries today. It was only our era that could produce the term and inevitably had to produce it] (Hartmann, quoted in Gassmeyer 1899: 349–50; my translation).

7. This term is not to be confused with the term *internationality* as used by Stead and Lawrence, nor with today's notion of *internationalization*.

8. His sense of mission can also be seen in his later involvement (from 1902) in the promotion of the international language Esperanto, which was also rooted in pacifist thinking (see Forster 1982: 269–70; Schleich 2015: 157, 230-31).

9. See also Reichel (1900: 724), Deniker (1901: 33–34), Markscheffel (1903: 9), Scott (1900), Loev (1901: 351), Bérenger (1900: 254).

10. See e.g. Rossmann (1897: 255), Kabisch (1896), Breymann & Steinmüller (1905: 108).

11. Dates taken from 'Hommage à Paul Mieille, promoteur de la correspondance scolaire internationale' (1934: 72).

12. This interest can be seen in his accounts of a private 'experiment', which he published in the *Review of Reviews*. This experiment involved Victor Bétis, who stayed with the Stead family for six months in 1892 in order to teach Stead's children French according to the system invented by François Gouin (see [Stead, William T.] 1892a, 1892b and 1893).

13. On Magill's life, see Magill (1907).

14. For similar advice in German, see, for instance Petri 1898: 514.

15. For a more complete analysis of the arguments put forward by the proponents of the Scholars' International Correspondence with regard to language learning and to fostering international understanding in a pacifist sense, see Schleich 2015: 328-49.

16. The German script was a topic in some of the penfriends' letters. It seems to have been a challenge for some but did not generally form an obstacle (see Schleich 2015: 403-04). See also McLelland 2015: 201-06.

17. See Buttjes (1991: 53) on *Realienkunde* and its link with the reform movement: 'But Vietor's [sic] call for reorienting language teaching was accompanied by a redefinition of the cultural content, too. Within the German context of modern language reform, the emphasis on some knowledge of the foreign realia (*Realienkunde*) can certainly be considered as one of the key demands of the reformers'. Brebner (1909: 32-33) explained the term as follows: 'The word *Realien* (real things or realities) is somewhat vague and comprehensive. It covers everything that is illustrative of a

nation's real life and thought — its literature, history and geography, its institutions, manners and customs. Till recently, even in Germany, the teaching of *Realien* in connection with languages, was mainly confined to literature: now, however, we can everywhere trace, in text-books and in teaching, the importance attached to the knowledge of the country and the people in almost every aspect'.

CHAPTER 4

❖

The Other in the History of German-Language Teaching: England and France, 1900–2000

Anke Wegner

This chapter examines the process of conceptualizing the Other in twentieth-century German-language teaching at secondary school level, with a special focus on the *premier cycle (collège)* in France and the Lower Certificate, the General School Examination and the O-level in England (i.e. to age sixteen). Concerning German-language teaching in France, it is obvious that the aim of developing a *culture générale* was closely connected to literary studies and — especially up until the Second World War — (pseudo-)historical information, which provided a portrayal of the other national character, the other *patrimoine national*, and offered insights into historical and contemporary characteristics of the people, their culture and nation. In contrast, German-language teaching in England was more focused on communicative skills and the promotion of mobility and professional qualification throughout the twentieth century. Thus, the Other in England was primarily constructed by everyday topics and real-life situations, by attractive geographical and tourist information and, after the 1980s and 1990s, educational concepts such as intercultural education or the focus on the European Dimension became dominant. The didactic discourse, official guidelines, and schoolbooks show how concepts of the Other in France and England in the twentieth century differed and how this is due to specific historical contexts.[1]

Introduction

The history of teaching and learning in Europe reflects the development of a plurality of education systems, especially primary and secondary schooling, and reveals specific politics and ideologies as well as traditions and changes in educational goals. The chapter focuses on the history of German language teaching in France and England during the twentieth century with special reference to teaching at the secondary level, at the *collège* in France and up to the Lower Certificate, the General School Examination and O-level in England (i.e. age sixteen). On one hand, this entails a comparison of tradition and innovation in the field of teaching and learning as determined by a common mind-set at the turn of the nineteenth to the twentieth century: the Reform Movement. During the nineteenth century, there was a tradition of literary and formal education with the aim of developing a *culture générale* in France and, in England, *exact scholarship* and training the mind, taste and character.[2] Adhering to the teaching of classical languages, this tradition was left intact despite the emergence of innovative approaches to modern language teaching during the nineteenth century. It was the Reform Movement at the end of that century which brought a major change to the main goals, contents and methods of modern-language teaching in accordance with the premise to communicate in a foreign language. On the other hand, the history of German-language teaching in France and England shows in a distinctive way that teaching and learning have been determined by national rather than common European concerns. The histories of German-language teaching in France and England reflect the differences in political and ideological standpoints and in pedagogical and didactic thinking in Europe. In France, this is due to forms of national education which imply the depiction and analysis of the *enemy* up until the end of the Second World War (e.g. Hovelaque 1910; Varenne 1935; curricula and ministerial guidelines from 1925, 1937 and 1938), whereas in England an orientation towards individual needs, the country's economic interests, and overcoming *insularity* dominated (e.g. Board of Education 1918; Atkins and Hutton 1920: 32-33).

This chapter outlines the ways in which the aims of German-language teaching and, consequently, concepts of the Other in France and England in the twentieth century differed from each other and how this was determined by an interplay of national interests, general goals of schooling and subject-specific aims and contents.

France 1900 to 1945: From Literary Impressions to Wotan and Krupp

At the end of the nineteenth century, the Reform Movement initiated a change in the goals, contents and methods of modern-language teaching due to its focus on communication and especially the emphasis on orality. This implied a rise of the object lesson (*leçon de choses*), everyday situations, and contemporary background studies. In France this reform only lasted a short while, beginning roughly in 1901/1902 with corresponding guidelines by the Ministry of Education and ending around 1908, when guidelines were again published in which a shift back to textual work on literature was agreed.[3]

At the end of the nineteenth century the overall aim of language teaching in France was to develop a *culture générale*, an intellectual, literary and moral culture understood as *formation désintéressée* — 'rien viser, mais rendre apte à tout' [aiming at nothing, but making fit for everything] (Basch 1892: 388)[4] — a concept defining the elite, *l'honnête homme*. Regarding German-language teaching, these general goals were interpreted in a particular manner up until the end of the Second World War because, since the Franco-Prussian War of 1870 to 1871, Germany had been the enemy, *l'inimitié héréditaire*, the *Erbfeind*. Thus, German-language teaching further implied the concepts of nation and action: *culture générale* meant national education, the appreciation of the French nation and culture — or national culture — and the defence of its superiority (e.g. Closset 1950: 142–45; Ministère de l'Instruction publique et des Beaux-Arts 1925: 600-01; Ministère de l'Éducation Nationale 1939: 84-85). The French and the German were constructed as two contrasting and conflicting characters representing the Latin and Germanic ideals:

> deux esprits impénétrables l'un à l'autre, entre deux conceptions qui s'excluent, l'idéal latin et l'idéal germanique qui à travers les siècles ont déterminé des croyances, des formes sociales, des politiques, des actions et des rêves, une esthétique et une philosophie opposées et inconciliables. (Hovelaque 1910: 378)

> [Two impenetrable minds, between two conceptions which exclude each other, the Latin ideal and the Germanic ideal which over the centuries have determined opposite and irreconcilable beliefs, social forms, politics, actions and dreams, an aesthetic and a philosophy.]

Although there had been a process of rapprochement between the German Chancellor Stresemann and French Prime Minister Briand on the political level after the Great War, there was — in the didactic discourse as well as in ministerial guidelines — a relatively strong demand for action in the interwar period which included 'étude défensive' (Douady 1917: 18) and mobilization against the enemy. The French Ministry of Education (1925: preamble) propagated the education of one, unified youth and one single culture, 'qu'il y ait un seul régime, une seule jeunesse, une seule culture', the teaching of colonial and military power and 'sentiment national'. Articles in *Les Langues Modernes*, a major modern-language teaching journal, called for the education of complete characters, with the resolve to act, 'caractères complets, décidés à l'action', an education in the character of the new generation 'ayant pris une claire notion des diversités, [...] capables de comprendre et de juger, dont le corps et l'âme auront été solidement trempés, seront pour la France la seule garantie d'un avenir meilleur et digne de son magnifique passé' [which has a clear idea of diversities, [...] capable of understanding and judging, whose body and soul will be solidly saturated, will be for France the only guarantee of a better future and a future worthy of its magnificent past] (Varenne 1935: 86). This nationalistic and chauvinistic ideology, the harsh critique of descriptive realism, a 'réalisme trop purement descriptif' and the mere teaching of geography and technique, 'leçon de choses géographiques ou techniques' ('Enseignement littéraire' 1907: 281), as well as the guidelines from 1908 all substantially influenced the development of background studies and the depiction of the Other in schoolbooks.

During the first two decades of the twentieth century, object lessons, *leçons de choses*, and tourist and geographical topics were reduced, while literature and (pseudo-) historical notes increased again. As a consequence, schoolbooks of the 1920s, like *L'Allemand et l'Allemagne par les textes*, did include geographical information, e.g. on the River Rhine, for the beginners' class (*sixième*), but the Other, the other national character or *génie national* was conceptualized by combining selected pieces of literature, myth and legend with historical elements.

This trend continued during the 1930s. The systematic selection of literature, literary history and of historical and mythological allusions led to ethnological and anthropological interpretations of the past and present soul and character of the German Other. Schoolbooks of that time started with the Germanic tribes and their gods and ended with a negative presentation of the contemporary German character and the superiority of the French.

Wer will, der kann (Bouchez 1934), for instance, states that the country of the Germanic people was poor and had a tough climate; and that this explained the 'dark' Germanic gods in contrast to the 'light' Greek gods and the urge to expand to the South and West. The Germanic people were presented as an ever-fighting people, whose greatest pleasure was fighting, and even the women were argumentative and belligerent and accompanied the men to battles, brought food and drink and encouraged them by their clamour:

> Die Germanen bildeten kein einziges Volk, sondern waren in Sippen geteilt, die bald miteinander, bald mit den Römern Krieg führten. Denn außer der Jagd war der Krieg ihre liebste Beschäftigung, ihr Hauptvergnügen. [...] Auch die Frauen waren zanksüchtig und kriegerisch gesinnt. Sie begleiteten die Männer in die Schlacht, brachten ihnen Speise und Trank und ermutigten sie durch ihr Geschrei. (Bouchez 1934: 44-45)

> [The Germanic tribes were not a single people, but were separated into clans which either fought against each other or against the Romans. For apart from hunting, war was their favourite occupation, their main pleasure. [...] The women were also quarrelsome and belligerent. They accompanied the men to battles, brought them food and drink, and encouraged them with their screaming.]

The combination of pictures and texts underlined the dark, mysterious soul of the Germanic people.

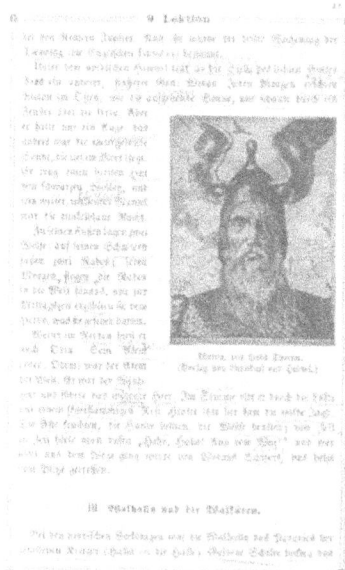

FIG 4.1. The Germanic Beliefs in Gods, Götterglaube bei den Germanen (Bertaux & Lepointe 1925: 21)[5]

Lessons about the gods of the Germanic people (see Figure 4.1), for example Wotan, explain that:

> the dark god Wotan appeared each morning in the east, like the rising sun, and watched through a window above the earth. But he had only one eye: the other was the setting sun which lies deep in the sea.

The text ends with a description of Wotan:

> riding in a storm through the air on a flaming horse, followed by a wild hunt that made branches crack, dogs bark and wolves howl, and those who did not get out of his way were struck by lightning (killed by his sword).

The author of *Wer will, der kann*, Maurice Bouchez, warns the reader in the same way about Krupp and its war economy, and about the German custom of students' duels:

> Daß Krupp und die deutsche Wirtschaft 'überhaupt sich ganz auf Friedenswirtschaft umgestellt' haben soll, darf uns doch nicht vergessen lassen, wie wenig friedfertig der Deutsche von jeher gewesen ist. Weil sein Land hier sumpfig, dort steinig, fast überall bewaldet war, hat er sich im Laufe der Jahrhunderte daran gewöhnt, bald über die Alpen, bald über den Rhein hinauszuschauen, wo ein fruchtbarer Boden, ein milderes Klima das Leben leichter machte.
>
> Daß das deutsche Volk eines der kampflustigsten, waffenfreudigsten ist, beweist nicht nur seine Geschichte, sondern auch manche Sitte, z.B. die Studentenmensur. (1934: 253)
>
> [The fact that Krupp and the German economy are said to have 'switched over entirely to a peacetime economy' should not make us forget how little the German has ever been peaceful in the past. Because his land was marshy here, stony there, wooded almost everywhere, the Germanic tribes became used in the course of the centuries to passing either over the Alps or the Rhine River to reach better soils and a milder climate to make life easier.
>
> That the German people are some of the most belligerent and militant can be proven by both history and customs like students' duels.]

Finally, these portrayals of the Other were combined with constructs of French superiority and, for instance in *Ich lerne Deutsch*, national strength; the power of the French army; the civility, education and courage of officers; the loyalty of soldiers; and the victory of the First World War:

> Frankreich ist *ein mächtiges Land*. Es hat eine wunderbare Armee. Die Höflichkeit, die Bildung und der Heldenmut seiner Offiziere sind in der ganzen Welt bekannt. Mutig scharen sich seine Soldaten um die blau-weiß-rote Fahne. Der hinreichende Gesang der Marseillaise führte sie zum Siege. (Fritsch 1928: 132)
>
> [France is *a powerful country*. It has a wonderful army. The civility, education and courage of its officers are known all over the world. Its soldiers troop together courageously around the blue-white-red flag. Sufficient singing of *La Marseillaise* led them to victory.]

Up until the end of the Second World War, the construction of the Other, *civilisation*, was based on literary pieces supported by legends, and myths as well as historical and ethnological impressions. A strong nationalistic and chauvinistic ideology meant that this tradition was combined with more or less excessive negation of the enemy, a stereotypical picture of an aggressive, expansionist people; the aim was to emphasize differences, 'les différences psychologiques irréductibles' (Hovelaque 1910: 386) and the need for national unity.

England 1900 to 1945: Bread and Butter Study and Hotel Scenes

In England at the turn of the century, academic traditions and 'exact scholarship', the appreciation of literature and the idea that language teaching 'should train the mind, the taste, and the character' (Board of Education 1918: 86) were perpetuated, as in France, but this was especially the case for modern-language teaching beyond the examinations for Lower Certificates and the General School Examinations.[6]

In contrast to France, a modern language was defined in England rather as a means for communication (e.g. Palmer 1955: 9) and a vehicle for everyday communication. Consequently, foreign-language teaching aimed at meeting individual needs — for instance those of personal contact and holidays, preparing the young generation to travel to France and Germany — and it also aimed to qualify the young generation to work abroad or in international contexts. Motivating students to learn modern languages and promoting mobility and professional qualification were closely linked to national interests. Aspects of 'national efficiency' became popular because of 'the widespread concern for Britain's survival' (Stray 1986: 18), which meant the 'needs of industry and commerce' (Board of Education 1918: 32) and, regarding the British Empire, the need to communicate and cooperate on an international level in order to overcome British isolation:

> The war has made this people conscious of its ignorance of foreign countries and people. [...] No country can afford to rely on its domestic stones of knowledge. The whole civilized world is a cooperative manufactory of knowledge. In science, technical and pure, in history, antiquities, law, politics, economics, philosophy, new researches are constantly leading to new discoveries (Board of Education 1918: 30-31).

In this respect, since the turn of the century the aims of 'friendly intercourse' and 'sympathy' as well as a policy of 'international understanding' and peace had become major goals of foreign-language teaching as well (Board of Education 1941: 115; IAAMSS 1949: 18, 38).

According to these aims of language teaching, the teaching of some knowledge of the other country and its people played an essential role:

> For none will this contact with a foreign mode of thought and point of view be more valuable than for an insular people like ourselves, who so rarely have the opportunity of coming into personal touch with the members of another nation. (Atkins and Hutton 1920: 3-4)

Further: 'for social intercourse we must know the people and their country through their language' (Atkins and Hutton 1920: 33). Getting to know the people and their country initially implied a focus on the *realia*, 'objects such as coins, newspapers, and the actual products of the country' (Brereton 1905: 19); and it also meant insights into 'experiences of everyday life' (ibid.) and 'real-life situations' (Findlay 1932: 329) in order to foster the ability to act appropriately in everyday situations abroad.

Schoolbooks consisted of these *everyday topics* and scenes in institutions, in restaurants, etc., and generally showed an attractive Germany through geographical, tourist, cultural and historical information. *Deutsches Leben*, for instance, contains dialogues like meeting businessmen in Berlin:

> Herr Märker. Wer ist dort? Jansen? Nanu, wo kommen Sie denn her? Ich dachte, Sie wären in England.
> Jansen. Heute früh bin ich zurückgekommen; ich will morgen nach Leipzig fahren, zur Messe. Kann ich Sie noch sprechen, wenn ich in Berlin übernachte?
> Märker. Selbstverständlich; ich freue mich sehr, wir haben uns ja so lange nicht gesehen.
> Jansen. Wo können wir uns treffen? [...]
> Märker. In Tempelhof. Sie müssen mit der Untergrundbahn fahren. Aber Sie haben recht, das ist zu umständlich. Das Beste ist, ich hole Sie von der Bahn ab, und wir essen dann im Kaiserhof, in der Friedrichstraße. Wenn ich nicht an der Bahn bin, fahren Sie gleich mit der Taxe dorthin. Ich werde einen Tisch auf meinen Namen bestellen. (Macpherson and Strömer 1931: 111-12)

> [Mr Märker. Who is there? Jansen? Oops! Where are you coming from? I thought you were in England.
> Jansen. I came back this morning I want to travel to Leipzig tomorrow, to the fair. Can I still talk to you if I stay overnight in Berlin?
> Märker. For sure; what a pleasure, we haven't seen each other for such a long time.
> Jansen. Where can we meet? [...]
> Märker. In Tempelhof. You have to take the Underground. But you are right, that is too much trouble. It is best that I pick you up from the train, and then we eat at the Kaiserhof, on the Friedrichstraße. If I am not at the station, take a taxi straight there. I will reserve a table under my name.]

This schoolbook, like others, corresponded to the predominant discourse on foreign language teaching which was focusing on the 'desirability of training in the ability to speak' as well as 'opportunities for travel, the development of the wireless and the interchange of modern films' (Board of Education 1938: 426).

Further, English schoolbooks showed a broader focus than in France on 'accurate knowledge of the civilization of modern Europe' (Kittson 1926: 158), especially in the fields of the economy, politics, science, industry and technical development. A photograph from *Deutsches Leben* (Macpherson 1939; see Figure 2) shows German industry, tanks of ammonium hydroxide in the Leuna factories in Merseburg. In the corresponding dialogue, one of the protagonists, Albert, says that the Leuna factories must be very large and that he wants to see them some day. His father answers that it takes minutes to pass by on the express train and that — in contrast to some isolated villages where farmers were ploughing their fields thirty years ago — it is one of the biggest industries, producing valuable substances that run

FIG 4.2. German Industry, Deutsche Industrie (Macpherson 1939: 32–33)[7]
Courtesy of Manuscripts and Special Collections, the University of Nottingham

our machines and make our soils fertile. Altogether, schoolbooks showed, even in 1939, an attractive contemporary Germany and its economic growth and technical development.

In sum, the construction of the Other followed different educational goals in England and France in the first half of the twentieth century. In France, literary, historical and mythological or ethnological facets of the Germanic people drew a complex but negative picture of the Other as an ever profoundly aggressive, militant soul, 'l'instinct le plus profond, le plus permanent et le plus enraciné' (Spenlé 1919: 6). In England, by contrast, everyday life and situational language teaching, the presentation of professional intercourse and economic growth in Germany remained predominant until the Second World War and after it. Both concepts of the Other reflected national interests as shaped by specific historical contexts — on one hand, perceptions of the enemy after the Franco-Prussian War and, on the other, an interest in economic power and a focus on national isolation which needed to be overcome in the course of the twentieth century.

France 1945 to 2000: *culture générale*, Continued

In France after the Second World War the aims of German-language teaching changed. Whereas before the Second World War only very few had defended impartiality, modesty and cosmopolitism (Rocher 1939), modern-language teaching was now supposed to foster sympathy and international understanding, friendship and peace.

De véritables écrans masquent aux uns et aux autres leurs réalités, leurs vrais visages. Écrans inconscients de l'ignorance ou d'une connaissance superficielle. Écrans voulu, destinés à servir certains intérêts, à justifier des politiques, par une information orientée qui souligne ce qui oppose, sépare, engendre la méfiance au lieu d'être au service de la sympathie et de l'amitié. (Bergès 1952: 224)

[Veritable screens hide their realities from each other, their true faces. Unconscious screens of ignorance or superficial knowledge. Deliberate screens, intended to serve certain interests, to justify politics, with information which underlines what opposes, separates, breeds distrust, instead of being in the service of sympathy and friendship.]

A new 'être cultivé', a 'culture de l'humanité et de l'humaine' (Handrich 1953: 65-66), was aimed at.

These changes in foreign-language teaching led to a revision of the concept of *civilisation*, which chiefly included a reduction of stereotypes and a more realistic representation of France's neighbour. Further, during the 1950s, 1960s and 1970s, situational contexts and a depiction of the way of life, tourist and geographical, economic, technological as well as social and political questions, contemporary topics or 'centres d'intérêt qui soient en rapport avec notre temps' (Compte rendu 1968: 649), took on a more important role. *L'Allemand facile* in the 1960s, for instance, provided everyday situations and information on correspondence or school exchanges, and contained *centres d'interêt* which presented relatively authentic pictures of contemporary Germany.

As at the start of the century, this development led to a harsh critique of cultural deficits as well as a trivialization of contents in German-language teaching — a 'spectaculaire déficit culturel' or a 'banalisation des contenus' (Lecomte 1985: 24) — and again, in consequence, the concept of a national culture and the definition of the Other and one's own national culture or *civilisation* remained the dominant point of reference: 's'ouvrir à une autre culture, c'est approfondir sa propre culture, développer son esprit d'analyse et son sens critique' (Puren 1988: 366). This again still implied the appreciation and analysis of literary pieces:

Quelle ne sera pas la joie des élèves auxquels seront rendus intelligible, à l'aide de beaux textes, la saveur concrète et la chaleur humaine de Goethe, la ferveur de Hölderlin, l'idéalisme de Schiller, la malice de Heine ou l'inquiétude d'un écrivain d'aujourd'hui en face des problèmes de notre temps. (Soulé-Susbielles 1985: 407)

[What a joy it will be for the students if they are given, with the help of beautiful texts, the concrete flavour and human warmth of Goethe, the fervour of Hölderlin, the idealism of Schiller, the malice of Heine or the concern of a contemporary writer dealing with problems of our time.]

Although a contemporary depiction of the Other and, to a certain extent, contemporary children's and youth literature served to teach the language and *civilisation allemande*, aspects of national heritage remained the core focus of German-language teaching. Literary constructs of the Other were still shaped by aspects of national identity and 'sentiment national' (Ministère de l'Éducation Nationale 1970:

23): 'Elle (la langue étrangère) exprime une culture. [...] Ce n'est que la connaissance profonde de la langue, à travers les œuvres littéraires abordées directement que l'on arrivera à comprendre le tempérament, la logique, les aspirations, l'originalité d'un peuple [It (the foreign language) expresses a culture. [...] It is only with profound knowledge of the language, by working directly with literary works that one masters an understanding of the temperament, the logic, aspirations, originality of a people.]

Finally, guidelines from 1985 defined the study of representative *oeuvres* of German culture as an essential element of civic education (Ministère de l'Éducation Nationale 1985: 94-95). Thus, the guidelines from 1992 proposed teaching facts of civilization — 'faits de civilisation' — of German-speaking countries (such as everyday topics, and political, social and economic aspects), but they also suggested focusing on 'la vie artistique, littéraire et culturelle proprement dite' as well as 'les événements historiques majeurs et les faits de la période moderne et contemporaine' (Ministère de l'Éducation Nationale 1992: 21). Again, poetry, songs and fairy tales, etc. were to allow pupils to become sensitized to the culture and 'civilisation germanique' (ibid.: 35) and to develop an awareness of differences between France and Germany: 'à sensibiliser les élèves aux différences culturelles entre la France et les pays de langue allemande' (ibid.: 48).

According to these developments, the schoolbooks of the 1970s, 1980s and 1990s contained everyday topics, 'thèmes de banalité des besoins de l'existence quotidienne' (Martin and Zehnacker 1972: 8), and information on German history and contemporary facts about geography, the economy and industry in German-speaking countries. And again these books presented 'thèmes de la connaissance objective et de la réflexion' (ibid.) which meant, in practice, legends, myths, saga, fairy tales and *Volksbücher* (folk tales), historicizing texts and literature as well as some information on great writers such as Heine, Goethe and Schiller and composers (Beethoven and Bach).

The schoolbook *Sag mal...* (Archer et al. 1993: 57-58), for instance, includes a page entitled 'Die neue Völkerwanderung' [The New Migration]. The text explains that rich Western European countries were under growing pressure from two sides. From the south ever more Africans were trying to find work in the European Union because economic growth in their homelands was not keeping pace with population growth. It added that in the East millions of people were dreaming of a better life in the West; and that there were refugees and those persecuted for political reasons from regions in crisis all over the world. The text refers to a map (apparently from *Stern*, a German magazine) showing the most important migration flows. This is reminiscent of the revival of the historical topic of the migration of peoples, the *invasion barbare* (the Barbarian Invasions), by instead presenting a Eurocentric interpretation of contemporary migration to Western Europe. Apart from topics concerning modern Germany, *Sag mal* (1993: 132) also contains literature and information about its authors: Goethe's *Zauberlehrling* (*Sorcerer's Apprentice*) is accompanied by an extra page on Goethe and Schiller with questions about Schiller's historical dramas and the historical events at the time of Goethe's fortieth birthday — which was in 1789.

At the end of the twentieth century, the concept of *civilisation* in France seems to have been particularly fuzzy and ambiguous. Although concepts of a contemporary and student-oriented *civilisation* or of inter- and transcultural education (e.g. Buffet and Willems 1995) were discussed, a 'didactique de la comparaison et du contraste' (von Bardeleben and Viselthier 1991: 131) continued to shape the concept of *civilisation* in France. Schoolbooks had not yet turned back to reconstructing a 'civilisation germanique' and major historical events (Ministère de l'Éducation Nationale 1992: 21, 35), but throughout the century *culture générale* was closely connected to an 'éducation à la différence' (Tournade 1986: 96-97) and 'citoyenneté nationale' (Sachot 1994: 34).

England 1945 to 2000: A Way of Life and a Reflection on Modern Societies

In England after the Second World War, sympathy, peace and international under-standing, together with countering the 'national isolation of the last century' (Harding 1967: 27) and 'narrow parochialism' (Incorporated Association of Head Masters 1966: 14) remained fundamental goals of foreign language teaching, international communication and cultural exchange:

> Cultural exchanges are a natural and necessary form of international intercourse. They must, in the long run, override ordinary considerations of both domestic and foreign policy. [...] If nations try to live on their own stocks of thought and sentiment, it will not be long before they all suffer from stagnation and decay. (Foreign Language Studies 1946: 5)

Still, foreign language teaching aimed to foster curiosity in other countries, a 'sympathetic attitude' (National Association of Language Advisors 1982: 3) and the ability to make contact with other people in Europe and beyond.

Although 'culturally broadening' and 'educationally humanizing' aspects of foreign-language teaching had a function in the discourse on the educational goals of foreign-language teaching (The Headmasters' Conference 1976: 1 ff.), pragmatic aims continued to play a major role: living and working abroad, the 'purposive, progressive citizen' (Mallinson 1953: 23) and an 'education of the child for life as a citizen, a worker and an individual in a changing world' (Ingram 1976: 12) and, finally, 'individual needs' and 'needs of the country' (Department of Education and Science 1988: 2) still dominated the discourse on foreign-language teaching.

From the 1970s onwards, societal and political changes prompted new educational concepts. The European dimension played, as it does today, an important role as far as the notion of common European citizenship and a better understanding between Great Britain and its European partners is concerned (see, e.g., The Headmasters' Conference 1976: 1 ff.; Department for Education 1991: 2). Vice versa, concerning the challenge of parochialism, just as today, foreign-language teaching was also thought to support educational goals focusing on tolerance and empathy within British society:

> A related characteristic of parochialism [...] is lack of 'empathy', the inability to see things as they are seen even by one's closest neighbours when they have different skin, colour or creed. Somehow the school curriculum must try to

> break down the barriers, whether in Belfast or Birmingham or Bradford, built by prejudice, which seems to be at its most virulent among post-adolescents. Lack of capacity for empathy disfigures national life in other ways. It is time, surely, to examine the school curriculum critically and insist that disciplines which combat parochialisms by their very nature have a secure place. [...] Doors and windows must be open, and be seen to be open, onto a polyglot, multicultural world. (Hawkins 1979: 75)

Educational concepts focusing on multicultural societies gained weight during the 1980s and 1990s, seeking to develop critical reflection on one's own and the other culture and national identity (Byram 1992: 11-12) and an 'awareness of the relativity of social environment, "culture" and way of life' (Garner 1981: 9). Consequently, like today, the GCSE and the National Curriculum highlighted insights into the culture and civilization of the other country and a sympathetic approach to other cultures and civilizations (Department of Education and Science 1985: 1); and called for the development of 'pupils' understanding of themselves and their own culture' (National Curriculum Council 1992: B1; Department of Education and Science 1990: 3) and 'a more objective view of their own customs and ways of thinking' (ibid.: 36), as well as the 'appreciation and enjoyment of diversity' and especially cultural and ethnic diversity as a part of modern societies (ibid.: 36, 81-82).

Finally, due to the development of comprehensive foreign-language teaching, the emphasis on communicative skills and the focus on general educational goals, foreign-language teaching was, like it is today, linked to other parts of the curriculum, particularly environmental or social studies (Broadbent 1984: 10). Cross-curricular themes and areas of study as well as the European dimension — e.g. the awareness of 'the need for joint responses in Europe to economic, ecological, social and political challenges' (Department for Education 1992: 3) — and 'Britain's place in a European and worldwide context' (NCC 1992: H8) played an important role in foreign-language teaching and continue to do so today.

The construction of the Other, after the Second World War and up until the end of the twentieth century, was determined substantially by the aim to motivate students and deepen their curiosity with authentic material, with background information about the way of life of the foreign country, and by presenting scenes of daily life and travel in the foreign country and 'some precise factual knowledge' (Modern Language Association 1968: 7):

> The subjects treated should be close to the everyday life and interests of the pupils; the vocabulary, limited to everyday experiences, should cover the treatment of such subjects as food; money; shopping; scenes in a café, in a restaurant, at a railway station, on a boat. (Modern Languages 1951: 22)

Schoolbooks in the 1960s and 1970s, like Nicholson's *Praktisches Deutsch* or *Wir lernen Deutsch*, highlighted travelling in Germany, introduced German radio and TV or provided information on journals and money; and to some extent focused on topics in the fields of the economy, politics, science, industry and technical development. Beyond this, textbooks of the 1960s and 1970s began to compare their own and the other contexts, experiences and viewpoints, and to present a plurality of individual perspectives and ways of life.

During the 1970s and 1980s, new approaches to background studies and the emphasis on educational goals had an influence on schoolbooks for German-language teaching. This primarily implied a broader perspective on European issues and world dimensions, a depiction of multicultural societies and a reflection on individual perspectives, on 'otherness outside the nation's boundaries' as well as 'otherness within it' (Byram 1993: 178). Schoolbooks still also contained educational topics, such as food, protection of the environment and European or global phenomena. For example, the schoolbook *Gute Reise!* (Gordon & Lanzer 1994: 37) shows teenagers talking about fast food and sweets; and the students are asked to do a class survey concerning the headline 'Teenagers are eating more and more sweets and fast food'. The schoolbook *Auf Deutsch!* (McNab & O'Brian 1995: 23 ff.) presents a lesson on 'The world — my home', with the task of comparing the weather in Melbourne and Darwin, and focusing on Australia, the Anangu and Uluru National Park, the protection area and desert eco-systems. The title 'The world — my home' might provoke allusions to the British Empire of past and present, but the lesson's focus instead hints at facets of intercultural and ecological education.

In England, constructing the Other was thus transformed from background studies which highlighted travelling, tourist insights and opportunities to work abroad — 'more fitting to travel agent than pedagogue' (James 1973: 43-44) — to educational, reflexive programmes which questioned contemporary society and made students discuss contemporary challenges in the fields of economics and ecology, of politics and societal change in a European and world perspective. The Other was thus becoming fluid here; and was being constructed as a mirror to contemporary challenges and tasks to consider.

Conclusion

The history of German-language teaching in France and England of the twentieth century shows that the construction of the Other depended on educational goals defined by both traditions and innovations of modern-language teaching, as well as by specific economic, political and ideological interests of the nation. The concept of the Other in France and England converged twice during the twentieth century: once due to the international Reform Movement at the start of the twentieth century; and again with the orientation towards communication and international understanding (and audio-visual language teaching) during the 1960s. Apart from this, concepts of the Other in France and England differed considerably. The Other in France was a literary one, constructed by literary texts, historical or ethnical elements, and intended to stress the differences between the German and French culture, nation, the German and French ethnic identity or *civilisation*. What can be seen here is, as Zygmunt Bauman puts it, that the invention of the Other, the 'stranger', was an uncircumventable aspect of the social production of identities. They are 'indeed, invented, zealously and with gusto, patched together with salient or minute and unobtrusive distinction marks. They are useful precisely in their capacity of stranger; their strangerhood is to be protected and caringly preserved'

(Bauman 1998: 30). The French version of the Other clearly implied such a construction of distinction marks, culture, the assumption of a superior people or nation on one hand; and, on the other, the aggressive enemy up until the end of the Second World War, and then the different people or *civilisation* until the 1990s.

 The German Other in England was an attractive country for tourists and those who wanted to work and live abroad, a country of economic wealth and a partner in commerce and trade. At the end of the twentieth century, individual, multicultural, European or world dimensions supported the focus on differences and similarities of individual perspectives, on a general, intercultural and political or civic education. The German Other in England changed from collective images of a tourist, attractive country, an economically successful nation and a modern society to an Other characterized by a plurality of viewpoints, lifestyles and aspirations and to the reflection on otherness outside and inside Great Britain, Europe and the world. In sum, comparing concepts of the Other in German language teaching reveals that, basically, these were shaped by discursive practices on a national scale, and especially by the differing didactic discourses, guidelines and examinations, and that neither a general European tradition nor convergence could be found by the start of the millennium.

Bibliography

ARCHER, C., ET AL. 1993. *Sag mal... 3^e* (Paris: Colin)

ATKINS, H. G., and H. C. HUTTON. 1920. *The Teaching of Modern Foreign Languages in School and University* (London: Arnold)

BARDELEBEN, M. VON, and B. VISELTHIER. 1991. 'Allemand: premier et second cycle', in *Enseignement/Apprentissage de la civilisation en cours de langue*, ed. by INRP (Paris: INRP), pp. 127-31

BASCH, VICTOR. 1892. 'De l'enseignement des langues modernes' *Revue Universitaire*, 1: 377-93

BAUMAN, Z. 1998. *Postmodernity and its Discontents* (London: Polity Press)

BEAUJEU, L. 1907. QUOTED IN 'Enseignement littéraire dans les classes du second cycle: réunion du 2 mars 1907', *Les Langues Modernes*, 5: 279-86

BERGÈS, F. 1952. 'Les Fins de l'étude des langues vivantes', *Les Langues Modernes*, 46: 221-24

BERTAUX, F., and E. LEPOINTE, 1925. *L'Allemand et l'Allemagne par les textes: classe de quatrième* (Paris: Hachette)

BOARD OF EDUCATION. 1918. *Modern Studies: The Position of Modern Languages in the Educational System of Great Britain* (The Leathes Report) (London: HMSO)

———. 1938. *Memorandum on the Position of French in Grant-aided Secondary Schools in England* (The Spens Report) (London: HMSO)

———. 1941. *Curriculum and Examinations in Secondary Schools: Report of the Committee of the Secondary School Examinations Council* (London: HMSO)

BOUCHEZ, M. 1934. *Wer will, der kann: Ein Buch für altere Anfänger. Zweiter Teil. Classe de Troisième A'- B, 2e langue* (Paris: Belin)

———. 1939. *Wer will, der kann: Ein Buch für Tertianer. Sonst und Jetzt II. Vierte Stufe. Classe de Troisième A — A'- B* (Paris: Belin)

BRERETON, C. 1905. *The Teaching of Modern Languages with Special Reference to Big Towns* (London: Blackie)

——. 1911. 'A Comparison between French and English Secondary Schools', Board of Education *Special Reports on Educational Subjects*, 24 (London: HMSO)

BROADBENT, J. 1984. 'Modern Languages', in *Curriculum Opportunities in a Multicultural Society*, ed. by A. Craft and G. Bardell (London: Harper & Row)

BUFFET, F., and G. WILLEMS. 1995. 'Communication transculturelle et "lingua franca"', in *Former les enseignants à l'international*, ed. by Chantal Paisant (= *Revue internationale d'éducation*, 6), pp. 61–72

BYRAM, M. 1992. 'Foreign Language Learning for European citizenship', *Language Learning Journal*, 6: 10–12

——. 1993. 'Foreign Language Teaching and Multicultural Education', in *The Multicultural Dimension of the National Curriculum*, ed. by A. S. King and M. J. Reiss (London: Falmer), pp. 173–86

CLOSSET, F. 1950. *Didactique des langues vivantes* (Brussels; Paris: Didier)

'Compte rendu d'un débat sur la reforme de l'enseignement des langues vivants'. 1968. *Les Langues Modernes*, 62: 648–50

DEPARTMENT OF EDUCATION and SCIENCE. 1985. *General Certificate of Education: The National Criteria — French* (London: HMSO)

——. 1988. *Modern Languages in the School Curriculum* (London: HMSO)

——. 1990. *Modern Foreign Languages for Ages 11 to 16* (London: HMSO)

——. 1991. *The European Dimension in Education: A Statement of the UK Government Policy and Report of Activities Undertaken to Implement the EC Resolution of 24 May 1988 on the European Dimension in Education* (London: DFE)

DEPARTMENT FOR EDUCATION. 1992. *Policy Models: A Guide to Developing and Implementing European Dimension Policies in the LEAs, Schools and Colleges* (London: DFE)

DOUADY, J. 1917. *L'Humanitarisme et les Langues Modernes* (Cahors: Coueslant)

'Enseignement littéraire dans les classes de second cycle: réunion du 2 mars 1907'. 1907. *Les Langues Modernes*, 5: 279–86

FINDLAY, J. J. 1932. 'The Psychology of Modern Language Teaching', *British Journal of Educational Psychology*, 3: 319–31

'Foreign Language Studies: Their Place in the National Life', 1946. *English Language Teaching*, 1: 3–6

FRITSCH, F. E. 1928. *Ich lerne Deutsch. Erster Teil. Lese- und Übungsbuch für das 3. und 4. Schuljahr der zweisprachigen Schulen im Elsass und in Lothringen*, 18th edn (Colmar: Union)

GARNER, E. 1981. 'Background Studies and "graded examinations"', *National Association of Language Advisors*, 12: 9–10

GORDON, A. L., and H. LANZER. 1994. *Gute Reise! Stage 3* (Cheltenham: Mary Glasgow)

HANDRICH, E. 1953. 'La Valeur culturelle de l'enseignement des langues vivantes', *Les langues Modernes*, Supplément: 57–67

HARDING, D. H. 1967. *The New Pattern of Language Teaching* (London: Longman)

HAWKINS, E. 1979. 'Why a Modern Language for All?', *Audio-Visual Language Teaching Journal*, 2: 71–76

HEADMASTERS' CONFERENCE. 1976. *Report on the Teaching and Examination of Modern Languages* (London: HMC)

HOVELAQUE, E. 1910. 'L'Enseignement des langues vivantes dans le deuxième cycle', *Les Langues Modernes*, 8: 375–90

INCORPORATED ASSOCIATION OF ASSISTANT MASTERS IN SECONDARY SCHOOLS. 1949. *The Teaching of Modern Languages* (London: University of London Press)

INCORPORATED ASSOCIATION OF HEAD MASTERS. 1966. *Modern Languages in the Grammar School*, rev. edn (London: [n. publ.])

INGRAM, S. R. 1976. *Teaching Languages in Great Britain — Why?* (London: CILT / The Modern Language Association)

JAMES, C. V. 1973. 'European Studies and the Study of Europe', in *Reports and Papers, 9 Modern Languages and European Studies*, ed. by CILT (London: CILT), pp. 42–51

KITTSON, E. C. 1926 [1918]. *Theory and Practice of Language Teaching, with Special Reference to French and German*, 2nd edn (London: Oxford University Press)

LECOMTE, P. 1985. '"Pourquoi votre fille est muette..." ou réflexions sur la motivation en didactique des langues', *Les Langues Modernes*, 79: 19–27

MCNAB, R., and A. O'BRIAN. 1995. *Auf Deutsch! 3* (Oxford: Heinemann)

MACPHERSON, A. S., and P. STRÖMER. 1931. *Deutsches Leben. Erster Teil* (London: Ginn)

——. 1939. *Deutsches Leben. Dritter Teil*, 2nd edn (London: Ginn)

MALLINSON, V. 1953. *Teaching a Modern Language* (London: Heinemann)

MARTIN, J., and J. ZEHNACKER. 1972. *Die Deutschen 4* (Paris: Didier)

MINISTÈRE DE L'INSTRUCTION PUBLIQUE ET DES BEAUX-ARTS. 1925. 'Instructions relatives à l'enseignement des langues vivantes', *Journal officiel*: 8665-68

MINISTÈRE DE L'ÉDUCATION NATIONALE. 1939. *Horaires et programmes de l'Enseignement secondaire des garçons et des jeunes filles. Nouveaux programmes de 6ᵉ à 3ᵉ (Arretés des 30 août 1937 et 11 avril 1938)* (Paris: Ministère de l'Éducation Nationale)

——. 1970. *Langues Vivantes. Horaires, Programmes, Instructions* (Paris: INRDP)

——. 1985. *Collèges, Programmes et instructions* (Paris: CNDP)

——. 1992. *Allemand, classes des colleges, 6e, 5e, 4e, 3e* (Paris: CNDP)

MODERN LANGUAGE ASSOCIATION. 1968. *Modern Language Courses in the Sixth Form* (London: MLA)

Modern Languages in the Secondary Modern Schools: Report on the Secondary Modern School Committee of the Modern Language Association. 1951. (London: Modern Language Association)

NATIONAL ASSOCIATION OF LANGUAGE ADVISORS. 1982. *Foreign Languages in Schools* (London: NALA)

NATIONAL CURRICULUM COUNCIL. 1992. *Modern Foreign Languages Non-Statutory Guidance* (York: NCC)

NICHOLSON, J. A. 1958/1960. *Praktisches Deutsch*, 2 vols (London: Harrap)

PALMER, H. 1955 [1921]. *The Oral Method of Teaching Languages* (Cambridge: Heffer)

PAXTON, N., and R. J. BRAKE. 1970-72. *Wir lernen Deutsch*, 3 vols (London: English University Press)

PUREN, CH. 1988. *Histoire des methodologies de l'enseignement des langues* (Paris: Nathan-CLE international)

ROCHER, M. L. 1939. 'Rapport de la Commission du 1er cycle sur les programmes: horaires et instructions de 1938', *Les Langues Modernes*, 37: 35-39

SACHOT, M. 1994. 'L'Éthique et l'enseignement des langues vivantes étrangères en tant que disipline scolaire', *Les Langues Modernes*, 88: 19-35

SOULÉ-SUSBIELLES, N. 1985. 'Lecture d'une nouvelle dans une clsse hétérogène', *Les Langues Modernes*, 79: 407-15

SPENLÉ, J. E. 1919. 'L'Impérialisme allemand', *Revue de l'enseignement des langues vivantes*, 36: 5-17

STRAY, CH. 1986. 'Culture or Discipline? The Redefinition of Classical Education', in *The Development of the Secondary Curriculum*, ed. by H. M. Price (London: Croom Helm), pp. 11-48

TOURNADE, J. F. 1986. 'L'Enseignement de civilisation en France: problèmes et questions', in *Journées d'études des germanistes. Leipzig 14–20 juillet 1986*, ed. by Association des Professeurs de Langues Vivantes (Paris: Association des Professeurs de Langues Vivantes), pp. 94-100

VARENNE, G. 1935. 'Les Vraies Humanités', *Les Lanuges Modernes*, 33: 80-87

WEGNER, A. 1999. *100 Jahre Deutsch als Fremdsprache in Frankreich und England* (Munich: iudicium)

Notes to Chapter 4

1. This chapter draws on my previous study of the history of German-language teaching in France and England in the twentieth century: a comparison of official guidelines, examination papers, didactic discourses and the development of schoolbooks (Wegner 1999).
2. Concerning France, see, for example, Basch (1892) and Lichtenberg (1902/03); concerning England, see, for example, Brereton 1911: 50, 54; Stray 1986: 13-14.
3. Ministerial guidelines in France had, and still have, a strong impact on teaching and schoolbooks; and this shift back to literature (and grammar) led to harsh discussions — les querelles des Anciens et des Modernes — in which teachers defended the oral approach, the direct method and a more realistic and tourist and geographical presentation of Germany (cf. Puren 1988: 55).
4. Translations from French or German into English are my own.
5. Every effort has been made to contact the copyright holder of the material contained in the figure and any information on this would be welcome.
6. In any case, there had been voices which spoke out for the academic rigour and intellectual content of the German language, which should be considered for teaching at the levels of Lower Certificates and the CSE as well (Brereton 1905: 15-16). Further, the school examinations still contained the translation of literature, a dictation, grammar and composition (Wegner 1999: 121-25).
7. Every effort has been made to contact the copyright holder of the material contained in the figure and information on this would be welcome.

CHAPTER 5

❖

Getting to Know the Other: Representation of 'the English' in German Cultural Readers of the 1920s

Felicitas Sharp

After the First World War the teaching of English as a foreign language faced a new orientation according to the principle of *Kulturkunde* [cultural studies], which was implemented in German schools with a new curriculum, the *Richert'sche Richtlinien*, in 1924/25. *Kulturkunde* used the discussion of examples of original foreign-language literature in the classroom: first, to offer students a better insight into the other culture; and, second, to reach an in-depth understanding of their own cultural background by comparing and contrasting. For this purpose, a new type of schoolbook, the cultural reader, was introduced. It offered various kinds of usually authentic literary and non-literary texts, which were intended to illustrate life in Britain (and in some cases also in the United States of America). This chapter looks at the requirements of the *Richtlinien* in the area of literature; outlines the different types of cultural readers; and takes a closer look at the different topics, authors and texts which found their way into these books in order to explore what were thought to be the typical characteristics of 'the English'.

Introduction

In the aftermath of the First World War, people in Germany were desperately trying to find reasons for their country's defeat. Probably the best-known explanation was the so-called 'stab-in-the-back' legend. It claimed a lack of support for the soldiers from the people at home, aiming to shift the blame especially onto the democratic politicians who had sought to end the war (Barth 2003). But the search for who was to be made accountable for the unpleasant outcome spread to all areas of society. And so another explanation was found by representatives of the German education system: the school system had failed. A famous example which illustrates this evaluation is the preface of Wilhelm Dibelius's highly successful book with the simple title *England*, an introduction to the history and geography of Great

Britain first published in 1922 (Dibelius [6]1931). It was extremely successful and was republished in seven editions until 1933. The author concludes that, despite the German school system providing the German people with the necessary attributes to win the wars of unification at the end of the nineteenth century, it had blatantly failed to do the same for the First World War. According to Dibelius, the Germans had been lacking the characteristics which would have made them a 'Weltvolk' (Dibelius [6]1931: xi), a people able to take over a leading role in the world:

> Der preußische Schulmeister hatte den Krieg von 1866 gewonnen, denn er hatte dem preußischen Volke all die [...] Eigenschaften gegeben, die es zur Hegemonie in Deutschland befähigten. Aber der preußische Schulmeister [...] hat den Weltkrieg verloren; denn die politischen Eigenschaften, die zu einem Weltvolke nötig sind, hat er dem Geschlechte nach 1870 nicht einpflanzen können. (Dibelius [6]1931: xi)

> [The Prussian schoolmaster had won the war of 1866, for he had given the Prussian people all the [...] qualities that made it capable of hegemony in Germany. But the Prussian schoolmaster [...] lost the World War; for he was not able after 1870 to instil in the new generations the political qualities that are necessary for a people of global standing (*Weltvolk*).][1]

Dibelius and his colleagues therefore supported a more nationalistic educational movement, *Kulturkunde*, which originated just after the end of the war. This new teaching principle, which could roughly be translated as 'cultural studies', was introduced by the guidelines for the Prussian school syllabus. As far as modern foreign languages were concerned, it aimed to encourage the students' examination of the foreign culture to gain a more in-depth understanding of both their own and the foreign cultural background.

The following chapter takes a closer look at how the implementation of the concept of *Kulturkunde* influenced the view of 'the English' in English-language classrooms in Germany after the First World War. It analyses how the cultural reader, a new type of schoolbook introduced during the time of the Weimar Republic in the Germany of the 1920s, aimed to illustrate and conceptualize 'the English' through fictional and non-fictional texts. Usually this meant a reduction to certain, almost stereotypical, aspects — an obvious danger which contemporaries were also aware of, the biggest criticism being that *Kulturkunde* paved the way for Nazi ideology in the German classrooms. It should be clarified that the cultural readers of the time used to talk about the 'English' despite referring to what should actually be called the 'British', as they also include information about the other parts of the United Kingdom. This substitution of 'Great Britain' by the term 'England' can still be heard in Germany today.

Historical Background

The main aspect that Dibelius and other German scholars complained about was a general lack of knowledge of Germany's opponents in the War, especially Britain and the United States, among educated Germans. According to them, universities, schools and especially the modern language subjects were therefore at least partly responsible for the fact that Germany had fatally underestimated these countries during the war (Dibelius [6]1931: xi).

At the same time, modern-language education started to lean towards a movement of nationalistic education, which had already been widely discussed for implementation in the so-called *deutschkundliche* subjects like German and History before the war (Hüllen 2006: 69). This *Deutschkunde* movement originated in the late 1890s. It aimed to shift school education away from the dominance of ancient Latin and Greek and place more emphasis on German as a subject, as well as on teaching students what it meant to be German instead of dealing with 'dead' languages and times long gone. The idea of *Deutschkunde* was to ensure that students developed pride in their native country, to make them aware of Germany's history and national culture, an aspect which could not necessarily be taken for granted in a country which had only been quite recently unified politically — the German nation state had only been founded as late as 1871 — and was still looking to unify culturally. Both school and university education were expected to contribute to *Kultureinheit*, which can be translated as 'cultural unity', a key concept at the time which had the aim of bringing together people from all over Germany under the umbrella of its glorious history (Hüllen 2006: 68-69). Ludwig (1988: 354) points out that *Deutschkunde* differed greatly from historical studies in that it aimed to look at Germany's history simply for the sake of its present: only what could be used to create a cultural unity was to play an important role in the classroom.

Scholarly discussion during the First World War was marked by a constant worry about the future of modern languages, which seemed doomed, as war propaganda on both sides had attempted to fuel mutual antagonism. No one knew when it was going to be possible again to resume peaceful relations between the opposing nations (Lohmann 1915). By adopting a more nationalistic concept, the representatives of English and French hoped to be able to show the importance of their subjects for the greater cause of the nation (Schöningh 1919). Among the arguments they put forward was the idea that especially the Anglo-Saxon countries ought to serve as an example for the German state. As the outcome of the war seemed to have proven they were politically strong and successful, in Germany they were renowned for their national pride; and especially the United Kingdom was admired for its worldwide Empire. Many German nationalists would have loved to see their country as a strong colonial power, too (Kaluza 1919; Schöningh 1919; Schiedermair 1920).

Many scholars argued that the new international political situation — the role of the United States of America during the war and their leadership in the establishment of the new League of Nations — also meant that English ought to take over a leading position in the curriculum of modern languages, which had traditionally been dominated by French (Kaluza 1919).[2]

A New School Syllabus: The *Richert'sche Richtlinien*

The end of the First World War led to considerable political changes in Germany: the Emperor, the *Kaiser*, had to flee the country. A year of political unrest followed, which was defined by a power struggle between Communists and more moderate political forces until finally, in the summer of 1919, a new democratic constitution was passed by a democratically elected National Assembly (Sturm 2011). The country had managed the transition from monarchy to republic. Following these political changes, Prussia, which was still the leading German *Land*, implemented a new school syllabus for secondary schools in 1924 to 1925, the so-called *Richert'sche Richtlinien* (Richert 1924). The name of this document goes back to Hans Richert, the head of division of the Prussian Ministry for Education who was the main author of the new educational guidelines. The syllabus was applied to the German higher schools, i.e. secondary schools leading up to university, and it influenced the secondary school syllabi in all the other German *Länder*. Its main aim was to introduce nationalistic education across all subjects. It did so using the concept of *Kulturkunde*. But what did this mean for the teaching of foreign languages and especially for the teaching of English? The educational guidelines demanded an introduction of the students to the 'Kultur- und Geisteswelt' of the foreign people, mainly through literature, in order to gain a deeper understanding of their own culture (Christ and Rang 1985: 135). The term *Geisteswelt* is especially important. It can be described as 'the way people in other cultures think'. Aiming to understand how people think, using their literature and culture as a basis for information, was the main goal of the *Kulturkunde* movement. This is also where the new concept differs from earlier approaches to teaching the history and literature of another culture in the foreign-language classroom, which was now despised as a simple accumulation of encyclopaedic knowledge (Aronstein 1926). *Kulturkunde* took the discussion of literature and culture to another level. By looking at the achievements of another culture and trying to understand how the geography and history of a nation had shaped the character of its people, the students were supposed to gain a deeper insight into their own cultural backgrounds by means of comparison. Thus, there was not only the aspect of utility (being able to use the foreign language for communication and reading), but a new concept of nationalistic meaning, which was supposed to give the students the necessary qualities to turn them into a people able to take over a leading role in the world (Aronstein 1926: 263).

So why was it that literature came to be at the very heart of *Kulturkunde* in the foreign-language classroom? The main reason for its strong position at the time was the fact that scholars believed that culture was expressed through literature. In the early twentieth century there were barely any other media available apart from books; travelling abroad and getting to know the other culture first-hand were expensive and not easily achievable for students (or teachers). Therefore, original texts from the target culture were considered the most effective way to introduce students to that culture (Schön 1929: 192). It is important to note that at the time, the term 'literature' was used in the wider sense, including both literary and non-literary texts.

These original texts were classified into two different types: *primär kulturkundliche Texte* and *sekundär kulturkundliche Texte* — primary and secondary cultural texts. Primary cultural texts illustrated certain characteristics of the other culture within themselves; the very way the texts were written by authors was seen as a representation of their culture (Graef 1930: 483). Richert himself calls language the *Spiegel der Nation* [the mirror of a nation] (Richert 1920), seeing both language and text as representatives of the culture they originated from. Usually, primary cultural texts are literary texts, such as excerpts from novels or poems. Secondary cultural texts, however, include pieces of writing in which the author intends to describe certain aspects of the target culture, for example religion, history or geography (Graef 1930: 483). The texts we find in cultural readers that fall into this category are usually taken from contemporary history books, for example James Anthony Froude's *Oceana* (Froude 1886) or Charles Lucas's *The Story of the Empire* (Lucas 1924).

Because such texts lent themselves so easily to the purpose of dipping into another culture and relating the findings to the students' own culture, the *Richtlinien* put fiction and non-fiction texts from the target culture at the very centre of foreign-language teaching. Consequently, a new type of schoolbook was introduced, the so-called *kulturkundliche Lesebücher* [cultural readers], in order to cater for the greater demand for reading material in the classroom. Soon there were many different kinds and editions on the market (see below).

Cultural Readers

The implementation of the *Richert'sche Richtlinien* in Prussia and their effect on the curricula in the other German states led to the appearance of a new type of schoolbook for the foreign-language classroom. Cultural readers were published in large numbers from 1925 onwards[3] and offered a collection of various authentic texts which were to be used in the foreign-language classroom to gain information about what was considered to be the 'ways of the English', as one of the titles suggests (Angermann 1931a).

Before moving on to the description of these readers it should be stressed that, naturally, the 'ways of the English' described in these books were limited to a certain number of aspects which appear almost stereotypical, especially when seen from today's perspective. Many contemporary scholars were also aware of this issue. It had its origin in the fact that the discipline of *Kulturkunde* used structural psychology to identify the character of a nation. This seemingly complicated approach tried to take many details into account, which then had to be simplified in order to make it possible to teach *Kulturkunde* at school. Several journal articles exemplify the debate as to what extent original texts were supposed to be shortened and altered, or printed with short introductory texts, in order to exemplify a certain 'characteristic trait' — if they were to be changed at all (Gerstenberg 1929: 4; Graef 1930; Hübner 1925a).

Cultural readers appeared in several varieties; and there are four different types which can be identified. Type A is closely related to the anthologies which had been used in foreign-language teaching until this point. These, usually earlier, cultural readers, were designed as literary histories spanning several literary periods. An example is Bauch (1925), which offered texts from the 'Elizabethan era' including Edmund Spenser and William Shakespeare, pieces from the Romantic Movement and the Victorian Period, all the way to 'Recent Literature', featuring authors such as Meredith, Hardy, Kipling, Wilde and Shaw.

Cultural readers of Type B focus on one main aspect of the target culture and use it as a focal point to look at the other areas as well. Bausenwein and Schnellenberger (1930), for example, identify different types of British imperialism in their cultural reader and use them to illustrate different aspects of British culture. Texts by John Milton consequently serve as examples of what Bausenwein and Schnellenberger describe as 'Puritan imperialism'; Daniel Defoe for them represents so-called 'mercantile imperialism'; the Romantic poets Wordsworth, Blake and Coleridge are portrayed as authors of patriotic poetry. The collection of 'imperialistic' texts culminates in the section on 'literary imperialism' with contributions by William Watson, Rudyard Kipling and Arthur Conan Doyle. Schmidt (1930) is a typical example of a Type C cultural reader. It offers a collection of contemporary non-fictional texts, adapted from newspaper articles. This type of reader was heavily criticized by contemporary scholars, who claimed that it was doubtful whether the texts, abridged and changed by the editor, could still be seen as original texts from the target culture (Graef 1930: 484). The most widely published was Type D, the classical cultural reader, which comprises a wide range of original texts from mainly British and American authors, generally shortened to excerpts, then annotated and grouped according to topics or in chronological order.

Topics and Sources

In order to find out how 'the English' were portrayed in the cultural readers in the Weimar era English-language classrooms, it is necessary to take a closer look at the cultural aspects the books covered and the authors and texts used to illustrate them. The choice of topics varies from one cultural reader to the next, but there are a number of aspects which can be found in the majority of them. These include the description of geographical features of the country; the historical development of the different peoples of Britain; the political history of the British Isles; as well as politics, philosophy, religion and the effects of the foundation of and the interaction with the British Empire. A crucial aspect of the concept of British culture, which was at the heart of *Kulturkunde* and its desire to understand the foreign *Geisteswelt*, was the question of the 'characteristics', the typical personality traits, of the British people. It featured in most cultural readers, even if it did not necessarily comprise a complete chapter on its own. I shall now expand on some of these topics and the texts used to illustrate them.

The field of geography generally features texts about the situation of Britain as an island (e.g. Gerstenberg 1929; Hartig and Krüper 1929); British cities, such as London and Sheffield (Gerstenberg 1929; Mack and Walker 1929); and other places of interest such as Stonehenge or Stratford-upon-Avon (e.g. Salewsky and Schwedtke 1930). Often they are also used to contrast life in the country with life in the city (e.g. Hartig and Krüper 1929; Mack and Walker 1929). Two popular sources for geographical chapters are Charles Lucas's *The Story of the Empire*[4] (1924) and William Ralph Inge's *England* (1926). But the coverage of geography also included poems, for example 'By the North Sea' by Swinburne (Angermann 1931a), or essays, especially from Washington Irving's *Sketch Book* (1819/20) (e.g. Mack and Walker 1929).

Another recurrent topic is the origin and development of the different British peoples — in the cultural readers often referred to as 'races' — generally including Celtic, Anglo-Saxon, Viking and Norman heritages (e.g. Mack and Walker 1929; Hartig and Krüper 1929; Angermann 1931a). From today's perspective it might seem strange to include such information in a book which is intended to make students more familiar with the British; at the time, it represented the scientific interest in the area of *Volkskunde* [ethnic studies] which was at the root of the *Kulturkunde* movement in the foreign-language classroom in an attempt to identify the main qualities of the British as a nation. The main sources that the editors of the cultural readers used for this purpose were contemporary history books, the most popular being Price Collier's *England and the English* (1909) with its chapter describing the influence each of these tribes had on the character of the English today (Gerstenberg 1929; Salewsky and Schwedtke 1930; Angermann 1931a).

Many cultural readers also contained an account of the political history of the British Isles. However, the question of whether historical aspects were to be included or not was a rather controversial one in *Kulturkunde* teaching, as the lack of focus on the present time had been one of the main aspects of the criticism of foreign-language teaching before the First World War (Graef 1930).

Another subject that features in practically all the cultural readers is philosophy, mainly political and economic philosophy, featuring texts by Francis Bacon, Thomas Hobbes, John Locke and John Stuart Mill, Adam Smith and David Hume. Excerpts from John Bunyan's *Pilgrim's Progress*, as well as texts by John Milton and Alexander Pope, were used to portray religious life in Britain, along with excerpts from contemporary history books.

As discussed above, one of the main goals of *Kulturkunde* was to enable school pupils to gain deeper insights into what were regarded as characteristic qualities of the British. How did the editors of the cultural readers meet this requirement? Some editors stated that almost every original text from the target culture lends itself to the identification of typically British characteristics. Their books generally use primary cultural texts (e.g. Salewsky and Schwedtke 1930). Others (e.g. Gerstenberg 1929; Mack and Walker 1929) include a whole chapter on the English character in which they explore different aspects, for example British common sense; the gentleman ideal (as depicted, for example, in John Milton's *Of Education* (1644) or William Makepeace Thackeray's *Vanity Fair* (1847)); or the British love of nature, illustrated by Romantic poems by authors like Wordsworth, Burns or Masefield (e.g. Gerstenberg 1929). John Locke and Adam Smith's works serve as examples of British individualism, whereas Jonathan Swift's *Gulliver's Travels* (1726) and Charles Dickens's *Pickwick Papers* (1836) were chosen to illustrate the British sense of humour and satire (e.g. Gerstenberg 1929). Sports and games were also considered an important aspect of life in Britain, contributing to British character qualities such as fair play and fairness in general, as the following excerpt of Dean Inge's *England* used in Hartig and Krüper (1929) illustrates:

> (3). The Love of Play
> It is no accident that the Englishman expresses his deepest moral convictions in the terms of a game. One of our chief contributions to the pleasure of the world is that we have invented most of the good games. The love of play is a very old English characteristic. Chamberlayne's 'Angliae Notitia,' [*sic*] published in 1660, at the end, it will be observed, of the Puritan domination, has this description; 'The common people will endure long and hard labour, insomuch that after twelve hours' hard work they will go in the evening to football, stockball, cricket, prison base, wrestling, cudgel playing, or some such like vehement exercise for their recreation.' [...]
> We may still congratulate ourselves that the words of an American Rhodes Scholar are true. Being asked, after a year's residence at Oxford, what struck him most in English university life, he replied: 'What strikes me most is that here are a thousand young men, every one of whom would rather lose a game than play it unfairly.' This spirit of fair-play, which in the public schools, at any rate, is absorbed as the most inviolable of traditions, has stood our race in good stead in the professions, and especially in the administration of dependencies, where the obvious desire of the officials to deal justly and see fair-play in disputes between natives and Europeans has partly compensated for want of sympathetic understanding, which has kept the English strangers in lands of alien culture (Hartig and Krüper 1929: 107, 108).

Accounts of football games, cricket matches and boat races are included in many of the cultural readers. A good example is Talbot Baines Reed's vivid description of the Parkhurst boat race, printed in Salewsky and Schwedtke (1930: 69-74).

An area that features prominently in most cultural readers is the British Empire and how it shaped the British character. The texts that were intended to be used in the classroom to illustrate the foundation of the Empire and the interaction between the Motherland and its colonies include speeches of politicians such as Chamberlain, Gladstone or Cecil Rhodes; excerpts from history books such as John Robert Seeley's *The Expansion of England* (1883) and Thomas Carlyle's *Past and Present* (1843); literature (especially poems by Rudyard Kipling); and contemporary newspaper articles (e.g. Mack and Walker 1929; Salewsky and Schwedtke 1930).

While all the cultural readers focus mainly on Britain and its Empire, some of them also include a chapter on the United States of America (Boek and Zorn 1928; Mack and Walker 1929; Salewsky and Schwedtke 1930); or feature a second volume which deals with the new Anglo-Saxon world power (Bauch 1926; Angermann 1931b). The texts concentrate on politics (speeches by Roosevelt, Wilson, Lincoln), economics and business (Henry Ford, Andrew Carnegie).

The Use of Cultural Readers in the Classroom

It is hard to tell how the cultural readers were really used in the foreign-language classroom at the time. When dealing with classroom practices of the age before videography, researchers must make do with contemporary accounts and teaching guidelines, which can still be obtained in journals and handbooks. The little we can say is that the readers were not meant to replace the reading of unabridged works of literature in the classroom. On the contrary, their task was to exemplify certain aspects of the other culture whenever students and teachers came across it in the classroom, for example when they were reading a novel, but also when they were discussing current political issues (Hübner 1925b: 107). Furthermore, the guidelines advise that the cultural readers be used inductively. Students were supposed to generate questions about the other culture through reading texts (whether full-length original books or texts provided by the readers), then their findings were to be discussed with the teacher in class (Christ and Rang 1985: 143).

Conclusion

Heavily influenced by the post-war discussion of the future of foreign-language learning, the new teaching principles introduced with the *Kulturkunde* movement and implemented by the *Richert'sche Richtlinien* clearly stated that German students of English as a foreign language were to gain a deeper insight into what were considered typical traits of the British character. One aim was to achieve a more profound understanding of what was going on in Britain, considered the former enemy but also admired for its achievements in the world. Another was to use these insights to compare and contrast them with the students' own culture, an aspect which was stressed especially in the context of cultural unification of the relatively young German nation state.

   The compilers of these cultural readers aimed to meet these requirements by providing teacher and students with a selection of fictional and non-fictional texts which covered all the aspects of British (and also American) life that were considered essential for the illustration of the character of its people. Naturally, they had to limit their selection and certain rather stereotypical elements were often chosen. They can be found in almost all the readers published at the time. The obvious fact that this method brought certain dangers with it was not unknown to contemporaries. To explore this more fully would go beyond the scope of this chapter; it is clear, however, that the National Socialists did not have to implement too many manipulations and changes to take over the concept of *Kulturkunde* for their own purposes.

Bibliography

ANGERMANN, ADOLAR. 1931A. *The Ways of the English* (Bielefeld: Velhagen & Klasing)
———. 1931B. *The Ways of the Americans* (Bielefeld: Velhagen & Klasing)
ARONSTEIN, PHILIPP. 1926. 'Die Kulturkunde im englischen Unterricht, *Monatsschrift für höhere Schulen*, 25: 260–67
BARTH, BORIS. 2003. *Dolchstoßlegenden und politische Desintegration* (Düsseldorf: Droste)

BAUCH, REINHOLD. 1925. *Literarisches Lesebuch zur Einführung in die Kultur- und Geisteskunde des englischen Volkes* (Dresden: Ehlermann)

——. 1926. *Die Literatur der Vereinigten Staaten von Amerika* (Dresden: Ehlermann)

BAUSENWEIN, JOSEF, and OTTO SCHNELLENBERGER. 1930. *Imperialismus: Das britische Grundproblem. Englands weltpolitische 'Sendung' beleuchtet durch sein Schrifttum aus drei Jahrhunderten* (Bamberg: Buchner)

BOEK, PAUL, and WALTHER ZORN. 1928. *England and the United States of America* (Berlin: Weidmann)

CHRIST, HERBERT, and HANS-JOACHIM RANG. 1985. *Fremdsprachenunterricht unter staatlicher Verwaltung. 1700 bis 1945. Allgemeine Anweisungen für den Fremdsprachenunterricht* (Tübingen: Narr)

DIBELIUS, WILHELM. 1931 [1922]. *England*, 6th edn (Stuttgart: Deutsche Verlagsanstalt)

ELLMER, W., and A. SANDER. 1925. *Englisches Lesebuch für die Mittelstufe höherer Lehranstalten* (Frankfurt am Main: Diesterweg)

FROUDE, JAMES ANTHONY. 1886. *Oceana, or England and her Colonies* (New York: Scribner)

GERSTENBERG, ERNST. 1929. *The Foundations of English Character: Englisches kulturkundliches Lesebuch für Oberklassen* (Brunswick: Westermann)

GRAEF, KARL. 1930. 'Kulturkunde und kulturkundliches Lesebuch', *Die Neueren Sprachen*, 38: 478-89

HARTIG, PAUL, and ADOLF KRÜPER. 1929. *England and the English: Ein Lesebuch zur Einführung in Volkstum und Kultur Englands* (Frankfurt am Main: Diesterweg)

HÜBNER, WALTER. 1925A. *Die englische Lektüre im Rahmen eines kulturkundlichen Unterrichts* (Leipzig: Teubner)

——. 1925B. 'Welche Aufgaben stellt die Schulreform dem neusprachlichen Unterricht?', *Neue Jahrbücher für Wissenschaft und Jugendbildung*, 1: 87-109

HÜLLEN, WERNER. 2006. 'Die Bedeutung der Richert'schen Richtlinien für den neusprachlichen Unterricht', in *Fremdsprachendidaktik im 20. Jahrhundert*, ed. by Sabine Doff and Anke Wegner (Berlin: Langenscheidt)

INGE, WILLIAM RALPH. 1926. *England* (New York: Scribner)

KALUZA, MAX. 1919. 'Für die Verstärkung des englischen Unterrichts an den höheren Schulen', *Zeitschrift für französischen und englischen Unterricht*, 18: 341-45

LOHMANN, OTTO. 1915. 'Die neuere Philologie und der Krieg. Betrachtungen eines alten Neuphilologen', *Die Neueren Sprachen*, 23: 1-8

LUCAS, CHARLES. 1924. *The Story of the Empire* (New York: Holt)

LUDWIG, OTTO.1988. *Der Schulaufsatz: Seine Geschichte in Deutschland* (Berlin: de Gruyter)

MACK, ALBERT, and THEODOR WALKER. 1929. *Formen und Gestalten angelsächsischen Kulturlebens: Ein Lesebuch für die Oberklassen höherer Lehranstalten* (Leipzig: Teubner)

OECKEL, FRITZ. 1920. 'Die Neugestaltung des höheren Schulwesens und die Neueren Sprachen', *Zeitschrift für französischen und englischen Unterricht*, 19: 241-50

RICHERT, HANS. 1920. *Die deutsche Bildungseinheit und die höhere Schule: Ein Buch von deutscher Nationalerziehung* (Tübingen: Mohr)

——. 1924. *Richtlinien für einen Lehrplan der deutschen Oberschule und der Aufbauschulen* (Berlin: Weidmann)

SALEWSKY, RUDOLF , and KURT SCHWEDTKE. 1930. *Angelsächsische Welten: Ein Lesebuch für die Oberstufe* (Kiel: Lipsius & Tischer)

SCHIEDERMAIR, RICHARD. 1920. 'Neusprachlicher Unterricht und nationale Erziehung', *Die Neueren Sprachen*, 28: 289-300

SCHMIDT, REINHOLD. 1930. *Modern England. Its problems and peculiarities* (Munich: Kellerer)

SCHÖN, EDUARD. 1929. 'Über das Verhältnis der Kulturkunde zum literarischen Werk', *Die Neueren Sprachen*, 37: 185-92

SCHÖNINGH, THEODOR. 1919. 'Zum Kampfe gegen den neusprachlichen Unterricht. Ein Wort zu seiner Beibehaltung und Vertiefung', *Die Neueren Sprachen*, 27: 53-66

STURM, REINHARD. 2011. *Vom Kaiserreich zur Republik 1918/19*, Informationen zur politischen Bildung, 261 (Bonn: Bundeszentrale für politische Bildung) <http://www.bpb.de/izpb/55949/vom-kaiserreich-zur-republik-1918–19?p=all> [accessed 6 November 2015]

Notes to Chapter 5

1. Translations into English are my own throughout.
2. French remained an important foreign language in Germany, even though France itself was no longer considered as significant as the United Kingdom or the United States (Oeckel 1920: 242).
3. The earliest publications of cultural readers I have been able to trace are: Ellmer and Sander (1925) and Bauch (1925). In 1926, several more cultural readers were published by different authors and publishing houses.
4. Charles Lucas's *The Story of the Empire* was part of a twelve-book series published by Collins for educational purposes during the British Empire Exhibition in London in 1924.

CHAPTER 6

Connecting Nations after the Third Reich: Culture in the English-Language Classrooms of Post-War Germany

Dorottya Ruisz

After the collapse of the Third Reich, Germany underwent fundamental change into a democratic state which valued international understanding. Where the teaching of modern languages is concerned, international understanding has often been associated with learning about the cultures of other nations, a notion which seems relevant for English-language teaching in post-war Germany but which needs to be explored further. *Kulturkunde*, a particular conception of studying culture, played a pivotal role both in the school curricula and in the professional discourse of modern language educators during the 1920s. Most of the proponents of this broad concept emphasized differences between cultures, an idea which was later perverted with the intention of showing Nazi Germany's superiority as compared to the cultures of other countries whose languages were taught. However, the *Kulturkunde* of the 1920s was also promoted by advocates of pacifism, whose attention was drawn to international understanding. This chapter sets out to examine thoroughly in what ways these ideas, as well as new concepts of studying culture, had an impact on the post-war discourses of language educators and of the regional governments in charge of curricula. The focus will be on Bavaria, a fruitful site for the study of possible shifts in the teaching of culture since it was in the sphere of influence of the American occupiers, who launched an ambitious re-education programme with the goal of democratization and international understanding and (to some extent only) the reshaping of English-language teaching.[1]

Introduction

In 1945 the Second World War was over and Nazi rule had been followed by the occupation of Germany: a new beginning of some sort was awaiting the country. Much has been written about the subsequent re-education programme for different areas of life in the American occupation zone and the two main goals of the programme: Germany's democratization and its transformation into a country with 'its place in the community of peaceful and law-abiding nations' (U. S. Department of State 1947: preface: iii). Recent research has also explored the ways in which English-language teaching was or was not a factor in re-educating the German nation.[2]

However, the role of teaching culture in English-language classrooms still needs closer scrutiny. After all, similarly to the post-war objectives of re-education, teaching culture had been seen, by some, as a vehicle for international understanding in the inter-war years within the modern-language education conception of *Kulturkunde*, even though this thread of discussion was a very minor one in the prevalent climate of nationalism. Indeed, combining the teaching of a foreign language with the teaching of culture had its own tradition in Germany within the (earlier) concept of *Realienkunde* as well as *Kulturkunde*. The key idea of *Realienkunde* was to approach the target nation through facts about its culture (e.g. Wendt 1965 [1898]: 188), as proposed by the *Neuphilologen*, the modern-language educators of Germany,[3] at the turn of the century. The term *Kulturkunde* became prevalent in the 1920s and continued to be used in the post-war discourse for discussing issues of teaching cultural contents; in the 1970s, it was replaced by *Landeskunde* [study of the country].

This chapter specifically examines three questions with regard to teaching of the target culture(s) in post-war English education: to what extent was understanding Germanness the underlying reason for learning about foreign cultures, especially compared to the discussion on *Kulturkunde* in the first half of the twentieth century ('Conceptualizing "the Other" or Understanding Germanness?' below); which cultures of the English speaking world were believed to be suitable content for English language classes ('Conceptualizing "the Other" — Which "Other"?'); and what ideas were shared about how to teach culture ('Conceptualizing "the Other" — How?'). Actual classroom practices are not looked at here, but rather the chapter aims to understand professional and political discourses. Two interdependent perspectives will be examined: that of the *Neuphilologen* and that of the educational policymakers of Bavaria, in particular as the policies became apparent in the curricula for the *höhere Schulen* (relatively academic secondary schools).[4]

Conceptualizing 'the Other' or Understanding Germanness?

Some of the essays on *Kulturkunde* featured in the journals of the *Neuphilologen* in the 1920s embrace international understanding when making suggestions on how to teach culture (e.g. Litt 1979 [1926]: 175).[5] However, the general tendency in this discourse was to emphasize teaching culture with the sole goal of understanding one's own identity through comparison with other nations (Lehberger 2007: 613). This led to the *Kulturkunde* of the Nazi period, which is often referred to as *Folientheorie* (Buttjes 1984: 143–44, 235, 255; Lehberger 1986: 54). The target nation was now merely studied in order to learn about the German nation's characteristics and at the same time the superiority of these characteristics, with *Folie* meaning the background which makes something more visible.

After 1945, published writings by the *Neuphilologen* frequently expressed disagreement with the views on *Kulturkunde* presented in the discourse of the 1920s and 1930s. Adolf Bohlen, the post-war head of the *Allgemeiner Deutscher Neuphilologenverband* (ADNV), the professional association of modern-language educators, declared that the aims of language teaching had to be reviewed after the experiences with the Third Reich, arguing also that the goal of understanding one's own culture had to be abandoned (Bohlen 1955: 57). The new purpose of language teaching was to introduce young people to the culture of 'neighbouring' countries (Bohlen 1952a: 76; see also Münch 1955a: 369).

But how — if at all — was this shift actually reflected in post-war language-teaching curricula? The first full-length curriculum for the *höhere Schulen* of Bavaria was published in 1964 (Bayerisches Staatsministerium für Unterricht [StMUK] 1964). Despite this late publication date, it makes sense to examine this document here since educational policies of this kind take a long time to become official, and so curricula can be seen as an outcome of prior discourse. The chapter on modern languages starts with the statement that young people must broaden their minds to become free of prejudice as well as open-minded to encounter the people and ideas of other nations (ibid.: 365). This introduction of objectives continues by drawing attention to the student's own culture, saying that consideration of another nation will lead to a revision of his/her attitude towards his/her own mother tongue and culture; thus, a relatively critical view is encouraged — the student's culture is to be 'revised' and the student is not asked to see his/her culture's superiority as required by Nazi pedagogy. This way of including the understanding of oneself as a cultural being indeed seems to point towards a 'modern' Byram-style definition of intercultural communicative competence (e.g. Byram 1997), a thread that leads too far from the historical focus of this chapter but which nevertheless needs at least to be mentioned. The goals which are set as the two main ones do not include reference to German culture at all (StMUK 1964: 365). The first goal concerns a good command of the target language, not just writing but also speaking, and therefore preparing the student for face-to-face encounters. The second refers to familiarizing the students with the culture of English-speaking countries.

All of this stands in stark contrast to the curricula issued before World War II, the so-called *Richert'sche Richtlinien* of 1925,[6] and the curriculum published under the Nazi regime in 1938.[7] At that time the foreign culture was to be studied in order to learn about the differences between nations. The change after the collapse of the Third Reich was well matched to the occupiers' ideal of international understanding. The dichotomy between learning about other people in order to understand German identity on the one hand and learning about the target culture for its own sake on the other had completely shifted towards the latter — in the Bavarian curriculum itself as well as in the discourse of the *Neuphilologen*.

This constituted a fundamental shift in the way cultural studies within language teaching were seen after the war. Nevertheless, a major limitation to this development needs to be mentioned. Contrary to the intentions of the Military Government, the willing acceptance of international understanding as goal only related to students of the *höhere Schulen*, thus just a minority. After Bohlen attended a UNESCO seminar in Ceylon on the 'Contribution of the Teaching of Modern Languages towards Education for Living in a World Community', he complained that the seminar had concerned objectives of language teaching for all students, regardless of what kind of school they were in (Bohlen 1954: 78; Bohlen 1955: 57). The Bavarian curricula presented a similarly elitist picture: learning modern foreign languages was only compulsory for the students of the academic *höhere Schulen* (see Ruisz 2014: 284–89). Thus, the discourse of the *Neuphilologen* and of the Bavarian authorities portrayed a view in which only an elite was entitled to international understanding, a view which did not correspond at all to the American objective of democratization.

Conceptualizing 'the Other' — Which 'Other'?

As we have seen, at least for the students attending *höhere Schulen*, getting to know 'the other' became the primary goal where teaching culture was concerned after World War II. But which target culture was indicated here? Until 1945 English-language teaching was, first and foremost, connected with the language and culture of 'England'.[8] However, there had been a shift in global power: the USA had gained prominence as a world-leading nation and had become the occupier of Bavaria. Especially with the beginning of the Cold War, the Military Government not only wanted Germany to establish true democracy and international understanding, they also wished to promote a favourable image of their own country as a land of democracy and liberty (further details: Ruisz 2013: 64–69). This means that closer examination is required with regard to which country was indicated when culture was being discussed in the context of English language teaching.[9]

The large number of papers and text passages dealing with the USA–England dilemma shows how important this question was in the post-war discourse of the modern-language educators. They unanimously wanted political and economic change to be reflected in classrooms and advocated the inclusion of more American studies,[10] including study of American literature, within English language teaching.[11] This suggests a truly positive view of the USA. A closer look, however, gives a different picture. It is true that there were constant suggestions that American issues and literature should be taught; however, the advocates of this also always tended to add that this should not occur at the expense of studies of England but only if hours could be increased (e.g. Bohlen 1952b: 6–7).

That the USA was to take second place to England in English-language teaching particularly holds true for the language standard aimed for. The 'King's English' continues to be seen as the default; and the teaching of American pronunciation and spelling is said to be disruptive (e.g. Utz 1950: 114), even if American English spelling is not to be marked as wrong (e.g. Rogge 1954: 490). Moreover, the USA are not seriously considered in contributions that do not specifically deal with the question of which target culture to choose — instead, England seems to be the only country considered. For example, when ways of teaching politics are discussed, neither the political system nor the newspapers of the USA tend to be mentioned (e.g. Geissler 1949: 313).

Comparing the curricula of 1925, 1938 and 1964, it becomes clear that there is a gradual shift towards the United States. The *Richert'sche Richtlinien* do not mention the USA except for naming some American book titles for fourteen- to sixteen-year-olds (four out of a total of twelve), and mention almost none for older learners (Zapp and Schröder 1983: 70–71). By contrast, the post-war curriculum equally includes British and American literature, sometimes using the word *angelsächsisch* [Anglo-Saxon] (cf. StMUK 1964: 365). This trend towards equality for British and American literature had started with the Nazi curriculum (Zapp and Schröder 1983: 102) and the short curriculum of 1952, which required English and American literature for fifteen-year-olds as well as a considerable portion of American literature for the last two years of secondary education (StMUK 1952a: 24–25; StMUK 1952b: 6–7). The document of 1964 is the first one that explicitly aims for pupils to be informed about American English but rejects it as the variety to be taught (StMUK 1964: 366). This kind of rejection evidently did not need to be expressed in the curricula before that: those of 1925 and 1938 contain no comment on the choice of target variety (Zapp and Schröder 1983: 49, 103–04). At that time apparently 'the King's English' was generally accepted and American English not considered for the classroom at all. Concerning culture *per se*, the *Richert'sche Richtlinien* require students to be taught about the British Empire, the history of England and the character traits of 'the English' but fail to mention anything American (quoted in Zapp and Schröder 1983: 70–75). The curriculum of 1938, on the other hand, gives the instruction that *Angelsachsentum* [the English-speaking world] is to be taught about, which is a clear shift towards including the United States (quoted in Zapp and Schröder: 109–19). The curriculum of the 1960s similarly refers to the culture of the *angelsächsisch* language areas (StMUK 1964: 365). All in all, the curricula issued after the Second World War show a marked increase in content related to the USA but at the same time still favour England.

One underlying reason for the relative continuing inattention to American issues could be the still deep anti-American sentiment resulting from the years of Nazi propaganda (Bohlen 1952b: 6–7). In the discourse of the *Neuphilologen*, negative characteristics, such as being ruthless capitalists, were still widely attributed to American citizens.[12] However, explicit hatred towards the United States was seldom shown (one of the very few exceptions being Zellmer 1954: 50). Additionally, comments in the modern-language educators' journals suggest that teachers saw it as too great a challenge to teach American literature: they complain about the editions not having annotations (cf. Utz 1950: 116) and suggest the use of German translations (e.g. Zellmer 1955: 83); or they simply do not feel sufficiently competent to explain anything about American culture (e.g. Fischer 1951: 412; Fischer-Wollpert 1954: 299; Geisler 1949: 50). This sense of a lack of competence could not easily be overcome either, because visiting the USA was generally out of reach for modern-language educators despite the occupiers' cultural exchange programme.[13] Another reason for the neglect is likely to have been the fact that teacher training did not include much in terms of American studies (cf. Buttjes 1991: 57; Fischer 1951; Geisler 1949: 50). It can reasonably be assumed that investigation of classroom level realities would show an even stronger Euro-centrism.[14]

Nonetheless, in contrast to attitudes in times before the unconditional surrender (Lehberger 1986: 160–67), the statements found on the USA in the post-war journals did show a distinct shift towards a preference for inclusion of American issues into English-language teaching. The United States had come to play too big a role in the world for the status quo to remain unchanged; and the Bavarian authorities were happy to implement anything which did not interfere with the school system but only changed the content of the curriculum. Nevertheless, the contents of the post-war curricula and especially the discourse of the *Neuphilologen* did not fully reflect the actual global importance which the United States had by now achieved.

Conceptualizing 'the Other' — How?

The focus of post-war English-language teaching at *höhere Schulen* thus became the target culture in contrast to studying a language for the sake of getting to know one's own culture; and there was increasing openness towards this target culture being American. The question of *how* the target culture was to be taught will now be addressed.

The Military Government proposed the broad framework of 'social education', a way of teaching democracy, which raises the possibility that there was an application of social education to the teaching of modern languages (Anderson 1949; see also Ruisz 2015). Social education was not only to be established as a separate school subject and as an overall guideline for school life but also as a fundamental principle for each school subject, involving the introduction of democratic practices through classroom activities such as discussions. This section will look at the options which were presented on how to teach the target culture in the discourse of the *Neuphilologen* and in the curricula; and the findings will be compared to guidelines on social education as drawn up by the Military Government.

In the 1920s ideas on how to teach culture had been explored at great length both in the journals of the modern-language educators and in the school curricula at a time when *Kulturkunde* played a pivotal role. Within this concept a so-called *Wesenskunde* was encouraged, which concerned getting to know other cultures via their specific character traits (Buttjes 1984: 145; 1991: 55). This was related, in turn, to certain racist aspects of language teaching during the Nazi period (see below). In the discourse after the War, however, identifying nations' distinctive character traits was usually explicitly rejected and comprehensive typifications had become out of date (see, for example, Hübner 1953: 309; Schmidt-Hidding 1952: 174; Münch 1955a: 368–69; all quite different from, for example, Münch 1936: 57–58). Nevertheless, various casual remarks show that there was not a total rejection: the change just involved either eliminating mention of unfortunate traits or including statements of positive traits alongside negative ones, in pairs. To cite an example, Americans could be seen as corrupt but at the same time as very religious (cf.

Münch 1955a: 370; similarly, Müller 1948: 1). This shows that the perception of an entire people as having one characteristic was still widespread. However, these findings also have to be assessed with the fact in mind that not too long before this the 'racial composition' of the target culture was to be studied.[15]

Since explicitly typifying the target nation was no longer considered theoretically appropriate, educators of the post-war period suggest other methods that they think could help students to get to know the characteristics of the target people. Mostly, they recommend that culture should be taught through literature rather than through non-fictional texts (see, especially, Hübner 1953). Additionally, they propose that the foreign language itself can usefully be focused upon for teaching cultural aspects. For example, drawing attention to the loss of suffixes in the English language is claimed to be a good way to tell students about the practical orientation of the English (Bohlen 1952a: 82), showing that *Neuphilologen* continued to see a close connection between language and people in the way they had done in their inter-war discourse (see, for example, Bohlen 1936: 81; see also Schmidt-Hidding 1952). The notion that culture could be taught through examination of the language was also present in the curricular requirements of 1951 (StMUK 1951: 334; also, in 1938, Zapp and Schröder 1983: 101) but was no longer mentioned in the requirements of 1964 (StMUK 1964). Associating certain phenomena of the language with the 'character' of the people who spoke it had clearly become out of date by then (cf. Hüllen 1969: 311, 319, 325).

The discourse of the modern-language educators also brought some new ideas on how culture should be taught. First and foremost, it is Heinz Fischer-Wollpert, a teacher of English and politics in Frankfurt am Main as well as Deputy Head of the ADNV, who deserves to be mentioned in this context (Fischer-Wollpert 1952: 535; 1954: 303; Zellmer 1954: 37). Fischer-Wollpert criticizes *Kulturkunde* for having used *Wesenskunde* as a tool for teaching culture (Fischer-Wollpert 1956: 163–64; see also Kellermann 1952: 292). Nor does he see literature as suitable for learning about culture — according to him, there is a lack of time for reading many books in foreign-language classes, sometimes only excerpts can be used, which leads merely to the production of stereotypes and makes students easy prey for propaganda (cf. Fischer-Wollpert 1956: 166–67). Instead, Fischer-Wollpert advocates *Sozialkunde* [social education][16] as an integral part of language teaching, promoting a concentration on topical issues and politics as the best way to get to know 'the other' and thus foster international understanding and democracy (Fischer-Wollpert 1956: 166–67; similarly, Wilhelm 1950: 134). He also reasons that methods which are useful for language learning anyway, such as discussing and debating, can be beneficial to social education, too: during such activities, listening to others' opinions, a vital democratic skill, could be practised (ibid.: 134–35). Furthermore, social education is said to be highly appropriate for the foreign-language classroom since thinking in a simple way can easily be achieved when there is a lack of ability to use a wide range of vocabulary and grammatical structures (ibid.: 134). Thinking in this manner is seen to be helpful for solving problems — something with which the Germans are said to have difficulties (ibid.: 134; thus popular stereotypes were not absent in this area of professional discourse either). English is understood to be particularly suitable for such thinking and its vocabulary is claimed to encourage problem-solving; indeed, the frequent usage in English of the verb 'to compromise' is given as a piece of evidence for this (ibid.: 134). Moreover, students can read English newspapers, which give them access to a press with a well-established tradition (Fischer-Wollpert 1952: 537). It is striking how much these thoughts on social education matched the guidelines of the occupying forces (for further detail, see Ruisz 2015).

Moreover, the concept of social education turned out not just to be a requirement by the Military Government or to be relevant in educators' discourse alone. Soon, it also came to be a part of the policies of the Bavarian Ministry of Education and was included in the Bavarian curriculum. In 1951, a sixteen-page curriculum on social education was issued (StMUK 1951) which required schools to teach the democratic way of living. The objective was to prepare students to be responsible citizens, which was to be achieved through teaching social education in the threefold way mentioned at the head of this section: as a separate school subject; as an overall guideline for school life; and as a method for the teaching of each subject (ibid.: 321–24, 336). This consistency between the American and Bavarian documents is not surprising considering the effective links between the Military Government and the Bavarian policy makers (for the channels of communication see Ruisz 2015: 173–77).

Taking a closer look at this curriculum, the so-called *Sozialkunde-Lehrplan*, one recognizes that the terms 'democracy' and 'international understanding' are not used in the passage on goals of social education. In this regard, the terminology of the Americans is not taken up, similarly to the way this is not done in the discourse of the *Neuphilologen* (see, for example, Hübner 1953: 312). This indirectly conveys the information that social education was not a serious concern for educators — literary extracts, for example, were still chosen for their aesthetic qualities and the choice was not necessarily based on usefulness for social education. Indeed, Fischer-Wollpert's appeals to choose newspapers as reading matter failed to be taken up with any enthusiasm (cf. Ruisz 2013: 174–77). Contrary to this discourse, however, the *Sozialkunde-Lehrplan* recommends reading matter to be at least sometimes chosen according to its potential usefulness to social education (cf. StMUK 1951: 334); this is very different from the *Richert'sche Richtlinien*, which only required choice according to literary and cultural considerations (Zapp and Schröder 1983: 48).

Roughly one page of the *Sozialkunde-Lehrplan* is explicitly dedicated to modern-language teaching, which is believed to be valuable because it offers an abundance of opportunities for discussion in the classroom (StMUK 1951: 323). A microcosm of democratic society with an active citizenry is to be created through letting students do independent and individual work and teaching them how to express themselves (ibid.: 321–24). The passage also provides some concrete information on what to read in English lessons, namely texts on topics such as the Industrial Revolution, political economy and imperialism (ibid.: 334–35).

To date, exactly what influence social education had on everyday teaching has not been studied. Although the Bavarian Ministry of Education and some *Neuphilologen* provided an institutional and theoretical framework, it can be assumed that social education did not become an integral part of English-language teaching after the War; it has to be considered that the majority of educators did not support this concept in print, nor presumably did other practising teachers. The finding that neither the Military Government nor the Bavarian authorities assigned a prominent role to English-language teaching (or to any other modern language) within social education is yet further evidence pointing towards this conclusion (cf. Ruisz 2015). Emphasis was placed, rather, on other school subjects, despite the fact that English was the language of the occupying force and that social education and English-language teaching could have been closely linked in the way suggested by Fischer-Wollpert. Among the reasons was the perception that the subject of History had to be dealt with as a first priority — false historiography was thought to have been one of the chief causes of the rapid spread of Nazi ideology before the war because it had helped the German people to believe in their superiority (cf. Müller 1995: 252–56).[17]

Conclusion: Connected Nations after the End of the Nazi Regime?

After the horrors of the Nazi regime, one automatically tends to imagine that one of two extremes occurred overall: either dramatic changes to all areas of life suddenly brought about by the unconditional surrender of 8 May 1945; or the restoration of traditional ideas generated in the past, especially during the Weimar Republic, at a time when any concepts to do with the Third Reich were to be eliminated. However, life is more complicated than this. The years after the War can be characterized neither as a period of restoration of the values of the Weimar Republic nor as an era of complete modernization but rather as a time with elements of both, or as a new beginning for later development (Hochgeschwender 2006: 292–93). A similarly diverse picture emerges when looking specifically into the area of teaching culture in English-language classes.

Contrary to the heated debates on *Kulturkunde* among the modern-language educators in the 1920s, the teaching of culture was discussed less often after 1945, although the assumption that it was not considered at all (as made by Buttjes in 1984: 353) is not true either (as also confirmed by Buttjes 1991: 61). It also has to be taken into account that focusing on reading works of great literary merit rather than on purely cultural issues could itself be seen as a sound alternative to the utilitarian kind of language teaching promoted by the Nazis.

The post-war discourse of the *Neuphilologen* on culture took up some elements of *Kulturkunde*, such as thinking of a nation as an individual with its own essential characteristics. Moreover, the educators explicitly aligned themselves with *Kulturkunde* at their first conference in 1947 (Münch and Willmann 1952: 157). Suggestions to include social education in this concept never came to be a key topic of debate. By the time the comprehensive curriculum was designed (StMUK 1964), the Bavarian Ministry of Education had forgotten about this fresh impetus, too, despite having issued guidelines on social education in 1951: for example, social education is not mentioned as a criterion for choosing literature for English lessons at all (ibid.: 225–26, 230–32). This is not surprising considering the fact that the Military Government also did not devote as much attention as might be expected to incorporating any sort of cultural studies into English-language teaching.

Nevertheless, it would not be true to say that views on teaching culture developed no new elements after the collapse of the Third Reich. The post-war curricula do not show traces of any requirement to typify another nation, in contrast with the *Richert'sche Richtlinien* and the curriculum of 1938 (Zapp and Schröder 1983: 73, 101). In the modern-language education journals, some contributions indeed elaborated upon ideas for working with social education in language classes, 'scientific' racism was unanimously condemned and there was a marked shift away from focusing on one's own culture. Furthermore, by issuing a curriculum for social education, the Bavarian educational authorities willingly accepted the Military Government's encouragement for internal reform. American studies played an evidently increasing role in both the curricula and academic discourse.

A direction for further research could be investigation of the classroom level, mainly via analysis of textbooks. However, on the basis of the exploration here of the framework for English language teaching after World War II, it can be stated that the way culture was to be taught matched efforts to connect people internationally more widely after the Hitler regime. Thus, culture in the English classroom did its share of work to form connections, even if a modest share.

Bibliography

Primary sources

AMERIKANISCHE ERZIEHUNGSKOMMISSION. 1946. *Der gegenwärtige Stand der Erziehung in Deutschland. Bericht* (Munich: Die Neue Zeitung)

ANDERSON, HOWARD R., et al. 18 November 1949. 'Report of the Social Studies Committee. Attachment to the letter of the Office of Military Government for Germany, United States, Education and Cultural Relations Division, to Warren M. Robbins, Bremen Enclave High School', in Office of Military Government for Germany, United States. 1 April 1947 to 30 November 1949, *Social Education in Germany* (microfiche, Institut für Zeitgeschichte, 5/300–3/37 [not published])

BAYERISCHES STAATSMINISTERIUM FÜR UNTERRICHT UND KULTUS. 1951. 'Politische Bildung (Sozialkunde) an den höheren Lehranstalten. Entschließung vom 17.9.1951 Nr. VIII 47994', *Amtsblatt des StMUK*, 14: 321–36

———. 1952A. *Stoffpläne für die höheren Lehranstalten in Bayern* (Munich: Pflaum)

———. 1952B. *Stoffpläne für die neue Oberstufe der höheren Lehranstalten in Bayern* (Munich: Pflaum)

———. 1964. 'Lehrpläne für Höhere Schulen in Bayern. Bekanntmachung vom 1.8.1964 Nr. VIII 72530', *Amtsblatt des StMUK*, 16: 341–465

BAYERISCHES STATISTISCHES LANDESAMT (ed.). 1960. *Die Entwicklung des bayerischen Schulwesens von 1945/46 bis 1959/60* (Munich: Bayerisches Statistisches Landesamt)

BOHLEN, ADOLF. 1936. 'Von der Sprachform zum Sprachgeist', *Neuphilologische Monatsschrift*, 7: 81–104

——. 1952A. 'Die Sprachtheorie Wilhelm von Humboldts und der Bildungswert des Englischen', in *Sprache und Literatur Englands und Amerikas*, ed. by Carl A. Weber (Tübingen: Niemeyer), pp. 61–83

——. 1952B. 'Zum USA-Thema im englischen Unterricht', *Mitteilungsblatt*, 5: 6–7

——. 1954. 'Zur Vorstandssitzung in Münster. 15.–16.10.1954', *Mitteilungsblatt*, 7: 77–78

——. 1955. 'Unser Beitrag zur Völkerverständigung', *Mitteilungsblatt*: 8: 57–59

FISCHER, WALTHER. 1951. 'Die Amerikanistik im gegenwärtigen Universitätsplan und in den Prüfungsordnungen der deutschen Länder', *Neuphilologische Zeitschrift*, 3: 412–17

FISCHER-WOLLPERT, HEINZ. 1952. 'Die Zeitungslektüre im Englischunterricht der Oberstufe: Eine Ergänzung', *Die Neueren Sprachen*, 51: 533–38

——. 1954. 'Die fremden Kulturen als Gegenstände des neusprachlichen Unterrichts: Zum Deutschen Neuphilologentag 1954', *Die Neueren Sprachen*, 53: 293–304

——. 1956. 'Das sozialkundliche Prinzip im englischen Unterricht der Oberstufe', *Gesellschaft, Staat, Erziehung*, 1: 162–72

GEISLER, FRIEDRICH. 1949. 'Der Neuphilologe entdeckt Amerika', *Neuphilologische Zeitschrift*, 1: 45–55

GEISSLER, ADOLF. 1949. 'Die Presse im neusprachlichen Unterricht', *Die lebenden Fremdsprachen*, 1: 312–17

HÜBNER, WALTER. 1953. 'Der Bildungsauftrag der englischen Lektüre', *Die Neueren Sprachen*, 52: 298–312

HÜLLEN, WERNER. 1969. 'Sprachwissenschaft und Landeskunde', *Praxis des neusprachlichen Unterrichts*, 16: 310–25

KELLERMANN, WILHELM. 1952. 'Der neusprachliche Unterricht als Erschliessung der Humanitas', *Neuphilologische Zeitschrift*, 4: 289–300

LITT, THEODOR. 1979 [1926]. 'Gedanken zum "kulturkundlichen" Unterrichtsprinzip', in *Didaktik des Englischunterrichts*, ed. by Werner Hüllen (Darmstadt: Wissenschaftliche Buchgesellschaft), pp. 144–80

MÜLLER, MAX. 1948. 'Die Tagung der westfälischen Neuphilologen in Iserlohn', *Mitteilungsblatt*, 1: 1–3

MÜNCH, RUDOLF. 1936. 'Doch noch Kulturkunde?', *Neuphilologische Monatsschrift*, 7: 49–60

——. 1952. 'Humanismus und Pragmatismus: Nachklänge zum Göttinger Neuphilologentag', *Neuphilologische Zeitschrift*, 4: 384–93

——. 1955A. 'Grundsätzliches zur Auslandskunde', *Die Neueren Sprachen*, 54: 367–73

——. 1955B. 'Zur Amerikakunde', *Aus der Praxis für die Praxis des neusprachlichen Unterrichts*, 2: 53–55

——, and FRIEDRICH WILLMANN. 1952. 'Die geschichtliche Bedeutung des Allgemeinen Deutschen Neuphilologen-Verbandes', *Die Neueren Sprachen*, 51: 153–64

ROGGE, HEINZ. 1954. '"American English" im Unterricht der höheren Schule', *Die Neueren Sprachen*, 53: 481–90

SCHMIDT-HIDDING, WOLFGANG. 1952. 'Leit- und Schlüsselwörter des Neuenglischen. (Zur Frage der Kulturkunde)', *Die Neueren Sprachen*, 51: 172–84

U.S. DEPARTMENT OF STATE (ed.). 1947. *Occupation of Germany. Policy and Progress. 1945–1946* (Washington, DC: U.S. Government Printing Office)

UTZ, KARL. 1950. 'Einige grundsätzliche Bemerkungen zu einer amerikanischen Lektüre', *Die lebenden Fremdsprachen*, 2: 114–16

WENDT, GUSTAV. 1965 [1898]. 'Die Reformmethode in den oberen Klassen der Realanstalten', in *Neusprachlicher Unterricht*, ed. by Karl-Heinz Flechsig, 2 vols (Weinheim: Beltz) 1, 179–89

WILHELM, THEODOR. 1950. '"Politische Erziehung" im Englisch-Unterricht?', *Schulverwaltungsblatt für Niedersachsen*, 2: 133–35

ZAPP, FRANZ-JOSEF, and KONRAD SCHRÖDER. 1983. *Deutsche Lehrpläne für den Fremdsprachenunterricht. 1900–1970. Ein Lesebuch* (Augsburg: Universität Augsburg)

ZELLMER, ERNST. 1954. 'Deutscher Neuphilologentag Hamburg 1954', *Mitteilungsblatt*, 7: 37–51

——. 1955. 'Amerikakunde in der Schule', *Mitteilungsblatt*, 8: 82–84

Secondary literature

APELT, WALTER. 1967. *Die kulturkundliche Bewegung im Unterricht der neueren Sprachen in Deutschland in den Jahren 1886 bis 1945: Ein Irrweg deutscher Philologen* (Berlin: Volk und Wissen)

BYRAM, MICHAEL. 1997. *Teaching and Assessing Intercultural Communicative Competence* (Clevedon: Multilingual Matters)

BUTTJES, DIETER. 1984. *Fremdsprache und fremde Gesellschaft: Politische Legitimation und landeskundliche Inhalte des Englischunterrichts an deutschen Schulen (1880–1960)* (Dortmund: [n. publ.]).

——. 1991. 'Culture in German Foreign Language Teaching: Making Use of an Ambiguous Past', in *Mediating Languages and Cultures: Towards an Intercultural Theory of Foreign Language Education*, ed. by Dieter Buttjes and Michael Byram (Clevedon: Multilingual Matters), pp. 47–62

HOCHGESCHWENDER, MICHAEL. 2006. 'Westernisierung und Amerikanisierung im Kalten Krieg', *Geschichte, Politik und ihre Didaktik*, 34: 282–99

LATZIN, ELLEN. 2005. *Lernen von Amerika? Das US-Kulturaustauschprogramm für Bayern und seine Absolventen* (Stuttgart: Steiner)

LEHBERGER, REINER. 1986. *Englischunterricht im Nationalsozialismus* (Tübingen: Stauffenburg)

——. 2007. 'Geschichte des Fremdsprachenunterrichts bis 1945', in *Handbuch Fremdsprachenunterricht*, ed. by Karl-Richard Bausch, Herbert Christ and Hans-Jürgen Krumm, 5th edn (Tübingen: Francke), pp. 609–14

MÜLLER, WINFRIED. 1995. *Schulpolitik in Bayern im Spannungsfeld von Kultusbürokratie und Besatzungsmacht. 1945–1949* (Munich: Oldenbourg)

RUISZ, DOROTTYA. 2013. '"Amerikakunde tut not!" Das Thema USA als Forderung für den Englischunterricht in der US-amerikanischen Besatzungszone im Nachkriegsdeutschland', in *Schulsprachenpolitik und fremdsprachliche Unterrichtspraxis (Historische Schlaglichter zwischen 1800 bis 1955)*, ed. by Friederike Klippel, Elisabeth Kolb and Felicitas Sharp (Münster and New York: Waxmann), pp. 63–78

——. 2014. *Umerziehung durch Englischunterricht? US-amerikanische Reeducation-Politik, neuphilologische Orientierungsdebatte und bildungspolitische Umsetzung im nachkriegszeitlichen Bayern (1945–1955)* (Münster and New York: Waxmann)

——. 2015. 'Social Education as Reeducation: The Implementation of US-American Policies in the English Language Classrooms of Bavaria (1945–51)', in *Die amerikanische Reeducation-Politik nach 1945: Interdisziplinäre Perspektiven auf 'America's Germany'*, ed. by Heike Paul and Katharina Gerund (Bielefeld: Transcript), pp. 161–84

SCHRÖDER, KONRAD. 1982. 'Vom Regulativ zum Rahmenplan: Versuch einer Entwicklungsgeschichte des neusprachlichen Lehrplans' *Die Neueren Sprachen*, 81: 5–29

Notes to Chapter 6

1. I wish to thank Robert Perneczky for proof-reading and Friederike Klippel for her invaluable advice.

2. At first sight the assumption that the American occupiers would have taken considerable interest in shaping English-language teaching seems plausible, as a form of 'soft power' within the

re-education programme. However, research shows that this was not the case (see Ruisz 2014, especially pp. 101–23, as well as the comments on related studies on pp. 58–64; also, Ruisz 2015). One explanation of the lack of interest in English-language teaching is that the main focus of the occupying forces was at first merely on reforming the structure of the school system: the socially selective vertically multi-track school system was regarded as anti-democratic (Amerikanische Erziehungskommission 1946: 26–28; Müller 1995: 129, 138–48; Ruisz 2014: 253–62). The occupiers were subsequently confronted with fierce opposition from the Bavarian authorities. By the time the Americans realized their lack of success, it was too late to focus on the curricula as the first post-war versions had already been in use and the occupation period was coming to its end.

3. The term 'modern-language educators' is used interchangeably with *Neuphilologen* in this chapter to designate specifically modern-language teachers and scholars involved in the professional association *Allgemeiner Deutscher Neuphilologenverband* (ADNV). The participants were mostly teachers at *höhere Schulen*, the schools that prepared for university admission (see next note). The geographical scope of their discourse reached all western parts of Germany; there was no separate discourse in existence only for the American zone.

4. The academic *höhere Schulen*, for pupils between the age of ten and university admission, were attended by less than a third of all children, in contrast to the more practically oriented *Volksschulen* (Bayerisches Statistisches Landesamt 1960: 11). The *höhere Schulen* will nevertheless be focused on in this chapter as only they offered compulsory modern-language education (cf. Ruisz 2014: 284–89). *Mittel-* or *Realschulen* were being established after the war as a third school type in some parts of Germany, being somewhat more academic than the *Volksschulen* (Müller 1995: 230–48). This three-tiered school system can still be found in most parts of Germany today.

5. For further information on the discourse of *Kulturkunde* during the Weimar Republic see, for example, Apelt 1967: 23–89. For more details of secondary literature on this topic cf. Ruisz 2014: 61–62.

6. The full name of the curriculum was *Richtlinien für die Lehrpläne der höheren Schulen Preußens*. Hans Richert was the Assistant Head of the Prussian Ministry of Education who was in charge of the curriculum; therefore, the document is usually referred to as *Richert'sche Richtlinien*. The requirements were to be followed in all *höhere Schulen* in Prussia and influenced all curricula in Germany in a major fashion at the time (Schröder 1982: 13). The reprint of the parts of the *Richert'sche Richtlinien* which are relevant to modern-language teaching: Zapp and Schröder 1983: 25–76; see especially p. 48.

7. The parts relevant to modern-language teaching are reprinted in Zapp and Schröder, 1983: 79–125; see especially p. 101.

8. This can be seen, for example, in the curricula of 1925 and 1938 (Ruisz 2013: 69–71). The sources mainly use the term 'England' without making clear whether they refer to England, Great Britain or the United Kingdom; their usage, however, suggests that usually it is only the area called England today that is being referred to (Ruisz 2014: 177). This can be observed also in the post-war sources (e.g. Münch 1952: 388–89). The term 'England' is therefore favoured over 'Britain' or 'UK' in this chapter.

9. For a more detailed discussion of this issue see Ruisz 2013. Although English-language teaching could, in theory, have been related to the culture of any English-speaking country, countries other than the USA and England were not in practice mentioned in the journals of the modern-language educators or in the Bavarian curricula.

10. The German sources of the time use the term *Amerikakunde*, American studies, which meant the study of present and past aspects of the culture of the United States. Sometimes the term also refers to American literature, i.e. novels etc. written by American authors.

11. As stated by, for example, Fischer-Wollpert 1951: 238; Geisler 1949: 46; Münch and Willmann 1952: 161; Münch 1955a: 372, 369; 1955b: 53; Rogge 1954: 488; Utz 1950: 114; Zellmer 1955: 82, to name just a few.

12. '[D]er Amerikaner [ist neben seinen guten Eigenschaften genauso] egoistischer Kapitalist, bestechlicher Machtpolitiker [weswegen] gewiß auch viele Deutsche von einer Umerziehung

in amerikanischem Geiste nicht viel wissen [wollen]' [The American not only has favourable character traits but is also a ruthless capitalist and a corrupt politician, which explains why many Germans want little to do with re-education along American lines] (Münch 1955a: 370; similarly, Müller 1948: 2).

13. The exchange programme was mainly for sending German 'experts' of various professions as visitors to the USA so that they would spread their experience of democracy when back in Germany (Latzin 2005; for participation by modern-language educators see Ruisz 2014: 101–12).

14. The classroom level requires further investigation, for example via comprehensive analysis of textbooks and carrying out of interviews (cf. Ruisz 2013: 71–73; 2014: 208–09).

15. My translation of *rassische[n] Zusammensetzung* from the curriculum of 1938, as quoted in Zapp and Schröder 1983: 101; similarly in the educators' journals: see, for example, Münch 1936: 55–56.

16. The terms 'social studies', 'training for citizenship', *Sozialkunde* and *politische Bildung* [political education] were used interchangeably in the post-war discourses. The American occupation power preferred to use the term 'social studies', whereas the *Neuphilologen* and the Bavarian Ministry of Education mainly used the term *Sozialkunde*. Sometimes 'social education' was understood as a broad term that referred not only to the school subject itself, which is the reason why the term was chosen for use in this chapter. For further detail see Ruisz 2015: 163.

17. For a thorough discussion of the reasons for the Military Government's neglect of English-language teaching within the concept of social education, see Ruisz 2015: 163–70.

CHAPTER 7

❖

Teaching Literature in the French-Language Classroom at German Grammar Schools (*Gymnasien*) between 1945 and 1985

Meike Hethey

Richert's concept of *Kulturkunde*, coined in the 1920s, influenced French-language teaching in higher secondary schools in Germany until 1970. 'High-class' literature as a 'value in itself' remained unquestioned until the 1960s. Rethinking started in 1964 with Georg Picht's notion of the 'German educational catastrophe' and culminated in the 1968 movement. The allegedly elitist aspects of general education (*Bildungsgut*) were replaced in upper secondary schools by a stronger focus on communication and language skills combined with sociological content; the ideal was an education system based on critical thinking and emancipation leading to a democratic society. In addition, the German–French Treaty of Friendship (1963) was a trigger for increasing (oral) exchange between German and French teenagers. From 1974 onwards, the communicative approach relegated literature to a place where it mainly served as a prompt for speaking; in addition, it provided geographical and historical input which helped to achieve a better understanding of the French and other francophone cultures. From the 1990s, especially since the 'Pisa shock' of 2001, in which the German education system was judged mediocre in the Organization for Economic Co-operation and Development's international test, there has been a general shift toward output and competence. The scientific debate has therefore been oscillating between the focus on utilitarian intercultural communication skills and a reinforcement of formal *Bildung*. An example of this development can be seen in the manner in which literature is used in and for French language teaching.

Introduction

Literature, in other words, poetic, dramatic and narrative texts, seems to be, and always to have been, an indispensable component of French-language teaching in German *Gymnasien* [grammar schools]. But from the 1990s, especially since the 'Pisa shock' of 2001 in which the German education system achieved only a mediocre ranking in the Organization for Economic Co-operation and Development's international tests, there has been a general paradigm shift towards an orientation towards output and competence. The scientific debate has therefore been oscillating between the focus on utilitarian intercultural communication skills and a reinforcement of formal *Bildung*. This is reflected in the discussion on the value of literature in the current foreign-language classroom at German grammar schools. Here, the role of literature seems to be reduced to one that provides cultural knowledge and fosters basic reading skills. Hallet considers literature to be in a difficult position, especially in middle-school classes (*Sekundarstufe I*) (Hallet 2007: 31). But is this present, and apparently critical, state of literature a new and therefore alarming phenomenon? With the aim of investigating this question, I examine the role of literature teaching in the years after World War II until the 1980s. I argue that the available evidence from textbooks and educational discourse of this period yields the following three observations:

• Literature has always played an important role in the foreign-language classroom at German grammar schools. Even though the educational aims associated with it have varied, its position has never been really questioned;

• Teaching literature, particularly in the French classroom, bridged the gap between Richert's 'knowledge of culture' (*Kulturkunde*) and a concept more orientated towards peacekeeping between France and Germany and the idea of a European union;

• The change in the choice of the reading matter as well as in approaches to deal with literature in the foreign-language classroom was (and still is) causally related to political and social discussions. In addition, it was influenced by new concepts in literary and pedagogic studies.

Below, these claims will be explained by analysing two main phases that were marked by important social developments: 1950 to the early 1960s, and 1963 to the early 1980s. After the National Socialist epoch ended with the end of World War II, a fundamental reorientation of the pedagogic and the didactic concept was necessary. Therefore, the question arises as to whether earlier approaches, for example Richert's *Kulturkunde* (1920/25), have been re-established or whether new ideas were developed. Beyond that, the social and political discussion in the 1960s left its mark in pedagogical debates, as we shall see below. I begin by presenting Richert's *Kulturkunde* as an important basis for teaching literature in the French-language classroom, before introducing Adolf Bohlen's notion of *Modern Humanism* (from 1957), in which he linked his ideas to Richert's concept. I thus argue that literature teaching was influenced by rather ambivalent central ideas, both traditionally in a more Humanist way, and as a means to foster peacekeeping in a newly bonded Europe.

Teaching Literature in the Foreign-Language Classroom after World War II: Back to the Roots?

Richert's Kulturkunde *(1920/25): An Important Basis for Teaching Literature in the French Classroom after World War II*

The 1920s brought fundamental progress in teaching modern languages. The methods finally deviated from the traditional way of teaching Latin or Ancient Greek. Learning English or French, it was believed, should no longer consist mainly of collecting as many facts as possible about another language area, something with which the 'knowledge of *realia*' (*Realienkunde*) was reproached. The concept of *realia* had been well established since the second half of the seventeenth century. As Risager points out, there are at least three dimensions in teaching and learning foreign languages in connection to this concept. Traditionally, it was linked to the reading of texts in the academic discourse. Beyond that, the knowledge of 'travel *realia*' became very important in the eighteenth and nineteenth centuries, preparing for any kind of the educational trips that were rather popular at that time. Finally, polite conversation in foreign languages was a common aim for young upper-class girls. In special institutes they worked on their oral proficiency by talking about their knowledge of *realia* (cf. Risager 2007: 24-25). This broad interest in relatively simple information about other cultures in foreign-language teaching incurred critical comments. It seemed to be far too superficial and only inspired by extrinsic motifs (cf. Risager 2007: 31). Rather, learning foreign languages should help in shaping the mind of those who were taught. (*Formung des Geistes*) (cf. Hüllen 2005: 115; Bohlen 1957: 41).

In 1925, Hans Richert's concept of *Kulturkunde* became the main principle of Prussian education policy. Five years earlier, the future secretary of the Ministry of Education and the Arts had published his monograph *Die deutsche Bildungseinheit und die höhere Schule*, in which he proposed his concept to reform the secondary school system, which arguably faced a crisis following the end of World War I. Richert criticized the fact that the German 'spirit of the nation' (*deutscher Geist*) had not developed after 1871, a shortcoming which had to be remedied. And while France and Great Britain were achieving substantial progress on their way towards shaping a national and cultural unity, Richert thought that Germany needed to catch up in the fields of religion, mind, social and moral unity, a shared law and a shared language and Arts (Hüllen 2005: 111).

The starting point of this so-called *Kulturkunde* was Richert's belief that each culture had a proper or genuine 'spirit'. In his opinion, the German 'spirit' (*deutsche Geistigkeit*) should be a key teaching objective in school, in order that pupils might understand it properly (Hüllen 2005: 116). He was convinced that *Kulturkunde* had not only the potential to explain the origins of cultures, but also to reconstruct their development (Christ 2011: 68). Awareness of one's own nation could be achieved through examining other cultures and comparing those to one's own culture (Risager 2007: 31). Richert defines cultures as entities, as integrated units existing in a permanent quarrel but which nevertheless influence each other constantly.

For Richert it was obvious that the interconnectedness of European cultures (*Kulturverbundenheit*) was deep and longstanding. He considered it necessary after World War I that a well-educated class in Germany should take part in this cultural struggle, especially because he was convinced of the cultural progress of France and Great Britain. Richert's idea of a 'cultural battle' (*Kulturkampf*) has led to the misinterpretation of his views by some, who believed that he assumed German culture to be superior to other cultures, culminating, for example, in the National Socialist ideologies of *Volkslebenslehre* and *Wesenskunde*. Despite the fact that Richert understood cultures as entities and the fact that he was acting out of a nationalist conviction, he was steadfast on the point that there had to be something like a European cultural synthesis (Richert 1920: 50, 58; Christ 2011: 68).

In Richert's approach to teaching, the most important tool to form the so-called German 'spirit' was the German language (Richert 1920: 19), which was also supposed to provide the basis for teaching foreign languages. His attitude towards modern languages provoked many critical reactions. He proposed an applied concept of teaching English or French in lower secondary school that focused on an active use of the language, on good pronunciation and an inductive approach to grammatical topics. English and French classes in higher grades, however, were supposed to treat the foreign culture on the basis of its literary text production (Richert 1920: 28). Richert's idea that other cultures could be understood in an objective manner by reading literary texts was one of the reasons that provoked a lively and critical discussion (Hüllen 2005: 116-17; Surkamp 2013: 196).

It is worth examining more closely Richert's explanations for using literary texts in the French language classroom in German schools:

> Die Lektüre steht im Mittelpunkt des neusprachlichen Unterrichts. Das zusammenhängende Lesen ganzer Werke oder selbständiger Abschnitte daraus soll möglichst früh einsetzen [...]. Für die Auswahl der Lektüre ist neben der Forderung hochwertiger Form der maßgebende Gesichtspunkt, besonders auf der Oberstufe, die Einführung in die verschiedenen Gebiete und Epochen des fremden Geisteslebens [...]. Dieser Gesichtspunkt gilt insbesondere auch für die Frage, inwieweit Erscheinungen des neuesten Schrifttums in den Unterricht einzubeziehen sind. Wichtiger als vielfältige Anregung ist die Klärung des jugendlichen Geistes, und diese kann im allgemeinen durch die erprobten Meisterwerke besser geschehen als durch Erzeugnisse, zu denen noch der nötige Abstand fehlt. [...] Es ist grundsätzlich zu erstreben, daß bei der Lektüre möglichst die fremde Sprache gebraucht werde, doch darf diese nicht auf Kosten der Klarheit und gedanklichen Ausschöpfung bevorzugt werden [...]. Auf der Oberstufe muß die Würdigung der künstlerischen Form und des darin ausgeprägten Geistes den krönenden Abschluß der Besprechung bilden. Dabei ist das Verhältnis des Werkes zum Gesamtschaffen des Schriftstellers, dessen Stellung in seiner Zeit und deren Bedeutung für die Geistesgeschichte herauszuarbeiten. (Richert, 1925: 119-20)

> [Reading is at the centre of teaching modern languages. Coherently reading whole works, or stand-alone extracts from them, should begin as early as possible [...]. When choosing literature the leading criterion — especially in higher grades — is, next to the quality of the form, an introduction to the

different areas and epochs of the foreign intellectual life [...]. This aspect is especially effective when asking which phenomena in the latest writings should be integrated into teaching. What is more important than multiple stimuli is the cleansing (*Klärung*) of the juvenile spirit, which can generally be better achieved through approved masterpieces rather than through works to which we lack the necessary distance. [...] One should generally strive for the use of the foreign language in the readings, although this should not be favoured at the expense of clarity and mental exploration of ideas [...]. In higher secondary school, the appreciation of the artistic form and the spirit expressed within must be the coronation of the coursework. As part of this process, the relation of the work to the writer's oeuvre, its status in its time and its importance for the history of ideas must be elaborated.][1]

The passage quoted emphasizes that literature or, to be more precise, the reading of literary texts, should play a central role in each lesson. By reading entire works the pupils would supposedly get to know the other culture. And to achieve this central aim, it was more important to Richert to work predominantly on the content and the topics of the texts rather than on the absolute and strict use of the target language. It is obvious that Richert is willing to neglect linguistic progress in order to support discussions with regard to the content. In Richert's opinion, in higher secondary school (*Obersekunda*/OII — *Oberprima*/OI, age sixteen to nineteen), the pupils were supposed to be able to analyse and to assess the aesthetic value of the texts. Additionally, they were expected to understand their social and historical context. Though the choice of the reading, pupils were meant to acquire an overview of the most important periods of the intellectual progress of other cultures. Therefore, Richert preferred pupils to work on reliable masterpieces rather than on contemporary literature. This statement is remarkable, because Richert provided recommendations, not intended to be canonical, for he was not interested in piling up encyclopaedic knowledge, but to assist teachers in making their own choices.

Pupils should acquire an idea of the development of a social culture through texts from the epochs of Louis XIV, Louis XV and Louis XVI. But they should become acquainted with problems of the contemporary economic, technical and social order, too. That is why Richert recommended reading some modern French authors (Richert 1925: 122–23). His suggestions were controversial, because he did not only recommend literary texts commonly known as established classics. He was even convinced that typical characteristics of other cultures could be more easily found in modern works than in literarily high-ranking texts (Surkamp 2013: 196).

Looking back at Richert's approach seemed important because, contrary to Surkamp's statement that *Kulturkunde* did not regain any influence after 1945 because of its ideological implications (Surkamp 2013: 196), Richert's ideas in fact heavily influenced the essential features of foreign-language teaching at German grammar schools after World War II and in particular the role of literature in the foreign-language classroom. Adolf Bohlen referred to Richert's concept in his *Moderner Humanismus* [*Modern Humanism*] (see next section). Having first published his well-received methodology in 1930, he further developed his central ideas on teaching modern languages at school in the 1950s, when he considered the German school system to be in absolute need of reorientation, having been under National Socialist influence for the past twelve years. In the next section, which examines Bohlen's concept more closely, the role of literature in teaching foreign languages until the 1960s will be described.

Key Considerations after World War II: Adolf Bohlen's Moderner Humanismus *(1957)*

Ten years after the end of World War II, *Kulturkunde* became once again the main educational approach adopted at the Düsseldorf conference in February 1955. In the Düsseldorf Agreement the Minister-Presidents of the West German states not only agreed about structuring the German school system into three different school types and about the order of the foreign languages that should be taught in lower and higher secondary education, but they also confirmed teaching approaches of the inter-war years (Doff 2008: 98; Hüllen 2005: 132). The resolutions of this conference tried to establish an image of a certain continuity of the ideas predominant during the Weimar Republic and did not show an innovative character. For Adolf Bohlen, an administration official in school supervision in Münster, this agreement guaranteed that the Humanist principle — the German idealistic tradition of shaping pupils' minds — would be maintained (Bohlen 1957: 32).

Two years later, in 1957, Bohlen proposed what he called a *Moderner Humanismus* to solve the cultural crisis in which he considered humanity to have been embroiled since the beginning of the twentieth century. To him it was obvious that all attempts to overcome this crisis had failed, especially the experiments that focused on a common external culture (*äußere Kultur*) applied by National Socialism or Bolshevism (Bohlen 1957: 21). He emphasized the importance of an inner culture or spiritual life (*Geistesleben*) based on tolerance (in an originally Humanist sense as we find it, for example, in the works of Montaigne (Bohlen 1957: 20-21)). For this very reason the author called for a fundamental reorientation of cultural education in the spirit of Humanism,[2] not only for the German culture but for other cultures as well. He did not comprehend this modern Humanism in a dogmatic way but rather as an attitude that allowed for mind-opening encounters with other cultures, international contacts and exchanges. Such an attitude also emphasized the importance of progress-oriented individuals who were not guided solely by their nation's cultural heritage. But nevertheless, Bohlen felt an obligation to the initial principle of Humanism. It was the principle of school *thinking* and therefore sought to ensure that every subject on the curriculum could contribute to shaping pupils' minds (cf. Bohlen 1957: 32).

Travelling and thus leaving behind one's own, at times narrow, cultural environment every now and again had always been an important characteristic of higher secondary education. As a consequence, learning modern languages became an important subject. The formula *foreign language = language + culture + literature* (*Fremdsprache = Sprache + Kultur + Literatur* (original emphasis (Bohlen 1957: 39)) meant that learning a foreign language meant not only to master the language in every different form of communicative situation, but to enter the intellectual life of another culture through its literature (Bohlen 1957: 38-40).[3] Bohlen demanded that 'Wir müssen dabei ferner im Auge behalten, daß unser Lehrziel ein humanistisches ist, d. h. daß *nicht eine Gebrauchssprache, sondern eine Bildungssprache* gelehrt wird' [We have to keep in mind that our learning objective is a Humanist one, that is to say, that we do not teach *a language in a utilitarian but in a way of classical education*] (Bohlen 1957: 91; original emphasis). It could be observed critically that Bohlen's ideas were not so very far removed from the approaches of the 1920s. For him, Germany, forming the buffer between the East and a civilized Western world was rooted in early educational concepts and their idea of teaching a language in a classical Humanist way (*Bildungssprache*).

Despite this fact, his reflections on the role of literature in the foreign-language classroom played an important role in his educational concept. And although we can see how he had been influenced by Richert's ideas, Bohlen was clearly progressive in integrating literary texts into his vision of cultural and political education, as we shall see in the next section.

Literature as the Highest Expression of a Nation's Mind

Elisabeth Stuck points out that literature had a predominant role in the foreign-language classroom at German grammar schools after World War II (Stuck 2013: 190), an observation which can be confirmed in Bohlen's reflections: 'Dort aber bietet der höchste Ausdruck der Geistigkeit eines Volkes, seine Literatur, Gelegenheit zu der im Sinne des Humanismus geforderten vertieften Sprachbehandlung' [There [in the German grammar schools], the highest expression of a nation's mind, its literature, gives the opportunity for a deeper treatment of the language in the Humanist way] (Bohlen 1957: 106).

For Bohlen, literature was one of four main components (history; geography; manners and customs; behaviour and literature) that could describe every single culture in all its particularities (Bohlen 1957: 14). Here, Bohlen took over Richert's concept of *Kulturkunde* and developed it further. Like Richert, Bohlen was convinced that we can understand other cultures through their literature (Bohlen, 1957: 150) and he believed that only a deep understanding of other national cultures (*Nationalkulturen*) would prevent misunderstandings and support international understanding. Here, it becomes evident that Bohlen followed some progressive ideas in thinking in a 'European' or even 'global' way in his vision of cultural and political education (Hüllen 2005: 139). A look at contemporary French textbooks shows that German pupils were expected to be equipped to help reconcile the two former arch-enemies through their reading of French literature. In Friedrich Schlupp's *Français vivant* ([5]1957), the author closes his preface with the following call:

> Jahrhundertelang kämpfen Frankreichs Denker und Dichter mit einer Glaubenskraft, die nie erlahmte, um die Erziehung des Menschen, kämpfen um seine Freiheit und Würde, gegen Diktatur und Krieg. Der heutige Unterricht muß mehr denn je dieser wenig beachteten Geisteshaltung der Franzosen Rechnung tragen und unsere reiferen Schüler zu einer ehrlichen

Auseinandersetzung mit dem Nachbarvolke anregen, sollen doch auch sie einmal mitwirken, die zwischen Deutschland und Frankreich bestehenden Spannungen zu beseitigen und die geistigen Brücken über den Rhein wieder aufzubauen. Soll Europa leben, dann muß die Feindschaft von gestern zur Solidarität von heute werden. Möge zur Erreichung dieses großen Zieles der vorliegende Band einen nützlichen Beitrag leisten! (Schlupp [5]1957: 7)

[French intellectuals have been fighting for centuries with an untiring belief for the education of the human being; they have been fighting for his freedom and dignity, against dictatorship and war. Today's teaching must consider more than ever this little-regarded spirit of the French and has to inspire our more mature pupils to an honest examination of the neighbouring people, as they will have to play their part in relieving the tensions between Germany and France and in rebuilding intellectual bridges across the Rhine. If Europe is to live, yesterday's enmity must become today's solidarity. May the book at hand make a useful contribution to this great goal!]

In these words, Schlupp suggests that a bi-national understanding and subsequently the European idea could only be achieved as a result of an understanding of other cultures. According to the author, this reconciliation was founded in analysing the texts of important French intellectuals, who represented the French attitude of mind.

Rather similar ideas can be found in the preface of *La Civilisation Française*, another textbook from 1957 (for pupils at the age of sixteen to nineteen). Its authors, Hofmann and Morlang, were convinced that only a constant cooperation between France and Germany could guarantee peace in Europe. In the authors' opinion, young Germans in the French classroom should retrace how the French 'spirit' had contributed to building up contemporary Europe, and this examination could be done through literary works:

Eine bedeutungsvolle Aufgabe fällt dabei dem französischen Unterricht zu; er muß bei der geistigen Elite unserer Jugend Verständnis dafür wecken, daß eine aufrichtige und freundschaftliche Zusammenarbeit zwischen Deutschland und Frankreich die grundlegende Voraussetzung für eine Befriedung Europas bildet. Der französische Unterricht wird durch die Beschäftigung mit der großen französischen Zivilisation zeigen, wie trotz aller Besonderheiten beide Völker seit Jahrhunderten aus den gleichen Wurzeln ihre geistige Kraft gezogen haben und wie trotz kriegerischer Verwicklungen ihr wechselseitiges Verhältnis reich und befruchtend gewesen ist. Es wird dabei sichtbar werden, in welch hohem Maße französischer Geist mitgewirkt hat, das heutige Europa zu formen. (Hofmann and Morlang [9]1957: 2)

[French language education plays a meaningful role: it has to awaken an understanding in our young intellectual elite that an honest and amicable collaboration between Germany and France is the basic condition for the pacification of Europe. In French language education, focusing on the great French civilization will clearly show that — in spite of some distinctive features — both peoples have drawn their intellectual capacities from the same sources; in addition — despite involvement in wars — their mutual relationship has been rich and fruitful. It will become apparent that the French intellectual spirit has played an enormous part in forming today's Europe.]

To judge by these two quotations, it becomes evident that Bohlen's progressive *thinking European* reflected the *zeitgeist* in guidelines for teaching modern languages.

One of the main challenges in modern-language classrooms was, and still is, '[*die*] *Fülle literarischer Meisterwerke*' [the multitude of literary masterpieces] (Bohlen 1957: 107) and the question of which works should be read in the classroom. Does it make sense to work on extracts from as many texts as possible, or should only a few representative works be analysed? Bohlen did not propose to seek to provide an overview of the most important periods and their main works. Rather, he believed the starting point should be the masterpiece itself (Bohlen 1957: 107). In keeping with the *New Criticism*, the predominant approach in literary studies in the 1950s, with its work-immanent character, Bohlen and many of his contemporaries (e. g. Schröder 1958) favoured an intensive examination of individual works. Surkamp also points out that under the influence of *New Criticism* literary texts were mostly treated without any reference to their historical or cultural background until the 1960s (Surkamp 2013: 196). For example, in 1959 Hüllen criticized the connection between *Kulturkunde* and literature. In his opinion, literary texts should not be chosen to teach cultural information. It must be recognized 'daß die Quellen, die ursprünglichen Zeugnisse des Geistes, also besonders die Literatur, die reinste Kulturkunde sind, die denkbar ist' [that the sources, as the original testimonies of the "spirit", particularly literature, are the purest form of *Kulturkunde* possible] (Hüllen 1959: 228). He demanded a literary text be considered as an important aesthetic and cultural reference itself and not as part of a corpus providing basic knowledge of another culture. Therefore *Kulturkunde* should not be a selection criterion to choose literary texts in higher secondary education (Hüllen 1959: 228-29). However, textbooks authors often did connect the chosen texts to their context. For Hofmann and Morlang, this approach had advantages: 'Dadurch entsteht ein Querschnitt durch die Literatur Frankreichs seit dem 17. Jahrhundert, der als Ersatz für eine Literaturgeschichte dienen kann' [Thereby is created a cross-section through French literature for the seventeenth century which could replace a literary history' (Hofmann and Morlang [9]1957: 3). They intended to connect the extracts as closely as possible to their context.

However, despite the fact that Bohlen called for pupils to read and to analyse a range of masterpieces from the OII (*Obersekunda*) to the OI (*Oberprima*), he refused to propose a canon. Instead, he supported modern curricula and teaching methodologies that included central ideas regarding the choice of representative texts to be taught in the foreign language classroom (Bohlen 1957: 107). It must be the teachers who decided on a specific selection for their classes (Bohlen 1957: 108). Because pupils should analyse formal elements of a text, Bohlen and others recommended 'high' literature (Surkamp 2013: 196). We can find some concrete topic proposals (Bohlen 1957: 108):

- the masterpieces of the Classical Period (the seventeenth century)
- prose of the Enlightenment and the Revolutionary epoch
- poetry of the Romantic and the Naturalist period
- main texts of the French idea of civilization and the European Conviction, etc.

Examining textbooks from the period suggests that these topics were often adopted. For example, in *La Civilisation Française* we can find these topics addressed in the explanations to Chapters IV (*L'Évolution politique et historique*), V (*L'Esprit français*), VI (*La Vie intellectuelle*) and VII (*Questions philosophiques et morales*) (Hofmann and Morlang [9]1957: 11-16).

Bohlen did not mention any concrete titles because he did not want to influence the teachers' decisions but he made it very clear that the latter were expected to guarantee to choose real classics (Bohlen 1957: 108-09). Without giving a concrete definition, some of his convictions about the choice of texts still indicate his understanding of a classical text. For him, judging the value of a literary work needed a certain temporary distance. He criticized a choice of subjects excessively relevant to the present day as alarming from a pedagogical perspective (Bohlen 1957: 109). In his Humanist approach to education the lasting value of a piece of literature was a central sign of its quality (Bohlen 1957: 108). With this conviction, Bohlen was not alone in the field of foreign languages. In 1958 Schröder shared Bohlen's opinion in his article 'Zur Lektüreauswahl im Englischen' in *Die Neueren Sprachen*. Schröder criticized the rather colloquial style of a great number of contemporary works and insisted on the Humanist value of classics (Schröder 1958). Schröder preferred to work on texts describing the human experience in its purest form (Schröder 1959: 276). It is evident that moral principles were important guidelines in his choice of classroom literature. He was not against a certain social realism in literature but in the classroom he preferred a choice of texts showing human beings as they should be (Schröder 1959: 276). This one-sided focus on the classics was not only typical for the foreign-language classroom but for the German classroom, too, and prevented the inclusion of contemporary works in the literary curricula. Although Bohlen, for example, did not exclude modern texts in an absolute manner, he only accepted them when they treated historical subjects (Bohlen 1957: 108). It is a fact that it provoked critical discussions in academic discourse (Stuck 2013: 189). Schrey, for instance, rejected the common view that modern English and American writers were unsuitable for the English classroom. Instead, he demanded that teachers should apply certain criteria to their choice of literature for the modern-language classroom such as, for example, 'unity, persuasiveness, truth of the reading matter' (Schrey 1959: 136). To Schrey's mind, those were real literary criteria and he reproached Schröder for having strictly formalistic expectations of classroom literature (Schrey 1959: 137). But for Schrey they were not helpful in deciding on the literary value of a text (Schrey 1959: 137). Because he was not convinced of a normative character of teaching literature in the foreign-language classroom, he pointed out that pupils should not only read texts showing people as they should be, but literature describing human beings as they were (Schrey 1959: 136).

But Bohlen's opinion also found support in the textbooks of the 1950s. Although both *La Civilisation Française* and *Français vivant* emphasized the importance of new literature in textbooks (Schlupp [5]1957: 6; Hoffmann and Morlang [9]1957: 4), they also demonstrated that masterpieces were expected to dominate the literary work in the French classroom: 'Es versteht sich von selbst, daß ein Lesebuch die Meisterwerke der Literatur nicht verdrängen kann. Diese werden immer im Mittelpunkt des

Unterrichts stehen müssen' [It goes without saying that a reading anthology can never replace literary masterpieces. They will always have to be at the centre of a lesson] (Schlupp ⁵1957: 6).

In conclusion, we can sum up that in the first twenty years after the end of World War II French as a foreign language was taught under rather ambivalent central ideas. On the one hand, it was rooted in the more traditional, Humanist concept of the *Kulturkunde* and proclaimed quite elitist educational standards. On the other hand, learning French and reading foreign literature were seen as an important contribution to peacekeeping and to a cultural understanding in a more connected Europe. These more progressive ideas left their mark on the 1960s, as we will see in the next part of this essay.

The New Role of Literature in the French Classroom

When, in the 1990s, Rück considered literature to be well established in the foreign-language classroom, he also pointed out that this had not always been the case. The role of literature faced a crisis in the late 1960s and into the 1970s (Rück 1990: 7). In retrospect we can find first signs of this change in the lively debate about the literary canon in 1959, when Schröder, Schrey and others were not only discussing which books could be agreed on to be read but also why pupils should work on literary texts and how such texts should be integrated into teaching literature (Schröder 1958, 1959; Schrey 1959; Hüllen 1959).

In the 1960s and 1970s the secure position of literary texts in the foreign-language classroom was facing challenges not only because of changes in pedagogical concepts but also because of important social and political developments. In addition, new approaches in literary studies influenced the status of literature in the classroom as well. At first, Structuralism and Behaviourism influenced the teaching of foreign languages fundamentally. The preference for an oral approach, supported by the technology of language laboratories, and for a more utilitarian attitude towards foreign-language learning did not help the status of literature. Weller describes the difficult position of literature in 1976: 'Nie zuvor war Literaturunterricht so radikal in Frage gestellt' [Never before has the teaching of literature been questioned in such a radical manner] (1976: 591). As everyday language and pattern drills were expected to be at the centre of the lessons, literature seemed to become an increasingly peripheral phenomenon.

But this change was not only prompted by the new theories of learning foreign languages. It was also influenced by the social and educational debates on the democratization of the German education system. In 1964 Georg Picht's notion of the 'German educational catastrophe' (*Deutsche Bildungskatastrophe*) set off a controversy about the improvements that would be necessary to guarantee the training of the university graduates needed. Picht lamented that the existing system failed to balance the training of specialists with economic needs:

> Aus den bisher vorgelegten Daten ergibt sich zwingend, daß wir die Zahl der Abiturienten mindestens verdoppeln und auch die Zahl der Akademiker erheblich steigern müssen, wenn Westdeutschland im Zuge der Entwicklung

der wissenschaftlichen Zivilisation nicht unter die Räder kommen soll. (Picht 1965: 19)[4]

[From the data produced so far it is necessary that the number of Abitur candidates must double and that also the number of academics must be increased substantially in order to prevent West Germany from falling behind with regard to the development of scientific civilization.]

These practical observations were accompanied by more social considerations. Picht and many of his contemporaries observed that social advancement was often prevented by lack of social mobility, especially in the context of equal access to educational institutions. Many education researchers accused the grammar schools of promoting an elitist and Humanist concept that did not meet the requirements of the labour market. As a consequence, these schools remained schools for the children of the educated middle class (Picht 1965: 22). Dahrendorf was very clear: 'Die Zielvorstellungen beruhen auf einem traditionellen, idealistischen Bildungsbegriff, der elitär mittelständisch ist und auf die Kinder der unteren Schichten wenig stimulierend und motivierend wirkt' [The aims are based on a traditional idealistic notion of education, which is elitist, middle-class and does not have a stimulating and motivating effect on lower-class children] (Dahrendorf 1970: 38). Dahrendorf asked 'ob ästhetische Erlebnisfähigkeit und Verständnis für Hochliteratur ein primäres Bildungsziel zu sein vermögen und ob die Schule sich nicht auf das rational Lehrbare zu beschränken hat' [whether the ability to experience aesthetics and an understanding for highbrow culture could be a primary aim of education and whether schools should not limit their focus to what can rationally be taught] (ibid.).

Another aspect influenced the reorientation in teaching literature in the French classroom. When Konrad Adenauer and Charles de Gaulle signed the Elysée Treaty on 22 January 1963, the former enemies did not merely make assurances about their mutual peaceful intentions and their wish to overcome Franco-German hostility. They also agreed an extensive and concrete programme whose purpose was to guarantee that these aims could be achieved. In addition to very precise co-operation agreements in matters of foreign policy and defence, the two governments agreed on the bi-national task of education and on the necessity for an extensive youth programme. Not surprisingly, teaching the language of the co-operation partner was one of the main aims. The two governments acknowledged that it would be imperative for Franco-German co-operation to know the 'other' language; and they signalled their intention to increase the number of pupils learning either French or German (Elysée Treaty 1963: 2). The decisions in this part of the Treaty explain that language acquisition had a concrete purpose. It should enable young Germans and French to participate in different forms of exchange. They were expected to become acquainted with their young neighbours and with their respective cultures, to build up or to intensify existing relations. Learning French now had a practical, communicative purpose, a significant difference compared to Richert's *Kulturkunde* and Bohlen's *Modern Humanism*. But did these developments really lead to a fundamental change in teaching literature in the French classroom? Or even to a dangerous crisis, as Weller diagnosed the situation in 1976 (Weller 1976: 591)? There were changes, on the one hand due to the social and political debate on the democratization of education; and on the other hand because of new approaches in literary studies. Texts were no longer expected to be analysed in a purely work-immanent manner. Rather, they were to be studied in their context, as we can find, for example, in the French educational guidelines of the city of Bremen:

> Für den Literaturunterricht gilt allgemein, daß die Behandlung literarischer Texte nicht auf werkimmanente Methoden beschränkt bleiben darf, sondern durch literatursoziologische Verfahren abgestützt werden muß. Hierunter sind die Einbeziehung des sozialgeschichtlichen Kontextes der literarischen Werke sowie die Berücksichtigung ihrer Rezeption zu verstehen. (Der Senator für Bildung, Sek. II Bremen 1978: 4)

> [For teaching literature it can be said in general that dealing with literary texts should not be limited to methods focusing purely on the work, but should be supported by methods from literary sociology. This reflects the integration of the social-historical context of the works and a consideration of their reception.]

Even according to the curriculum of North Rhine-Westphalia from 1973, a curriculum that still focused heavily on the traditional textual analysis, novels were to be read as a means and as a result of critical social reflections, as well as a means to influence social processes (Kultusministerium NRW 1973: 57).

Beyond that, the perspective of the reader was to be taken into account (Kultusministerium NRW 1973: 57; Der Senator für Bildung, Sek. II Bremen 1978: 4). Shaped by German and North American reader-response theories, the focus on the question of how literary texts affected pupils as readers became a new and important approach in teaching literature in the foreign-language classroom.

Besides the described changes with regard to the question of how to work with literature, there was also a change in the choice of recommended texts for the French classroom. From the 1970s onwards we can find more recently published texts in the guidelines, as well as new genres such as detective stories and children's literature that had become more accepted and valued in the literary debate (Stuck 2013: 189-90). In the North Rhine-Westphalian reading lists, for example, we find Camus's *L'Hôte* (1957) and *La Chute* (1956); Ionesco's *Rhinocéros* (1957) as well as Sartre's *Huis clos* (1944); *Le Square* (1955/57) by Marguerite Duras; and even some of Simenon's Maigret stories (e.g. *La Pipe de Maigret* (1945); *Maigret et le clochard* (1962)) (Kultusministerium NRW, 1973: 52, 57-58). This development was also the result of the discussion on a more democratic education system. Dahrendorf, for example, even advocated the integration of popular literature:

> Um der massenhaft verbreiteten Literatur besser gerecht zu werden, mache man sich ihre sozialintegrative Funktion deutlich. Sie bewirkt Kommunikation und ermöglicht Bestätigungserlebnisse, die Sicherheit verschaffen. [...] Während sich der intellektuell geschulte Mensch der Mittelschicht den prickelnden Genuß verunsichernder Lektüre leisten kann, wären Menschen der Unterschicht ihr ziemlich hilflos ausgeliefert. (Dahrendorf 1970: 47-48)

[In order to do justice to popular literature we must understand its social-integrative function. It fosters communication and enables experiences of affirmation that enforce security. [...] While the intellectually trained middle-class person can afford the sparkling pleasure of reading works that produce insecurity, people from the lower classes are helplessly exposed.]

The Bremen guidelines from 1981 emphasized *French popular culture* as the first topic in the eleventh grade (pupils aged sixteen to seventeen). It was justified by its clear structures and its comprehensible language (Der Senator für Bildung, Bremen Sek. II 1981: 5, 7).

Conclusion

To summarize, teaching literature has played and continues to play an important and permanent role in the French classroom at German grammar schools after World War II. As a fundamental component in Bohlen's *Modern Humanism* it was part of a quite elitist educational concept. At the same time, however, teaching literature was supposed also to foster cultural understanding in a more connected Europe. This idea predominated in the French classroom after the reorientation in foreign-language teaching in the 1960s and early 1970s. New approaches in literary studies influenced and changed the educational aims, in the choice of texts as well as the methods. Sociological approaches in literary studies influenced the concentration on texts and genres beyond the traditional 'trinity' of prose, drama and poetry. Empirical approaches mirrored an increasing interest in literary texts that actually circulated in society. However, contrary to Weller's fears regarding the position of literature, its status has never really been questioned in the foreign-language classroom at German grammar schools. While this is a rather positive conclusion, it should not be overlooked that the position of literary texts in the foreign-language classroom at German secondary modern schools (*Realschulen*) was a different one. Literary texts had been integrated in the textbooks in the 1950s and 1960s but after the paradigm shift in the 1970s mentioned above, teaching French in secondary modern schools followed a predominantly pragmatic approach.

Bibliography

Primary sources

Abkommen zwischen der Regierung der Bundesrepublik Deutschland und der Regierung der Französischen Republik über die Errichtung des Deutsch-Französischen Jugendwerkes, veröffentlicht am 31.12.1963. 1963. Bundesgesetzbl. II, p. 1613 <http://www.deutschland-frankreich.diplo.de/Elysee-Vertrag-22-Januar-1963,347.html> [accessed 13 February 2018]

BAUMGÄRTNER, ALFRED CLEMENS, and MALTE DAHRENDORF (eds). 1970. *Wozu Literatur in der Schule? Beiträge zum Literaturunterricht* (Brunswick: Westermann)

BOHLEN, ADOLF. 1957. *Moderner Humanismus* (Heidelberg: Quelle & Meyer)

DAHRENDORF, MALTE. 1970. 'Voraussetzungen und Umrisse einer gegenwartsbezogenen literarischen Erziehung', in *Wozu Literatur in der Schule? Beiträge zum Literaturunterricht*, ed. by Alfred Clemens Baumgärtner and Malte Dahrendorf (Brunswick: Westermann), pp. 27-50

Elysée-Vertrag vom 22. Januar 1963 <www.deutschland-frankreich.diplo.de/Elysee-Vertrag-22-Januar-1963,347.html> [accessed 13 February 2018]

HOFMANN, FRITZ, and WILHELM MORLANG. 1957. *La Civilisation Française*, 9th edn (Frankfurt am Main: Hirschgraben)

HÜLLEN, WERNER. 1959. 'Gesichtspunkte zur Lektüreauswahl im Englischunterricht', *Die Neueren Sprachen*, 5: 225-33

KULTUSMINISTERIUM DES LANDES NORDRHEIN-WESTFALEN. 1973. *Empfehlungen für den Kursunterricht im Fach Französisch* (Düsseldorf: Henn)

PICHT, GEORG. 1965. *Die Deutsche Bildungskatastrophe* (Munich: Deutscher Taschenbuch Verlag)

RICHERT, HANS. 1920. *Die deutsche Bildungseinheit und die höhere Schule. Ein Buch von deutscher Nationalerziehung* (Tübingen: Mohr)

—— (ed.). 1925. *Richtlinien für die Lehrpläne der höheren Schulen Preußens* (Berlin: Weidmann)

SCHLUPP, FRIEDRICH. 1957. *Français vivant. A la découverte de la France*, 5th edn (Paderborn: Schöningh)

SCHREY, HELMUT. 1959. 'Noch einmal: Zur Lektüreauswahl im Englischen', *Die Neueren Sprachen*, 3: 134-38

SCHRÖDER, AUGUST. 1958. 'Zur Lektüreauswahl im Englischen', *Die Neueren Sprachen*, 12: 552-66

——. 1959. 'Zur Lektüreauswahl im Englischunterricht: Eine Antwort', *Die Neueren Sprachen*, 6: 275-77

DER SENATOR FÜR BILDUNG. 1978. *Rahmenrichtlinien für den Unterricht in der gymnasialen Oberstufe Sek. II — Französisch – Entwurf* (Bremen)

DER SENATOR FÜR BILDUNG. 1981. *Rahmenrichtlinien für den Unterricht in der gymnasialen Oberstufe Sek. II — Französisch* (Bremen)

WELLER, FRANZ-RUDOLF. 1976. 'Auswahlbibliographie zur Didaktik des fremdsprachlichen Literaturunterrichts', *Die Neueren Sprachen*, 6: 591-606

Secondary sources

BREDELLA, LOTHAR, and WOLFGANG HALLET (eds). 2007. *Literaturunterricht: Kompetenzen und Bildung* (Trier: Wissenschaftlicher Verlag Trier)

CHRIST, HERBERT. 2011. 'Die Stunde der Politik: Drei Beispielfälle für Versuche der staatlichen Regulierung des Fremdsprachenunterrichts', *französisch heute*, 2: 65-74

——, and HANS-JOACHIM RANG. 1985. *Fremdsprachenunterricht unter staatlicher Verwaltung 1700 bis 1945,7 vols, II: Allgemeine Anweisungen für den Fremdsprachenunterricht* (Tübingen: Narr)

DOFF, SABINE. 2008. *Englischdidaktik in der BRD 1949–1989* (Munich: Langenscheidt)

FRICKE, DIETMAR, and ALBERT-REINER GLAAP (eds). 1990. *Literaturen im Fremdsprachenunterricht — Fremdsprache im Literaturunterricht* (Frankfurt am Main: Diesterweg)

HALLET, WOLFGANG. 2007. 'Literatur, Kognition und Kompetenz: Die Literarizität kulturellen Handelns', in *Literaturunterricht: Kompetenzen und Bildung*, ed. by Lothar Bredella and Wolfgang Hallet (Trier: Wissenschaftlicher Verlag Trier), pp. 31-64

HÜLLEN, WERNER. 2005. *Kleine Geschichte des Fremdsprachenlernens* (Berlin: Erich Schmidt)

RIPPL, GABRIELE, and SIMONE WINKO (eds). 2013. *Handbuch Kanon und Wertung: Theorien, Instanzen, Geschichte* (Stuttgart/Weimar: Metzler)

RISAGER, KAREN. 2007. *Language and Culture Pedagogy: From a National to a Transnational Paradigm* (Clevedon: Multilingual Matters)

RÜCK, HERIBERT. 1990. 'Fremdsprachenunterricht als Literaturunterricht', in *Literaturen im Fremdsprachenunterricht — Fremdsprache im Literaturunterricht*, ed. by Dietmar Fricke and Albert-Reiner Glaap (Frankfurt am Main: Diesterweg), pp. 7-20

STUCK, ELISABETH. 2013. 'Schule im deutschsprachigen Bereich', in *Handbuch Kanon und Wertung: Theorien, Instanzen, Geschichte*, ed. by Gabriele Rippl and Simone Winko (Stuttgart and Weimar: Metzler), pp. 188-93

SURKAMP, CAROLA. 2013. 'Geschichte der Kanones englischsprachiger Literatur an deutschen Schulen', in *Handbuch Kanon und Wertung: Theorien, Instanzen, Geschichte*, ed. by Gabriele Rippl and Simone Winko (Stuttgart and Weimar: Metzler), pp. 193-200

Notes to Chapter 7

1. All translation are the author's own.
2. 'Es erscheint richtiger, angesichts der das Ganze bedrohenden Kulturkrise auch einen Ganzheitsanspruch zu vertreten und *eine im humanistischen Geiste erfolgende Neubesinnung und Neuorientierung* zu fordern' [Facing a cultural crisis which threatens the whole, it seems more appropriate to claim absoluteness and to require a *reorientation in a humanist spirit*] (Bohlen 1957: 22; emphasis in the original).
3. Bohlen developed his approach to a modern Humanism exclusively for the two modern types of the German *Gymnasium*: the German grammar schools specializing, on the one hand, in modern languages or, on the other hand, in mathematics and natural sciences. In both forms, pupils were required to learn at least two foreign languages (English and French or Latin (Düsseldorf Agreement 1955) (Hüllen 2005: 131-32)).
4. The German *Abitur* is a school examination usually taken at the end of the thirteenth year. It is equivalent to the British A level.

CHAPTER 8

❖

'A Dragoman for Travellers'

Popular Arabic Instruction Books and their Authors in Late Nineteenth-Century Egypt

Rachel Mairs

In the nineteenth century, ever larger numbers of Europeans visited Egypt. In earlier decades, those visitors who learnt Arabic (and many did not) did so through a combination of formal grammatical study of the language, and immersion and practice with native speakers. In the late nineteenth century, however, publishing houses in the Middle East and Europe responded to the desire of many travellers to learn basic conversational Arabic with a number of dedicated publications, simple in format and reasonably priced. The same books were often designed to be used by Arabic speakers learning European languages. This chapter reviews a number of works, including Yacoub Nakhlah's *New Manual of English and Arabic Conversation* (Cairo: the Khedive's Press, 1874) and *Arabic Self-Taught: The Dragoman for Travellers in Egypt* by A. Hassam (first of many editions, 1883). As well as the content of these handbooks, I review the professional backgrounds of their authors, most of whom were first-language Arabic speakers, and examine contemporary accounts of the experiences of their users.

Arabic at a Glance

The Arabic language, when spoken, sounds very much like an agitated person trying to dislodge a fish bone. It is one of the most unmusical tongues in the world and offers no tempting inducements to the student, yet Mr. Peasley actually bought one of those 'Arabic at a Glance' books and started to learn some of the more useful sentences. He said that if he could get Arabic down pat he would pass as a native and be enabled to buy things at about half price. After two days of hard study he attempted a conversation with a military policeman standing on the river bank at Dendera. Mr. Peasley strolled up to him, careless like, and said, 'Ana awez arabiyet kwayesset min shan arookh el balad.' That was supposed to mean, 'I want a first-class carriage for driving in the town.' The stalwart soldier gazed at Mr. Peasley with a most bewildered look in his jet black eyes and then began to edge away.

'Hold on,' said Mr. Peasley. 'How about hal yel zamna ghafar yerafegua bill tareeg?'

Mr. Peasley thought he was asking, 'Shall we require a guide or an escort in this town?'

The soldier beckoned to us to come over and help him out.

'Tell him, please, that I am educate at the Presbyterian Mission,' said he. 'I speak only English and Arabic.'

We questioned him later and learned that he took Mr. Peasley to be a Russian. This one little experience rather discouraged our travelling companion. He said it was foolish to waste important dialogue on a lot of benighted ignorami who did not know their own language. (Ade 1906: 209-11)[1]

In the late nineteenth and early twentieth centuries, a publishing industry sprang up to cater to those travellers, like the American humourist George Ade's friend Mr Peasley, who wished to enhance their foreign travels by acquiring a smattering of the local language. Academic Arabic Studies have a long and distinguished history in Europe, a history bound up with the ever-changing priorities of commerce, diplomacy, scientific research, theology and imperialism. The history of the *study* of European Arabic Studies — or the wider, but now no longer so-described, discipline of Orientalism — is also long and distinguished. Important recent projects include those supported by the Centre for the History of Arabic Studies in Europe at the Warburg Institute in London, such as The Teaching and Learning of Arabic in Early Modern Europe.[2] This chapter addresses, in contrast, a sub-group of Arabic learners, outside institutional academe, who wished to learn some Arabic without having the inclination and/or the resources to indulge in formal, long-term study. Casual learners may well have greatly outnumbered dedicated scholars of Arabic, although figures are difficult to come by. The large number of European and American tourists who visited the Middle East and North Africa in the second half of the nineteenth-century (facilitated by European colonialism and by companies such as Thomas Cook) created a new market for Arabic teaching materials of a practical nature, which did not require (or claimed not to require) access to a teacher.

The focus of this chapter will be on English-language materials published for use in Egypt, with some discussion of French and German. This focus necessitates omitting full discussion of some important early works in other languages or for use in other regions of the Arab world, such as Philipp Wolff's *Arabischer Dragoman für Besucher des Heiligen Landes* (Wolff 1857). Wolff was a German Protestant pastor who travelled and undertook research in Palestine; and his book, tailored to the type of Arabic vocabulary and phrases travellers might need, went through several editions over the following decades.

The books which I discuss are principally those authored or revised by five men: Khalīfah ibn Maḥmūd al-Miṣrī, Yacoub Nakhlah, Muhammad Anton Hassan, Naser Odeh and Anton Tien. I have several questions about these materials. What were the professional backgrounds of the authors of language books and how did these influence their teaching methods? What expectations did authors have of their audience and the latter's needs? How did this audience use these books and what were their experiences of them? (In some cases, owners' inscriptions inside copies of phrasebooks tell us something about who used them and how.) I also wish to draw to attention to a neglected aspect of these already neglected books: namely, the extent to which they address themselves to an audience of Arabic-speakers learning European languages as well as to learners of Arabic.

Sørensen's recent publications on 'popular language works' point out that the method of 'Teach Yourself' guides has changed little between her nineteenth-century case study of Scandinavian works for learners of English and the present day. Such books focus on the spoken language and have an emphasis on practicality, in two senses: as learning to be put into practical application, and on practice as a means of learning (Sørensen 2011: 30-33). They have often been viewed as ineffective tools, although learning outcomes are also the product of user motivation and discipline. Nineteenth-century Arabic phrasebooks and self-instruction manuals share a great many features with their cousins for other languages. Many, indeed, were published in series with instruction manuals for other languages and contain advertisements for them. They use the same methods of grammatical drill, vocabulary lists and practice phrases. They also require the same degree of dedication from learners in order to be effective. Ade presents what was doubtless the experience of many a foreign traveller in Egypt: phrases crammed from a book, with no idea of how the language sounded or what individual elements of the sentence meant, were not going to get a learner very far. Some indication of what was required to use popular language manuals effectively is offered by the British archaeologist Sir W. M. Flinders Petrie (1853-1942), who lived in Egypt and Palestine for extended periods of time and learnt colloquial Arabic to a high standard. He advises travellers to start with the brief guides to Arabic in popular guide books and move on from there:

> Learn first of all what you want in Baedecker's vocabulary; refer to Murray, or better, to a dictionary, for any further words you want; and absorb the addenda of very common words which come at the end of this chapter; then a week or two in Cairo, talking to the natives as much as possible, would quite suffice to float the active tripper. (Petrie 1892: 188)

Petrie's method takes popular language works as only a starting point for a more thorough self-guided programme of study, which requires dedication and motivation in seeking out conversation with native speakers. In his own list of useful vocabulary, which he advises the learner to 'absorb', he clearly marks the separate elements of sentences, and which word means what. 'The engine it.leaves when? — *El wabur ye.safir emta?*', with its unidiomatic English translation, helps the user understand how the Arabic sentence fits together. For an archaeologist, popular language works do not cover all the relevant situations, so Petrie fills the gaps in their vocabulary. 'The peasants (are) foolish like cattle — *el fellahin maganin zeyeh behaim*' may not be a phrase everyone would need, or care, to use, but it does teach the learner an important grammatical point: that Arabic does not mark the verb 'to be' in the present tense.

The nineteenth-century Arabic instruction manuals and phrasebooks which I review here were not inherently deficient. They did, however, require hardworking and proactive users. Many of my own copies, even those in paper covers, are in very good condition indeed. Bought with enthusiasm in London or Cairo, and skimmed with panic and confusion on the deck of a Mediterranean steamer or the terrace of that famous Cairene institution, Shepheard's Hotel, they sat unopened at the bottom of a trunk for the duration of a Nile cruise.

Pearls before Translators

The publication of popular language works in Egypt dates back to at least the mid-nineteenth century. Several early examples, published by the government press at Būlāq in Cairo, rather than by private printing houses, speak to two potential audiences — foreigners learning Arabic and Egyptians learning foreign languages — simultaneously. In 1850, the Būlāq press issued a book with a bilingual title page. At the top, enclosed in an ornamental border, in French we read 'Instructions aux Drogmans'. A fuller Arabic text occupies the bottom of the page, which gives the title as the more poetic *Qalāʾid al-jumān fī fawāʾid al-tarjumān* — 'Necklaces of Pearls for the Benefit of Translators'. The pages are to be turned from left to right, in the Arabic style, so that to a European reader it appears as if the book opens from the back cover, and the page numbers are in Arabic numerals. The author, Khalīfah ibn Maḥmūd al-Miṣrī, had studied languages and law in Cairo, and had been French teacher to a Khedive's son 'Moustafa Bey' (probably Mustafa Fazl Pasha, 1830-1863) during a stay in Constantinople. Khalīfah Effendi is also described as head of the Translation Bureau, an attaché at the Ministry of Public Instruction, and the translator of a number of works from French into Arabic.

The term 'dragoman' ('drogman', 'tarjumān') is used by Khalīfah Effendi in a literal sense: his work is addressed to professional translators and to those who need languages for their professional role. In the following decades, 'dragoman' appeared again and again in the titles of popular language works for foreign learners of Arabic, but in a metaphorical sense: the book was to act as a dragoman, a guide, to a country and its language in the same way as professional dragomans, translators and guides, in the tourist industry (Mairs and Muratov 2015). The *Qalāʾid al-jumān*, however, is designed primarily for the use of Arabic speakers: an 'Ouvrage très méthodique, destiné à ceux qui desirent apprendre à parler les trois Langues, Arabe, Turque et Française' (al-Miṣrī 1850: no pagn).

The first part of the book comprises a trilingual vocabulary list in three columns: French on the left, Arabic on the right, and Turkish in the middle. Because of the different directions in which the scripts are read, it is not immediately apparent which, if any, language has priority — although it is certainly not the Turkish. The vocabulary lists words in categories: starting with the human body; then human emotions and qualities, ailments; then animals and plants; and so forth. Categories of especial interest to a professional diplomatic translator include religion, the army and the professions. An equally large section of the book then lists common verbs by their conjugation, not by their meaning.

The second third of the book begins with phrases used in greetings, courtesies and social niceties (such as 'Pour refuser ou s'excuser'). It then incorporates these, and the vocabulary already learnt, into dialogues. The topics include leisure activities and conducting a range of transactions, from being fitted for a suit at a tailor to buying a country house. Some dialogues relate specifically to travel (touring a strange town, taking a sea voyage, etc.), and the user, naturally, learns how to haggle: 'C'est fort cher; dites moi le dernier prix' (al-Miṣrī 1850: 160). The final third of the book is occupied by an outline of French grammar and syntax, in Arabic and Turkish, with French examples.

The *Qalāʾid al-jumān* is an interesting work for a number of reasons. It is accessible to users with a range of needs, from learning set phrases and vocabulary for specific situations to making a more in-depth grammatical study of French. French is the target language: the user needs to know either Arabic or Turkish, and the Arabic script. It is set, however, within an already established European tradition of phrasebook writing with which the French-educated Khalīfah Effendi was evidently familiar. Although it might be used in the same manner as one of these phrasebooks, it has a serious scholarly purpose: the formal training of translators. It appears, in fact, to have been the very first grammar of French published in Arabic (Bechraoui 2001).

This fascinating book has received little scholarly attention. I have been unable to find out more about the elusive Khalīfah ibn Maḥmūd al-Miṣrī than is stated in the book itself, other than that he trained at the language school in Cairo established by Rifāʿa Rāfʿi al-Ṭahṭāwī, an Egyptian scholar who had studied in Paris (Newman 2004). It sets the scene for my remaining discussion in two important ways. Like most of the popular language works I shall discuss, it was written by a native speaker of Arabic with a professional interest in the teaching of languages. It was also a book that could potentially be used by learners with a range of needs and levels of competence.

The New Manual of Arabic and English Conversation

One of the earliest Egyptian-published examples of a phrasebook and grammar aimed, at least in part, at speakers of European languages learning Arabic is Yacoub Nakhlah's *New Manual of Arabic and English Conversation* (Nakhlah 1874), published, also at the Khedival Press in Būlāq, in 1874. Khalīfah Effendi had opened his *Qalāʾid al-jumān* by addressing it 'à ceux qui desirent apprendre à parler les trois Langues, Arabe, Turque et Française' (al-Miṣrī 1850: no pagn), although its contents reveal that his principal concern was teaching Arabic speakers French. Nakhlah's book is more determinedly aimed at two separate readerships — Anglophone and Arabophone — although to someone who knows only English, this is not clear. On the title page, English has priority: it is at the head of the page, in a larger font than the Arabic. The Arabic title of the *New Manual of English and Arabic Conversation* is slightly different. It is a *tuḥfa*, a 'gift', *fī taʿallum al-lughat al-inglīziyya* 'for learning the English language'.

In the English and Arabic prefaces, the balance continues — again, invisible to the English reader. The English Preface states that: 'This work is intended to be a practical hand-book for the use of English and American travellers on the Nile; and a useful manual of conversation for the interest of natives desirous of acquiring the English language'. The Arabic Preface, on the page facing, begins with the ubiquitous *bismillah al-raḥmān al-raḥīm* [In the name of God, the most gracious, the most merciful]. It includes Qur'ānic and poetic quotations, and notes that the English language has come to be associated with *al-rifa'a wa al-makāna* [greatness and prestige].

In common with the *Qalā'id al-jumān*, the *New Manual* contains no information on the script or phonology of either language. For the Anglophone user, the Arabic is presented in Roman transcription, but the transcription of Arabic is a notoriously messy business, and no guidance is given on the many 'new' consonants for an English speaker. Confronted, on the very first page, with *al-àoolâd* (a more modern transcription would be *al awlād*: 'the boys'), one can imagine different users of the book coming up with very different pronunciations. (This is the essence of Mr Peasley's problem.) On the second page, we find *Massr* 'Egypt', with the Arabic letter Ṣād rendered by a double 's' — but the user is not told that this is significant. The Arabic speaker learning English is faced with a similar problem in transposing what is on the page to what he or she actually needs to articulate in that no guidance is given on how to pronounce English words whose spelling is illogical. What to make, for example, on page 169, of 'though' and 'thought'? Unlike speakers of some European languages, Arabic speakers (although not in all dialects) have the advantage that their own language differentiates between the phonemes /θ/ and /ð/ as English does. But no explanation is given that these words are pronounced differently.

Overall, the *New Manual* prioritizes the English-speaking user, although not to the same extent as the *Qalā'id al-jumān* does the Arabic. The book's pages turn in the European manner and page numbers are in the numerals used in Europe. The introductory grammar is of 'Vulgar Conversational Arabic', as befits its intended audience of travellers rather than scholars. There is more than one way to view the ensuing presentation of nominal paradigms and verb conjugations. We might argue that Arabic is here being inappropriately crammed into a Latinate model of grammatical description; and that memorizing the imperfect tense of the verb 'to govern' is not likely to be of much use to a tourist on the Nile. (Not least because the British did effectively govern Egypt for much of the nineteenth century, not 'used to govern'.) On the other hand, those of the social class to be able to afford to travel in Egypt will probably have received an education in their own language, and others such as Latin, French and German, along these same grammatical lines. The use of this familiar method of instruction may have helped them to make sense of Arabic more quickly.

Forty-two pages of grammar are followed by a vocabulary, listed according to English alphabetical order, with the English, transcribed Arabic, and Arabic in Arabic script, in three columns. The Arabic-speaking user, referring to the Arabic script in the right-hand column, will have found it difficult to be an active user of this portion of the book. It will have been easier, however, for an English-speaking user to find the word he/she needs and point to the Arabic. The following section of familiar phrases and conversation opens with greetings and enquiries after the person's health and that of their family, one's comings and goings, eating and drinking. There are passages which will have been of equal interest to English tourists and Egyptians who came into contact with them: numerous ways of apologizing; making requests; and affirming or denying things; expressing surprise; assessing probability; and apportioning blame. There is little here that is specific to any one situation. The user could refer to this for help in everything from negotiating the price of a boat trip to making polite chit-chat. The following dialogues are, however, more securely social in nature, with only some small samples of conversations with a laundress or a donkey boy, or haggling in a shop. The user learns not only how to say 'Will you have a glass of beer?' (*tereed kâss beera*) but 'Will you have another glass of beer?' (*tereed kâss beera kamân*). If the traveller is not a beer drinker, he can respond *biddi ashrab kâss nebeed* [I like to have a glass of wine]. The *New Manual* concludes with a remarkably long section on playing cards. The loser has the final line of the book: *iza kân gâni warah tayyib kont àla'b ahhsan* [I could play better if I had a good hand]. A tourist who bought Nakhlah's book would be well equipped for a night out in the 'coffee' houses of Cairo. On the other hand, the book glosses over differences between the spoken dialect of Egypt and formal written Arabic. This is clearest, to the Arabophone user, in the dialogues, where the romanized Arabic presents the dialect version (*ma tehottish feeh sokkar keteer* [Don't put much sugar in it]), but the Arabic script gives the formal standard (*lā taḍ'a fîha sukkar kathīran*). These problems of register and dialect were confronted more directly by later writers.

Arabic Self-Taught

More tourist-oriented Arabic language instruction books catering to Europeans date back at least as far as Philipp Wolff's *Arabischer Dragoman* of 1857. From the 1880s, an increasing number of works were published that were specifically marketed to tourists in Egypt by publishers who were already catering to the tourist market within Europe. These often ran through several editions and revisions; and the changes — or lack of change — they underwent can be revealing. One of the most frequently reissued was *Arabic Self-Taught, or the Dragoman for Travellers in Egypt*, first published in 1883 in Franz Thimm's series of 'Classical, European and Oriental Grammars, after an Easy and Practical Method', published in London and Leipzig. While earlier popular Arabic instruction manuals had not vaunted the easiness, or otherwise, of learning the language, Thimm's series promised results.

The author of *Arabic Self-Taught* is named on the title page of the 1883 edition as 'A. Hassam', an error for (Muhammad) Anton Hassan. Hassan came to Austria in 1837 with a group of Egyptian students who had been sent to study mining engineering (Chahrour 2007). After several years' study, Hassan dropped out and found a job as proof-reader for Oriental languages in the government printing office in Vienna. In

1852 — Christian baptism in the meantime having improved his career prospects — Hassan took up a post teaching Arabic at the Kaiserlich-Königliches Polytechnisches Institut to students who needed Arabic for commerce and professional use. He was respected as a teacher of colloquial Arabic, but his attempts to gain an academic position at the University of Vienna were unsuccessful, because he did not know Classical Arabic. Hassan's teaching philosophy was that, although grammar might be taught well by a European teacher, practice with a native speaker was essential to learn to speak the language well. Speaking and reading were two separate skills: 'I know well that a person can speak a language and yet not be in a position read it' (Chahrour 2007: 134). Hassan ran popular Arabic courses at the Polytechnic and at the Oriental Academy, but he suffered from financial problems and poor health. He made an extended visit to Egypt in 1871–75 to recuperate. He died after his return in Vienna — during an especially harsh winter — in March 1876.

How did Hassan, an Arabic-German bilingual who died in Austria in 1876, come to be the author of an English guide to self-instruction in Arabic that was published after his death in 1883? Trying to puzzle out the answer tells us much about the language-publishing business in the late nineteenth century. Hassan had produced an *Arabisches Lesebuch* in 1855 for German-speaking students of colloquial Arabic. This was informed by his own experience as an Arabic teacher, and in particular by his frustration at the lack of good teaching materials then available for colloquial, as opposed to classical, Arabic. In 1869, he brought out a more comprehensive textbook, his *Kurzgefasste Grammatik der Vulgär-Arabischen Sprache, mit besonderer Rücksicht auf den Egyptischen Dialekt*. After many years of teaching colloquial Arabic to students in Austria, he still felt that the available teaching materials were not up to scratch, and that there was a great need for a concise and moderately priced textbook. As he put it in the Preface: 'So mancher Hörer und wohl auch so mancher Lehrer des Vulgar-arabischen an öffentlichen Anstalten wird das Bedürfniss eines kurzgefassten und nicht zu kostspieligen Lehrbuches dieser Sprache langst gefühlt haben' [Many a student and probably many a teacher of colloquial Arabic in public institutions will have long felt the need of a short and not too expensive textbook of this language]. Although this is a textbook for students in an academic institution, Hassan introduces some touches more commonly found in popular phrasebooks. Grammatical points, for example, are typically illustrated with more than a dozen sample sentences which might be used for conversation practice in class or social interaction. It is made clear to the student that the grammar they are learning has a practical application. As well as reading exercises, Hassan's *Kurzgefasste Grammatik* also contains conversational phrases. In the section 'Vom Sprechen' [On Speaking], we find Hassan's hope for his students: *ílli jásma' kalâmak jazúnn ánnak ibn 'árab* — 'Wenn man Sie sprechen hört, hält man Sie für einen Araber' [To hear you speak one would take you for an Arab].

Hassan's grammar of 1869, however, has no material in common with *Arabic Self-Taught*. The latter is not simply a translation of an earlier German work. The format it follows is that of the rest of the series in which it was published, Thimm's 'Self-Taught' manuals for various European and Asian languages. Franz Louis Julius

Thimm (1820-1889) was a German bookseller with business premises in Manchester and London — Friedrich Engels was a customer (Reed 2007: 110-11). His first 'Self-Taught' books were for German and Italian, both issued in 1861. The format was successful, and the range of languages offered expanded greatly until it included most of the major languages of Europe, the Middle East and Asia — or at least those that might be needed by a British tourist or soldier. Later, the series was taken over by Franz's son Carl, who led a colourful personal life and was frequently in debt. Contemporary reviewers noted a consequent decline in the books' quality.

Where, then, does Anton Hassan's *Arabic Self-Taught* of 1883 fit into the chequered history of Thimm language books? The book has not been compiled from any surviving publications by Hassan of which I am aware; no text, for example, is taken from his 1869 grammar. It may be a manuscript that was left unfinished or unpublished at his death. It may be a project on which he worked during his stay in Cairo in the early 1870s, at the same time as Nakhlah and others were publishing guides to Arabic for English speakers. Franz Thimm, as a German bookseller, may have stocked Hassan's publications and come to know his work in that way, and then approached him to contribute to the *Self-Taught* series. Or it may even be that Hassan had no involvement in the work at all, but that his name was 'borrowed' because he was a well-known teacher of colloquial Arabic. We are simply not in a position to know. In my following discussion, the reader may wish to imagine the author 'Hassan' in inverted commas. I shall review the original 1883 publication, and then examine its place within the evolving *Self-Taught* series.

Hassan's *Arabic Self-Taught* follows the method and format of other books in the series: pronunciation; vocabulary in categories; a grammar; practical phrases; and a dictionary. All books in the series are short and in a compact format; they are very portable. A tourist might walk around a town with a copy in his/her bag or pocket, referring to it where necessary. Inside the front cover of *Arabic Self-Taught* we find advertisements for other books published by Franz Thimm on a wide range of other languages, according to the same learning method. The books are priced at between three and five shillings, an affordable sum for middle- or upper-class tourists.

Arabic Self-Taught addresses a number of new subjects to those in the less exclusively touristically minded Arabic manuals published in Cairo in the preceding decades: dialect, phonology, script — and the challenge of Arabic for a European learner. Hassan's initial advice to the student may be best summarized as 'Don't panic'. He describes the beauty, history and spirituality of Arabic, and continues:

> To an English eye, the Arabic Letters appear at first sight very puzzling and difficult and this is chiefly the reason why travellers think it impossible to learn Eastern Languages; besides which, the manner of imparting these languages has hitherto been of an old grammatical and forbidding form; but Eastern languages are not difficult to acquire, on the contrary, they are easily learnt, and any ordinary capacity can acquire a knowledge of them in a short time. (Hassam 1883: vi)

The secret, Hassan claims, is slow and steady practice, not taking on too much at a time. The learner should learn vocabulary by speaking and listening to words as well as reading them. Throughout the grammar and vocabulary, the English is accompanied by the Arabic in Arabic script, and in Roman script, so that even a learner who has not mastered the alphabet can still use the book.

Hassan cautions that it is not possible to transcribe Arabic sounds precisely, and that the beginner should learn by listening to native speakers — drawing upon his own experience of teaching colloquial Arabic. The descriptions and rules he adopts include some which will be familiar to many more recent learners of Arabic. Guidance is given on the pronunciation of vowels in transcription, to get by the problem of irregularities in English spelling and pronunciation. I shall take two Arabic consonants as 'canaries in the mine' of Arabic phonology in the popular language works I discuss: *ḫa'*, the voiceless velar or uvular fricative; and *'ayn*, the voiced pharyngeal fricative. *ḫa'*, according to Hassan, 'is pronounced like the German *ch* in *ich*, or like the Scotch word "loch"'. *'ayn* 'is a guttural, peculiar to the Semitic languages, which can only be learned by ear. [...] It also sounds like the bleating of a goat'. We shall see how other authors handle these.

The list of practical phrases is shaped closely to a traveller's needs, beginning not with the typical courtesies, but with the interactions they are likely to need to have in Arabic at the very beginning of their stay: making requests or orders to servants or hoteliers. The reader learns first to say 'Give me some bread' and 'Bring me some milk', before proceeding to greetings. Less immediate concerns, such as telling the time and talking about the weather, follow, then more complex scenarios: giving directions, discussing prices, and language difficulties. Words to use to a bothersome person escalate quickly from *rûḥ bakâ* [Be gone] to *rûḥ lil-gehennum* [literally: Go to Hell], expressed with Victorian circumspection as 'Go to the d — l'. The phrases conclude with the tourist, having settled into Eastern life, ready to go out on a trip, giving orders to dragomans about starting times and horses.

The closing pages of *Arabic Self-Taught* mirror its opening pages: it concludes with an advertisement for Thimm's forthcoming series on other Oriental languages, which makes the Thimm 'unique selling point' clear:

> All Oriental Grammars hitherto published have been for the learned, nothing has been done for the general Public, and for them this Series is intended. That it shall be possible for any one to take up the study of an Eastern Language without a master has been the Editor's ruling idea. (Hassam 1883: no pagn)

Anton Hassan may not have agreed that learning colloquial Arabic without a teacher was either possible or desirable.

The first edition of *Arabic Self-Taught*, in 1883, was published while Franz Thimm was still alive, although his son Carl was already involved in the business. Despite the decline in the quality of the *Self-Taught* books during Carl's tenure in the 1890s, Arabic was not severely affected. *Self-Taught* books in the latter part of the 1890s and into the 1900s were now published under the aegis of 'E. Marlborough & Co.' — perhaps a sale to help relieve Thimm's debt. Thimm was, however, still credited as author, and the language instruction was advertised as according to 'Thimm's Method'. A new edition of *Arabic Self-Taught*, under the title *Egyptian Self-Taught*, appeared in 1897/98. Reviews praised its user-friendliness:

> with a little book like this in one's hand, a traveller will enjoy a sojourn
> in Egypt in a much greater degree than when he is totally ignorant of the
> languages. The series of books in which it is included is now very well known,
> and this volume seems no exception to the carefulness usually exercised in their
> production. (*Booksellers' Review*, 8 April 1897)

The fifth edition of *Egyptian Self-Taught (Arabic) for Tourists, Travellers, Soldiers & c.*
appeared in 1914, and shows a dramatic evolution from Hassan's original *Arabic
Self-Taught* of 1883. Aside from the title and the place in Thimm's series, little is the
same. Hassan's name is long gone from the title page, replaced with that of Major
R. A. Marriott, who had been responsible for the work's more militarily minded
revision some years before. Marriott (1857-1930) had served with the Egyptian Army
in the 1880s, including with the Camel Corps on the Gordon Relief Expedition
in the Sudan in 1884-85. Inside, we find one Negib Hindié credited for providing
supplementary vocabulary; no further information is given on him. Flinders Petrie
reviewed the proofs. In place of Hassan's reassuring words about mastering Arabic,
Marriott opens with a defence of the Egyptian dialect. Some of the explanatory text
is reproduced verbatim from Hassan, although a slightly different system is used for
transcribing Arabic. Although the Arabic alphabet is introduced, it is not used in the
book. The pronunciation of the letters *ḥa'* and *'ayn* is described slightly differently
from Hassan's book. For *ḥa'*, the same comparison is made with German and the
Scottish word *loch*, but the (presumably bemused) reader is further told that '[i]n
Egyptian it is rendered harder by placing the muscles of the throat as in clearing it'.
For *'ayn*, the user is reassured that '[i]t can be attained by practice, and is a vowel-
sound produced far back and down in the throat. Special throat muscles must be
developed to produce it, so that a European can never imitate the sound at first
attempt' (Marriott & Hindié 1921: 8). Hassan's descriptions of the sounds, as a native
speaker and experienced teacher, offer clearer guidance than Marriott's, although
neither necessarily ensures that the user will pronounce these sounds correctly.

Like Hassan, Marriott divides his vocabulary and phrases into functional categories, but new to this version is an extensive section of military terms, as might
be expected from Marriott's own experience, and terms for use by Christian missionaries. The grammatical section which follows is much shorter than Hassan's,
and tailored to the Egyptian dialect. Like Hassan, Marriott leads his practical
phrases with instructions rather than greetings, but the former are harsher and more
numerous. By the third page, the reader already knows to say *huwa sakrān* [He is
drunk] and *huwa taḥt 'eydi* [He is under my orders], and many other statements and
reprimands in a similar vein. The reader is provided with a section on Egyptian
weights, measures and currency, but the extensive dictionary of Hassan is lacking.
I shall return to the practical uses of this book below.

In 1911, Marlborough issued another variation on the theme of Hassan's,
Thimm's and Marriott's book under the title *Marlborough's Arabic (Syrian) Self-Taught*.
It announces on the cover that: 'This system teaches you the essentials of a lang-
uage (for travel and enjoyment) without the drudgery of prolonged study'. This

time it did bear Hassan or Hassam's name on the cover, with a note that it had been revised and enlarged by Rev. N. Odeh. Naser Odeh was a Syrian clergyman resident in England, who was one of T. E. Lawrence's first Arabic teachers. The Preface explains that '[t]he present enlarged edition of *Arabic-Self Taught* is to all intents and purposes a new work. It has practically been rewritten throughout', and that the text has been adapted to 'modern requirements'. Hassan's comforting words on learning a challenging language are then reproduced, long after Marriott had excised them from his Egyptian version of the work. Odeh teaches the Arabic script, and, in contrast to Marriott, does use it throughout the book, alongside English transcription. He uses a more modernized form of transcription for Arabic. His explanations of how to pronounce *ḥa'* and *'ayn* are identical to Hassan's. We find the same kind of listing of useful vocabulary as in Hassan and Marriott (minus the military obsession, but keeping the religious section). The grammar, for the first time, explains Arabic grammatical categories and terms, and gives the user exercises to practice, all with example sentences tailored to the needs of travellers. The section on the expression of the English Potential and Subjunctive in Arabic is not as dry as it sounds, and includes phrases that a traveller might actually hear or use, such as *la naqdar nakhruj al-yaum bisabab-il-maṭar-il-qawi* [We cannot go out today on account of the heavy rain] or *'alaik an tat'allam al-'arabīyah* [You should learn Arabic]. The section of conversational phrases begins with instructions and greetings; and the sections on a traveller's needs in terms of catching trains, shopping or staying at a hotel are extensive. The leisure traveller's every need is catered for, from *nārīd naṭla' lifauqi-l-nadīdh* [We want to go up the minaret], to *la tansa-l-nabīdh* [Do not forget the wine].

Using the Books

The various editions and revisions of *Arabic Self-Taught*, from the 1880s to the 1910s, reveal much about the changing needs — or perceived changing needs — of learners and about European colonial activity in the Middle East. Major Marriott's is the most overt. Yet even Hassan's 1883 work already taught military terms such as 'deserter', 'infantry', 'officer', 'squadron (fleet)', 'squadron (cavalry)'. My own copy bears an inscription inside the front cover: 'S. Churchill Lt RSF [Royal Scots Fusiliers] Thayetmyo B.B. [British Burma] 26/11/85'. The owner (not a member of the famous Churchill family) was evidently a soldier who had served in Egypt in the British campaigns of 1884-85, although why the inscription was written in Burma, presumably his next posting, is unclear.

In 1890, Rev. Joseph Llewellyn Thomas published a memoir of his travels in the Middle East, in which he offered the following advice:

> You cannot always fall back upon a dragoman; so, if you are a monoglot, you will be a very helpless being indeed in the East. [...] As regards languages, my next advice to the reader who contemplates a visit to Egypt is, 'Get up a little Arabic.' Even French will not go everywhere. A slight acquaintance with Arabic will go far to make you feel at home in Egypt. It is very generally taken up by foreign residents in that country. General Grenfell is fast becoming a proficient in that language, and the subordinate English officers have also set themselves

to learning it. There is a very useful handbook, written by an English officer, which makes the acquisition of conversational Arabic a comparatively simple matter. (Thomas 1890: 32)[3]

The book mentioned by Thomas is probably Major Arthur Octavius Green's *Practical Arabic Grammar* (Green 1883). This was dedicated to Lt-General Stephenson, Commander of the British Army of Occupation in Egypt, and was issued to British soldiers and police. My copy of the second edition, of 1887, reveals its history of ownership and use. I can find no trace of the first owner of the book. Thirty years after it was printed, it was rebound and the cover labelled in gilt letters 'Lieut. A. H. Corble, R.G.A. Khartoum'. Archibald Harrison Corble (1883-1944) served with the Royal Garrison Artillery in the Sudan and Egypt during the First World War. Corble, or a subsequent owner, took good care of the book, reinforcing torn pages neatly with paper backing. In 1947 a new owner signed his name (now illegible) inside the front cover, below Corble's, with the subscription 'Medani, Sudan Dec '47'. This single copy was put to practical use by British soldiers over at least sixty years.

Marriott's *Egyptian Self-Taught* is a product of his military service in Egypt some decades earlier, but annotations in my copy of the 1915 edition reveal an ongoing relevance to the British military. Inside the front cover is a list headed 'Nautical Terms' in English and romanized Arabic. The user has practised a few words in Arabic script on the appropriate page. He has also added some items of vocabulary: crab, lobster, prawn, cockroach, sweater, 'snappy piece' referring to a woman (*helwa*, *bint zeyn*), and a discreet word for toilet (*mahall el adeb* [place of politeness]). He notes Arabic numerals, and Arabic military ranks, with drawings of the appropriate insignia. He also makes corrections: *mushīr* is not the term used for Field-Marshal in Egypt; and 'pipe' is pronounced *bib*.

These annotations offer an insight into how these language books were actually used, in a colonial context, by soldiers and sailors, whether trying to communicate about technical matters, or picking up girls. Sometimes, as with 'pipe' and 'bib', they reveal the differences users might encounter between what the book told them, and what they heard from native speakers in Egypt. Most of all, they show that practice with native speakers, and learning new words in context, had the best results.

The Dragoman

The dragoman — guide and interpreter — is a constant presence in these books. A book may be aimed at dragomans as language learners (*Instructions aux Drogmans / Qalā'id al-jumān fī fawā'id al-tarjumān*); or it may present itself as a substitute for a dragoman, as in Hassan's *Arabic Self-Taught, or the Dragoman for Travellers in Egypt*. In his Preface, Hassan offers the reader the possibility of becoming 'his own dragoman' by learning Arabic (Hassam 1883: vi). The metaphor of the language book as dragoman recurs in a number of works which I do not have the space here to discuss, over more than a hundred years: *Arabischer Dragoman* (Wolff 1857); *Le Drogman arabe* (Harfouch 1894); *Le Dragoman — vocabulaire du voyageur* (Elias 1935); and *The Dragoman in the Pocket* (Gayed 1965). At least one actual dragoman published

Arabic instruction books for foreigners: Rev. Anton, or Antonio, Tien (1834-1920), author of a *Manual of Colloquial Arabic* which went through many editions (Tien 1885).

Tien's early life is recounted in a history of his alma mater, St Augustine's College, Canterbury:

> A member of one of the most ancient families of the Lebanon Maronites, he was in early life selected to succeed to the patriarchate, and with this intent was sent to Rome to pursue his studies at the Propaganda, where he remained for several years. The course of events however led to his taking a sea-voyage as tutor to a devout Englishman, and the result of their reading their bibles and praying together was that Tien recognised the superior purity of the Anglican faith, and, sacrificing his prospects of becoming Patriarch of the Maronites, came to England, bearing letters of introduction to Mr. Gladstone. [...] [H] e went out in 1860 to Constantinople, where he found that his knowledge of oriental languages and religions equipped him with a store of arguments to be used in controversy with the Turks. (Boggis 1907: 195-96)

In Constantinople, Tien found that instruction in English and other European languages was a great enticement to Muslim Turkish parents to send their sons to Mission schools — where they might be evangelized.

Tien served in the Crimean War (1853-56). He had some contact with Prince George, Duke of Cambridge, to whom the *Manual of Colloquial Arabic* is dedicated. It is this service that is hyped on the title pages to Tien's publications. His *Levant Interpreter* of 1879 introduces him as '[f]ormerly first-class interpreter to the Allied force in the Crimea', while the *Manual of Colloquial Arabic*, among his other positions and qualifications, notes that he was '[f]ormerly Oriental Secretary on Lord Baglan's staff during the Crimean campaign'.

During the 1870s and 1880s, Tien pursued his career in England. In 1871, a newspaper reported — erroneously — that he had 'abjured the Christian faith and embraced Mohammedanism' (*Courier Journal* (Louisville, Kentucky), 16 July 1871). In 1874 he attended the International Congress of Orientalists in London, where *The Times* noted his presence: 'This gentleman is a native of Turkey, in whose official hierarchy he bears rank' (21 September 1874). He worked with the resident Muslim community in London and in 1878 reported to the General Conference on Foreign Missions on his efforts. The culmination of this career as a respectable Victorian clergyman and Orientalist came in 1886 in a meeting between a visiting Sheikh from Muscat, in charge of Arab horses for Queen Victoria, and the Queen's representatives, Lord Cross and Sir Henry Ponsonby.: 'Rev. Antonio Tien acted as interpreter, and has been requested to attend on the Sheikh during his stay in England' (*The Times*, 2 December 1886).

Why this excursus into Reverend Tien's life and career? Because it offers insights into how and why he produced the language books he did, and for what audiences. *The Levant Interpreter: A Polyglot Dialogue Book for English Travellers in the Levant* (Tien 1879) is one of his earliest publications. By this date, Tien's career had taken him from Lebanon, to Rome, to London, the Crimea and Constantinople. He knew several languages and had worked professionally as an interpreter. The *Levant Interpreter* offers words and phrases in four columns: English, Turkish, Italian and

Greek. The layout is simple and elegant. The Preface states: 'Owing to the number of nationalities dwelling in the Levant, language there is necessarily cosmopolitan; and as English travellers are seldom conversant with Oriental tongues, this Interpreter is offered to them' (no pagn). He explains that he has used romanized renderings of Turkish and Greek, and that the Greek is colloquial, not classical. The book comprises around 150 pages of words and phrases useful to a traveller, and concludes with Bible passages. There is no section on grammar. Tien's *Egyptian, Syrian and North-African Hand-Book* of 1882 was billed as 'a simple phrasebook in English and Arabic for the use of the armed forces and civilians'. It is, as the title suggests, a pared down version of some of the other works I have discussed, with only listings of vocabulary by category, phrases and a dictionary with transcribed Arabic, and no grammar or phonology. It was reprinted as late as 1954.

It was Tien's *Manual of Colloquial Arabic* which enjoyed the greatest success: it ran through at least six editions, into the 1900s. Tien's Preface contains reflections on the utility of teaching Arabic to English speakers, and the means by which it is best achieved. The colonial and military context is constantly in the background. He does not need to specify why 'there is no country in Western Europe to which the encouragement of the study of Arabic should be a matter of more vital interest than England' (Tien 1885: v). The imperative for the learning of colloquial Arabic, in Tien's view, was more than demonstrated by previous British military difficulties in communicating with troops and prisoners. He notes his encounters with Russian officers in the Crimean War who spoke excellent, idiomatic Arabic, and the success of Arabic teaching schools for the Italian Army. He does not need to press his point. Previous instruction books glossed over the differences between Arabic dialects. Tien explains these clearly, and states that he will be giving precedence to the Egyptian and Syrian dialects. He also acknowledges the difficulties in transcribing Arabic. The 'unique selling point' of his book, he claims, is that:

> an attempt has been made for the first time to adapt the construction of Arabic Grammar to the Western mind, with the object of removing what has hitherto been the greatest stumbling-block to the acquisition of the Arabic language by European students. (Tien 1885: x)

What does Tien mean by this? His grammar turns out to proceed by Arabic grammatical categories and terms, and not to force Arabic to confirm to the grammar of English or Latin — for the most part. On page 21, however, we find a nominal declension of the nouns *walad*, *bayt* and *kitâb*. Arabic, or at least Classical Arabic, does have case endings (nominative, accusative and genitive), but these are not what this table teaches. Instead, the reader is told either than the noun does not modify in a particular case, or is given a 'case' created with a preposition.

And so to Tien's phonology of Arabic. *ḥa'* is 'a strong guttural, as in the Scotch *loch*'. (What someone who knew nothing of Scotland was to make of this now-standard description, I do not know.) *'ayn* is simply a 'guttural sound'. As the book progresses, it becomes clear that this is not simply a phrasebook but, as the title suggests, a manual. There is an extensive grammar and syntax, and reading exercises, as well as dialogues and vocabulary.

Tien's *Manual of Colloquial Arabic* spoke to a different audience from that of his simpler *Egyptian, Syrian and North-African Hand-Book* of a few years previously. It was intended for serious study, by an educated user. Remarks throughout suggest that this is an army officer. In my copy of the fifth edition, we find confirmation of both intent and result. The advertisements inside the cover offer books on other languages of the British Empire: Andamanese, Bengali, Burmese, Chinese, Hindustani. An ink inscription inside reads 'Thomas B. Matheson, Capt. Staff Capt (P) Government Jerusalem 14:VIII:18'. Tien's manual was being used by a British officer in Jerusalem, recently captured from the Ottomans, in the First World War.

Tien later published similar grammars of Modern Greek and Turkish, and translations (including the Book of Common Prayer and the Apology of al-Kindi), from Arabic into English and English into Arabic. He was a versatile user and teacher of languages. At the time of the 1911 English census he was living in Hampstead, and is listed as a clergyman in the Church of England and also as a 'Professor, King's College London'; he was perhaps teaching Arabic in his retirement.

Conclusion

Examining the professional and personal lives of their authors, publishers and users offers us a perspective on popular Arabic language instruction manuals which takes us beyond the words on the page. Over the course of the nineteenth and early twentieth centuries, the market for such books changed. Early pioneers in Egypt, such as Khalīfah ibn Maḥmūd al-Miṣrī and Yacoub Nakhlah, were interested in teaching Egyptians European languages as well, or even more than, teaching Europeans Arabic. Arabic teachers and the manuals they produced responded to the changing needs of European learners. From the 1860s, the period at which Egypt opened to mass tourism, tourists were a dependable market for language books — so long as these were simple in format, portable, moderately priced, and taught them phrases they might actually need on their holiday. Whether these enabled many tourists to speak more than a few words of Arabic, badly mispronounced, is in many ways irrelevant. Tourists wanted to try some Arabic, authors set out to help them, and publishers sold books.

Between the casual leisure learner and the scholar of Classical Arabic there was a wide spectrum of abilities and needs. Many authors and revisers of popular Arabic manuals had specific groups of learners in mind. As a teacher of colloquial Arabic, Anton Hassan knew that learning to read Arabic and learning to converse in it were two very different things. In his publications for use by his students, or other learners for commercial or tourist purposes, he aimed to demystify Arabic and to help learners acquire phrases that they might use in specific, practical contexts. This social context of language acquisition and use had also been stressed, less explicitly, by Nakhlah some years earlier. Nakhlah's readers learn how to socialize with Egyptians over beers and games of cards.

The chequered history of the *Self-Taught* series of language books helps us to place

Arabic materials in their wider context. The lure of being able to learn a language quickly and easily attracted buyers to 'Thimm's Method' and the results it promised. The quality of individual books within this series varied — especially after Carl Thimm took over from his father. The many revisions of *Arabic Self-Taught* show that language books were not just for tourists. The British Army was an important market, and annotations in contemporary copies of Arabic manuals show that these were indeed bought and used by soldiers.

Mr Peasley's growing frustration as he tried to use his 'Arabic at a Glance' to talk to an Egyptian policeman was doubtless shared by many initially keen purchasers of phrasebooks. His experience, told though it is for comedic effect, reveals the critical weakness of popular Arabic self-instruction manuals: the user must convert the written word into the spoken word. I very much doubt that a user of any of the books which I have discussed would have been able accurately to produce an *'ayn* from the instructions in the book alone. Writers such as Hassan and Petrie who told readers that there was no real alternative to practice with native speakers offered the best advice of all.

Bibliography

ADE, GEORGE. 1906. *In Pastures New* (New York: McClure, Phillips)

BECHRAOUI, MAHAMMED-FADHEL. 2001. 'La Grammaire française à l'usage des Arabes (1854) de Gustave Dugat et Fārès Echchidiāk', *Histoire Épistémologie Langage*, 23: 107-26

BOGGIS, R. J. E. 1907. *A History of St. Augustine's College, Canterbury* (Canterbury: Cross and Jackman)

CHAHROUR, MARCEL. 2007. '"Vom Morgenhauch aufstrebender Cultur durchweht." Ägyptische Studenten in Österreich 1830-1945', in *Von Soliman zu Omofuma: Afrikanische Diaspora in Österreich 17. bis 20. Jahrhundert*, ed. by Walter Sauer (Innsbruck: Studien), pp. 131-50

ELIAS, MITRI. 1935. *Le dragoman — vocabulaire du voyageur: français, anglais, arabe* (Cairo: Elias' Modern Press)

GAYED, RIAD. 1965. *The Dragoman in the Pocket* (Cairo: Anglo Egyptian Bookshop)

GREEN, ARTHUR OCTAVIUS. 1883. *Practical Arabic Grammar* (Cairo: Boulack Printing Office)

HARFOUCH, JOSEPH. 1894. *Le Drogman arabe, ou, Guide pratique de l'arabe parlé en caractères figurés: pour le Syrie, la Palestine et l'Egypte* (Beirut: Librairie de l'imprimerie catholique)

HASSAM, A. 1883. *Arabic Self-Taught, or the Dragoman for Travellers in Egypt* (London: Thimm)

MAIRS, RACHEL. 2016. *From Khartoum to Jerusalem: The Dragoman Solomon Negima and his Clients, 1885–1933* (London: Bloomsbury)

——, and MAYA MURATOV. 2015. *Archaeologists, Tourists, Interpreters: Exploring Egypt and the Near East in the late 19th–early 20th Centuries* (London: Bloomsbury)

MARRIOT, REGINALD ADAMS. 1911. *Arabic (Syrian) Self-Taught. Thimm's system*, Marlborough's Self-Taught Series (London: E. Marlborough)

——, and NEGIB HINDIÉ. 1921. *Egyptian Self-Taught (Arabic). Thimm's system*, Marlborough's Self-Taught Series (London: E. Marlborough)

AL-MIṢRĪ, KHALĪFAH IBN MAHMŪD. 1850. *Qalā' id al-jumān fī fawā' id al-tarjumān / Instructions aux drogmans* (Būlāq: al-Maṭabaʿ ah al-ʿ Āmirah)

NAKHLAH, YACOUB. 1874. *New Manual of English and Arabic Conversation* (Būlāq: The Khedive's Press)

NEWMAN, DANIEL L. 2004. *An Imam in Paris: Account of a Stay in France by an Egyptian Cleric (1826–1831)* (London: Safi)

PETRIE, W. M. FLINDERS. 1892. *Ten Years' Digging in Egypt (1881–1891)* (New York: Revell)

REED, SUSAN. 2007. 'German Printers, Publishers and Booksellers in Nineteenth-century Britain', in *Migration and Transfer from Germany to Britain, 1660–1914*, ed. by Stefan Manz, Margrit Schulte Beerbühl and John R. Davis (Berlin: de Gruyter), pp. 107-18

SØRENSEN, LOUISE MUNCH. 2011. 'Popular Language Works and the Autonomous Language Learner in 19th-Century Scandinavia', *Histoire Épistémologie Langage*, 33: 28-38

THOMAS, JOSEPH LLEWELLYN. 1890. *Oxford to Palestine* (London: Leadenhall)

TIEN, ANTON. 1879. *The Levant Interpreter: A Polyglot Dialogue Book for English Travellers in the Levant* (London: Williams and Norgate)

——. 1885. *Manual of Colloquial Arabic* (London: Allen)

WOLFF, PHILIPP. 1857. *Arabischer Dragoman für Besucher des Heiligen Landes* (Leipzig: Weber)

Notes to Chapter 8

1. An unkind critic might point out that Mr. Peasley, who does not know that the correct English plural of ignoramus is ignoramuses, not ignorami, is not much of a linguist either.
2. See <www.kent.ac.uk/ewto/projects/teaching-of-arabic/index.html>.
3. On Thomas and his dragoman in Syria, see further Mairs 2016: 185-90.

CHAPTER 9

❖

The History of Teaching and Learning German in Africa: The Case of Cameroon

Vera E. Boulleys

One of the notable changes which the annexation of Cameroon by Germany on 14 July 1884 brought in Cameroonian society was in the domain of education, and, more precisely, in the establishment of formal school systems. It is worth noting that this initiative to establish formal schools in Cameroon had nothing to do with charity; rather, it was part of overall colonial policies. The establishment of schools was one of the demands of the Congo Acts of November 1884, which required that schools be opened in the colonized and annexed territories (Schlunk 1914: 14). The opening of schools brought along its own problems: which language should be used as the language of instruction in these schools? The discussions and debates about the language of instruction were summarized under the theme *Sprachenfrage* [language question],[1] at the end of which German was adopted as the main language of instruction from the second school year. With the defeat of Germany in 1916, another drastic change occurred in the educational landscape of the colonies and protectorates. Under the League of Nations the former German colonies and protectorates in Africa came under the Mandate governance of Britain and France. Seven eighths of Cameroon (East Cameroon) came under French administration and one eighth (West Cameroon) under British administration. During this period, German ceased both to be the official language and to be offered as a subject in schools in Cameroon. When Cameroon gained independence in 1960, German and Spanish were re-introduced in Cameroon alongside English and French, which had earlier been adopted as the official languages of Cameroon.[2] The teaching and learning of German, which was then resumed, continues to the present day. This chapter thus seeks to trace the evolution of the teaching and learning of German in Cameroon from the colonial period to the present, where it still occupies a firm place in the educational system of Cameroon.

Introduction: Background to the Study

The annexation of Cameroon by Germany on 14 July 1884 opened a new page in the history of Cameroon. It brought with it great changes in the geo-political and economic domains, as well as changes in the socio-cultural and linguistic domains. German became the official language of Cameroon. With the establishment of schools, German also became the principal language of instruction. With this decision, the basis for the teaching and learning of German in Cameroon was laid.

However, it is worth noting that the establishment of schools was part of the overall colonial policies. The European powers agreed that the colonizing power not only had rights over the colonies and protectorates but also had obligations to 'develop' their territorial possessions. This in part led to the establishment of schools in the colonies. As the organization of schools was left in the hands of each colonizing power, the teaching and learning of German was done in line with the goals of the German colonial language policy and not according to the communicative need of Cameroonians.

With the defeat of Germany in World War I, former German colonies and protectorates like Cameroon came under the Mandate governance of Britain and France until 1960, when Cameroon gained independence. During this Mandate period German lost its status as the official language of Cameroon as well as its function as the language of instruction.[3]

If Cameroon is often described as 'Africa in miniature', it is due to the multitudes of languages and cultures within its national territories. The major language families in Cameroon include the Afro-Asiatic languages, the Niger-Congo and the Nilo-Saharan languages. The Afro-Asiatic and the Nilo-Saharan languages are spoken mostly in the northern zone of Cameroon and the Niger-Congo languages are spoken in the southern zone. Despite the multitude of Cameroonian languages, only a few of them are widely spoken or even used beyond their geographical locations. The languages that are widely spoken include: Fulfulde (northern regions); Duala (coastal regions); Ewondo and Bulu (south-east and central regions); Mendumba, Ghomala, Yemba and Bamum (western regions); and Lamnso and Kom (north-west regions) (Ethnologue 2009).

Other language varieties include English and French (official languages, L2); Arabic; German and Spanish (foreign languages taught in schools, L3); and recently also Chinese and Italian. The learning of German and Spanish in Cameroon came as a result of demands from the advocates of Cameroon independence in the late 1950s, who demanded an educational system similar to that in France. Consequently, German and Spanish, which were learnt as foreign languages (L2) in the French school system, were also adopted as foreign languages (L3) in the French-speaking part of Cameroon from 1960 onwards when Cameroon gained independence. Recently, due to Cameroon's developing economic relations with countries such as China and Italy, Chinese and Italian are now also learnt in some state universities in Cameroon.

There is also the widespread use of Pidgin English (Cameroon Pidgin English — CPE). CPE is a contact variety which developed along the coastal regions of

Cameroon in the 15th century. Another contact variety is 'Camfranglais' which developed in the 1980s and spoken mostly in the French-speaking of Cameroon. The vocabulary list is drawn from English, French, CPE and the indigenous languages. Since the end of 2000, a social variety 'Kamerdeutsch' (a.k.a. Camfrangdeutsch') has rapidly developed in the Departments of German Studies in Universities in the French-speaking part of Cameroon. It is exclusively used by students of German studies, and its vocabulary list is drawn from German, English, French, CPE and the indigenous languages. But our focus here is mainly on the German language, especially the teaching and learning of German in Cameroon.

This chapter examines the teaching and learning of German in Cameroon from the colonial period to the present, considering the main reasons for teaching and learning German; the main organs for the teaching and learning of German; and the organization of the teaching and learning of German during the different periods in Cameroon's history. The consultation of archive materials, documents and discussions will serve as basis for analysis. This chapter is structured as follows: the first section that follows examines the reasons for the teaching and learning of German during the German colonial period in Cameroon. The main organs for teaching German, the teaching of the German (organization of German lessons) in government and mission schools as well as the motives of Cameroonians for learning German will also be discussed. The second section provides an overview of the teaching and learning of German under the Mandate governments, while the third section considers the circumstances that led to the reintroduction of the teaching and learning of German in Cameroon shortly before and after Cameroon gained independence. The teaching and learning of German in post-colonial Cameroon, as well as the motives of Cameroonians for learning German, will also be examined. Finally, in the last section, the outcome of the teaching and learning of German in Cameroon from the German colonial period to the present day will be looked into.

The Teaching and Learning of German during the German Colonial Period in Cameroon (1884–1916)

The teaching and learning of German in Cameroon during the German colonial period was part of the general policy of political and socio-economic colonization. Education, like the development of infrastructure, was done for the benefit of the colonizing governments and their home countries and not for the colonized. Consequently, the education administered to Cameroonians was tailored to meet the economic needs and goals of the colonizing states. The opening of schools and like-wise the teaching of German were the main instruments used to attain these goals.

For the German colonial government, the use of German was necessary for the daily administration of their territory. Consequently, German was taught to a few Cameroonians who later served as clerks, interpreters and messengers in the colonial government. The reduction of administrative costs was another factor which prompted the teaching of German. Local administrative personnel were far cheaper to employ than those from Germany, whose salaries were extremely high (Hausen 1970:113). The establishment of schools and likewise the teaching of German were intended to produce the skilled labour which was necessary to achieve an increase in production and to transmit German culture to the colonized people. The rivalry between Britain and Germany for dominance in Cameroon, especially in the economic domain, was another motivating factor for the teaching of German. Even though Cameroon was officially recognized as a German territory, British influence was still dominant in Cameroon due to the pre-colonial trade ties that had developed between the two countries.[4] The massive use and spread of German undertaken by the German colonial government was therefore intended to reduce British's influence and also to serve as a symbol of German authority in Cameroon. The teaching of German was thus meant to serve as a political stamp or mark of German authority in Cameroon.

The teaching of German was also used as an instrument to check the development of a sense of belonging among the local population, according to the maxim *divide et impera* [divide and rule]. This sense of belonging was a potential threat to the colonial government, one that necessitated the teaching of German. A memorandum of the Basel Missionary Society in 1913 gives full expression to this hidden motive:

> So far as we know, the intention that none of the indigenous languages should be allowed to become a unifying language, is politically motivated; it is the motto: Divide and conquer! [...] On the one hand, one wants to take away the possibility of binding ethnic groups and people with one another through the use of a common language, and on the other hand one wants to weld the population of the whole colony into a unified people by imposing the use of German on them. (Basler Missionsgesellschaft, E-2, 11 Nr. 18, Bl. 1)[5]

From the above report, one can conclude that the teaching of German was greatly shaped by the political and economic ambitions of the German colonial government.

In addition, for all the missionary societies the teaching and spread of German was seen as a weapon to combat Islam, which was transmitted through Fulfulde, the principal medium of communication in the north of Cameroon.[6] Missionary societies that received subsidies from the government were likewise obliged to teach German in their schools. The Basel Missionary Society was the only missionary society which did not receive any subsidy and consequently continued to teach indigenous languages in most of its schools and was largely free to manage the organization of teaching in its schools with very little interference from the government.

The principal organs for the teaching of German were the government itself and the missionary societies. Three categories of schools were put in place by the German colonial government to maximize their economic goals: the government schools (*Regierungsfortbildungsschule* or *Regierungsschule*); the agricultural schools (*Ackerbauschule*); and the trade schools (*Handwerkerschule*). However, it was only in the government schools that great emphasis was laid on the teaching and learning of German due to the demands in the administrative, educational or commercial domains. In the agricultural schools, greater emphasis was laid on the production of skilled labour.

The Teaching of German in Government Schools and in Subsidized Missionary Schools[7]

Two types of language policy were adopted in the colonized and annexed territories during the German colonial period: a liberal language policy (1884-1910) and a non-liberal language policy (1910-16).[8] The initial liberal language policy facilitated research, codification and standardization of some indigenous languages and also the teaching of these languages — Duala, in the south and Fulfulde in the north — alongside German in government and mission schools. The School Law of 1910 (*Schulordnung*), however, marked the end of the liberal language policy of the German colonial government.[9] From 1910 onwards the government initiated and promoted a more aggressive language policy aimed at spreading the German language. In schools that were opened after 1910, German became the sole language of instruction, but in earlier schools it was still taught alongside the indigenous languages. The outbreak of World War in 1914 put a temporary end to the teaching and learning of German in Cameroon. Until that time, the teaching and learning of German in Cameroon was structured as follows.

The goal of German lessons was the promotion of the knowledge of German and speaking (communicative) skills. Schlunk (1914: 125-26) sums up the teaching goals as follows:[10]

> The pupils should be able to understand German; make themselves understood and express themselves correctly in oral and written German; translate accurately from German into the indigenous language and vice versa, so far as the subjects are simple in content and the language structure does not cause great difficulties.

The total duration of German teaching was five years, introduced from the second school year.[11] The following subjects were offered in the second year: reading, writing and word and sentence formation. For reading, the *Deutsche Fibel* [*German Primer*] was used.[12] In the third and fourth school year, reading, writing and word and sentence formation were likewise taught. In the fourth school year, reading, dictation in German, writing, word formation, suffix structures and interrogative structures of verbs were taught. In the fifth school year, an in-depth study of the subject matter and essay writing in German were programmed.[13]

The teaching aids used were boards, chalks, ink, reading boards and pictures for visual instruction. For German lessons in particular, a slate and an exercise book were used in addition. For reading the *Deutsches Lesebuch* (Eduard Bock 1876) and the *Deutsche Fibel* (Theodor Christaller 1888) were used.[14] Examples of themes in the *Deutsches Lesebuch* included *Herbstfreuden* [the joys of autumn], *die Erdbeere* [the strawberry] and *die Birnbaum* [the pear tree].[15] The themes in the *Deutsche Fibel* included basic knowledge of grammar (conjugation and declension). Writing and translation from the Duala language into German and vice versa were also learnt.

Compared to the teaching personnel of the mission schools, the teachers of the government schools who came from Germany had some educational training. Only the local personnel had no educational training. With the passing of the School Law in 1910, schools created before the School Law of 1910 maintained German and Duala and Fulfulde as the languages of instruction, but for the newly created schools, German became the sole language of instruction from the first school year.

The Teaching of German in the Basel Mission Schools

The goal of teaching German in the Basel Mission schools was to promote oral and written skills in German. Knowledge of German grammar, reading and the understanding of short essays in German were also aimed at. For German in the middle schools in Bonaberi, Lobethal and Buea in 1897 the syllabus was conceived as follows (Basel Mission Archive, E-10.25, 7; Boulleys 1998: 87-88): German was taught for six hours a week and the content was taken exclusively from Christaller's primer. Translation exercises, the learning of poems and word construction were also part of the syllabus. Visual aids were used. The majority of teachers had no pedagogical training, not even the European teachers themselves. Furthermore, they had a heavy workload because they were preachers and pastoral workers at the same time.

After the School Laws of 1910 the teaching program for the German lessons and other disciplines in all the schools were harmonized.

	Government schools	Basel Mission Schools	Catholic mission schools	American Presbyterian schools	German Baptist mission schools	Total
No. of schools	6	275	112	97	41	531
No. of pupils	879	131,129	10,456	7013	2 640	152,117
No. of teachers	18 (9 Europeans and 9 indigenous teachers)	311 (25 Europeans and 286 indigenous teachers)	176 (37 Europeans and 139 indigenous teachers)	175 (13 Europeans and 162 indigenous teachers)	62 (13 Europeans and 49 indigenous teachers)	742 (97 Europeans and 645 indigenous teachers)

TABLE 1. Pupils Learning German in Schools in Cameroon before the Outbreak of World War I (1913) (Boulleys 1998: 90)

Table 1 shows that education in Cameroon was principally in the hands of the missionary societies, which were mainly based in the south. Only one government school was opened in the North (in Garoua). Consequently, the majority of Cameroonians who attended school and learned German were based in the south. Likewise, the influence of German on the structure of the indigenous languages was stronger in the south than in the north of Cameroon. There were 152,117 Cameroonians learning German and 742 teachers teaching that language during the German colonial period in Cameroon.

Motives of Cameroonians for Learning German during the German Colonial Period

Motivation — whether integrative or instrumental (Gardner 1981: 510-25) — constitutes one of the affective variables of language learning. It includes all the factors that contribute positively to the learning of a second or target language. Integrative motivation is backed by the learner's desire to be integrated into the target community. Instrumental motivation has to do mainly with the social and economic benefits attached to learning the target language. This was the motivation that many Cameroonians had in learning German during the German colonial period. One of the motivational factors for the learning of German during the German colonial period was the desire to acquire a western education. Western education and, more precisely, a knowledge of European languages was one of the preconditions for gaining a 'prestigious' job with the government, most missionary societies and commercial houses. With the annexation of Cameroon, the indigenous economic system was largely replaced by the Western economic system. The search for lucrative business activities was a motivational force behind the acquisition of German (Austen and Derrick: 1999). That is, the desire for higher living standard was the driving force behind the learning of German.

Even though knowledge of German was a major prerequisite for gaining a job, the level of acquisition also played an important role in the recruitment and salary scale of local employees. Cameroonians with a better knowledge of German had higher salaries than those with low or no knowledge of German (Hausen 1970: 132; Boulleys 1998: 56). This factor — an increment of salary — also contributed positively towards the learning of German by Cameroonians. Cameroonians with better knowledge of German were treated as 'civilized'. They were exempted from corporal punishment. To escape such punishment and shame, the learning of German became a necessity (Boulleys 1998: 56).

Another factor that contributed to a positive attitude towards the learning of German was fear of being defrauded in business dealings. Little or no knowledge of German could lead to loss of property, as indicated in a report by Pastor Joseph Wilson of the Baptist Mission:

> One must go far to get a person to read and explain to him a piece of German writing which may require him to acknowledge a debt he does not owe, or to declare that he sold and received payment for a piece of land he never sold. Otherwise he must blindly submit to sign a document, only to discover afterwards, when it is too late, that he has been duped beyond remedy. (DZA, RKA Nr. 10.01 4665 Bl. 92)

In conclusion, the motives behind the learning of German in Cameroon were basically instrumental.

The outbreak of World War 1 in 1914, however, marked a temporary end to the teaching and learning of German in Cameroon. From 1919 to 1940 Cameroon was governed by the British and French Mandate governments under the League of Nations. From 1946 until independence in 1960, it came under the trusteeship of the United Nations and was still governed by both governments. Under the League of Nations, seven eighths of Cameroon came under French rule and one eighth under British.

The Teaching and Learning of German during the British and French Mandate in Cameroon (1918–60)

World War I marked the end of German as the official language of Cameroon and also put a temporary end to the teaching and learning of German in schools in both the British and French Mandate territories. The British government pursued a liberal language policy in all their colonies, but German was no longer taught as a subject in any of the schools. Meanwhile, the French government pursued a policy of assimilation which was intended to absorb all its colonies and territories into the socio-cultural life of France (Marchand 1971: 352). There were no special administrative-organization and language policies specially designed for Cameroon. The teaching and learning of German or other foreign languages as well as of the indigenous languages of Cameroon was strictly forbidden in schools, just as in the other French colonies in Africa.[16] With the adoption of the French school curriculum in the French-governed part of Cameroon in the late 1950s, German and Spanish were also adopted and were now learned as foreign languages in Cameroon (L3). Since then, both subjects have been taught in Cameroon. With regard to the teaching of German during this second period (1950 to 1968), when the German teachers who were of French nationality were withdrawn from Cameroon, the teaching of German in Cameroon was organized in the same way as in France since they had no clear vision with regard to the teaching of German (see Kum'a Ndumbe III 1989).

German was taught for three hours a week in the *4ème*, the *3ème* and the *2nde*; and for two hours a week in the *1er* and the *Terminale*. The indirect method was used in teaching German. French was the principal language of instruction in the teaching of German. The teaching personnel were French citizens and had the same pedagogical training as their counterparts in France. Table 2 summarizes the teaching aids used for the teaching and learning of German (Mbassi 1985: 93).

Class	Teaching aids
4ème	*Deutschland* by P. Isler and P. Deghaye, published in 1962 (Nouvelle Collection Deutschland (Paris: Masson))
3ème	*Von Gestern und Heute* by L. Bodevin and P. Isler, published in 1948 (Collection Deutschland (Paris: Masson))
2nde	*Phantasie und Wirklichkeit* by L. Bodevin and P. Isler, published in 1949/50 (Collection Deutschland (Paris: Masson)
1er	*Cours d'allemand – Classe de 1er* by J. Chassard and G. Weil published, in 1965 (Paris: Colin-Bourrelier)
Terminale	*Pages allemandes d'hier et aujourd'hui* by A. Spaeth, published in 1954 (Grenoble: Didier & Richard)

TABLE 2. Textbooks in Use in Teaching German in French-Speaking Cameroon, 1950s–1960s

Some examples of the themes taught from the textbook *Phantasie und Wirklichkeit* are: 'Feeling for Nature' (*Naturgefühl*); 'Dream and Reality' (*Traum und Wirklichkeit*); and 'From the German Past' (*Aus der deutschen Vergangenheit*).

The motives of Cameroonians for learning German during this period were largely similar to those of Cameroonians during the German colonial period. For the Cameroonian government, political and economic factors played an essential role in the adoption or reintroduction of German as a foreign language in the secondary schools of the French-speaking part of Cameroon.[17]

German in Post-Colonial Cameroon (1960–Present)

Since independence, German and Spanish have been taught as foreign languages (L3) in schools in the then East Cameroon. In the then West Cameroon, neither language was taught; and this remains the case today despite the interest shown by some private schools in this part of the country.

From the third school year or *4ème*, the students are expected to choose between German and Spanish. Since German, like Spanish, is not offered in English-speaking Cameroon, both languages have become the exclusive domain of French-speaking Cameroonians. This socio-cultural and linguistic imbalance between the English- and French-speaking Cameroonians can negatively affect the political unity of the country since economical and socio-cultural issues cannot be separated from political issues. Besides, there is also a socio-economic imbalance. A majority of French-speaking Cameroonians benefit more from the scholarships offered by the governments representing the different foreign languages. The introduction of German and all the other foreign languages in English-speaking Cameroon should therefore be given serious consideration.

With the adoption of German and Spanish as foreign languages in francophone schools, the teaching goals, syllabus, teaching aids, teaching contents and teaching methods from France were also adopted. Indeed, Kum'a Ndumbe III summarizes the teaching and learning of German in Cameroon from 1950 to 1968 as follows:

> The system of teaching has not changed and the programmes have practically remained the same for several years after political independence. We have even noticed a revealing phenomenon. When a teaching reform was introduced in France many francophone countries hastened to put the same reform in place in their countries. (Kum'a Ndumbe III 1984/85: 20)

However, with the withdrawal of French teachers of German by the French government in post-colonial Cameroon in 1968, Germany took over the training of teachers for German.[18]

From 1970 a new textbook — *Yao lernt Deutsch* — was introduced as a teaching aid.[19] The teaching goal as stated in *Yao lernt Deutsch* was the acquisition of grammatical competence. Other skills included listening, speaking, reading and writing. The teaching aids used included texts from the series *Vorwärts international*, a revised German grammar in French (Chassard and Weil 1970), or *Deutsch 2000* (Schäpers 1974)). Other didactic teaching materials and aids included tape recorders and cassettes. Three teaching methods were used in the teaching and learning of German before the replacement of *Yao lernt Deutsch* in 1991/92: the Grammar-Translation method; the direct method; and the audio-lingual method.

From 1991 *Yao lernt Deutsch* was replaced with *Ihr und Wir plus*[20] because of the concern that the strong dominance of German culture in *Yao lernt Deutsch* could lead to the cultural alienation of the learners of German. The teaching approach of the textbook *Ihr und Wir plus* (Vol. III), is also based on the communicative competence of the learner and on intercultural learning. With regard to the teaching content, the themes include: 'Contact beyond Barriers'; 'Keeping Fit'; 'Learning for Life'; 'Getting Along'.

A closer look at some of the topics still reveals clichés and stereotypes which intercultural learning aims to reduce or eliminate. The sub-topic, 'Schüler engagieren sich' (Chapter 5: 'Schulen in Aktion' (p. 62)) describes how pupils in German schools dedicate a day to working in firms, flower shops and hairdressing salons among other places to raise money. The money collected is used to finance educational projects in five African countries. Africa is presented here again as the receiving nation and Germany as the giving nation. Such texts can hardly contribute to the reduction or elimination of clichés and stereotypes.[21]

A new syllabus for the teaching and learning of German has been developed, but is still in the experimental phase.[22] Communicative competence is aimed at. The total number of hours allocated for the teaching and learning of German in the first cycle is 216 (three hours a week). German has a coefficient of three (out of a maximum of four — the coefficient is graded from 1 to 4. The higher the coefficient attributed to a subject, the more important that subject is). The learners' profile at the end of the first cycle is equivalent to the level A1, the norm required by Common European Framework of Reference for Languages.

In the *2nde*, which is the beginning of the second cycle, the emphasis in the teaching and learning of German is placed on the didactics. There are six didactic sequences:[23] information and clichés; writing and reading a letter; talking about the problems of employment; talking about problems of lodging; talking about problems of youth; and talking about music and the Arts.

There are eight hundred thousand pupils currently learning German in secondary and high schools in Cameroon and two thousand teachers teaching German (Mbia 2016). Learners' motives for learning German are to a great extent similar to those of their predecessors. Securing a job in the government secondary schools qualifies one as a civil servant with benefits including a monthly salary, paid annual leave and a pension on retirement. The benefits that knowledge of German confers have greatly and positively contributed to its acquisition. The desire to study in Germany has positively affected the attitude of Cameroonians towards German. Furthermore, Germany also offers scholarships to students and lecturers to study and carry out research in Germany. This has also contributed positively to the attitude of Cameroonians towards learning German.

Outcome of Teaching and Learning of German in Cameroon from the German Colonial Period to the Present Day

The teaching of German alongside indigenous languages (Duala and Fulfulde) in schools greatly contributed to the structural development of these languages. Loan words from German have passed into Duala in everyday life; some examples are given in Table 3 (see Ittmann 1978: 7). Bilingual Dictionaries (German-Duala; German-Bassa; Banôho-German) were also produced.

German	Duala
Tisch (Table)	Tisi (n.b. The German sound 'sch' was replaced with 's' and 'z' with 's')
Maschine (Machine)	Masin
Zigarre (Cigar)	Sika
Kaiser (Emperor)	Kaisa
Pfingstmontag (Whit Monday)	Montag na bie Pfingsten
Johannes (John)	Yohannes ('J' was replaced by 'Y')

TABLE 3. Loan Words from German into Douala

In post-colonial Cameroon the teaching of German has led to the development of a student variety of German called *Camfrancallemand* (*Camfrancdeutsch*; *Kamerdeutsch*),[24] a mixture of French, English, Cameroon Pidgin English, German and the local indigenous languages of Cameroon. Unlike Cameroon Pidgin English and *Camfranglais* which have simplified grammars and are spoken even by uneducated young Cameroonians in urban areas, *Camfrancallemand* has a well-structured grammar and it is spoken exclusively by students of German studies in Cameroon. An example of a sentence combination in *Camfrancallemand* is:

> **Mensch**, voilà Charles, il geht mbidiment **zur Schule**.[25]
> (Translation: Man, look at Charles, he is going slowly to school). **Mensch (German), voilà (French), il (French), geht (German), mbindi-ment (Duala + French), zur Schule (German)**

Conclusion

One of the greatest challenges facing the teaching and learning of German in Cameroon today is the absence of an official syllabus. The use of textbooks conceived by the Inspectorate of Pedagogy will greatly contribute to a balanced teaching and learning of German in Cameroon. Also, it will contribute to the development of the cultural identity of the learners of German and at the same time open them up to the global scene. From the above presentation and discussion one can also conclude that the teaching and learning of German in Cameroonian society has a bright future since German is a subject in the educational curriculum. Furthermore, the teaching and learning of German have created and are creating employment and job opportunities for many Cameroonians who are paid by the government of Cameroon (unlike in the 1960s and 1970s, when such civil servants were paid by the German government).

Bibliography

Archive Materials

Basler Missionsgesellschaft (BMA) E-2, 11 Nr. 18, Bl.1
Basel Mission Archive E-10.25, 5
Deutsches Zentralarchiv (DZA) 10.10 RKA Nr. 4441
DZA, RKA Nr. 10.01 4665 Bl. 92

Secondary literature

Austen, Ralph A., and Jonathan Derrick. 1999. *Middlemen of the Cameroons Rivers: The Duala and their Hinterland, c. 1600 — c. 1960* (Cambridge: Cambridge University Press)

Bock, Eduard, *Deutsche Lesebuch für die Bedürfnisse des Volksschul-Unterrichts* (Breslau: Hirt, 1876)

Boulleys, V. E. 1998. *Das Deutsche in Kamerun* (Bamberg: Collibri)

Breton, R., and B. Fohtung. 1991. *Atlas administratif des langues nationales du Cameroun* (Paris: Yaoundé)

Chassard, J., and G. Weil. 1970. *Cours d'allemand: Classe de 1er* [1st edn 1965] (Paris: Colin-Bourrelier)

Christaller, Theodor. 1888. *Fibel für die Volksschulen in Kamarun* (Berlin: Heymanns)

Ethnologue. 2009. Ed. by M. Paul Lewis (Dallas, TX: SIL) <http://www.ethnologue.com/16/home/> [accessed 23 October 2017]

Fishman, J. 1971. *Advances in the Sociology of Language, 1: Basic Concepts and Theories: Alternative Approaches* (The Hague and Paris: Mouton de Gruyter)

Gardner, R. C., and P. C. Smythe. 1981. 'On the Development of the Attitude/Motivation Test Battery', *Canadian Modern Language Review*, 37: 510-25

Hallden, E. 1968. *The Culture Policy of the Basel Mission in the Cameroons 1886–1905* (Lund: Berling)

Hausen, K. 1970. *Deutsche Kolonialherrschaft in Afrika: Wirtschaftsinteresse und Kolonialverwaltung in Kamerun vor 1914* (Zurich; Freiburg i. Br.: Atlantis)

Illy, H. F. 1976. *Politik und Wirtschaft in Kamerun* (Munich: Weltform)

Ittmann, J. 1978. *Grammaire du Duala. Traduit de l'allemand par I. A. Boumard* (Douala: Collège Liebermann)

Kerker, E. 1989. 'Germanistik im frankophonen Afrika: Das Beispiel Kamerun und Madagaskar. Ein Erfahrungsbericht', in *Afrikanische Germanistik*, ed. by Peter Kasprzyk and Norbert Ndong (Bonn: Deutscher Akademischer Austauschdienst), pp. 41–46

Kum'a Ndumbe III, Alexandre. 1985: 'Les Traités camerouno-germaniques: 1884 -1907', in *L'Afrique et l'Allemagne: de la coopération à la colonisation*, ed. by Kum'a Ndumbe III (Douala: Afric Avenir)

——. 1984/85. 'Finalité de l'enseignement de l'allemand en Afrique Noire : l'exemple du Cameroun', in *Études Germano-Africaines*, 2/3: 27–32

——. 2008. *Das deutsche Kaiserreich in Kamerun* (Douala: Afric Avenir)

Mackey, W. F. 1989. 'Determining the Status and Function of Language', in *Status and Function of Languages and Language Varieties*, ed. by U. Ammon (Berlin & New York: de Gruyter), pp. 3-20

Madiba, Essiben. 1980. *Colonisation et Evangélisation en Afrique: l'héritage scolaire du Cameroun (1885–1956)* (Bern etc.: Lang)

——. 1986. 'Enseignement scolaire et expansion économique au Cameroun sous administration allemande', in *L'Afrique et l'Allemagne: de la coopération à la colonisation*, ed. by *Kum'a Ndumbe III* (Douala: Afric Avenir)

Marchand, C. 1971. 'Idéologie coloniale et enseignement en Afrique noire francophone', *Canadian Journal of African Studies*, 5: 349-58

MBASSI, J. 1985. 'L'Evolution de l'enseignement de l'allemand au Cameroun depuis l'indépendance', in *Cent ans de Relations entre le Cameroun et les Allemagnes*, ed. by Kum'a Ndumbe III et al. Vol I, Numéro 2 (Yaoundé)

MBIA, C. M. 2016. *Hundert Jahre Deutschunterricht in Kamerun 1910–2010: Von Deutsch als Unterrichtssprache zu Deutsch als Unterrichtsfach* (Paris: L'Harmattan)

MENDE, H.-W. 1982. *Sprachpolitik im Dienste der Entwicklungspolitik* (Göppingen: Kümmerle Verlag)

MOUSSA, A., et al. 2012. *Ihr und Wir plus* (Munich: Goethe Institut)

NDONG, N. 1993. 'Afrikanische Germanistik: Eine Entwicklungshilfeprojekt oder eine interkulturelle Wissenschaft', in *Kultureller Wandel und die Germanistik in der Bundesrepublik*, ed. by J. Janota, 4 vols (Tübingen: Niemeyer), IV, 119-28

NJEUMA. M. 1978. *Fulani Hegemony in Yola (Old Adamawa) 1809 –1902* (Yaounde: CEPER)

OROSZ, K. J. 2005. 'An African Kulturkampf: Religious Conflict and Language Policy in German Cameroon, 1885–1914', *Sociolinguistica*, 25: 82-91

SCHLIEBEN-LANGE, B. 1992. 'Die Kolonialisierung der Sprache und Diskurse', in *Sprache und Kolonialismus, Zeitschrift für Literaturwissenschaft und Linguistik*, 85: 7–11

SCHLUNK, M. 1914. *Die Schulen für Eingeborenen in den deutschen Schutzgebieten* (Hamburg: Friederichsen)

SCHRÖDER, M., and R.-D. BEISSNER. 1976. *Yao lernt Deutsch* (Dakar: Nouvelles Éditions Africaines du Senegal)

STOECKER, H. (ed.). 1977. *Drang nach Afrika: Die koloniale Expansionspolitik und Herrschaft des deutschen Imperialismus in Afrika von den Anfangen bis zum Ende des zweiten Weltkrieges* (Berlin: Akademie Verlag)

STRUMPF, R. 1979. *La Politique linguistique au Cameroun de 1884 à 1960* (Bern etc.: Lang)

WILDE-STOCKMEYER, M. 2001. 'Landeskunde = Kulturwissenschaft?', in *Kommunikative Fremdsprachendidaktik: Theorie und Praxis in Deutsch als Fremdsprache. Festschrift für Gerhard Neuner zum 60. Geburtstag*, ed. by H. Funk and M. Koenig (Munich: Iudicium), pp. 69-92

Notes to Chapter 9

1. Deutsches Zentralarchiv (DZA). 10.01 Reichskolonialamt (RKA) Nr. 4441; Schlunk 1914.
2. The North of Cameroon came into contact with Islam as early as the fourteenth century. With the conquest of this region by Osman dan Fodio in the eighteenth century, Arabic was introduced (Boulleys 1998: 21).
3. This important issue has been treated elsewhere (Boulleys 1998).
4. A series of treaties was also signed during the pre-colonial period between Britain and the indigenous chiefs. Politically Cameroon was a German Protectorate, but in socio-economic and linguistic terms it was under the influence of Britain (Kum'a Ndumbe III 2008).
5. See Boulleys 1998: 47 for original text in German. All translations are by the author.
6. The north of Cameroon, with the Adamawa Emirate as the seat of administration, became part of the Sokoto Empire (1809–1902) when Modibo Adama, a sub-officer of Osman dan Fodio, conquered the region and imposed Islam on the people. This region had a well-structured organization before the arrival of the Europeans and the colonization of Africa (Njeuma 1978). Up until the present day this region is still dominated by Islam. There are very few Christians in this region of Cameroon.
7. Missionary societies which received a subsidy from the colonial government adopted the same curriculum as the government schools.
8. The liberal language policy of the German colonial government was similar to that of the British colonial government (indirect rule) and the non-liberal language policy (direct rule) to that of the French colonial government (direct rule).
9. The School Law (*Schulordnung*) restricted the use of Duala in newly created schools. The purpose

was to facilitate the spread and use of German over their colonial territories and protectorates (Basel Mission Archive (BMA), E-10.21,5 Bl.2; Boulleys 1998: 47)

10. See also Boulleys 1998: 72

11. Deutsches Zentralarchiv, RKA Nr. 4073: 'Lehrplan für die Regierungsschulen in Kamerun und Togo von 1892'. Before the passing of the School Law in 1910 all the lessons were taught in the indigenous languages in the first school year.

12. For reading in second, third and fourth year, the German primer (*Deutsche Fibel*) was used.

13. Ibid.

14. Theodor Christaller was the first government schoolteacher in Cameroon.

15. See Boulleys 1998: 76-77.

16. It should be noted that Cameroon was not a French colony; nevertheless, it was governed as part of French Equatorial Africa (AEF) (Stumpf 1979: 79).

17. For details of the discussion with regard the reintroduction of German in Cameroon just before independence in 1960 see Kerker 1989: 41-46; Calvet 1978: 117; Boulleys 1998: 107.

18. The teaching of German experienced the least development under the British and French Mandates. As Stumpf (1979: 93) rightly states, there were few teaching aids for the teaching of French, on which much value was placed, which implies that very little value at all was placed on the teaching of German. Thus, when France came under financial difficulties as a result of its participation in the Vietnam and Algerian Wars, it withdrew the French German teachers from Cameroon after agreements with Germany. Consequently, Germany took over the training of teachers for the teaching of German in Cameroon (Mende 1982: 264-65).

19. M. Schröder and R.-D. Beißner. 1986/1989. *Yao lernt Deutsch* (Hamburg).

20. *Ihr und Wir plus*, a joint regional textbook language project put together by scholars from Germany and some African countries: Moussa Anoumatacky, Côte d'Ivoire; Essi Kpogli, Togo; Malick Ndao, Senegal; Jean Nyankam, Cameroun; Alexis Ngatcha, Cameroun; Dieudonné Ouédraogo, Burkina Faso; and Anja Schümann, Germany

21. For detailed criticism, see Bassock 2010: 93-95.

22. Programme d'Etudes de l'Allemand Langue Vivante II en classes de 4ème et de 3ème; Ministry of Secondary Education; Inspectorate General of Education; Inspectorate of Pedagogy for German; Foreign Languages' Section; Department of German, 2010.

23. *Progression sequentielle d'Allemand; Classe de 2nde Allemand*. Ministry of Secondary Education; Regional Delegate of Littoral; Regional Inspectorate of Pedagogy/LAL.

24. The term was coined by students of German studies in the Department of English and Foreign Languages, University of Douala, following a new variety of French in Cameroon called *Camfranglais*.

25. *Mbindi* is a Duala word which means *small* (or *junior*). The word *–ment* is from the French adverb *lente* + *ment*. *Mbindiment* is a composition from *small* in Duala and *–ment* in French. A direct translation would mean *Man, look at Charles, he is taking 'smaller steps' to school* (Yvette Ekobe, native speaker of Duala, personal communication).

CHAPTER 10

❖

Westerners Learning Chinese: Nineteenth-Century Didactic Materials

Mariarosaria Gianninoto

During the nineteenth century, the increase in contacts between Western countries and China resulted in a rising number of foreigners eager to learn Chinese languages. This promoted the compilation of different kinds of language-learning and teaching materials, such as pedagogical grammars, language textbooks, and phrasebooks, written in Western languages (e.g. English, Latin, French and Portuguese). These works were essentially written by and for Westerners: the authors as well as the intended learners were Westerners. The first grammars were compiled by missionaries, who played a pivotal role in the development of this field. During the nineteenth century, diplomats and civil servants working in China also wrote several language textbooks. Moreover, the rise of Sinological Studies in Europe and the institution of university chairs promoted the production of works related to Chinese language-teaching and learning written by Western academics. The authors generally adopted the linguistic as well as the pedagogical approaches that they were already used to, adapting Western paradigms to the Chinese context. Even though the Western model was predominant, these bilingual or multilingual works progressively integrated aspects of Chinese linguistic and didactic traditions, amalgamating native and Western linguistic categories and language-learning methodologies.

Introduction

The first Western works on the Chinese languages were compiled between the end of the sixteenth century and the beginning of the seventeenth century in Asia, and were essentially conceived as tools for missionary language training, the knowledge of the local languages being considered of great importance for missionary work (Masini 1993: 5; Levi 2007: 228). As far as we know, the *Arte de la lengua chio chiu* (1620) is the earliest existing treatise on a variety of Chinese, written in the Philippines.[1] It described 'a koine of urban Southern Min dialects, as spoken at that time' (Chappell 2006: 441), labelled Early Manila Hokkien by Klöter (2011: 19); while the first existing treatise on Mandarin Chinese was the *Grammatica sinica*, compiled between 1651 and 1652 by the Jesuit Martino Martini (1614–1661) (Paternicò 2011: 231-32).[2] Between the seventeenth and eighteenth centuries several grammars, glossaries and manuals of the Chinese languages were compiled in different Western languages, including Latin, Portuguese, Spanish, French and English (Chappell and Peyraube 2014: 113-19).

Nevertheless, it was during the nineteenth century that this production of grammars and manuals developed considerably, due to the increase in contacts between Western countries and China after the Opium Wars (1839-42; 1856-60) and thanks to the rising number of foreigners needing to acquire a basic knowledge or a good command of Chinese. Moreover, all these later grammars and manuals were printed and this contributed to their widespread diffusion. The compilation of Chinese teaching materials in Western languages was also promoted by the development of Sinological Studies in different European countries: while the first classes of Chinese in Europe had probably been taught at the *Collegio dei Cinesi*[3] in Naples between the end of the eighteenth and the beginning of the nineteenth centuries (Castorina 2014), the first Sinological chair in Europe was established at the *Collège de France* in 1814, when Jean-Pierre Abel-Rémusat (1788–1832) was appointed Professor of *Langue et littérature chinoises et tartares-mandchoues* (Chinese and Manchu Tartar Languages and Literatures). Two decades later the appointment of Samuel Kidd as Professor of Chinese Language and Literature at University College, London, inaugurated British Chinese Studies (McLelland 2015: 113).

Hence, this period saw the publication of important reference grammars and linguistic treatises essentially composed by European academics, such as J.-P. Abel-Rémusat's *Elémens de la grammaire chinoise* (1822), S. Julien's *Syntaxe nouvelle de la langue chinoise* (1869), and G. Gabelentz's *Chinesische Grammatik* (1881). Even though these reference grammars were also used as teaching tools, the analysis of these works, which have been the object of various studies (e.g. Peyraube 2001; Pellin 2009; Chappell and Peyraube 2014), goes beyond the aim of the present chapter, which focuses on nineteenth-century pedagogical grammars and manuals, specifically conceived as language teaching and learning tools, a field that has generally been less investigated.

The nineteenth century saw the publication of different kinds of Chinese learning materials. We can find examples of pedagogical grammars, essentially compiled by missionaries serving in China, like R. Morrison's *A Grammar of the Chinese language* (1815) and J. Gonçalves's *Arte China* (1829), sharing a markedly practical approach. We can also find examples of native monolingual primers translated into Latin, French, English and Italian, which were widely adopted for teaching Chinese as a foreign language in Asia as well as in Europe and became a source of inspiration for the compilation of Western-language manuals of Chinese.

The second half of the nineteenth century witnessed a considerable development in the publication of manuals of Chinese in English and French, whose titles ('course', 'progressive course', *leçons progressives*)[4] make explicit their nature as pedagogic manuals and differentiate them from the contemporary reference grammars and linguistic treatises. This production was very diverse, being aimed at various kinds of learner and responding to various pedagogical needs: we find concise self-instruction manuals as well as multi-volume manuals of both written and spoken Chinese, treating also the language for specific purposes (Wade 1867).

This chapter analyses a corpus of grammars and manuals compiled or translated by Western missionaries (e.g. Morrison 2008 [1815], 1816; Gonçalves 1829; Mateer 1922 [1892]; Martin 1897), diplomats (Giles 1873, 1887; Wade 1867a, 1867b, 1867c) and academics (Julien 1864a, 1864b, 1864c; Kleczkowski 1876) during the nineteenth century. Of course, these works do not represent the whole production of nineteenth-century language-learning tools, but are chosen as representative examples of the wide range of materials for teaching and learning Chinese as a foreign language compiled in this period.[5]

Our aim is to describe the main characteristics of this production of didactic tools, which deserves an important place in the history of Chinese language-learning and teaching. In particular, we shall see that these works are characterized by an interplay of Western and Chinese linguistic categories and pedagogical methodologies, and merge the legacies of both Western and Chinese traditions with innovative approaches to face the challenges of presenting and teaching Chinese to Westerners.

Western Pedagogical Grammars of Chinese in the First Half of the Nineteenth Century

While there is sometimes an overlap between reference grammars and pedagogical grammars, the latter are characterized by a clear didactic purpose and a practical approach, aiming to assist language learning and teaching practice instead of providing theoretical linguistic descriptions. Hence, in these works the grammatical explanations are generally extremely concise, while a considerable place is reserved to dialogues, illustrative sentences, and eventually exercises. *A Grammar of the Chinese Language* (Chinese title *Tongyong hanyan zhi fa* 通用漢言之法)[6] by the English Presbyterian missionary R. Morrison (1782-1834), published in Serampore in 1815, can be regarded as an example of this kind of grammar. Chappell and Peyraube (2014: 120) rightly affirm that these types of work 'could be better described as kinds of textbooks or manuals, introducing the learner to the language by translated examples, rather than being real grammars'. Moreover, the didactic purpose of this manual is explicitly identified by Morrison in his preface (2008: iii):

> The object of the following work is to afford practical assistance to the students of Chinese. All theoretical disquisitions respecting the nature of the language have been purposely omitted. On this subject much has already been said; but, as yet, in our language, little practical assistance has been afforded to the student.

In this work, the explanations of grammatical rules are extremely brief, and the rules are illustrated through several examples with transcription and word-for-word translation. For instance, the first lines of the section devoted to the relative pronouns are as follows:

The Relative

Pronouns 'who, which and that' are made by sò 所, preceding the verb, or chày 者, closing the member of sentence. Thus,

'The man is happy who lives virtuously.'

矣 è !⁷ 福 fŏ happiness 有 yeù has 者 chày he who 善 shén goodness行 hǐng practices (Morrison 2008: 106)

The reference to Western grammatical categories (here, the relative pronoun) is extremely frequent in missionary grammars of Chinese and can be considered as a didactic device, to facilitate language-teaching and learning through familiar categories (Zwartjes 2011: 14; Breitenbach 2000: xxxiii).

Morrison's practical approach is also shown in the way of treating the Chinese tones. He affirms (2008: 21): 'They are not absolutely necessary to be understood in speaking Chinese; but are yet essential to good speaking. Hence an early attention to them is advisable'. Hence, while the importance of tones for acquiring a good mastery of Chinese is underlined, their importance for people needing to learn the language quickly is relativized. It is worth stressing that the space given to tones in teaching Chinese as a foreign language is an issue still much debated in Chinese linguistics and didactics (for instance, Raini 2007).

In presenting the tonal system, Morrison briefly mentions the long-standing Chinese phonological tradition (making reference to the original names of the tones and to the opposition between direct and oblique tones), while he includes in his grammar a table of syllables and suggests learning tones by 'reading over the Table of syllables with different natives' (2008: 3) in order to become familiar with the pronunciation of the different varieties of Chinese.

Some twenty pages (25-37) are devoted to the description of the writing system, and the attempt to render the Chinese script easily understandable and more accessible to learners is evident in different passages of this work. For instance, Morrison writes (2008: 27), 'though the Chinese character appears complicated, it is, generally reducible to a very few primary parts which the Chinese call 部 poó' (i.e. the radicals or keys). A table of the 214 radicals is followed by a section 'On the mode of finding out words in the Chinese dictionary', which gives examples of how to find characters according to their radicals and remaining strokes. For example, we read 'Pīng, 兵 a soldier, is found under the Radical pǎ 八, and eight strokes' (Morrison 2008: 35).

In *A Grammar of the Chinese Language*, there are no dialogues, because, as Morrison indicates in his preface (2008: iv), this work was accompanied by his *Dialogues and detached sentences in the Chinese language*. This work, published in Macao in 1816, consists of dialogues in Chinese, with Latin-letter transcription, English translation and word-for-word translation, completed by some samples of written documents in Chinese (e.g. a letter, a petition, a proclamation), followed by their 'free translation' (Morrison 1816: 252) in English.

The use of bilingual texts in dialogue format was common to both Western and Chinese traditions. In Europe, the use of bilingual dialogues dealing with 'frequent communicative situations' can be traced back to the Greek and Latin *hermeneumata* in the third century AD (Sanchez 2014: 60), and was widely adopted during the Middle Ages (Germain 1993: 9).

As for Chinese as a foreign language, among the earliest manuals we find the *Putongshi* 朴通事 and the *Laoqida* 老乞大, two textbooks for Korean learners composed at the end of the Yuan period (1279-1368), both presenting examples of everyday conversation, such as dialogues about travelling, doing business and local customs (Zhang 2009: 37), in Chinese characters.[8]

In Morrison's work we find dialogues 'With a Shopman and Visitor', 'With a Tea Merchant', 'With an Assistant in Learning Language', 'A Person Ill', presenting situations of everyday life in China. For example, the first sentence of Dialogue XIV, 'On Purchasing Silk' (Morrison 1816: 98):

A. Shopman, I want a piece of Blue Silk.
Sze 事 Business
t'how 頭 head   Shopman,
kung, 公 man,
wo 我 I
yaou 要 want
mae 買 to buy
yĭh 一 a
pëïh 疋 piece of
lan 蓝 blue
töan. 緞 silk
tsze 子

Other sections, like 'An Ambassador Introduced' (Dialogue XVIII), the four dialogues (XVIII to XXI) 'On the Mode of Visiting in China' (i.e. devoted to the ways of receiving visitors and going to visit someone according to Chinese etiquette) as well as the Dialogue 'Mandarin and Visitor' (III) focus on pragmatic and socio-cultural competence and reflect Morrison's attention to the specific context and needs of his intended readers, i.e. foreigners (diplomats, civil servants, missionaries) living and working in China.

The *Arte china constante de alphabeto e grammatica comprehendendo modelos das differentes composiçoens*, with the Chinese title *Hanzi wenfa* 漢字文法 (1829), by the (Catholic) Lazarist missionary J. A. Gonçalves (1781-1841), occupies a central position among the pedagogical grammars that appeared during the first half of the nineteenth century. This work was originally composed for the students of the Colégio de São José in Macao, the institute where Father Gonçalves taught, and was to 'be used by young (and not-so-young) students learning Chinese, in this case European priests and missionaries, most of whom spoke Portuguese as their first, second, or third language' (Levi 2007: 219). However, its influence was much wider, as this work was not only used for decades as a Chinese language textbook in Asia, but it was also translated into French (see below) and adopted in European institutions (Pino and Rabut 1995: 323-27).

Lusophone students of Chinese being his intended readers, Gonçalves adopts a contrastive approach, comparing Portuguese and Chinese. For instance, when he briefly introduces the Chinese tonal system in the *Prologo*, Gonçalves claims that 'in our language we have these tones, we call them accent' (*Na nossa lingua temos estes tons, que chamamos accento*) (1829: V) and compares the tones with the accents and intonations familiar to Portuguese speakers. For example, the author explains that (1829: v) the Portuguese interjection *hui* is usually pronounced with the same intonation of the 'high and level' tone in Chinese (*Assim a interjeiçaõ Hui! a proferimos no tom Plano Alto*).

In this work, considerable space is allocated to the Chinese writing system. Not only are the first seventy pages of this work (the *Alphabeto china*) devoted to the Chinese script, listing strokes, radicals and characters (from the simpler to the more complex), but also the second section, the *Frases vulgares e sublimes*, is structured according to progression in learning the script. This section consists of Portuguese sentences[9] translated into both vernacular and classical Chinese, composed or chosen according to the number of strokes of the characters that they are written with. For instance, we have a list of sentences composed of characters counting up to six strokes, sentences composed by characters of up to seven strokes, and so forth. This content organization aims to motivate students and 'relieve the tedium of learning the script' (*satisfazer a curiosidade do Estudante, allivia-lo do tedio de estudar letras*), giving the opportunity to learn sentences to use in every-day life and practicing the characters learned (*exercita-lo ñas ja conhecidas*) (Gonçalves 1829: vi), without having to learn all the characters listed in the first part of the book before starting to read and write the first sentences in Chinese.

While the titles of following chapters refer to grammar points (e.g. *grammatica, syntaxe, syntaxe figurada, excercicios de syntaxe*), grammatical explanations are almost absent, and the grammatical notions or categories (such as adjective, superlative) are usually merely illustrated by some sentences, the grammatical rules having to be deduced from these examples. For instance, in the fourth chapter (entitled *Syntaxe*) we read (1829: 147):[10]

> Accusativo depois do verbo [Accusative after the verb] [...]
> Volton para casa [Go back home] 回家去 Δ[11] 歸家

The reference to Western linguistic terms and categories, like 'accusative' and 'subjunctive', to describe a language with neither declension nor conjugation, was a pedagogical device, as underlined by Gonçalves (1829: 127):

> Servi-me dos casos Nominativo Genitivo &c. como e meio mais claro para exprimier as regras. devendo-se subentender: O quem em Latin he Nominativo &c.; e delles, e das particulas tratei so na syntaxe, para a hum tempo ver o modo de os formar, usar, e o lugar, que occupao na oraçao.

> [I use the [terms] Nominative case, Genitive case etc. as a clearer device to express rules. These [terms] are to be understood as: what is called Nominative in Latin etc.; the particles are treated in the section Syntax, where we will see the way they are formed, used and the place they occupy in discourse.]

Beside these references to grammatical categories, grammar is far from central in Gonçalves's *Arte*. A great part of the *Arte* consists of illustrative sentences (for instance, the chapter *Frases vulgares e sublimes*); dialogues (such as buying things or talking about weather, time, travels); lists of proverbs and idiomatic expressions (in the chapter *Proverbios*); and models of written compositions, ranging from poetry to samples of petitions, warning, notes (in the chapter *Composições Chinas*).

As an example of dialogue, we give some lines from Dialogue XXXVI, entitled *Doente* 病人 [A Sick Person]) (Gonçalves, 1829: 265):

> Estoa doente ; vai chamar o medico. Ja vou. 我有病請大夫去。就去
> [I'm ill; please go call a doctor. I go.]
> Quem officio tem aquelle ? 這個人有什麼手藝
> [What is his craft ?]
> Elle tem huma pequena botica, e tamben cura. 他開一門小藥舖子也行醫
> [He has a small pharmacy, but he also practices medicine.]

The *Cours graduel de chinois parlé et écrit*, published in Paris in 1876 was a French translation (with explanations and commentaries) of the illustrative sentences and dialogues of Gonçalves' *Arte china*. It was compiled by a French diplomat and teacher of Chinese, Michel Kleczkowski (1818-1886), for his classes at the *École nationale des langues vivantes* in Paris (Kleczkowski, 1876: 47-48). The transcription, the French translation, the word-for-word translation, and some lexical or grammatical explanations are added to Gonçalves' text. For example (Kleczkowski, 1876: 322-23):

> 有人麼。
> Yéou jenn mo
> 一個也沒有不過有一位客人來見。
> Y ko yé me yéou, pou kouo yéou y oueǐ k'o jenn lai kienn. [...]
> *Traduction française*
> Quelqu'un de ce côté-là ? [Is there someone there?]
> Il n'y a absolument personne (il n'y a même pas un seul individu), il n'y a qu;une visite. [...] [There is no one at all, there is just one visit.]
> *Traduction littérale*
> avoir — gens — ? —
> Un — p.n.g. — aussi — pas — avoir, — pas (ne) — passer (que) — avoir — un — personne (particule numérale s'appliquant aux personnages) — hôte (convive) — créature humaine (c.s.) — venir — voir.

The prominence of dialogues and examples, the conciseness of grammatical explanations, the attempt at simplifying the presentation of tones and scripts, 'two of the challenges of learning Chinese' for foreigners (McLelland 2015: 131), characterize these manuals. These works were essentially composed by missionaries and diplomats, living in China or having worked in the country, and share a markedly practical approach. They can be regarded as representative examples of 'practical Sinology' (*sinologie pratique*), rather than examples of 'scholarly Sinology' (*sinologie savante*), to use Galy's words (1995: 131).

Chinese Primers in Nineteenth-Century Teaching of Chinese as a Foreign Language

Among the didactic materials for Western learners of Chinese, the translations of native monolingual primers, like the *Qianziwen* 千字文 (*Thousand Character Text*) by Zhou Xingsi 周興嗣 (470–521) and the *Sanzijing* 三字經 (*Three Character Classic*), attributed to Wang Yinglin 王應麟 (1223–1296), deserve mention. These texts, composed of three-character and four-character couplets, using rhyming verses to facilitate memorization, had been adopted for centuries in China to teach language and characters to children (Julien 1864a: i–ii), and had been employed by the missionaries for learning Chinese characters and vocabulary since the late sixteenth century, as witnessed by the evidence preserved in the Roman Archives of the Society of Jesus (Brokey 2008: 248). Their translations and adaptations were widely used to teach Chinese as a foreign language to European learners during the nineteenth and early twentieth centuries (Castorina 2014; Rabut 1995: 223).

The *Qianziwen* was translated into French by the Sinologist Stanislas Julien (1797–1873) under the title *Thsien-tseu-wen, Le livre des mille mots* and published in Paris in 1864. Julien's version opens with the Chinese text, followed by the section 'Analyse de tous les éléments des mille caractères' [Analysis of every component of the thousand characters], indicating the number of the radical (i.e. the key component of a character) and the remaining traits of each character of the text. For instance, for the first character *tian* 天 [sky], we read: '1 天 37+1 大 37 一' (Julien 1864a: 1), 大 being the radical no. 37 and one being the number of remaining strokes necessary to form the character 天. At the end of this section we find a table of radicals.

In the second part of the book we have the transcription of the Chinese text in Latin letters, accompanied by the word-for-word translation, by the so-called 'developed translation' (*traduction développée*) (Julien 1864a: 1), and by some philological and historical remarks. Each character of the Chinese text is progressively numbered in order to be identified in the second part of the book (where only the transcriptions and translations are presented). For instance, we quote the first lines of the Chinese text and the first lines of Julien's transcription and translation (Julien 1864a: 1, 5):

天1地2玄3黃4宇5宙6洪7荒8

1–4

Thien, ciel ; *hiouen*, bleu ; *ti*, terre ; *hoang*, jaune. Le ciel est bleu, la terre est jaune.

The sky is blue, the earth is yellow.

5–6

Yu-tcheou, l'univers ; *hong*, vaste ; *hoang*, désert. (Au commencement du monde), l'univers était vaste et désert. -*Yu* signifie 'les côtés d'un toit, grand, ailes d'oiseau' et *tchou*, 'depuis l'antiquité jusqu'à nos jours'. Ces deux mots réunis veulent dire l'univers. [At the start of the world, the universe was vast and empty. *Yu* signifies the sides of a roof, big wings of a bird, and *tchou* 'from antiquity to our day'. These two words combined mean the universe.]

Julien was also the author of three translations of the *Sanzijing* (*Three Character*

Classic), in English, Latin and French. The English version appeared in 1864 under the title *San-tsze-king, The Three Character Classic Published in Chinese and English by S. Julien.* The work is organized in a similar way to the *Thsien-tseu-wen, Le livre des mille mots*: in the first part of this work, we find the Chinese text with indications of radicals and additional traits (indicated by numbers on the right side of each character), while the second part presents the translation and the transcription in Latin letters. For instance, below we quote the first lines of Julien's translation and Latin letter transcription, which corresponds to the first four verses of the Chinese text [人之初 性本善 性相近 習相遠] (Julien 1864c: 1):

> 1-6
> *Jin-che-thsoo-săng-pung-shen*
> The nature of man, at his birth, is fundamentally good.
> 7-12
> *Săng-seang-kin-seĭh-yuen*
> Man resembles his fellowman in his nature, and differs from him in his habits.

Julien's Latin translation was published in 1864 under the title of *Institutio prima linguae sinicae San-tseu-king, triumlitterarum liber a Wang-Pe-Heou*, while the French edition appeared in 1873 under the title *San tseu king, ou Le livre de phrases de trois mots*.

The British Sinologist and diplomat Herbert A. Giles (1845–1935) published in 1873 the English translation of both the *Qianziwen* and the *Sanzijing* under the title of *The San Tzǔ Ching: or Three Character Classic, and the Ch'ien Ts~u Wên, or Thousand Character Essay, Metrically Translated by Herbert A. Giles*, while Guo Dongchen 郭棟臣 (Giuseppe Maria Kuo (1846-1923)), student and later teacher at the Collegio dei Cinesi in Naples, published in 1869 an Italian edition of the *Sanzijing* under the title of *Classico dei tre caratteri* (Castorina 2014: 145).

The American Presbyterian missionary William A. P. Martin (1827–1916) represents an example. Martin explicitly quoted the *Qianziwen* as 'its model' (Martin 1897: 10). In Martin's work we find poems (on religious topics as well as on everyday life) composed for didactic purposes by the Chinese scholar He Shimeng 何師孟 (Martin 1897: 6). For each verse, the Chinese characters, the transcription with tones and Martin's English translation are indicated. For example, we quote a strophe from Chapter 1 (Martin 1897: 19-20):

> 六⁴ 日⁴ 力⁴ 作⁴
> Luh jih lih tsoh
> 先¹ 闢⁴ 天¹ 地⁴
> sien p'ih t'ien ti
> 萬⁴ 物⁴ 多¹ 焉¹
> wan wuh to yien
> 既⁴ 希¹ 且³ 異⁴
> ki hi ts'ie yi [...]

> Six days *he* mightily wrought,
> First divided Heaven and Earth,
> Myriads of things multiplied,
> Both rare and strange.

As Martin emphasized in his introductory section (1879: 1–5), the rigorous selection of the characters and their arrangement on the basis of their frequency of occurrence are to be considered among the main improvements of his work. The frequency lists that guided character selection and arrangement resulted from the analysis of '4,166 octavo pages' published by the Presbyterian Mission Press (i.e. a corpus of about 'one million two hundred thousand characters'), which it had taken two Chinese scholars two years to compile (Martin 1897: 3). The author specifies that this investigation was initially motivated by typographic concerns, i.e. 'to ascertain the proportion in which the several letters would be required in casting a font of metallic type and to determine in what order the types should be arranged, so as to bring those in most common use nearest to the hand of compositor' (Martin 1897: 2). As Martin underlines, this was the application to Chinese of the method of computing the frequency of the letters to facilitate composition in Western language typography.

However, in the case of the Chinese characters, this investigation had important linguistic and pedagogical outcomes, allowing Martin to conclude that 'a very few characters, from the great frequency with which they occur, constitute the great body of those in a book, and that the great majority occur seldom' (Martin 1897: 5) and to identify different frequency lists, for a total amount of 6000 characters in general use. Hence, this selection was extremely useful 'to save the time expended in learning rare or useless characters, and abbreviate for foreign students [...] the tedious task of acquiring the written language' (Martin 1897: 2). It is important to underline that the selection of characters according to their frequency and the reduction of the space allocated to the characters in language learning are main concerns of contemporary pedagogy of Chinese as a foreign language (Zhang 2009: 132; Allanic 2015; Droucourt 2015).

Hence, Martin's work is to be considered as particularly significant from the point of view of the history of linguistic and didactic studies: on the one hand, it was characterized by the combination of Western and Chinese pedagogical paradigms, on the other hand, the systematic use of corpus-based frequency lists in compiling teaching materials was innovative in the pedagogy of Chinese as foreign language and more generally in language teaching.

Late Nineteenth-Century Manuals

The production of didactic manuals of Chinese as a foreign language underwent a dramatic expansion in the second half of the nineteenth century as a result of the increase in contacts between Western countries and China. This period saw the publication of numerous pedagogical grammars and manuals in different European languages, including the above mentioned *The Analytical Reader* by Martin (1897) and the translations due to Kleczkowski (1876), Giles (1873) and Julien (1864a, 1864b, 1864c). In this section we shall introduce just three more examples of the didactic materials published in the late nineteenth century.

The *Tzŭ-erh chi* [*Zi'erji*] 自邇集 represents one of the most outstanding examples of this production and can be considered a 'landmark textbook of Chinese for English-speaking learners' (McLelland 2015: 114). Compiled by Thomas Fr. Wade (1818-1895), British diplomat and professor of Chinese, this work is composed of two main parts: the *Yü-yen tzŭ-erh chi* [*Yuyan zi'erji*] 語言自邇集 (with the English subtitle *A Progressive Course Designed to Assist the Student of Colloquial Chinese as Spoken in the Capital and the Metropolitan Department*); and the *Wên-Chien tzŭ-erh chi* [*Wenjian zi'erji*] 文件自邇集 (*A Series of Papers Selected as Specimens of Documentary Chinese, Designed to Assist Students of the Language as Written by the Officials of China*), devoted respectively to colloquial and written Chinese, completed by volumes of exercises and keys.

This detailed and well-structured manual was intended to meet 'the requirements of the official student rather than those of any other class of readers' (Wade 1867d: iii), and 'to direct the studies of the gentlemen destined to recruit the ranks of Her Majesty's Consular Service in China' (Wade 1867b: xii). Hence this work can be also regarded as a manual of Chinese for specific purposes. For instance, in the volumes of the *Wên-Chien tzŭ-erh chi* we find the Chinese texts and the English translations of dispatches, semi-official notes, petitions, memorials, private letters, and commercial forms *inter alia*. The extensive use of authentic materials in this section is worth stressing.

In the sections of the *Yü-yen tzŭ-erh chi* we find the description of the Chinese tonal system, writing system and radicals; followed by *The Forty Exercises* (consisting of illustrative sentences in Chinese and English, with grammatical explanations or word-use explanations, plus translation exercises); the *Ten Dialogues* (with Chinese text in the first volume, English text in the second volume); and *The Hundred Lessons*, dialogue-format illustrative examples in Chinese (in the first volume), with English translation (in the second volume), plus glossaries and grammatical explanations.

As an example, we quote two lines from Lesson XII (from the section 'The Hundred Lessons'):

> 1兄台, 恭喜咯 說放章京揀選上了。 2 是啊,昨爾揀選的,把我擬了正了。(Wade 1867b: 221)
>
> 1[*Junior*] I congratulate you, sir. They said you've been selected for a *chang-ching*-ship₁.
>
> 2[*Senior*] Yes, the selection₂ yesterday they decided on proposing₃ me as the effective nominee. [...]
>
> 1.章京*chang-ching*: the words are supposed to give nearly the sound of the Manchu word *chanyin*, signifying assistant.
>
> 2. 選 *hsüan* ³ to choose; 揀*chien*³ to select: *chien-hsüan* colloquially used only of choosing officers, not in their turn, but by merit; *shang* is an auxiliary verb, but indicating at the same time the *superior* merit of the person chosen
>
> 3.擬 *ni*³ commonly, to suggest; here, of submitting a name to the Throne. (Wade 1867c: 261)

Among the manuals published in the late nineteenth century we also find self-instructional manuals, like H. A. Giles's *Chinese Without A Teacher, Being a Collection of Easy and Useful Sentences in the Mandarin Dialect, with a Vocabulary* (Chinese title *Wu shi zi ming* 無師自明 (1887)), destined 'to assist those who wish to acquire quickly a temporary or superficial knowledge of the Chinese language' (Giles 1887: i).

This simple phrase book contains a very short chapter on 'Grammar' (two pages), consisting of a few remarks on nouns, adjectives, and verbs with illustrative sentences, while most of the units present examples of colloquial sentences, thematically organized (for instance, among the chapters we have 'The Tourist', 'The Merchant', 'The Housewife', 'The Sailor'). In these chapters, the English sentences are followed by the Chinese translation in characters and in romanized transcription: for instance, some lines from the unit 'In a Shop' (Giles 1887: 21):

> Have you any good skins here? 你們這兒有好皮子沒有 *Neemun-cher yo how p'eedza mayo ?*
> What kind do you want? 你要什麼樣兒皮子 *Nee yow shunmo yahnger pee'dza?*
> [...]
> This jacket is Tls.[*taels*]150.00 這個馬褂 一百五十兩銀子 *Chayka mahkwah yee pi wooshirt layang yeendza*

Pages 33–65 consist of a simple glossary, listing alphabetically the English entries and the Chinese equivalents, in characters and transcription.

As these examples show, the aim of this work was to prepare learners to be in contact, to live and work with Chinese native speakers, a goal being very similar to the 'social goals' (*objectifs sociaux*) identified by Puren (2005: 6–7) for the communicative and action-oriented approaches to foreign language teaching elaborated in recent decades.

By contrast, *A Course of Mandarin Lessons based on Idiom* by the American Presbyterian missionary Calvin W. Mateer (1836–1908), first published in Shanghai in 1892, can be regarded as an example of manuals characterized by the prominence of grammar. The content is organized in units devoted to topics like 'The general classifier 個'; 'Demonstrative pronouns 這, 那'; 'Personal pronouns'; 'The possessive particle 的'; and the examples of sentences are clearly composed or selected to illustrate grammar points.

For instance, in the second lesson we find the following examples of the way of using the demonstrative adjectives and pronouns (Mateer 1922: 5):

> ¹ 這個人沒有學問。²那個人沒有錢。 [...]
> 1.This man has no learning 2. That man has no money

These illustrative sentences are followed by grammatical and lexical explanations (Martin 1922: 5):

> 這, 那 This That
> These words, when not followed by a special classifier, are generally followed by 個 and 些. Sometimes the 個 and 些 are omitted, the sense remaining approximately the same. When followed by 些, the meaning is plural; viz. these and those. The 些 sometimes takes an 一 before it, which modifies the sense a little, making it equivalent to this or that lot of, etc. Thus, 這些東西means these things, 這一些東西 means rather this lot of things.

Among the characteristics of this textbook, the author emphasized the place reserved to authentic materials ('all extant Mandarin literature was considered a legitimate field from which to gather') and the important role of Chinese informants (Mateer 1922: iv), claiming that:

> The manner of their preparation implies that the sentences are truly Chinese in thought, style, and idiom. With the exception of the short, simple sentences in the first twenty or thirty lessons; the author has scarcely composed a single sentence in the book.

Conclusion

Nineteenth-century Chinese language learning materials were extremely diverse, ranging from concise phrasebooks for beginners to structured manuals of spoken and written Chinese for professional purposes. Different models and methodologies were adopted and often combined. The influence of Western grammar studies, introduced since the seventeenth century in China, was noteworthy: on the one hand, pedagogical grammars were numerous among the nineteenth-century didactic tools; on the other hand, different language textbooks were built on grammatical progression, or included concise grammatical treatises. Nevertheless, the Chinese pedagogical tradition was also taken into account: native monolingual primers were translated into Western languages, adapted as foreign language teaching materials; and they inspired Western authors in compiling their manuals of Chinese. Hence, we can underline that this period, just as in other linguistic and didactic traditions, was characterized by 'continuity and overlap among teaching theories and practices' (Howatt and Smith 2014: 75).

Nineteenth-century didactic grammars and language textbooks, mainly composed by China-based missionaries and diplomats, were all characterized by a markedly practical approach, distinguishing them from the reference grammars of the same period (essentially compiled by academics in Europe). Among the innovations and the peculiarities of this kind of work, we can underline the space allocated to authentic materials and the role of Chinese informants. In some works we also find the attempt at presenting the most frequent and useful words and expressions, in the case of Martin (1879) thanks to the selection of characters and words based on corpora and frequency lists.

It is worth stressing that some pedagogical and methodological issues raised in these works, for instance about the ways of dealing with Chinese grammar, tones, script or the space to allocate to authentic materials are still debated in the pedagogy of Chinese as a foreign language (for instance, Zhang 2009: 132–36; Drocourt 2015; Raini 2007; McLelland 2015). I hope to have demonstrated in this chapter that the rich production of such nineteenth-century pedagogical materials, amalgamating Western and Chinese linguistic and didactic traditions, occupies an important place in the history of Chinese as a foreign language learning and teaching, and deserves further investigation.

Bibliography

Primary sources

ABEL-RÉMUSAT, JEAN-PIERRE. 1822. *Elémens de la grammaire chinoise ou principes généraux du Kou-wen, ou style antique, et du Kouan-hoa, c'est-à-dire de la langue commune généralement usitée dans l'empire chinois* (Paris: Imprimerie Royale)

BAZIN, ANTOINE. 1856. *Mémoire sur les principes généraux du chinois vulgaire* (Paris: Imprimerie royale)

GABELENTZ, GEORG VON DER. 1881. *Chinesiche Grammatik mit Ausschluß des niederen Stiles und der heutigen Umgangssprache* (Leipzig: Weigel)

GILES, HERBERT ALLEN (ed. and trans.). 1873. *The san tzŭ ching: or three character classic [by Wang Ying-lin], and the ch'ien tzŭ wên, or thousand character essay [by Chou Hsing-Ssu] Metrically Translated by Herbert A. Giles* [Shanghai: de Carvalho]

———. 1887. 無師自明, *Chinese Without A Teacher-Being a Collection of Easy and Useful Sentences in the Mandarin Dialect, with a Vocabulary* ([Shanghai: Kelly & Walsh])

GONÇALVES, JOAQUIM A. 1829. *Arte china constante de alphabeto e grammatical* (Macao: Real Colégio de São José)

JULIEN, STANISLAS (ed. and trans.). 1864a. *Thsien-tseu-wen. Le livre des mille mots, le plus ancien livre élémentaire des chinois* (Paris: Duprat)

—— (ed. and trans.). 1864b. *San tseu king. Trium litterarum liber a Wang-Pe-Heou sub finem XIII. saeculi compositus* (Paris: Duprat)

—— (ed. and trans.). 1864c. *San -tsze-king: The three character classic published in Chinese and English by S Julien* (Paris: Duprat)

———. 1869. *Syntaxe nouvelle de la langue chinoise* (Paris: Maisonneuve)

KLECZKOWSKI, MICHEL. 1876. *Cours graduel et complet de chinois parlé et écrit* (Paris: Maisonneuve)

MARTIN, WILLIAM A. P. 1897. *The Analytical Reader: A Short Method for Learning to Read and Write Chinese* (Shanghai: Presbyterian Mission Press)

MATEER, CALVIN W. 1922 [1892]. *A Course of Mandarin Lessons, Based on Idiom* (Shanghai: Presbyterian Mission Press)

MORRISON, ROBERT. 2008 [1815]. *A Grammar of the Chinese Language* (Zhengzhou: Henan chubanshe)

———. 1816. *Dialogues and detached sentences in the Chinese language, with a free and verbal translation in English, collected from various sources by the Rev. Morrison* (Macao: East India Company's Press)

WADE, THOMAS FRANCIS. 1867A. *Wên-Chien tzŭ-erh chi, A Series of Papers Selected As Specimens Of Documentary Chinese, Designed To Assist Students of The Language as Written By The Officials Of China* (London: Trübner)

———. 1867B. *Yü-yen Tzŭ-erh chi, a Progressive Course Designed to Assist the Student of Colloquial Chinese, as Spoken in the Capital and the Metropolitan Department, in eight parts, with Key, Syllabary and Writing Exercises*, I (London: Trübner)

———. 1867C. *Yü-yen Tzŭ-erh chi, a Progressive Course Designed to Assist the Student of Colloquial Chinese, as Spoken in the Capital and the Metropolitan Department, in eight parts, with Key, Syllabary and Writing Exercises*, II (London: Trübner)

———. 1867D. *Key to the Tzŭ Erh Chi — Documentary Series*, I (London: Trübner)

Secondary sources

ALLANIC, BERNARD, 2015. 'Une expérience d'enseignement-apprentissage raisonné des caractères', *Les Langues Modernes*, 4: 27–34

BREITENBACH, SANDRA. 2000. 'Introduction: The Biographical, Historical, and Grammatical Context of Francisco Varo's *Arte de la lengua Madarina* (Canton, 1703)', in *Francisco Varo's Grammar of the Mandarin Language, 1703: An English Translation of 'Arte de la Lengua Mandarina'*, ed. by W. South Coblin and Joseph A. Levi (Amsterdam; Philadelphia: Benjamins), pp. ixx–liii

BROCKEY, LIAM MATTHEW. 2008. *Journey to the East: The Jesuit Mission to China, 1579–1724* (Cambridge, MA: Harvard University Press)

CASTORINA, MIRIAM. 2014. 'I materiali didattici del Collegio dei Cinesi di Napoli: una ricerca preliminare', in *Atti del XIII Convegno dell'Associazione Italiana Studi Cinesi*, ed. by C. Bulfoni and S. Pozzi (Milan: Angeli), pp. 145-55

CHAPPELL, HILARY. 2006. 'From Eurocentrism to Sinocentrism: The Case of Disposal Constructions in Sinitic Languages', in *Catching Language: The Standing Challenge of Grammar Writing*, ed. by F. Ameka, A. Dench and N. Evans (Berlin: Mouton de Gruyter), pp. 441–86

——, and ALAIN PEYRAUBE. 2014. 'The History of Chinese Grammar in Chinese and Western Scholarly Tradition', *Language & History*, 57: 107-36

DROCOURT, ZHITANG. 2015. 'L'écriture chinoise: entre universaux et spécificités', *Les Langues Modernes*, 4: 15-26

FATICA, MICHELE. 2005. 'Giacomo Lignana, Michele Kerbaker, Angelo De Gubernatis e la fondazione a Napoli dell'Istituto Orientale (1888)', *Scritture di storia*, 4: 165–230

GALY, LAURENT. 1995. 'Entre sinologie pratique et sinologie savant: les interprètes professeurs de l'école des langues orientales vivantes, 1871-1930', in *Un siècle d'enseignement du chinois à l'Ecole des langues orientales*, ed. by M.-C. Bergère and A. Pino (Paris: L'Asiathèque), pp. 131-67

GERMAIN, CLAUDE. 1993. *Évolution de l'enseignement des langues: 5 000 ans d'histoire* (Paris: CLÉ International; Montréal: HMH)

HOWATT, A. P. R., and RICHARD SMITH. 2014. 'The History of Teaching English as a Foreign Language, from a British and European Perspective', *Language and History*, 57: 75–95

KLÖTER, HENNING. 2011. *The Language of the Sangleys: A Chinese Vernacular in Missionary Sources of the Seventeenth Century* (Leiden and Boston: Brill)

LEVI, JOSEPH A. 2007. 'Padre Joaquim Afonso Gonçalves (1781-1834) and the Arte China (1829): An Innovative Linguistic Approach to Teaching Chinese Grammar', in *Missionary Linguistics III / Lingüística misionera III: Morphology and Syntax*, ed. by Otto Zwartjes, Gregory James and Emilio Ridruejo (Amsterdam and Philadelphia: Benjamins), pp. 211-32

McLELLAND, NICOLA. 2015. 'Teach Yourself Chinese — How? The History of Chinese Self-instruction Manuals for English Speakers, 1900-2010', *Journal of the Chinese Language Teachers Association*, 50: 109-52

MASINI, FEDERICO. 1993. *The Formation of Modern Chinese Lexicon and its Evolution toward a National Language: The Period from 1840 to 1898*, Journal of Chinese Linguistics Monograph Series, 6 (Berkeley: University of California)

PATERNICÒ, LUISA M. 2011. 'Martino Martini and the First Grammar of Mandarin Chinese Ever Written and Published', *Hanxue Yanjiu*, 29: 229–66

PELLIN, TOMMASO. 2009. *Lessico grammaticale in Cina (1859–1924)* (Milan: Angeli)

PEYRAUBE, ALAIN. 2001. 'Some Reflections on the Sources of the Mashi Wentong', in *New Terms for New Ideas: Western Knowledge and Lexical Change in Late Imperial China*, ed. by Michael Lackner, Iwo Amelung and Joachim Kurtz (Leiden: Brill), pp. 341-56

PINO, ANGEL, and ISABELLE RABUT. 1995. 'La Chaire de chinois à l'affiche de l'École des Langues O', 1843-1945', in *Un siècle d'enseignement du chinois à l'École des langues orientales: 1840–1945*, ed. by Marie-Claire Bergère and Angel Pino (Paris: L'Asiathèque), pp. 315-38

PUREN, CHRISTIAN. 2005. 'L'Evolution historique des approches en didactique des langues-cultures, ou comment faire l'unité des 'unités didactiques', in *Congrès annuel de l'Association pour la Diffusion de l'Allemand en France (ADEAF), École Supérieure de Commerce de Clermont-Ferrand, 2–3 novembre 2004, Le Nouveau Bulletin de l'ADEAF*, 89: 40-51

RABUT, ISABELLE. 1995. 'Un siècle d'enseignement du chinois aux Langues O': éléments d'une enquête sur la didactique de la langue chinoise en France du milieu du XIXe siècle à la fin de la Seconde Guerre mondiale', in *Un siècle d'enseignement du chinois à l'École des langues orientales: 1840–1945*, ed. by Marie-Claire Bergère and Angel Pino (Paris: L'Asiathèque), pp. 213-69

RAINI, EMANUELE. 2007. 'Osservazioni sulla ridondanza fonologica e prosodica del *putonghua*', in *La Cina e il Mondo, Atti del XI Convegno dell'Associazione Italiana di Studi Cinesi*, Roma, 22–24 febbraio 2007 (Rome: Nuova Cultura), pp. 659–72

——. 2010. 'Sistemi di romanizzazione del cinese mandarino nei secoli xvi-xviii' (unpublished doctoral thesis, Sapienza-Università di Roma)

RIMSKY-KORSAKOFF DYER, SVETLANA. 1983. *Grammatical Analysis of the. Lao Ch'i-ta. With an English Translation of the Chinese Text*, Faculty of Asian Studies Monographs: n.s. No. 3 (Canberra: Faculty of Asian Studies, Australian National University)

SÁNCHEZ, AQUILINO. 2014. 'Spanish as a Foreign Language in Europe: Six Centuries of Teaching Materials', *Language and History*, 57: 59-74

ZHANG, XIPING 张西平. 2009. *Shijie Hanyu jiaoyu shi* 世界汉语教育史 (Beijing: Shangwu yinshuguan)

ZWARTJES, OTTO. 2011. *Portuguese Missionary Grammars in Asia, Africa and Brazil, 1550–1800* (Amsterdam and Philadelphia: Benjamins)

Notes to Chapter 10

1. The composition of this work was probably tied to the proselyting activities of Dominican missionaries to the Chinese community who had settled in the Philippines (Chappell and Peyraube 2014: 115). The Dominicans arrived in Manila in 1587 and reached southern China at the beginning of the seventeenth century (Klöter 2011: 34; Chappell and Peyraube 2014: 112).

2. The Jesuit Mission was established in southern China in 1579 (Klöter 2011: 34). In the following decades the Jesuits moved towards the inner and the northern regions of the Empire (including the capital), and by 1631 the mission had residences spread over eight of the fifteen imperial provinces (Brockey 2008: 49, 61, 89).

3. The Collegio dei Cinesi was founded in Naples in 1724 by the Italian missionary Matteo Ripa (1682-1745) and formally approved by Pope Clement XIII in 1732. This institute, created with the aims of training Chinese priests and forming interpreters of Oriental languages, was destined to become the Naples Oriental University (Fatica 2005; Castorina 2014: 146-47).

4. For instance, we can quote the *Leçons progressives pour l'étude du chinois parlé et écrit* by A. Mouillesaux de Bernières, published in Beijing in 1886, which is not investigated in this chapter; or Wade's *Progressive Course* (see below).

5. It is important to stress that several grammars and manuals were devoted to other Chinese languages and regional varieties. The analysis and description of the different varieties represented in nineteenth-century didactic materials are topics for further research and go beyond the purpose of the present chapter.

6. In the body of the text we use the *pinyin* transcription of Chinese characters, the official transcription system adopted in the People's Republic of China. In the quotations we have maintained the original transcriptions. The different transcription systems elaborated by Western missionaries and scholars are not analysed in this paper. On some of these romanization systems, see Raini (2010).

7. The final particle (矣) is rendered as an exclamation mark in the word-for-word translation, while we find a full stop in the illustrative sentence.

8. For instance, we quote the first sentences of the *Laoqida*: 大哥你從哪裡來。我從高麗王京來。Elder brother, where do you come from? I come from the Royal Capital in Korea (quoted from Rimsky-Korsakoff Dyer 1983: 304–05).

9. The *Advertência* (Gonçalves 1829: 89) indicates that this section and the following could also be used by Chinese learners of Portuguese (*Como esta parte, e seguintes servirão também os Chinas aprender português*), even though no specific parts of the work are dedicated to the description of the Portuguese language.

10. English translations are by the author.

11. The symbol Δ is used in this work to separate the examples in vernacular and in classical Chinese.

CHAPTER 11

Isawa Shuji and Visible Speech in Japan: An Early Application of Phonetics to the Teaching of Chinese Pronunciation

Chang Zou

This article introduces Isawa Shuji's method of Chinese pronunciation teaching. In Japan, the history of Mandarin pronunciation teaching can be traced back to the Meiji period (1868-1912). Due to the fact that Chinese was not considered an academic subject at that time, instead of a methodology grounded in best practices of contemporary linguistics, the method adopted in Chinese teaching was mainly based on tradition, or based on each teacher's idiosyncratic experience. Being dissatisfied with this situation, Isawa Shuji found and trialled a special method in his pronunciation study and teaching practice, the application of 'visible speech'. The learners were mainly Japanese people, as well as Chinese speakers who suffered from stuttering. 'Visible speech' is a system consisting of symbols that show the position and movement of the vocal organ (articulator) which produce the sounds of language. Instead of using the ear to listen to pronunciation, students use their eyes to confirm which articulator should be moved and how to move it. The method was invented by Alexander Melville Bell, father of the inventor of the telephone, Alexander Graham Bell. This article mainly focuses on the following three topics: 1. How Isawa Shuji became familiar with the method; 2. The content of the method, Isawa Shuuji's conception of it, and his application of the novel method to the study and teaching of Chinese pronunciation; 3. The efficacy, influence and acceptance of the method on the basis of available evidence.

General introduction to Chinese Teaching in Japan in the Meiji Period (1868–1912)

During the Meiji period (1868-1912), Japan underwent tumultuous changes from a feudal to a modern society. Western culture came to be regarded as advanced and worthy of imitation; on the other hand, Chinese culture — which had been the main source of imported wisdom for thousands of years — began to be regarded as backward and worthy of rejection. Japan made every effort to study and catch up with Western culture, including wholesale adoption of political and economic systems and even extending to life-style (see 佐藤直助 [Sato Naosuke] 1968). On the other hand, in order to achieve the recognition it coveted as a leader on the world stage, Japan continued to expand its power and influence in neighbouring countries such as China. These thought patterns are clearly reflected in the language teaching of the time.

Scholars agree that there was little methodology grounded in linguistics governing Chinese teaching during the Meiji period.[1] To be more exact, there was no possibility for language teaching to be grounded in linguistics. English, French and German were taught academically for the purpose of learning about advanced culture and science. Chinese, by contrast, was mainly taught for the purpose of political, diplomatic and business use. In modern Japan, the first school opened to teach Chinese, the 漢語学所 [School of Chinese Learning], was set up by the Ministry of Foreign Affairs in 1871. It served the purpose of diplomatic needs. Although it became a department of the 東京外国語学校 [Tokyo School of Foreign Studies] in 1873, the contents of teaching did not change and its aim was still to train up practical interpreters (Rokkaku 1989: 11).

The curriculum of other universities also reveals that Chinese was never considered a language worthy of study for academic purposes. According to the publications of Rokkaku Tsunehiro (1919-), the leading scholar in the field of Chinese-language teaching in the Meiji period, few universities offered modern Chinese language courses; and the aim of Chinese courses was to meet practical needs. For example, the Imperial University of Japan at Tokyo (later renamed the University of Tokyo) established a Chinese-language course (Colloquial Chinese) in 1886 (Rokkaku 1984: 53). 'Colloquial Chinese' indicated that the course was for ordinary communication, as opposed to Classical Chinese.

In private universities such as WASEDA University, modern Chinese language lessons were first offered as an elective under the Department of Politics, Economics and Commerce in 1902 to 1903. At this time, Chinese was not available in public high schools. Meanwhile, some schools privately organized by volunteers — such as the 日清社 [Sino-Japanese Association], 興亜会 [Asia Promotion Society], 日清貿易研究所 [Institute for Sino-Japanese Trade], 善隣書院 [Zenrin Shoin, a Chinese academy], 東亜同文書院 [Toua Doubun Shoin, the East Asian Literary School] — were established, though these toed the line of the dominant foreign and domestic policy (Rokkaku 1984: 38-107).

The method adopted in the teaching of Chinese pronunciation was mainly based on the traditional way of reading texts aloud, or based on each teacher's idiosyncratic experience. For example, in the Chinese school managed by the Asia Promotion Society, teachers made students read the 三字経 [*Three Character Classic*], the 千字文 [*Thousand Character Classic*], and 中庸 [*The Doctrine Of The Golden Mean*] (Rokkaku 1984: 61). Reading books like this provided no guidance at all on pronunciation, since they are standard works used for teaching literacy in Chinese as a first language.

There was at least one effort before Isawa Shuji to improve the teaching of pronunciation in language teaching: the Romic Alphabet proposed by Henry Sweet (1845-1912) was adopted in teaching of English pronunciation by Ralph G. Watkin (1873-?), who taught in Tokyo Higher Normal School. 杉森此馬 (Sugimori Konoma (1858-1936)), who taught at Hiroshima Higher Normal School, introduced the knowledge of phonetics, which was learned from Henry Sweet. The use of the International Phonetic Alphabet to describe English pronunciation can be dated back at least to the book 『英語発音と綴字』 [*English Speech and Spelling*] published in 1919, which was written by 岩崎民平 (Iwasaki Tamihei (1892-1971)) (Tanabe 2015). However, it was not adopted in teaching Chinese pronunciation at that time. Dissatisfied with the current conditions of Chinese teaching, Isawa Shuji made an effort to find an effective way of teaching Chinese pronunciation.

A Brief Introduction to Isawa Shuji (1851–1917)

Isawa Shuji was active in many fields of education, and was especially well known in modern music education and education for persons with hearing and speech impediments. He was born on 30 June 1851 and died on 3 May 1917. He had a cosmopolitan upbringing. In early childhood, he began reading ancient Chinese books at home and at a local private school. In his youth, he was sent to America as a foreign-exchange student by the Japanese government. There, he was exposed to various pedagogical theories and methods. After returning to Japan, he helped to establish the Tokyo Normal School, the Tokyo School for the Deaf and the Tokyo School of Music; and he acted as Principal at each of these schools for a time. In 1895, just after The First Sino-Japanese War, Taiwan was ceded to Japan and Isawa was appointed Director of Education to Taiwan to help establish the Taiwanese public school system. In order to facilitate open communication with the local Chinese people and better to perform his duties for this educational project, Isawa Shuji trained several Japanese teachers to speak Chinese and brought them along. From this time on, he showed a great interest in Chinese pronunciation study and wrote several books with titles such as 『視話法』 [*Visible Speech*] or 『視話応用支那語正音韻鏡』 [*The Application of Visible Speech: A Chinese syllable chart*], which included Chinese pronunciation, Japanese pronunciation and Korean pronunciation. In the last few years of his life, he even went abroad to China to spread his method and sought to correct the pronunciation of local Chinese people who struggled with stuttering. He continued this work until he passed away at the age of sixty-seven (Isawa 1912; Kaminuma 1989).

Isawa's Encounter with 'Visible Speech'

From 1875 to 1878, Isawa Shuji studied in America. He entered Bridgewater Normal School in Massachusetts to study in 1875, and then graduated from senior class in 1877. After that, he spent an additional year studying in the Department of Science at Harvard University. In 1876, he first encountered 'Visible Speech' when he attended an exhibition for the centennial anniversary of American Independence held in Philadelphia. There he noticed a strange chart on the wall, which, he learned from the staff, had been produced by Alexander Melville Bell. This is the chart of 'Visible Speech'. Bell's system of Visible Speech was elaborated over a period of years; its 'Principles of Speech' — which only dealt with English sounds — was brought out in 1849; and the system for universal use was completed in 1864 (Bell 1867: 14–19). Bell's son, Alexander Graham Bell, had adopted and popularized this system for use in treating people with hearing and speech impediments. Isawa recognized in the chart, however, potential for application to foreign-language study, especially phonetics. As Isawa himself was very insecure about his own English pronunciation, he decided to visit Graham Bell in Boston to have it corrected. Isawa reasoned that if people with hearing and speech impediments could learn to speak using this method, he should be able to master the correct pronunciation of English. Having finally achieved this goal, he brought the method to Japan and applied it to pronunciation treatments for conditions like stuttering among native Japanese speakers, to the correction of pronunciation among Japanese learners of Chinese, and to the teaching of foreign languages in Japan.

'Visible Speech' and How Isawa Shuji Himself Conceived of It

In his book 『視話法』 [*Visible Speech*], published in 1901, Isawa Shuji explained the theory and introduced the application of the theory to Japanese and English pronunciation. The book opens with an explanation of how to produce speech sounds, which is similar to the thought of articulatory phonetics today. Isawa wrote that in order to produce sounds, we need airflow from the lungs and vocal organs. 'Visible Speech' is a system consisting of symbols that show the position and movement of the vocal organs (articulators) which produce the sounds of language. The symbols indicate the parts that include the throat, tongue, lips, vocal cords, etc. Together they function as a type of phonetic notation. Bell himself called it 'Physiological letters'.

Figure 11.1 shows the consonants in the book *Visible Speech*: the symbols on the left half of the Figure represent, from left to right, the vocal cords; back of the tongue; top of the tongue; front of the tongue; lip; and the symbol at the soft palate means nasal; and the 'greater-than' sign (>) means to breathe. In the chart to the right, vertical columns are arranged with the part of the articulator to be used, and horizontal rows are arranged with the state or shape of articulation. For example, the symbol in the eighth column, second row should indicate alveolar nasal.

The vertical line down the centre of the cross-section of the vocal tract in Figure 11.2 indicates the central reference point of the tongue. The point on the left indicates the placement (height) of the back of the tongue. The point on the right of the line indicates the height of the front of the tongue. The point on the left and right simultaneously indicates the placement of the middle of the tongue. For example, the second symbol from the left in the left-hand picture indicates that the back of the tongue should be raised, and the sixth symbol from left means that the

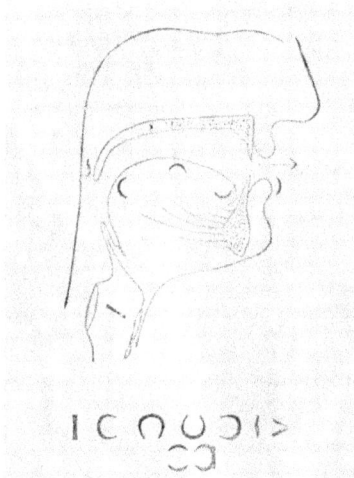

FIG. 11.1. Symbols of the Consonants (Isawa 1901: 18-20)

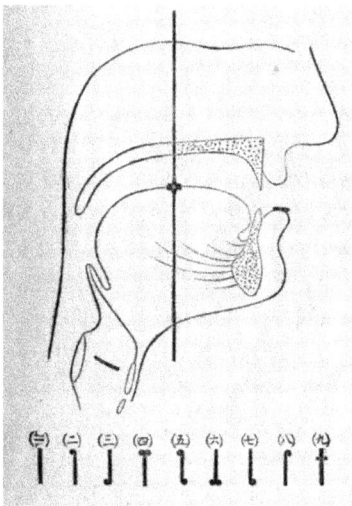

FIG. 11.2. Symbols of the Vowels (Isawa 1901: 27-30)

middle of the tongue should be lowered. So in this way, consonants and vowels are translated into visible symbols that represent the vocal organs (articulators) that we use when we pronounce. With the combination of these symbols, we can see how to shape the oral cavity in different ways, and to produce the sounds we wish.

Figure 11.3 below is an example of its application, which shows the symbols representing the Japanese sound system.

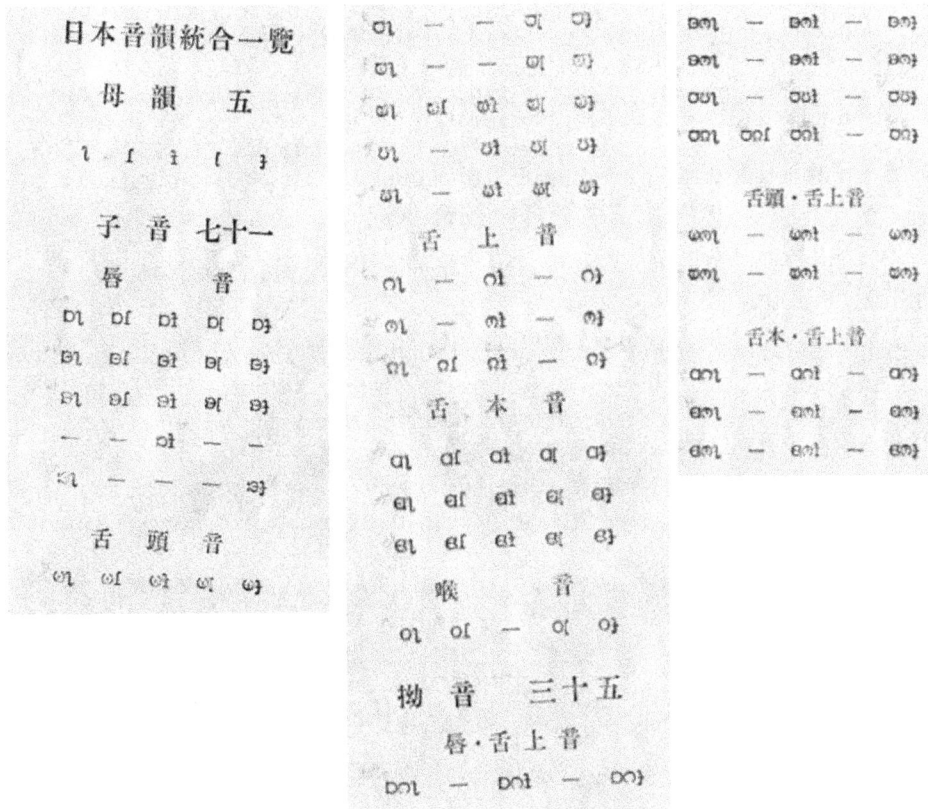

FIG. 11.3. The Sound System of Japanese (Isawa 1901: 73–75)

Compared to a phonogram writing system such as Latin alphabets or Japanese *kana*, or a logographic writing system such as Chinese or Ancient Egyptian hieroglyphs, 'visible speech' directly shows the act or manner of uttering a speech sound. Since all of the sounds of language are produced by human vocal organs, and humans around the world share virtually the same vocal organs, Isawa thought that the 'visible speech' symbols might also be applied to the writing systems of other foreign languages. Besides the Japanese sound system, Isawa also tried it with Chinese.

In the book *Visible Speech*, Isawa mentioned nine significant applications of 'visible speech':

1. Helping to establish standard pronunciation of any national language;

2. Helping to correct the personal pronunciation habits that people may have in different regions;

3. Helping to investigate the system of dialects both for posterity and for protection against loss;

4. Helping foreign-language learners to master correct standard pronunciation;

5. Helping to diffuse suzerain languages to colonies (e.g. Japanese in China);

6. Helping to establish a phonetic symbol system which can be adapted to all languages;

7. Promoting the smooth exchange of information between different countries, reducing the labour of translation;

8. Helping people with hearing and speech impediments to speak;

9. Helping to eliminate illiteracy around the world, preparing any pupil to read and write in only a few weeks. (Isawa 1901: 2–8)

The Application of this Novel Method in the Study and Teaching of Chinese Pronunciation

As mentioned above, one of Isawa's applications of 'visible speech' was to try it with Chinese. He established a writing system for Chinese pronunciation by using the 'visible speech' symbols. At the same time he created another writing system using symbols that he transformed from Chinese radicals and Japanese *kana*. Figure 11.4 is the chart Isawa made to show the entire structure of Chinese pronunciation, which is similar to the syllable chart we use in teaching Chinese as a Foreign Language today.

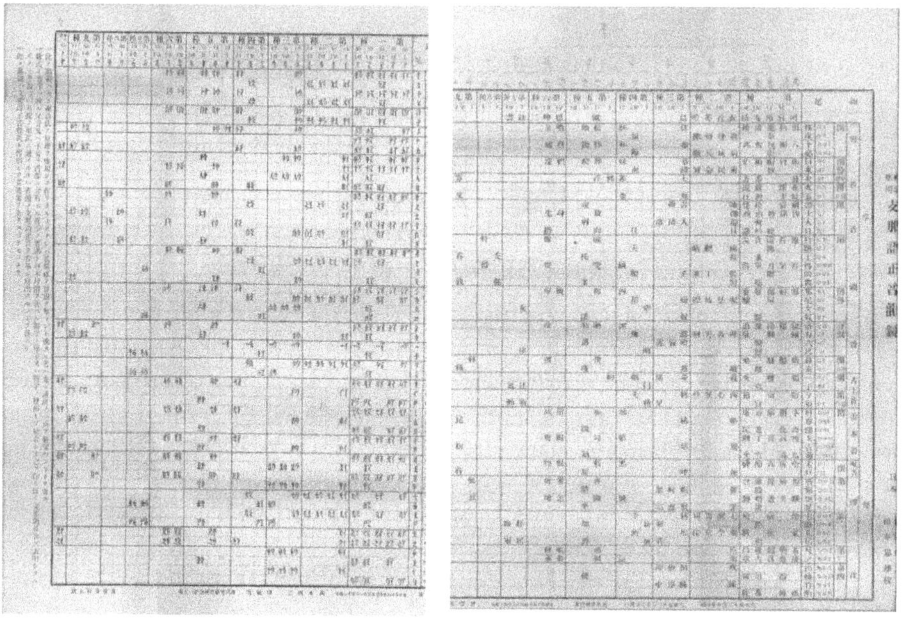

FIG. 11.4. Chinese Syllable Chart (Isawa 1916)

中国語音節表

	a	o	e	-i	-i	er	ai	ei	ao	ou	an	en	ang	eng	ong	i	ia	ie	iao	iou	ian	in	iang	ing	iong	u	ua	uo	uai	uei	uan	uen	uang	ueng	ü	üe	üan	ün
	a	o	e			er	ai	ei	ao	ou	an	en	ang	eng		yi	ya	ye	yao	you	yan	yin	yang	ying	yong	wu	wa	wo	wai	wei	wan	wen	wang	weng	yu	yue	yuan	yun
b	ba	bo					bai	bei	bao		ban	ben	bang	beng		bi		bie	biao		bian	bin		bing		bu												
p	pa	po					pai	pei	pao	pou	pan	pen	pang	peng		pi		pie	piao		pian	pin		ping		pu												
m	ma	mo	me				mai	mei	mao	mou	man	men	mang	meng		mi		mie	miao	miu	mian	min		ming		mu												
f	fa	fo						fei		fou	fan	fen	fang	feng												fu												
d	da		de				dai	dei	dao	dou	dan	den	dang	deng	dong	di	dia	die	diao	diu	dian			ding		du		duo		dui	duan	dun						
t	ta		te				tai		tao	tou	tan		tang	teng	tong	ti		tie	tiao		tian			ting		tu		tuo		tui	tuan	tun						
n	na		ne				nai	nei	nao	nou	nan	nen	nang	neng	nong	ni		nie	niao	niu	nian	nin	niang	ning		nu		nuo			nuan				nü	nüe		
l	la	lo	le				lai	lei	lao	lou	lan		lang	leng	long	li	lia	lie	liao	liu	lian	lin	liang	ling		lu		luo			luan				lü	lüe		
g	ga		ge				gai	gei	gao	gou	gan	gen	gang	geng	gong											gu	gua	guo	guai	gui	guan	gun	guang					
k	ka		ke				kai	kei	kao	kou	kan	ken	kang	keng	kong											ku	kua	kuo	kuai	kui	kuan	kun	kuang					
h	ha		he				hai	hei	hao	hou	han	hen	hang	heng	hong											hu	hua	huo	huai	hui	huan	hun	huang					
j																ji	jia	jie	jiao	jiu	jian	jin	jiang	jing	jiong										ju	jue	juan	jun
q																qi	qia	qie	qiao	qiu	qian	qin	qiang	qing	qiong										qu	que	quan	qun
x																xi	xia	xie	xiao	xiu	xian	xin	xiang	xing	xiong										xu	xue	xuan	xun
zh	zha	zhe	zhi				zhai	zhei	zhao	zhou	zhan	zhen	zhang	zheng	zhong											zhu	zhua	zhuo	zhuai	zhui	zhuan	zhun	zhuang					
ch	cha	che	chi				chai		chao	chou	chan	chen	chang	cheng	chong											chu	chua	chuo	chuai	chui	chuan	chun	chuang					
sh	sha	she	shi				shai	shei	shao	shou	shan	shen	shang	sheng												shu	shua	shuo	shuai	shui	shuan	shun	shuang					
r			re	ri					rao	rou	ran	ren	rang	reng	rong											ru	rua	ruo		rui	ruan	run						
z	za		ze	zi			zai	zei	zao	zou	zan	zen	zang	zeng	zong											zu		zuo		zui	zuan	zun						
c	ca		ce	ci			cai		cao	cou	can	cen	cang	ceng	cong											cu		cuo		cui	cuan	cun						
s	sa		se	si			sai		sao	sou	san	sen	sang	seng	song											su		suo		sui	suan	sun						

FIG. 11.5. One Example of Chinese Syllable Charts in Use Today

In Figure 11.4, vertical columns show the consonants and horizontal rows show the vowels. The crossed grids in the middle show the pronunciation of Chinese syllables, which come to 410 in total, even without considering semantically significant tones. (Incidentally, the syllable chart in use today only accounts for around four hundred syllables, independent of tone.) According to Isawa, his chart was checked by a Chinese native teacher; to some extent it could be regarded as a reflection of Chinese pronunciation of that time. It also indicates that Chinese pronunciation has changed slightly from that time to today. For example, in Isawa's chart, the pronunciation '[io]' — which does not exist in today's syllable chart — is indicated.

In Isawa's key work on Chinese pronunciation, 支那語正音発微 [*Getting to the Core of Correct Chinese Pronunciation*], he sorted and explained the consonants and vowels, basing his explanation on the theory of Visible Speech. 'Visible speech' symbols invented by Melville Bell were supplemented by a hybrid Japanese-Chinese writing system to show the pronunciation of Chinese characters. For the convenience of learners, every pronunciation was specifically written in all four tones, and each was followed by some examples of characters and common phrases. Exercises were added to each pronunciation. A further practice book (Isawa 1915b) was produced to supplement this text. One of the features worth mentioning is that Isawa already clearly marked the tonal modification, neutral tone and stress of words. Stress of words had not been generally noticed in Chinese teaching at that time.

Figure 11.6 below shows the title page and the contents page of the text of 支那語正音発微 [*Getting to the Core of Correct Chinese Pronunciation*].

FIG. 11.6. Title page and contents page of 『支那語正音発微』(Isawa 1915a)

Isawa's practice of teaching Chinese pronunciation was mainly implemented during his time in Taiwan (1895-99) and Manchuria (1916). As mentioned above, for the purpose of communicating and educating, Isawa trained some Japanese teachers to speak Chinese. According to the speech at the graduation ceremony of the first teacher-training programme held on the 1 July 1896 in Taiwan, Isawa reported that after a mere two and half months of training, the teachers already felt no difficulty in daily conversation. And in a speech entitled 台湾教育に対する今昔の感 [A Retrospective View of Education in Taiwan], he mentioned that, at first — for about three weeks — instead of conversation, only the pronunciation of vowels according to the Taiwanese dialect was practised in eight tones[2] from morning to night (Isawa 1958: 643-58). He emphasized that learning the pronunciation of a foreign language is different for children and adults. So, when teaching adults, the effective way is to teach some basic knowledge of phonetics first, then to let them see the action of vocal organ and to train their ear to become used to the pronunciation. He said that this thought came from the theory of 'Visible Speech'.

According to the record of his time in Manchuria in 1916 in the book 楽石伊沢修二先生 [Our Teacher, Isawa Shuji], in order to check the effectiveness of the book Getting to the Core of Correct Chinese Pronunciation, Isawa assembled thirty people around twenty-five-years old to teach them Chinese pronunciation for ten days (Memorial Association of Isawa Shuji 1919: 310). He used the method of 'Visible Speech', which meant, firstly, using the eyes to remember how properly to position the vocal organs.

The Efficacy, Influence and Acceptance of the Method

There is little record of Isawa's time in Taiwan. In his speech 'A Retrospective View of Education in Taiwan', Isawa mentioned that the teachers mastered the pronunciation of eight tones after twenty-one days of effort. After another forty days' worth of training in conversation, these teachers were sent to the 国語伝習所

[Japanese Language School] to teach Japanese in Taiwan. Isawa reported that some of the teachers' pronunciation was so good that sometimes they were thought to be natives of Taiwan (Isawa 1958: 652–53).

Speaking of the results of the practice of the method during Isawa's time in Manchuria, Isawa's juniors recorded that Japanese students had mastered correct Chinese pronunciation after six months' effort. Furthermore, Isawa tried to treat twenty-three Chinese people who suffered from stuttering in 大連公学堂 [Dalian Public School]. According to the record, the training lasted for twenty-three days and had positive results. One of the students reportedly made a good speech at the graduation ceremony in front of high-ranking officials and wealthy merchants (Memorial Association of Isawa Shuji 1919: 312).

As to the influence and acceptance of the method in Chinese teaching, Isawa's method was not accepted by mainstream Chinese education. However, one thing worth mentioning is that his son-in-law later published a book called *Phonetics: Visible Speech*.[3] This book explained phonetic knowledge and visible speech in more detail, emphasizing that this writing system was suited to recording the pronunciation system. It is thought to be influenced by Isawa's book.

There are some reasons that can be considered why Isawa's methods appeared unacceptable to contemporary Chinese education in Japan. Firstly, the purpose of learning Chinese at that time was mainly for practical uses such as diplomacy or business, so students cared more about the speed of learning than accuracy or any academic theory. Secondly, the symbols of Visible Speech were unfamiliar to Japanese people; students preferred to use Japanese *kana* or roman letters to transcribe Chinese pronunciation, despite the limitations of these systems in expressing Chinese pronunciation correctly. Thirdly, although the symbols may show the act or manner of uttering sound, they cannot describe it precisely. For example, we cannot tell to which point we should put our tongue above when we see the symbol 'ɯ', which would be used for an alveolar consonant.

The Mainstream Writing System in Parallel with and after the 'Visible Speech' Writing System

While Isawa was trying the 'Visible Speech' writing system, the mainstream of Chinese pronunciation education was using 'Japanese *kana*' and 'Wade–Giles'. Wade–Giles is a romanization system for Mandarin Chinese. It developed from a system produced by Thomas Wade,[4] who acted as a British diplomat in China from 1842 to 1883, and was given completed form with Herbert Giles's Chinese–English Dictionary of 1892. After the Republic of China National Ministry of Education released the 'Bopomofo' system in 1913, Chinese teaching in Japan turned to use this system. The symbols of this system, taken mainly from the forms of ancient Chinese characters, remain to this day in Taiwan's school education and dictionaries. In 1958, the 'Bopomofo' system was replaced by 'Hanyu Pinyin', which we use today to transcribe Chinese pronunciation.

Even the writing system 'Hanyu Pinyin' that we use today still has some deficiencies or misalignments between its orthography and phonetic value. For example, the Chinese character '天' is rendered as *tian*, but the *-an* is not pronounced as '[tʰian]', as we might expect by analogy with *-an* in words like 看 *kan* [kʰan], but as '[tʰien]'. Hence, we still have some way to go in finding a better form of writing and teaching Chinese in foreign contexts.

Conclusion

Testimonies of the time suggest that Isawa Shuji's method had some effect. However, it was not accepted by mainstream Chinese education. The reasons for its lack of acceptance are probably as follows: first, the purpose of learning Chinese at that time was mainly for practical uses such as diplomacy or business; speed, rather than perfect pronunciation, was the priority. Second, the symbols of Visible Speech were unfamiliar to Japanese people, and there were few learning materials produced using Visible Speech, so students preferred to use Japanese *kana* or roman letters to transcribe Chinese pronunciation. Third, the rise in popularity of romanization in general in early twentieth-century Japan made roman letters more popular; and some reformers in the Taisho era (1912–26) even recommended that the roman alphabet should replace *kana* and *kanji* for written Japanese. Fourth, although the symbols can show the act or manner of uttering sound, they cannot describe it precisely.

Due to the promotion of the language policy issued by the Chinese government in 1958, the writing system 'Hanyu Pinyin' become popularized and today we still use it to learn the pronunciation of Chinese. However, it too still has some deficiencies or misalignments between its orthography and phonetic value. We still have some way to go in finding a better form of writing and teaching Chinese in foreign contexts.

Bibliography

Primary sources

遠藤隆吉 [ENDO RYUKICHI]. 1906. 『発音学 : 視話音字』 [*Phonetics: Visible Speech*] (Tokyo: Hakubunkan)

後藤朝太郎 [GOTO ASATARO]. 1908. 『現代支那語学』 [*Modern Chinese*] (Tokyo: Hakubunkan)

伊沢修二 [ISAWA SHUJI]. 1901. 『視話法』 [*Visible Speech*] (Tokyo: Dainippon Tosho)

伊沢修二 [ISAWA SHUJI]. 1912. 『楽石自伝教界周遊前記』 [*An Autobiography of Isawa*] (Tokyo: Isawa Shuji's sixtieth birthday celebration group)

伊沢修二 [ISAWA SHUJI]. 1915A. 『支那語正音発微』 [*Getting to the Core of Correct Chinese Pronunciation*] (Tokyo: 楽石社 [Rakusekisya])

伊沢修二 [ISAWA SHUJI]. 1915B. 『支那語正音練習書』 [*An Exercise-book of Chinese Pronunciation*] (Tokyo: 楽石社 [Rakusekisya])

伊沢修二 [ISAWA SHUJI]. 1916. 『視話応用支那語正音韻鏡』 [*The Application of Visible Speech: A Chinese Syllable Chart*] (Tokyo: 楽石社 [Rakusekisya])

故伊沢先生記念事業会 [MEMORIAL ASSOCIATION OF ISAWA SHUJI]. 1919. 『樂石伊澤修二先生』 [*Our Teacher, Isawa Shuji*] (Tokyo: Memorial Association of Isawa Shuji)

伊沢修二 [ISAWA SHUJI]. 1958.『伊沢修二選集 』 [*Selected Works of Isawa Shuji*] (Nagano: 信濃教育会 [Shinano Educational Association])

魚返善雄 [YOSHIO OGAERI]. 1942.『支那語の発音と記号』 [*The Pronunciation and Writing System of Chinese*] (東京 [Tokyo]: SANSEIDO)

BELL, ALEX MELVILLE. 1867. *Visible Speech: The Science of Universal Alphabetics* (London: Simpkin, Marshall)

WADE, T. F. and W. C. HILLIER. 1886.『語言自邇集』[*Yü-yen tzu-erh chi: A Progressive Course Designed to Assist the Student of Colloquial Chinese*], 2nd edn (ShangHai: The Statistical Department of The Inspectorate General Of Customs)

Secondary sources

上沼八郎 [KAMINUMA HACHIRO]. 1989.『伊沢修二』 (Isawa shuji) (Tokyo: Yoshikawa Kobunkan)

佐藤直助 [SATO NAOSUKE]. 1968.『西洋文化受容の史的研究』 [*A Historical Study of Japan's Absorption of Western Culture*] (Tokyo: Tokyodo Publishing)

——. 1992.『明治文化全集』[*The Complete Series of Meiji Culture*]

六角恒広 [ROKKAKU TSUNEHIRO]. 1984.『近代日本の中国語教育』 [*Chinese Language Education in Modern Japan*] (Tokyo: Fuji shuppan)

——.1989. 『中国語教育史論考』 [*The Study of Chinese Education History*] (Tokyo: Fuji shuppan)

——.1991-98. 『中国語教本類集成』 [*A Compilation of Chinese Teaching Resources*] (Tokyo: Fuji shuppan)

田邉祐司 [TANABE YUJI]. 2015. 「日本英語音声教育史：岩崎民平『英語 発音と綴字』における"教育的まなざし 'A History of English Phonetic Education: The Pedagogical Perspective Involved in Iwasaki Tamihei's English Pronunciation and its Spelling',『専修人文論集 [Humanities Papers of Senshu University],』97: 31-49

Notes to Chapter 11

1. See Rokkaku (1984) and Goto (1908). Goto Asataro was a famous Chinese specialist in Japan during the Meiji and Showa periods.
2. At that time, most people in Taiwan spoke Min Nan dialect, which has eight tones.
3. 遠藤隆吉 (Endo Ryukichi (1874-1946)), Japanese sociologist, educator and thinker, Isawa's son-in-law. He published the book『発音学:視話音字』[*Phonetics: Visible Speech*] in 1906.
4. Thomas Francis Wade (1818-1895) came to China with the British Army in 1842. He also acted as a Chinese teacher for overseas employees. In 1871, he was appointed British Minister to China, and in 1883 he returned England. In 1888, he was elected the first Professor of Chinese at the University of Cambridge. His work 語言自邇集 [*Yü-yen tzu-erh chi: A Progressive Course Designed to Assist the Student of Colloquial Chinese*], published in 1867, was widely accepted, and his writing system 'Wade–Giles' was widely used by Chinese teachers and scholars in Japan during the Meiji period.

CHAPTER 12

❖

Chinese Language Educators in Meiji-Era Japan: Miyajima Daihachi and Zhang Tingyan

Yang Tiezheng

This chapter presents two key figures in the history of Chinese-language teaching in Japan: Miyajima Daihachi (1867-1943) and Zhang Tingyan (1864-1929). Miyajima Daihachi was one of the most famous Chinese educators in Meiji-era Japan. The Chinese institute that he set up in 1895, the Zenrin Syoin (善隣書院 [Zenrin Academy of Classical Learning]) soon became the centre of Chinese-language teaching in Japan, publishing a series of Chinese textbooks to meet the Chinese learner's needs at that time. His textbook of colloquial Chinese, *Kyūsyūhen* (急就篇) was seen as the 'Bible' of Chinese learning that every Japanese learner of Chinese had to use at the time. It was published more than 190 times between 1904 and 1945 and monopolized the market of basic-level Chinese textbooks. Zhang Tingyan (1864-1929) was a key native Chinese educator in Meiji-era Japan about whom little was previously known, but who also assisted with the production of the *Kyūsyūhen*. His Chinese textbooks were used widely as intermediate-level textbooks. This article traces how Miyajima Daihachi's *Kyūsyūhen* became a popular Chinese learning text and adds to our knowledge of Zhang Tingyan by analysing newly found materials.

Previous Research on the History of Chinese Language Education in Japan

The first research on the history of Chinese language education in Japan appeared after World War II. Although more than half a century has passed, the research achievements in this field are still relatively limited. Rokkaku Tsunehiro (六角恒廣, 1919-),[1] one of the scholars who participated in building the field of the history of Chinese education in Japan, wrote in his book *Tyūgokugo Kyōikushi no Kenkyū* (中国語教育史の研究 [*A Study of the History of Chinese Education*]) (Rokkaku 1988:12) as follows:

中国語教育史の研究は、昭和三0年（一九五五）前後の時期から生まれた研究分野である。この分野での研究はこれまで限られた二、三の研究者によっ

ておこなわれているにすぎない。したがって研究の成果も、他の諸研究の分野のものと比べてごく少数しか発表されていない。また中国語学界一般においても、中国語学研究が本筋であるため、中国語教育史の研究にはほとんど関心を示さないのが現状である。そのため中国語教育史の研究は、他の分野からあまり知られていない。

[The study of the history of Chinese language education [in Japan] was born around 1955. By now [1988], there are only two or three researchers working in this area. Due to this, the research achievements in this field are not as numerous as in other fields. In the area of Chinese language study, the research on Chinese language itself is the main trend, thus the current research status is that almost no attention is paid to this field. And it makes the study of the history of Chinese language education an almost unknown area.][2]

However, the situation that Rokkaku Tsunehiro described in 1988 has been changing. More researchers have started to work in this field and more research achievements have emerged. Two key researchers have built a solid research foundation in this field. The first landmark publication is the *Tyūgokugo Kankeisyo Syomoku* (中国語関係書書目 [*List of Chinese Textbooks*]) (Rokkaku 1968), by Rokkaku Tsunehiro (六角恒廣), a bibliography of 1437 Chinese textbooks published between 1867 and 1945, including the name of textbook, date of publication, the press, and the library where it is held. Also by Rokkaku, the *Tyūgokugo Kyōhonrui Syūsei* (中国語教本類集成 [*A Compilation of Chinese Textbooks*]) (Rokkaku 1991-98) is a huge compilation of forty volumes, containing 274 major Chinese textbooks, dictionaries and Chinese learning materials published in the Edo period (1603-1868) and in the Meiji era (1868-1912). Many items from Rokkaku's own collections, which are difficult to find or cannot be found in other libraries, are also included. We must also note *Tyūgokugo Kyōikushi no Kenkyū* (中国語教育史の研究 [*A Study of the History of Chinese Language Education*]) (Rokkaku 1988), which can be seen as a textbook on the basic status of the history of Chinese-language education in Japan. It introduces how the main Chinese schools in the Meiji era were established, and how those schools changed or disappeared. School curricula are included, and a number of Chinese teachers are also introduced. The final chapter provides an introduction to Chinese language education in the Edo period.

Also important is the *Tyūgokugo to Kindai Nihon* (中国語と近代日本 [*Chinese Language and Modern Japan*]), published in 1988 by Andō Hikotarō 安藤彦太郎 (1917-2009).[3] This small volume introduces the position of Chinese language education in Japanese society from the end of the nineteenth century to the beginning of the twentieth century, including the system of Chinese language education in Meiji-era Japan; the tradition of Montōtai Kyōhon (問答体教本 [Ask-and-Answer style Chinese textbook]); how Japanese people saw classical Chinese and the modern Chinese language, etc.

Background: Chinese Education in Meiji-era Japan: The Transition from Nanjing to Beijing Dialects

Japan has a long history of teaching and learning Chinese. Spoken Chinese has been taught in Japan since the Edo period (1603-1868). In the Edo period, spoken Chinese, known in Japan as Tōwa (唐話 [the language of the Tang Dynasty]), was used, studied and taught by so-called Tōtsūji (唐通事 [Chinese translators]) and their descendants at the Nagasaki port for international trade between Japan and China and other countries of South Asia. At that time, almost no attention was paid to the Beijing dialect in Japan, for most of the ships that arrived in Nagasaki were from South China. The sailors and migrant traders on the ships could only speak dialects of Southern China, so the main dialects used in Nagasaki were the Nanjing and Fuzhou dialects.

In 1870, the beginning of the Meiji era, Japan started to build diplomatic relations with China. In response to a shortage of Chinese translators, an official Chinese translator's training school *Kango Gakusyo* (漢語学所 [Chinese Institute]) was set up by the Ministry of Foreign Affairs (外務省) in 1871. At the same time, Tōtsūji began to go to the ports of Tokyo and Yokohama to seek better opportunities. Several found teaching positions in the *Kango Gakusyo*. Those teachers inherited the Chinese teaching system from Nagasaki and applied it in the *Kango Gakusyo*, including Chinese textbooks, curriculum and teaching method. Thus, Chinese teaching in the Meiji era was at first still in essence that of the Edo period. However, the Sino-Japanese Friendship and Trade Treaty in 1871 sparked the first governmental negotiations between Japan and China. During these negotiations, the Japanese realized that the Beijing dialect, rather than the Nanjing dialect, was used in the government of China. The Japanese now realized their dire need for Beijing-dialect-speaking officials, and started cultivating a Beijing style education system. Beijing dialect teachers were soon hired from Beijing, and appropriate textbooks[4] were soon adopted into the school curriculum. In 1876, the *Tokyo Gaikokugo Gakkō* (東京外国語学校 [Tokyo Foreign Language School]) switched its curriculum from teaching the Nanjing dialect to the Beijing dialect. Every school set up after that adopted the Beijing dialect.

The Chinese Language in Japan's Educational System

When considering the teaching of Chinese in Meiji-era Japan, the wider circumstances of foreign-language learning must be mentioned. After the Meiji Revolution, the whole of Japanese society turned its eyes towards Europe. The Japanese were eager to learn the advanced technology of Europe. People learned English, French and German for the purposes of understanding European culture and literature, and above all for pursuing advanced technology. In another words, learning European languages was seen as a way to acquire knowledge. The status of Chinese as a foreign language was quite different.

During that time, Japanese society had very complicated feelings towards China, especially when China lost the Sino-Japanese War of 1894 to 1895. The complicated feelings can also be reflected in the various names for the Chinese language in Japan. It was called Shinago 支那語 [the language of China]; Kango 漢語 [the language of the Han]; Shingo 清語 [the language of the Qin]; Shinkokugo 清国語 [the language of the Qing Dynasty]; Kago 華語 [the Chinese language]; and Mansyūgo 満州語 [the language of Manchuria]).[5] Unlike European languages, Chinese was learned for practical purposes — for business and for military action, for at that time Japan began to notice the commercial opportunities in China, and Chinese was taught in order to meet the needs of international trade. Further, Chinese was an important tool for the army. Each time military conflict occurred or war broke out between China and Japan,[6] the number of Chinese learners soared. Many 'Sensō Gogaku 戦争語学 [Chinese for war] textbooks' were published and were used in military schools. *Heiyō Shinago* (兵要支那語 [*Chinese for Military Use*]) and *Nisshin Kaiwa* (日清会話 [*Chinese–Japanese Conversation*]) are two examples. In these two textbooks, phrases like '若在路上要跑就打死你 [I will kill you, if you run away]' (Konoe Hohei Daiichiryodan 1894: 10) and '把他押到牢獄裡去 [Send him to the prison]' (Sanbō Honbu 1894: 11) can be seen. It is worth mentioning that Fukushima Yasumasa 福島安正 (1852-1919), who was the Captain General in the Imperial Japanese Army and who also helped build the system of Intelligence assessment of Japan, published a popular Chinese textbook, *Jijisyū Hyōsokuhen Shiseirenjyu* (自邇集平仄編四声聯珠 [*Combination of Four Tones*]) in 1886.

The difference in status between European languages and Chinese was also reflected in Japan's educational system (see Figure 12.1).

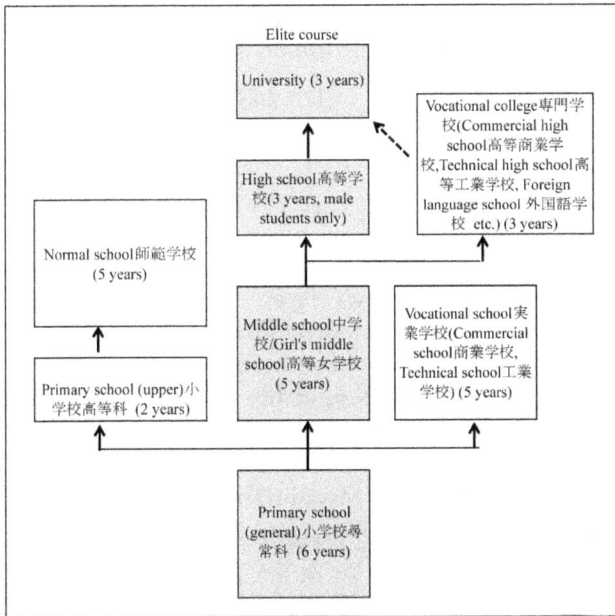

FIG. 12.1. The education system in Japan before World War II (after Andō Hikotarō 安藤彦太郎 *Tyūgokugo to Kindai Nihon* (中国語と近代日本 [*Chinese Language and Modern Japan*]) (1988: 2)

As shown in Figure 12.1, the progression from primary school to middle school, high school and finally university was the elite route that students from rich or powerful families could choose. Most senior officials in government and many upper-class people took this path at that time. However, before they entered university, a compulsory foreign-language course had to be taken in high school for three years. The foreign languages that could be selected were normally English, French and German. Chinese was not one of the options.

Someone who graduated from middle school and wanted to learn Chinese could find a way to learn it in vocational colleges such as a *Kōtōsyōgyō Gakko* (高等商業学校 [commercial high school]) or a *Gaigokugo Gakko* (外国語学校 [foreign language school]). Many of these students became junior officials with the job of interpreting and international trade between China and Japan.

This educational system created a situation that Kuraishi Takeshiro (倉石武四郎, 1897-1975)[7] described in his book *Shinago Kyōiku no Riron to Jissai* (支那語教育の理論と実際 [*The Theory and the Practice of Chinese Language Education*]) (Kuraishi 1941: 84) as follows:

> 北京なり南京なりに駐在している人たちで、支那語を上手に話すのは、おほむね、下僚であって、要職にある人は、ほとんど、支那語らしい支那語が話せない（中略）外交官として高い地位に進むために、欧州の教養は相当以上に重んぜられているが、支那語はまるつきり関係がない

> [Amongst those who were stationed in Beijing or Nanjing, the ones who could speak Chinese well were almost all junior officials. In contrast, almost all who held important positions could not speak Chinese. [...] For a diplomat, cultural knowledge about Europe was highly valued and decided whether he could get promoted or not. However Chinese had nothing to do with it.]

Having outlined the status of Chinese-language education in Meiji-era Japan, we turn now to two key figures: Miyajima Daihachi and Zhang Tinyan.

Miyajima Daihachi 宮島大八 (1867-1943)

Miyajima Daihachi 宮島大八 (courtesy name字: Eishi詠士; see Figure 12.2[8]), was born on 20 October 1867 in Yonezawa, Japan. Daihachi's father Miyajima Seichiro 宮島誠一郎was a warrior of the Yonezawa Domain (米沢藩). In the year of 1871, Seichiro began work for the Meiji Government, so Daihachi's family moved to Tokyo in 1872. At the age of thirteen, at his father's suggestion, Daihachi began learning the Chinese language in the Qing dynasty embassy (清国公使館). It was Daihachi's first time learning Chinese. Recalling his lessons in the Qing dynasty embassy sixty years later, Daihachi (Miyajima 1942: 21) wrote:

> いよいよ習うことになると、どんな教科書を使つたら適当かということになつたが、（中略）親父の案で、とにかく漢字を支那音で覚えたらよかろうということになつて、詩の韻をことごとく支那音で習うことになつて、一東の韻から始めて、若干字づゝ先生が楷書で丁寧に認めて教えて呉れられた（後略）

> [The Chinese learning would soon begin, but choosing an appropriate Chinese textbook became a problem. [...] On my father's suggestion, learning

FIG. 12.2. Miyajima Daihachi 宮島大八

the pronunciation of Chinese characters was decided first, then we could read ancient poetry in Chinese. My teacher started to teach me from the first Chinese rhyme characters '東 East'.[9] He taught me how to write those characters in the script of Kaisyo 楷書.[10]]

Daihachi's study of Chinese at the Qing dynasty embassy did not last long, for Daihachi's teacher quit the job. In 1881, in order to continue learning Chinese, Daihachi entered the *Kōakai Shinago Gakko* (興亜会支那語学校 [the Chinese school of Kōakai]). Kōakai was the first organization set up in Japan by a group of politicians and soldiers who believed Asia should unite against European imperialism. Daihachi's father was a vital member of the board of Kōakai. In Kōakai, Daihachi received a strict reciting education ('Ansyō Kyōiku 暗誦教育'), each day reciting everything that was taught the previous day; every student had to turn his back to the teacher and then start to recite the texts with the textbook closed. Talking about his study life in Kōakai, Daihachi (Miyajima 1942: 22) wrote:

これは支那のといふやりかたを倣つたものであらうと思われた（中略）、その
間に自然に自分のものになるというやりかた、語学の研究などには、これが最
もよいやりかた、 （中略）、このやり方のおかげで、語学にも文学の根底にも
なつたと思う。これは実に興亜学校に入つたおかげだとおもう。この恩義は忘
れられない。この興亜学校ほど思い出深き所はない。

[This was called '背 reciting' in Chinese, a teaching method we learned from
China. [...] By reciting, the texts naturally become a part of us. It is the best way
to master a foreign language. [...] This kind of education that I received helped
me lay the foundation of Chinese language and Chinese literature. I am really
thankful to Kōakai. I owe the school a favour. It is a place full of memories.]

Daihachi was deeply affected by this teaching method, and this is reflected in the
Chinese textbook he edited called *Kyūsyūhen* 急就篇 which we discuss below.
However, after Daihachi had been learning Chinese for one year, the Chinese
school of Kōakai was closed down due to lack of funds, and Daihachi transferred to
the *Tokyo Gaikokugo Gakkō* (東京外国語学校 [Tokyo Foreign Language School])
and then to the *Tokyo Syōgyō Gakkō* (東京商業学校 [Tokyo Commercial School]).
At these two schools Daihachi learned Chinese for a further four years. In 1887, aged
twenty-one, Daihachi went to China with the recommendation of the Ambassador
of China. He studied Chinese language, Literary Chinese and calligraphy under
Zhang Lianqing (張廉卿, 1823-1894), a Confucian teacher, for more than seven
years until 1894, when he was forced to return Japan due to the outbreak of the
Sino-Japanese War of 1894 to 1895.

On his return to Japan, Daihachi began his forty-nine-year career as a Chinese
educator, and taught in many official schools including the *Tokyo Teikoku Daigaku*
(東京帝国大学 [Tokyo Imperial University]) and *Tokyo Kōtōsyōgyō Gakkō* (東京
高等商業学校 [Tokyo Higher Commercial School]). The private Chinese school
Zenrin Syoin (善隣書院 [Zenrin Academy of Classical Learning]) that Daihachi
set up in 1895 (originally called the *Eikisya* 詠帰舎) then became the core school
of Chinese teaching in Meiji Japan. In Daihachi's Chinese-teaching career, he
published more than thirty Chinese textbooks and dictionaries.

When Daihachi set up his school, there was only one official school offering
Chinese lessons, the *Kōtōsyōgyō Gakkō* 高等商業学校 [Tokyo Higher Commercial
School], and no private Chinese school existed in Tokyo. Many people who saw
the prospect of doing business with China or who wanted to join the army could
not find a way to learn Chinese; the establishment of the *Zenrin* Academy helped
to fulfil this need.

Initially, the *Zenrin* Academy offered two courses, a Chinese literature course
and a Chinese language course. The Chinese literature course, as its name suggests,
focused on literature, and included many Confucian works in its curriculum. The
Chinese language course focused on colloquial Chinese and consisted of dialogue,
translation, Chinese characters, etc. However, in 1900 the Yihetuan Movement (or
Boxer Rebellion, 義和団の乱) took place in China. As a member of the Eight-
Nation Alliance, Japan dispatched troops to China. The war greatly accelerated the

FIG. 12.3. The ticket for asking questions

passion for learning colloquial Chinese in Japan, as the enrolment figures for the *Zenrin* Academy show, increasing from twenty-three and sixteen students in May and October 1900 respectively to 118 in April 1901 (Rokkaku 1999: 211).

As the number of Chinese learners in the *Zenrin* Academy soared, the school launched a new educational policy in March 1901, focusing its teaching activity on colloquial Chinese and dropping the Chinese literature course. At the same time, a correspondence course also started from March 1901, to cater for students who did not live in Tokyo and who had no way to learn Chinese in their own cities. Self-learning materials were published monthly. In these materials, the Japanese pronunciation system — Hiragana — was used to help students memorize the pronunciation of Chinese. Besides, a 'ticket for asking questions' (質疑券, see Figure 12.3) was attached to every self-learning material. If a student had a question, he could write a letter to the *Zenrin* Academy to ask with the ticket attached. Selected questions and their answers would be published in the next issue of self-learning material.

Miyajima Daihachi's Chinese Textbook, the *Kyūsyūhen* (急就篇)

The *Kyūsyūhen* is a Chinese textbook compiled by Daihachi. Its first edition was published in 1904 and originally bore the title *Kanwa Kyūsyūhen* 官話急就篇. The first part of the name of the textbook — 'Kanwa 官話 [*Official Language*]' — indicates that it is a textbook of Beijing-based Mandarin. The second part of the title — 'Kyūsyūhen 急就篇' — was adopted from an ancient textbook for the practical and rapid learning of Chinese characters, the *Jíjiùpiān* (急就篇), which was written under the Former Han Dynasty (206 BC– 9 AD) and known widely both in China and Japan. It can be assumed that Daihachi intended to emphasize that *Kanwa Kyūsyūhen* was a practical and rapid-progress textbook by using the name of the earlier, famous textbook. As soon as *Kanwa Kyūsyūhen* was published, it was adopted by many Chinese learners and schools. After being revised twice, the third edition was published in October 1933 and the name was changed to *Kyūsyūhen*. Up until 1945, *Kyūsyūhen* was issued 197 times. It has been called the 'Bible' of Chinese learning and was recommended to all the beginners learning Chinese.

The contents of the *Kyūsyūhen* are listed in Table 1. Part 1 contains 736 basic words. Part 2 and Part 3 offer basic dialogues and intermediate level dialogues. Thirty-two upper intermediate level dialogues and passages are provided in Part 4. Part 5 is an appendix containing dialogues for everyday life which were written by Zhang Tingyan (張廷彥).

Part	Section	Contents
1	*Mingci* (名辞 [Words])	736 words: number, time, animal, food, weather and so on.
2	*Wenda zhishang* (問答之上 [Ask and Answer I])	100 groups of basic dialogues (average number of Chinese characters per dialogue: 9.05).
3	*Wenda zhizhong* (問答之中 [Ask and Answer II])	163 groups of intermediate level dialogues (average number of Chinese characters: 35.6).
4	*Wenda zhixia* (問答之下 [Ask and Answer III])	32 upper-intermediate level dialogues/ passages (from 50 characters to 400 characters) and one short novel, the *Momotarō* 桃太郎 story.
5	Appendix: *Jiating Changhua* (家庭常話), *Yinghui Xuzhi* (応回須知)	Dialogues for everyday life. This part was written by Chinese teacher Zhang Tingyan 張廷彥.

TABLE 1. The contents of *Kyūsyūhen*

Unlike previous basic Chinese textbooks, no Chinese pronunciation was introduced in the *Kyūsyūhen*; and no Japanese pronunciation system was used to help students memorize the pronunciation of Chinese. Besides, the contents of the book were all written in Chinese only. No Japanese translations or explanations of grammar were included, which makes the textbook a very portable size. In 1916, twelve years after *Kyūsyūhen* was published, the Japanese translations and the explanations of grammar were published for the first time.

The *Kyūsyūhen* has no curriculum guideline for teachers, and there is no known record of how exactly the *Kyūsyūhen* was taught. However, some descriptions of how the *Kyūsyūhen* was learnt were recorded by its learners. Through these fragments of information, we can glean some clues of the *Kyūsyūhen*'s teaching method:

(1) Reciting all the texts was required

As mentioned earlier, reciting texts from a book was considered an important way to learn a foreign language in the Meiji era. This way of learning was also reflected in the *Kyūsyūhen*. Andō Hikotarō learnt Chinese from a teacher who was Daihachi's student. Andō mentioned how he studied the *Kyūsyūhen* in his book *Tyūgokugo to Kindai Nihon* [*Chinese Language and Modern Japan*] (Andō 1988:15):

> 善隣書院出身で、国士的風格をのぞかせた渡俊治という老先生が、『急就篇』一冊を三年がかりでアタマから暗記させる、という授業ぶりであった。

> [The old teacher Mr Watari Syunji seemed to be a patriot. He was a graduate of the *Zenrin* Academy. In his Chinese class, he asked us to memorize the whole *Kyūsyūhen* in three years (and that is all we did in his Chinese class).]

Li Xianglan 李香蘭 (1920-2014)[11] talked about how she learnt the *Kyūsyūhen* in her father's Chinese class in her autobiography *Ri Kōran, Watashi no Hansei* (李香蘭 私の半生 [Li Xianglan, *The Story of my Early Life*]) (Li 1990: 8):

> 父が、単語一つ一つの発音や文章の音読の模範を示し、意味や使い方を丁寧に教え、ついで全員が復唱する。それから、生徒一人一人に復唱させる。大人が終わると最後に「淑子、発音してごらん。よし、其の意味は？ 」私が答えると、父は満足気にうなずくのだった。

> [First, my father reads those words and passages. Then he tells us their meanings and the usages of them. Then he asks all the students to repeat the pronunciations and the meanings together. Finally students have to repeat them again one by one. After those adult students all finish, my father says 'Yoshiko [Li Xianglan's Japanese name], try the pronunciation. And what is the meaning?' When I finish, my father is satisfied and nods his head.]

From the examples above, it can be seen that the *Kyūsyūhen* also followed the traditional way of language teaching: all the texts were required to be memorized. And in a Chinese class, teachers spent a lot of time asking students to repeat what they had just learnt in order to check whether they had memorized everything or not.

(2) Grammar patterns were not emphasized

Around 1900, the conception of grammar was still vague. Even many Chinese teachers preferred to avoid talking about Chinese grammar in Chinese classes. Andō Hikotarō (Andō 1988: 8) also wrote about his experience of learning Chinese from Mr Watari Syunji:

> 文法について質問しようものなら、「支那語に文法があるか!」と大喝された。

> [I tried to ask some questions about Chinese grammar, but my teacher shouted: 'Do you think the Chinese language has a grammar?']

Grammar patterns were not emphasized in the class. However, this did not mean that grammar was not learnt. As Daihachi said in the passage cited above: 'By reciting, the texts naturally become a part of us. It is the best way to master a foreign language'. Students memorized the grammar patterns naturally by reciting the whole texts.

念就篇

問答之上

（一）來了麼。（二）走了麼。（三）去了麼。（四）到了麼。（五）是不是。（六）好不好。（七）買不買。（八）可以不可以。

來了。走了。去了。到了。是。好。不買。可以

一八

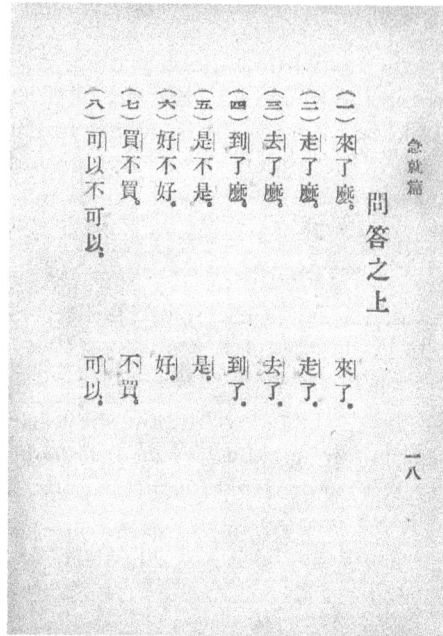

FIG. 12.4. *Kyūsyūhen* Wenda zhishang 問答之上 (Ask and Answer I, page 18)

The success of the *Kyūsyūhen* can be attributed to two main factors. First, the dialogues of the *Kyūsyūhen* are extremely short and easy for beginners to memorize. As can be seen in Table 1, a large portion of the *Kyūsyūhen* is in the format of dialogues. In Part 2, every dialogue consists of just one question and one answer (see Figure 12.4). The average number of Chinese characters per dialogue is only 9.05. Although the dialogues in Part 3 become much longer, the average number of Chinese characters is still only 35.6, and every sentence was still very short. The first dialogue '來了麼? (Laileme?)' '來了。(Laile)' [Has [...] come? [...] has come] has only five characters. This dialogue with no subject soon became a symbol of the *Kyūsyūhen* as an easy textbook to learn from. For a Chinese learner, a short dialogue can definitely be much easier to memorize than a longer one. The *Kyūsyūhen* thus matched the teaching method and the needs of the user well. Learners found that it was easier to learn Chinese with *Kyūsyūhen*.

Second, besides the main *Kyūsyūhen* textbook, a series of reference books accompanying the *Kyūsyūhen* were also published, intended to make learning Chinese with the *Kyūsyūhen* more efficient: Japanese translations of the dialogues (1–3 in Table 2), a romanization (4), a pronunciation dictionary (5), and *Kyūsyūhen* II (6).

In the Meiji-era, many popular Chinese textbooks had their own accompanying reference books like these. However, there were no other textbooks with as many supporting reference books as the *Kyūsyūhen*. The publication of reference books can be seen as evidence of the *Kyūsyūhen*'s popularity amongst Chinese learners. However, the publication of the reference books itself offered convenience to learners and so could further promote the use of *Kyūsyūhen*.

Daihachi's *Zenrin* Academy offered those students who could not enter vocational

FIG. 12.5. Zhang Tingyan 張廷彥

	NAME	YEAR OF PUBLICATION	PUBLISHER	CONTENTS
1	Kanwa Kyūsyūhen Sōyaku官話急就篇総訳(Japanese translation of Kanwa Kyūsyūhen)	1916	Mansyodō満書堂	Japanese translation of Kanwa Kyūsyūhen and explanations of grammar
2	Kanwa Kyūsyūhen Syōyaku官話急就篇詳訳(Jananese translation of Kanwa Kyūsyūhen)	1917	Buneidō 文英堂	Japanese translation of Kanwa Kyūsyūhen and explanations of grammar
3	Kyūsyūhen Sōyaku急就篇総訳 (Japanese translation of Kyūsyūhen)	1934	Zenrin Syoin 善隣書院	Japanese translation of Kyūsyūhen and explanations of grammar
4	Rōmaji Kyūsyūhen羅馬字急就篇 (Kyūsyūhen written in Latin alphabet)	1935	Zenrin Syoin	Reference book to learn the pronunciation of the texts of Kyūsyūhen. It was the first time that Miyajima Daihachi adopted the Latin alphabet in his book.
5	Kyūsyūhen Hatsuon急就篇発音 (The pronunciation dictionary of Kyūsyūhen)	1935	Zenrin Syoin	A pronunciation dictionary for Kyūsyūhen adopted both Latin alphabet and Zhuyin system
6	Zoku Kyūsyūhen続急就篇(A sequel to the Kyūsyūhen)	1941	Zenrin Syoin	A textbook for advanced level learners

TABLE 2. A Series of Reference Books of Kyūsyūhen

college a chance to learn Chinese. Between 1895 and 1943, about five thousand students graduated from the *Zenrin* Academy. Many graduates went to China to work as interpreters, and many became Chinese teachers in Japan and China (*Tokyo Asahi Shinbun* (東京朝日新聞 [*Tokyo Asahi News*] 15 July 1943). Once the *Kyūsyūhen* was published, various Chinese textbooks that imitated it were also published. In sum, Daihachi had a great influence on Chinese language education in the Meiji era.

Zhang Tingyan 張廷彦 (1864–1929)

Zhang Tingyan (courtesy name字: Shaopei 少培, see Figure 12.5[12]) was born on 7 March 1864 in Shuntianfu Daxingxian 順天府大興県 (a part of Beijing). He was known as the reviewer of the *Kyūsyūhen* before it was published, and the author of the *Kyūsyūhen*'s appendix. The autobiography of Chinese language educator Inoue Midori 井上翠 (1875-1957), *Syōtō Jijyutsu* (松濤自述 [*Inoue's Autobiography*]) provides evidence that Zhang Tingyan also participated in the compilation of the texts of *Kyūsyūhen*. In Zhang's thirty years in Japan, he published more than twenty Chinese-learning textbooks and Japanese-learning textbooks. As a Chinese native speaker, he co-operated with other Japanese educators and reviewed their Chinese textbooks. He was a key figure in the teaching of Chinese in Meiji Japan, although he and his Chinese textbooks have not previously been researched, and information about him is limited. However, his résumé[13] was found in the General Library of the University of Tokyo, through which we can get a glimpse of his teaching career in Japan. The beginning of Zhang Tingyan's résumé (Figure 12.6)[14] reads:

> 中華民国直隸省順天府大興県 [Daxing xian, Zhili Shuntian prefecture, the Republic of China]
> 東京赤坂区青山南町二丁目六十六番地 [2–66, Aoyama Minamityō, Akasak-ku, Tokyo]
> 文生員　張廷彦 [Wen Shengyuan, Zhang Tingyan]
> 同治三年三月七日生 [7 March 1864 Tongzhi 3].

The first line mentions the hometown of Zhang Tingyan in '中華民国', i.e. 'the Republic of China', indicating that this résumé was not written in the Qing Dynasty, but some time after 1906, when the Republic of China was established. The second gives the address of Zhang Tingyan in Japan. The third and the fourth lines are the title and the birthdate of Zhang Tingyan respectively.[15]

In September 1897, a foreign language affiliated school 附属外国語学校 was set up under the *Tokyo Kōtōsyōgyō Gakkō* (東京商業高等学校 [Tokyo Commercial School]). As we saw above, at that time, the Nanjing dialect had already been replaced in teaching by the Beijing dialect, but former Tōtsūji could only speak dialects of Southern China. Thus qualified Beijing dialect teachers were desperately needed. In order to meet this need, the Japanese Ambassador in Beijing, Uchida Kōsai (内田康哉), undertook the job of recruiting Chinese teachers from Beijing to *Tokyo Kōtōsyōgyō Gakkō*. Zhang Tingyan was one of those Chinese teachers that Uchida Kōsai invited, a fact which was recorded in his résumé, which reads:

> 明治三十年五月卅日大日本国駐京公使内田康哉代政府聘任東京高等商業学校華語教師

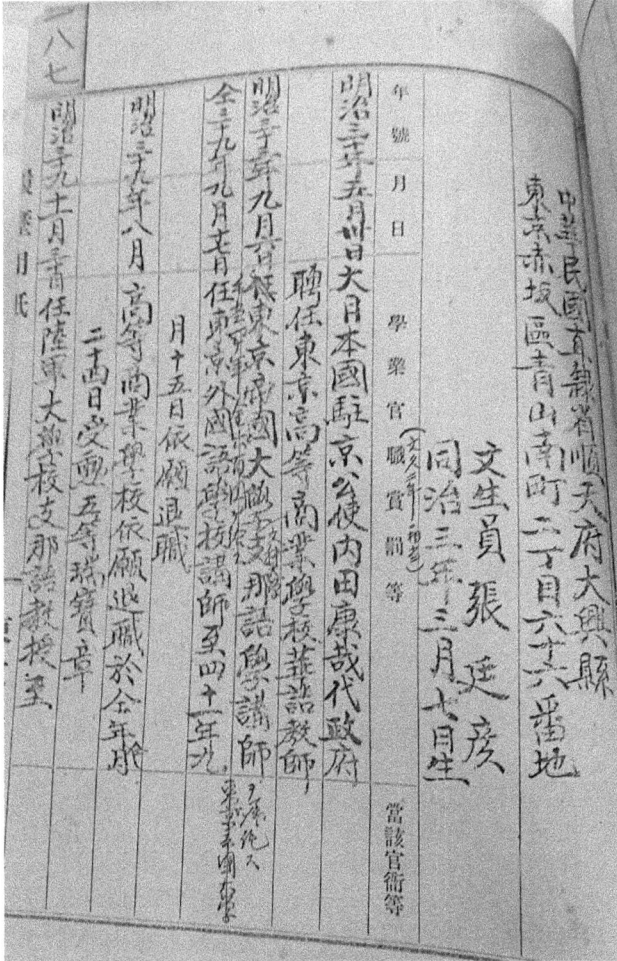

FIG. 12.6. First page of Zhang's résumé.

[On 30 May 1897, Zhang Tingyan was recruited as a Chinese teacher of *Tokyo Kōtōsyōgyō Gakkō* by the Japanese Ambassador Uchida Kōsai, who was stationed in Beijing and represented the Japanese government to invite Chinese teachers to Japan.]

Zhang Tingyan received his job offer on 30 May 1897, and in September 1897 he began work in *Tokyo Kōtōsyōgyō Gakkō*. At the same time, Daihachi also started his work in *Tokyo Kōtōsyōgyō Gakkō*. According to the documents and the materials found, there are two reasons why Zhang Tingyan came to Japan to teach Chinese. First, he was ideally qualified. Zhang Tingyan was born in Beijing, had graduated from *Tongwen Guan* (同文館 [School of Combined Learning]), and was qualified to teach Chinese. Tanaka Keitaro 田中慶太郎 said in *Syuppan to Shinago* (出版と支那語 [*Publication and the Chinese Language*]) (Tanaka 1942: 41):

張さんも金さんも、ともに同文館出身です。（中略）ふたりとも、それだから英語がわかったのです。

[Mr Zhang and Mr Jin [Mr Zhang = Zhang Tingyan, Mr Jin = Jin Guopu 金国璞] were graduates from *Tongwen Guan*. [...] Both of them could speak English.]

The *Tongwen Guan*, mentioned above, was the first educational institute founded for teaching Western languages in Beijing in 1862. Zhang Tingyan learned English in the *Tongwen Guan*. Unusually, then, he had language-learning experience, and he could speak the Beijing dialect. These two points were enough to qualify him to be a Chinese teacher.

Second, there was a personal reason. In the late Qing Dynasty, Chinese society was unstable. Zhang Tingyan felt it was difficult to fulfil his potential, and so started to consider going to Japan. In the preface of Zhang Tingyan's Chinese textbook *Pekin Kanwa Tyūgai Mōgyū* (北京官話中外蒙求 [*Mandarin Textbook, Chinese and Foreign Stories for Children*]) (Zhang 1911:1) Zhang Tingyan's friend Shen Baoru (沈保儒) wrote:

吾友张子少培,博学通儒,凤娴著述力,以生逢乱世,遭际不偶,惟抱道自重,又不甘尽弃其学,听之湮灭,于是远游东瀛,以教化之责自任。

My friend Zhang Shaopei [= Zhang Tingyan] is very knowledgeable. He knows Confucian works well and he is good at writing. However he was born in an unstable society and had no chance to achieve his own self-worth. He did not want to abandon what he had learnt. Then he went to Japan and devoted himself to teaching.]

During his teaching career, Zhang Tingyan taught at Tokyo Imperial University, the Tokyo Commercial School (*Kōtōsyōgyō Gakkō* 高等商業学校), the Tokyo Foreign Language School (*Tokyo Gaikokugo Gakkō* 東京外国語学校), the Army War College (*Rikugun Daigakkō* 陸軍大学校), the Army Accounting College (*Rikugun Keirigakkō* 陸軍経理学校) and the *Zenrin* Academy. In recognition of his work, in 1906 Zhang Tingyan was awarded a Fifth Order of the Sacred Treasure;[16] he died in Japan in 1929. His son Zhang Yuling 張毓靈, who also came to Japan when he was young, followed his father's path in becoming a Chinese teacher later.

In his thirty years in Japan, Zhang Tingyan published several kinds of Chinese textbooks, including grammar books and textbooks of Chinese. These are listed in Tables 3 and 4.

	Name	Year	Publisher
1	Shinago Dōji Yōhō (支那語動字用法 [The usage of Chinese verbs]	1904	Bunkyūdō 文求堂
2	Kanwa Bunpō (官話文法 [Grammar of Chinese-Kanwa]	1905	Kudō Syooku 救堂書屋
3	Dōjibunrui Taizen (動字分類大全 [Category of Chinese Verbs]	1906	Bunkyūdō 文求堂

TABLE 3. Grammar Books by Zhang Tingyan

	Name	Year	Publisher
1	Shinago Kyōkasyo Pekinhūdohen (支那語教科書北京風土編 [*Chinese Textbook, Beijing's Natural Features and Cultural Climate*])	1898	Tetsugaku Syoin 哲学書院
2	Pekin Kanwa Tyūgai Mōkyū (北京官話中外蒙求 [*Mandarin Textbook, Chinese and Foreign Stories for Children*]	1911	Bunkyūdō 文求堂
3	Hutsū Kanwa Shinkagensyū (普通官話新華言集 [*Mandarin Textbook, New Chinese Collection*])	1918	Bunkyūdō Syoten 文求堂書店
4	Saishin Kanwa Danronhen (最新官話談論篇 [*New Mandarin Conversation*]	1921	Bunkyūdō Syoten 文求堂書店
5	Kokkei Sōdan (滑稽叢談 [*Collection of Humorous Stories*]	1928	Bunkyūdō Syoten 文求堂書店

TABLE 4. Intermediate/ Advanced Level Chinese Textbooks by Zhang Tingyan

According to Rokkaku Tsunehiro's bibliography of Chinese textbooks *Tyūgokugo Kankeisyo Syomoku* (中国語関係書書目 [*List of Chinese Textbooks*]), in the Meiji era there were overwhelmingly more basic conversation textbooks than any other kind of textbook. Only a few intermediate or advanced-level Chinese textbooks were published before Zhang Tingyan's publications listed above, which filled this gap.

Beside Chinese textbooks, Zhang Tingyan also reviewed several Japanese textbooks for Japanese educators. For instance, the Japanese textbook *Tōbun Ikai* (東文易解 [*Easy to Learn Japanese*]) was written in Chinese by Ohya Tōru 大矢透 (1851-1928), a Japanese educator. It was called the first Japanese textbook for Chinese learners. After Zhang Tingyan checked the contents and its language, the book was presented to the Emperor of the Qing Dynasty.

Conclusion

To summarize, Miyajima Daihachi and Zhang Tingyan were two key Chinese educators in Meiji-era Japan. Their efforts fulfilled the changing needs of Japanese society and improved the development of Chinese-language education in Japan. However, about Zhang Tingyan and Miyajima Daihachi and their works we still know relatively little, and some questions — such as how Miyajima Daihachi's works affected Chinese teaching in the Meiji era, or how Zhang Tingyan's grammar textbook influenced Chinese grammar teaching in Japan — remain unresolved. Further research is still needed.

Bibliography

ANDŌ HIKOTARŌ. 1988. *Tyūgokugo to Kindai Nihon* [中国語と近代日本 *Chinese Language and Modern Japan*] (Tokyo: Iwanami Shinsyo 岩波新書)

MIYAJIMA DAIHACHI. 1942. *Eikisya Kanwa* [詠帰舎閑話 *Essays in the Eikisya*] Tyūgoku Bungaku [中国文学 *Chinese Literature*], 83 (Tokyo: Kyūko Syoin 汲古書院)

INOUE MIDORI 井上翠. 1950. *Syōtō Jijyutsu* [松濤自述 *Inoue's Autobiography*] (Osaka: Ōsaka Gaikokugo Daigaku Tyūgokugo Kenkyūkai大阪外国語大学中国研究会)

KONOE HOHEI DAIICHIRYODAN [近衛歩兵第1旅団 THE FIRST GUARDS INFANTRY REGIMENT OF THE JAPANESE IMPERIAL GUARD]. 1894. *Heiyō Shinago* [兵要支那語 *Chinese for Military Use*] (Tokyo: Tōhō Syoin 東邦書院)

KURAISHI TAKESHIRO 倉石武四郎. 1941. *Shinago Kyōiku no Riron to Jissai* [支那語教育の理論と実際 [*The Theory and the Practice of Chinese Language Education*]] (Tokyo: Iwanami Syoten 岩波書店)

LI XIANGLAN 李香蘭, FUJIHARA SAKUYA 藤原作弥. 1990. *Ri Kōran, Watashi no Hansei* [李香蘭 私の半生 [Li Xianglan, *The Story of my Early Life*]] (Tokyo: Shintyō Bunko Press 新潮文庫)

MIYAJIMA DAIHACHI. 1942. 'Eikisya Kanwa' [詠帰舎閑話 'Essays in Eikisya'] *Tyūgoku Bungaku* [中国文学 *Chinese Literature*], 83: 20–26

OHYA TŌRU大矢透. 1902. *Tōbun Ikai* [東文易解 [*Easy to Learn Japanese*]] (Tokyo: Taitō Dōbunkyoku Press 泰東同文局)

ROKKAKU TSUNEHIRO 六角恒廣. 1968. *Tyūgokugo Kankeisyo Syomoku* [中国語関係書書目 [*List of Chinese Textbooks*]] (Tokyo: Fuji Syuppan 不二出版)

——. 1984 *Kindainihon no Tyūgokugokyōiku* [近代日本の中国語教育 [*Chinese Education in Modern Japan*]], 2nd edn (Tokyo: Fuji Syuppan 不二出版)

——. 1988. *Tyūgokugokyōikushi no Kenkyū* [中国語教育史の研究 [*A Study of the History of Chinese Language Education*]] (Tokyo: Tōhō Syoten 東方書店)

——. 1991-98. *Tyūgokugo Kyōhonrui Syūsei* [中国語教本類集成 [*A Compilation of Chinese Textbooks*]] (Tokyo: Fuji Syuppan 不二出版)

——. 1999. *Kango Shikaden* [漢語師家伝 [*The Biography of Great Masters of Chinese Teaching*]] (Tokyo: Tōhō Syoten 東方書店)

SANBŌ HONBU 参謀本部 [IMPERIAL JAPANESE ARMY GENERAL STAFF OFFICE. 1894. *Nisshin Kaiwa* [日清会話 [*Chinese-Japanese Conversation*]] (Tokyo: Sanbō Honbu 参謀本部)

TANAKA KEITARO 田中慶太郎. 1942. 'Syuppan to Shinago' [出版と支那語 ['The Publication and the Chinese language']], *Tyūgoku Bungaku* [中国文学 *Chinese Literature*], 83: 39–44

TOKYO ASAHI SHINBUN [東京朝日新聞 [*Tokyo Asahi News*]]. 15 July 1943, p. 4

Yō Gaikokujin Kyōshi•Kōshi Rirekisyo. 1971. [傭外国人教師•講師履歴書 [*The Résumés of Foreign Teachers•Instructors*]] (The University of Tokyo)

ZHANG TINGYAN 張廷彦. 1911. *Pekin Kanwa Tyūgai Mōgyū* [北京官話中外蒙求 [*Mandarin Textbook, Chinese and Foreign Stories for Children*]] (Tokyo: Bunkyūdō Syoten 文求堂書店)

Notes to Chapter 12

1. Former professor at Waseda University, scholar of the history of Chinese education in Japan.
2. Translations into English are my own throughout.
3. Former professor of Waseda University, scholar of the history of China–Japan relations.
4. Sir Thomas Francis Wade's (1818-1895) Mandarin Chinese textbook 語言自邇集 [*Yü-yen tzu-erh chi: a progressive course designed to assist the student of colloquial Chinese*] was adopted. It had a major influence on Chinese language education in Japan.
5. Manchuria (1932-1945) in Northeast China and Inner Mongolia was a puppet state of the Empire of Japan. The language in Manchuria was Chinese; however many people in Japan called Chinese 'the language of Manchuria' around 1930.
6. Two wars broke out between China and Japan in the modern history of China (1840-1949): the Sino-Japanese War of 1894 to 1895 and the Second Sino-Japanese War (1937-1945).
7. Former professor at the University of Tokyo, scholar of modern Chinese literature, Chinese linguistic, etc.

8. Figure 12.2 was provided by Miyajima Daihachi's grandson Miyajima Yoshisuke 宮島吉亮 (1925-).

9. The Chinese classical poem (Lüshi 律詩) has a very strict tonal pattern and rhyme scheme where certain rhyme characters on the 'list of rhyme characters' have to be used; 東 [East] is its first Character. It is very important for writing a poem or appreciating a poem, which is why Daihachi started to learn Chinese from rhyme characters.

10. Kaisyo or Kaishu is a standard Chinese handwriting script.

11. Li Xianglan (Japanese name: Yamaguchi Yoshiko 山口淑子) was a Chinese-born Japanese actress and singer. Li Xianglan's father learnt Chinese from *Pekin Dōgakukai Gogakkō* (北京同学会語学校 [Beijing Alumni Chinese School]); and Li Xianglan learnt Chinese from her father when she stayed in Wushun 撫順, China. The *Pekin Dōgakukai Gogakkō* that her father attended had been built in 1903 by a group of Japanese who learnt Chinese from the Chinese teacher Jin Guopu 金国璞. Jin Guopu was a former Chinese teacher in the *Zenrin* academy. In 1903, he came back from Japan to Beijing. His students worried about him because of his great age, and hoped he could still have a stable income after coming back to Beijing. Finally, some of his students decided to set up the *Pekin Dōgakukai Gogakkō*, where Jin Guopu could be Deputy Head Teacher of the school and could enjoy his later years. Because of this, many Chinese textbooks used in the *Zenrin* academy were also applied in this school.

12. Figure 12.5, Zhang's photo, was provided by Miyajima Daihachi's grandson Miyajima Yoshisuke.

13. Zhang Tingyan's résumé was found in *Yodoi Gaikokujin Kyōshi•Kōshi Rirekisyo* (傭外国人教師•講師履歴書 [*The Résumés of Foreign Teachers and Instructors*] 1971). This material consists of 442 résumés of foreign teachers who were hired in the University of Tokyo.

14. Figure 12.6 was taken by the author of this chapter.

15. Students who have qualified to take the imperial examination were called Shengyuan.

16. The Order of the Sacred Treasure (瑞宝章) was established in January 1888 by Emperor Meiji of Japan. It is awarded to mark distinguished achievements in research fields, business industries, healthcare and so on.

CHAPTER 13

❖

Der Schüler ist fleissig. Wir sind Freunde [The Pupil is Diligent. We are Friends]: Teaching German Language and Cultural Values in China, c. 1906–08[1]

Nicola McLelland

While the history of Europeans' discovery and study of the Chinese language is relatively well charted, the history of Chinese encountering and learning European languages remains almost entirely unexplored. It is in this context that this chapter examines one of the very earliest textbooks for Chinese learners of German, Carl Teufel's *Grammatik für Chinesen zur Erlernung der deutschen Sprache* (1906–08), used in German missionary schools in early twentieth-century China, showing its significance in both the histories of linguistic ideas and of language teaching, and specifically in the history of German as a Foreign Language. It also illustrates the role of language teaching in German cultural diplomacy and cultural exchange, and thus in the exercise of Germany's soft power. The chapter outlines the historical context in which Teufel's book was published, before analysing his approach to the teaching of culture and values, and his linguistic and pedagogical approach compared to contemporary trends in Europe. It demonstrates that this first tentative footstep in the teaching of German to Chinese speakers is a fascinating hybrid: a combination of both localization to a local teaching context, and a proud assertion of German cultural values. It is also pedagogically innovative.

Introduction

Carl Teufel's *Grammatik für Chinesen zur Erlernung der deutschen Sprache* (1906-08) is one of the very earliest textbooks for Chinese learners of German. Written by a German missionary in China, it sits at the intersection of several currents in the history of language teaching and learning. It shows a debt to the treatment of grammar in nineteenth-century Latin grammars for Chinese learners; but there are also some apparent influences from the European language-teaching Reform

Movement with which it is contemporaneous; and yet other features that reflect the author's concern to cater to the specific context of missionary teaching in German-colonized China, mostly obvious in the values and cultural information presented to learners. As the first analysis of this intriguingly hybrid grammar and reader, the earliest-known materials for German as a foreign language in China, this chapter therefore makes a contribution to the histories of linguistic thought and of language teaching, specifically to the history of German as a Foreign Language outside Europe; and also illustrates how language teaching can contribute to cultural diplomacy and cultural exchange. In examining a textbook for Chinese learners of a European language, the study also complements existing work on the reverse case, the history of Chinese as a Foreign Language learnt by Europeans (e.g. McLelland 2015a). Below I outline the historical context in which the book was published; examine Teufel's approach to teaching of culture and values in that context; and, finally, analyse his linguistic and pedagogical approach and the possible influences on it. I shall demonstrate that his work is a fascinating hybrid, a combination of both localization to a local teaching context, and a proud assertion of German cultural values; it is also innovative in its approach to teaching the language.

The Historical Context: Missionary Education and the German Presence in China

Teufel's grammar was written for use in the German-controlled concession of Jiaozhou Bay (then Kiao-Chau, or in German Kiaotschou, with its port Qingdao) and its hinterland in Shandong Province, situated between Beijing and Shanghai. Germany came late to the colonial race; and its activities in this small part of China in the late nineteenth century never achieved full colonialization, and are sometimes considered, in Marxist terms, semi-colonialization. But they were often presented by German commentators as offering the potential to create a 'model colony', exemplifying enlightened imperialist policy (more explicitly so from about 1905 until the territory was lost in World War I (Leutner & Mühlhahn 1997: 36, 48). The goal was a *deutsches Kulturzentrum* [German cultural centre], in the words of a 1907 document cited by Leutner & Mühlhahn (1997: 45), that would present a positive image of Germany's cultural and scientific achievements to China and the world.[2] Germany's trade advantages were to be pursued through cultural diplomacy: '[W]ir sollen [...] in umfassender Weise auf Geist und Charakter einwirken und das Mittel sein zu einer Durchtränkung der ganzen Provinz, des von Qingdao abhängigen Hinterlandes mit deutschem Wissen und deutschem Geiste' [[W]e should [...] have an influence in a comprehensive way on spirit and character, and be the means of saturating the whole province, the hinterland dependent on Qingdao, with German knowledge and German spirit] (cited by Leutner & Mühlhahn 1997: 449; my translation; see also 450).[3] The author of the *Grammatik für Chinesen zur Erlernung der deutschen Sprache* was a member of the Catholic *Societas Verbi Divini* missionary society, as the title page makes clear. German missionaries had been in China since 1860, when the freedom to proselytize was granted, first under French protection, then under German protection from 1890 (Leutner & Mühlhahn 1997: 39, 41); and the German government was fully aware of their potential importance as bearers of German culture (Reinbothe 1992: 90). The *Societas Verbi Divini* (*SVD* [Divine Word Missionaries]), also known as the Steyler Mission, had been founded in the Dutch town of Steyl, just beyond the German border and so beyond the reach of Prussian control, during the years of the so-called *Kulturkampf*, the time of Prussian efforts to limit the power and influence of the Catholic Church (1871-78). The Society's involvement with the German colonial concession can thus be seen as part of a rapprochement between the Catholic Church and Prussia after the *Kulturkampf* (Kim 2004: 118-19). The first Steyler mission was established in China in 1879 (Mühlhahn 2000: 348), first primarily and then (from 1889 onwards) exclusively in south Shandong Province (Mühlhahn 2000: 321), hoping to build on the existence of a small number of Christians who had been converted by the Franciscans three hundred years earlier (Mühlhahn 2000: 337). Their first schools did not open until after 1900, beginning with a Middle School in Yanzhou and in Jinning (Mühlhahn 2000: 349).

The author, Carl Teufer, was born on 30 October 1869 in Baisingen, near Tübingen in south-western Germany: his southern origins are evident in occasional vocabulary choices such as *Trottoir* and *Brosamen* (Teufel 1907: 77; 1908: 60). He went to China with the *SVD* in 1895, at the age of twenty-six or twenty-seven, and seems to have remained there until his death on 24 February 1948. In China, his surname was misspelt as Teufel, and he ended up using this as his family name.[4] The grammar, written when he was in his mid- to late-thirties, was published in three parts, progressing from beginner level to advanced (on the structural grading, see below). Below, I refer to Volume I as Teufel (1906), Volume II Part 1 as Teufel (1907) and Volume II Part 2 as Teufel (1908).[5] All three were published by the Catholic Mission's press (*Verlag der Katholischen Mission*), located outside the German concession itself, in Yanzhoufu (兗州, German *Jentschoufu*), where the *SVD* had founded a seminary in 1884 (Gianninoto 2014a: 239), in the west of Shandong Province, about 570 kilometres south of Beijing and 770 kilometres north-west of Shanghai. Yanzhoufu is also where the prefaces were signed, with the exception of the preface to the fourth edition of Volume I, signed in *Dschutscheng*, i.e. Zhucheng (诸城) in the south-east of Shandong Province.

During the seventeen years of the German concession in China, twenty-seven elementary schools (teaching Chinese pupils according to the Chinese curriculum) were set up, as well as ten mission schools, four *Berufsschulen* [vocational colleges], and a *Fachhochschule* [senior technical college] (Leutner & Mühlhahn 1997: 431, n. 1, 432), schools in which German was taught as a foreign language, and so offering a respectable market for a textbook to teach German to Chinese learners.[6] Indeed, the lack of suitable materials for teaching German was keenly felt according to contemporary sources cited by Reinbothe (1992: 160, 241). Demand is evident in the fact that the second edition of the first volume was published almost as soon as the final volume had been completed (Teufel 1906: iii); two thousand copies of the third edition of the first volume were sold within nine months, prompting the printing of the fourth edition (Teufel 1908: iv).

Teufel's materials make an effort to avoid the fatal flaw in language materials for Chinese learners identified by teacher Richard Cordes in 1909. Writing in a journal for teachers of German in East Asia, Cordes lamented that language teaching materials were 'so dreadfully remote' from Chinese pupils' experience (*so furchtbar fern* (cited by Reinbothe 1992: 160)). By contrast, Teufel's grammar was tailored to its local users. First, the geographical frame of reference is Shandong Province. In Teufel (1906: 30-31) pupils learn to say that they come from *Tientsin*, i.e. Tianjin, a large city in Shandong Province 140 kilometres south of Beijing, and within which the Qing Dynasty ceded concessions to several European powers in 1900; or from Tsinanfu, modern Jinnan, lying in Shandong Province about 370 kilometres south of Tianjin). Tsinanfu, the provincial capital, is the city mentioned most frequently, often as a place that might have been visited or from which post might be expected (e.g. Teufel 1907: 58, 82, 85, 119). Other places mentioned are Tsining (Jining), lying, like Tianjin, on the Grand Canal, and apparently a place with much trade and where one can buy an attractive inkpot (Teufel 1907: 95, 149, 178); and Beilou (apparently lying behind a mountain that is in view); Lintsing; and a small village called Wangsiolo which I have not been able to identify (Teufel 1907: 125, 142, 178). Peking (Beijing) is sufficiently remote that it is worthy of an exclamation (*Sie kommen aus Peking!* [You come from Beijing!] (Teufel 1906: 31)).

Two of Teufel's lessons describe the daily life of pupils. They suggest that some were day-pupils, others boarders — boarders might receive visitors from friends or family at times (Teufel 1907: 104-06); the life of the boarder is presented first, so was possibly the more typical experience. If the timetable outlined can be believed, pupils might have had two hours of German a day, alongside other subjects including maths, *Turnen* (gymnastics, in practice probably military exercises (see Reinbothe 1992: 120)), drawing, singing, and calligraphy (Teufel 1908: 1). German might not be the only language learned — French, English and Japanese are all listed as possibilities (Teufel 1907: 51, 57, 115), and just as in Germany's African colonies (cf. McLelland 2016), German seems to have had an uphill struggle to compete against English, already the dominant European language (Reinbothe 1992: 123-27).

Teaching Culture, Teaching Values

Despite the practical focus of parts of Teufel's grammar — with lessons on weights and measures, calculations, simple commercial correspondence, and culminating in applying for a post — the teaching of German was not driven purely by the learners' practical needs. The wider goal was to engender interest in and sympathy for Germany and German culture, and to inculcate German (and, for the Mission, Christian) values, which would, ultimately, promote Germany's economic and diplomatic interests in the region. There was concern at the time that the image of Germany portrayed by existing American, British or Japanese materials was either wildly inaccurate (e.g. geography books that presented Germany as virtually uninhabited) or simply showed Germany in an unfavourable light (Reinbothe 1992: 261).

As already noted in the introduction, Teufel made an effort to meet pupils half way in their encounter with German culture, as we saw above in the references to their local geography. This effort is also evident in descriptions of daily life. For example, Teufel's description of a living room depicts a conspicuously simpler room than the upper-middle-class living rooms typically portrayed in European language materials of the time. In the elegant living room in Rees and Baumann's *Pictorial German Course* (Rees & Baumann 1910: 14), for example, a piano is prominent, but for Teufel's learners, the piano is a curiosity, to be seen only in the teacher's room (Teufel 1907: 149). The living room described by Teufel is a room used for work as well as relaxation (1908: 44) — it may be warm or cold, dry or damp, healthy or unhealthy; there are sewing materials, an embroidery frame, and a spinning wheel. The broom, brush and duster are also all kept in the living room; for children who misbehave, there is a rod in the corner (Teufel 1908: 42-44). It is not clear to what extent Teufel was describing a simple home from rural Germany, rural China, or both — but at any rate, it was less remote from his pupils' experience than one with a piano in it. At the same time, a more prosperous lifestyle is also described in one lesson. There are napkins; a servant clears the plates; the meal consists of three courses, accompanied by diluted wine; the father takes sugar in his coffee and smokes a good cigar (Teufel 1908: 149). Mother prepares meals, but some finer (*vornehmere*) families have a cook (Teufel 1908: 56). The countryside is compared unfavourably with the city, which is *schöner* — 'nicer' — than the country, for in the city, the houses are built of stone, the roof is of tiles or slate; there are pavements, gas lighting, and running water.

While making an effort to acknowledge Chinese pupils' life experience, Teufel is also relentless in modelling ideal pupil behaviour. The 'diligent pupil' is never far away in the example paradigms and sentences for translation, occurring literally hundreds of times. Lesson 1 of the reader describes pupils entering the room and taking their places silently, washed, combed and in clean clothes. They are quiet and attentive; they obey the teacher, and do not chatter or laugh; they always tell the teacher the truth; and reply thoughtfully to his questions (Teufel 1908: 1). To write, they sit upright and hold the pen correctly (Teufel 1908: 7). At meals, they sit up straight, without leaning on the table (Teufel 1908: 49). Diligent pupils keep their books clean (Teufel 1907: 24); they have somewhere particular to store their school things safely at home (Teufel 1908: 8). Talented students who do not work hard make little progress; others, with little talent, make good progress because they are diligent (Teufel 1907: 125). Good pupils are rewarded by the teacher (Teufel 1907: 47). Pupils are told: 'Remember, first work, then play' (*merke dir: Erst arbeiten und dann spielen* (Teufel 1908: 10)). All people should work (*Alle Menschen sollen arbeiten* (Teufel 1908: 18)). Hard work features far more prominently than in typical German textbooks for English learners of the same period, presumably because the pupils are assumed to be of a less privileged social class. For example, the mother, an adornment in most European textbooks of this time, here runs the household: she does the shopping; grows hemp and flax; spins; takes the thread to the weaver; and then bleaches the cloth to make shirts, bedlinen and the like. When they have finished their homework, pupils may help their parents with their work (Teufel 1908: 131).

It is no accident that a description of the teacher's room tells us that two pictures hang over the piano, one of the German Kaiser and one of the Chinese Emperor (Teufel 1907: 125). For, crucially, Teufel's passages do not just promulgate European values, but seem to highlight values that are common both to Germany and to Chinese, Confucian values, including love and respect for one's parents and elders (e.g. one must not mock the elderly (Teufel 1908: 23)). The tale of a boy who smokes his father's pipe in his absence and feels ill as a result illustrates the moral that children must obey their parents, even when there is no one to see (Teufel 1908: 14). Good children love their parents (Teufel 1907: 3), and they should do their best to earn their parents' love by their obedience and diligence (*Gehorsam und Fleiß* (Teufel 1908: 89)). They are honest — a father is pleased when his daughter owns up to having broken a teapot (Teufel 1907: 164-65). The father is the head of the family; the head commands, the limbs obey (Teufel 1908: 17). These are the kind of morals that an elementary education in Germany would also have inculcated — and here too a fable by the popular German moralist Gellert is included (Teufel 1908: 67), also a common choice in earlier textbooks for English learners (McLelland 2015b: 58, 76 n. 38). More than this, though, Teufel represents a social order in which the relationship between a benevolent Emperor, his representatives, and his people is like that of a father to his family. Children must obey their parents swiftly and promptly (Teufel 1908: 22-23). Just as the father is head of the family, so the Emperor is the loving head of his people: 'Wir haben einen gerechten und volksliebenden Kaiser' [We have a just Emperor who loves his people] (Teufel 1908: 13; likewise p. xiii). The civil servant must be just; he must be the father of the people. If a civil servant is just and loves the people, the people honour him like their father. The Chinese have just civil servants: 'Der Beamte muss vor allem gerecht sein. Die Beamten müssen Vater des Volkes sein. Wenn ein Beamter gerecht und volksliebend ist, so ehrt ihn das Volk wie Kinder ihren Vater. [...] Die Chinesen haben gerechte Beamte' (Teufel 1908: 58).

Alongside this sensitivity to Chinese values, however, Teufel alludes in his third volume to the habits of the Christian life: when parents lament the bad behaviour of their children, 'God hears these laments and punishes such children' ('Der liebe Gott hört diese Klagen und straft solche Kinder' (Teufel 1908: 16)); the father prays with his family (Teufel 1908: 18); the family pray together in the living room (Teufel 1908: 44). Parents send their children to church and to school, and pray to God to protect them; children are to be reverent and quiet in church (Teufel 1908: 23). Six lessons describing how a house is built culminate in a reference to the eternal dwellings of heaven: 'Im Himmel sind die ewigen Wohnungen' (Teufel 1908: 40).

Finally, German nationalist sentiment is also in evidence in the reader. The Germans are described as a bold, hardworking and educated people (*ein tapfres, arbeitsames und gebildetes Volk* (Teufel 1907: 58)), all values that Chinese people too would value. Just as China has its great men (*grosse Männer*), so too does Germany, though no examples are named in either case (Teufel 1907: 125). Boys play at soldiers wearing the typically German pointed helmet, the *Pickelhaube* (Teufel 1908: 29-30). But soldiering for one's country is a serious sacrifice too — the first of a small number of short poems in the reader is 'Der gute Kamerad' [The Good Comrade] by J. L. Uhland (1787-1862), narrating the death of the I-persona's comrade in battle, now *im ew'gen Lebem* [in eternal life] (Teufel 1908: 31-32). 'Dem Vaterland' [To the Fatherland] by Hoffmann von Fallersleben (1798-1874) swears loyalty until the grave (Teufel 1908: 85). Likewise, the I-persona in the poem 'Mein Vaterland' [My Fatherland] by Julius Sturm (1816-1898) calls the Kaiser his hero, and is proud to say his land is *das deutsche Reich* [the German Empire] (Teufel 1908: 87-88). The book ends with the German national anthem of the time, *Heil dir im Siegerkranz* ['Hail to Thee in the Victor's Laurels'] (lyrics by Heinrich Harries, 1762-1802).

The Linguistics and Pedagogy of the *Grammatik für Chinesen*

I turn now to Teufel's method for teaching German to Chinese learners. The title of Volume I promises the 'Elementary foundations of the German language and the most important rules of syntax' (*Die Anfangsgründe der deutschen Sprache und die wichtigsten Syntaxregeln*). In it, nearly all verbal morphology, including subjunctive (but not passive) is introduced, but only two cases, nominative and accusative, are introduced — and even the accusative comes relatively late (see below). Such a sequencing of German grammar is, to my knowledge, unique in the history of German as a Foreign Language. Volume II is titled *Die Deklinationen* [*The Declensions*]. Part 1 revisits the noun phrase, but now in all cases and with all kinds of declension. With the exception of the passive, which is presented only at the beginning of Part 2 (Teufel 1908: 9-14), all remaining major topics in German grammar are introduced (e.g. *da*-compounds, *wo*-compounds, reflexive verbs, indefinite pronouns, relative pronouns), interspersed with lessons on greetings, a meal at home, and a pupil's daily routine. Part 2 of Volume II takes the form of a reader of 102 pages, each lesson consisting of a short passage (typically of about half a page or less), with additional vocabulary to be built on during the lesson. Whereas in the first two books the language of instruction is Chinese, this third book is entirely in German, using Chinese only to translate new vocabulary.

Influence from Earlier Grammars of Latin for Chinese Learners

The *Grammatik für Chinesen* shows influences from a range of traditions, both indigenous Chinese and European. A Chinese influence is apparent in the presentation of the sounds of German (Teufel 1906: xi-xii) with which the book begins, using a method that was familiar from native Chinese rhyme dictionaries, that of listing syllables or 'combined sounds' (hé yīn 合音) in a tabular layout, as in Table 1. Similar tables also present the possible combinations of initial consonants with the diphthongs *au, ai, ei, eu,* and with *ä, ö, ü, äu* (grouped together because of their diacritic; in fact the fourth sound is a diphthong identical in standard German with *eu*). Rather than direct influence from Chinese texts, however, it seems likely — given certain other, terminological, similarities (see below) — that this approach was influenced, directly or indirectly, by a Latin grammar for Chinese learners, the

Lading ziwen 辣丁字文 , published in 1828 in Macao, and written by the Portuguese Lazarist missionary Joaquim Afonso Gonçalves (1781-1841) (Gianninoto 2014c: 33).

	b	p	d	t
a	ba	pa	da	ta
e	be	pe	de	te
i	bi	pi	di	ti
o	bo	po	do	to
u	bu	pu	du	tu

TABLE I. An Excerpt from the Presentation of German Sounds in Teufel (1906: xi)

Teufel also introduces the various possible spellings for long vowels (*ei, ih, ah, eh, oh, uh*), illustrating their use in real words, e.g. for long /i/ *ie wie nie sie viel*. Consonant clusters are also dealt with: initial *pf, qu, x, z* and *st, sp, str, spr*, and final *ng, nk*. The capital letters and syllabification follow: e.g *U Uhr Ur-sa-che Un-ter-richt Un-ter-tan* (Teufel 1906: xiii-xiv).

The terms *consonants* and *vowels* (*zì yīn zì* 自音字 and *tóng yīn zì* 同音字) are then introduced: vowels can be either simple (*dān zì yīn zì* 單自音字) or 'double', i.e. diphthongs (*shuāng zì yīn zì* 雙自音字). There is no description of the individual sounds — no hint of the phonetic script now beginning to appear in some textbooks of German for foreign learners published in England by this time (see McLelland 2012: 209-14 for examples). However, the grouping of the consonants suggests some awareness of developments in phonetics, for the consonant graphemes are grouped by place of articulation, into 'lip-sounds' (*b p w f v (ph) m*); 'tongue-sounds' (*d, t, s, ss, sch, l, n, r*); 'throat sounds' (*g k c j ch h*); as well as 'mixed' sounds, presented as *pf, qu = (kw), x = (ks)*, and *z = (ts)*. (Since the sounds are listed by their graphemes, the voiced /z/ is not distinguished from voiceless /s/, both represented by <s>.) Such a grouping of consonants — according to the broad place of articulation, without categorizing the manner of articulation — was less fine-grained than that of the International Phonetic Association that had been active since the 1880s; evidently the teacher was relied upon to model the correct pronunciation.[7]

Teufel then introduces ten parts of speech: the article; noun; adjective; numeral; pronoun; verb; adverb; preposition; conjunction; and interjection. In each case, the Chinese terms are given, along with both the Latinate terms and the native German terms (which had been in use alongside the Latinate terms in German since the seventeenth century (see McLelland 2011 and references there)), e.g. 指名 *das Fürwort oder das Pronomen* [pronoun], (Teufel 1906: xvi). This places the grammar firmly in the very long tradition of teaching Latin grammar since Antiquity, where grammars typically begin by defining the parts of speech in turn. From the Renaissance onwards, it became common to begin by introducing the letters first of all, as Teufel does. The explicit definitions are kept simple. For example, Teufel defines the numeral as follows: '数名者,形容人物之多者也.如 [the numeral describes how many of a person, as in]':

ein(s) 一個   der erste 第一   einmal 一次
zwei 兩個   der zweite 第二   zweimal 二次

The examples given illustrate the difference between cardinals (first column), ordinals (middle column), and adverbs of frequency (in Chinese actually a numeral plus verbal classifier; third column), but these are not defined — in this instance they all correspond in a straightforward manner to a distinction made in Chinese. As for the grammatical terminology used, some terms — e.g. adverb and preposition (*zhuàngcí* 狀辭 [adverbs]; *qiáncí* 前辭 [prepositions]) — correspond to those used in Latin grammars for Chinese learners, such as Zottoli's grammar of 1859 (see Gianninoto 2014c: 37), others do not (e.g. *jiēcí* 接辭 [lit. continue-word] and *kǒu wěncí* 口吻辭 [lit. mouth-word] (Teufel 1906: xvii)). The term *zuò* 座 [position] for 'case', introduced in Lesson 15, can be traced back to Gonçalves's influential Latin grammar of 1828, noted above, though Teufel does not use Gonçalves's labels for the individual cases.[8] The Chinese terms that he uses are closer than Gonçalves's to the Latinate forms: 名坐 *míng zuò*; 至坐 *zhī zuò* ([lit. name case]; and [arrive or destination case]). Gianninoto notes that Gonçalves's manner of describing the Latin cases, through a series of questions (e.g *who* for nominative, *whose* for genitive), was imitated in subsequent works into the twentieth century, including a grammar published in Yanzhou (Gianninoto 2014a: 239), but this technique was also well-established in the grammatical tradition of German, too, by this time, as is obvious from the German names *Werfall* [who-case], *Wenfall* [whom-case] in common use and given by Teufel alongside the Latinate *Nominativ, Akkusativ*.

In sum, Teufel's grammar draws on established European grammatical categories, but somewhat adapted to the Chinese context, in terminology and in layout, with some possible influence from Gonçalves's 1828 grammar of Latin for Chinese learners; but some other Chinese terms, that are closer to the Latin terms, differ from those used by Gonçalves. Unfortunately it is impossible to say to what extent Teufel himself (or any possible Chinese collaborator?) knew the Gonçalves grammar itself, or perhaps a missionary training tradition that drew on it, and to what extent he (or they) innovated themselves.

Sequencing Grammar: Teufel's Step-by-Step Approach

After defining the parts of speech, Teufel's next step in providing his learners with the *Anfangsgründe* [initial foundations] is to show how to analyse a sentence (here called *chéngyǔ* 成語, although the term is more commonly used to refer to fixed four-character idiomatic phrases in Chinese). The first three sentences presented to the learner in German are: 'Der Schüler lernt' [The pupil learns]; 'Der Schüler ist fleissig' [The pupil is diligent]; and 'Wir sind Freunde' [We are friends], illustrating the principle that 每成語有三事 [every sentence has three items], the sentence structure consisting of subject, predicate and copula (一 首領 *Satzgegenstand (Subjekt)*; 二歸語; *Satzaussage (Prädikat)*; 三联络 *Satzband (Kopula)*) — the Chinese terms indicate in essence the 'first', 'second' and 'third' elements (Teufel 1906: xviii). The so-called 'naked' simple sentence (*nackte[r] einfache[r] Satz* 裸單成語) may be extended to an 'extended' sentence (*erweiterte[r] einfache[r] Satz* 加單成語), for example by adding an adverb (Teufel 1906: xix), as in *Dieser Schüler lernt fleißig* 此徒弟子的用心 [This pupil learns diligently]. Finally in this introductory section, pupils are introduced to the concepts of singular and plural, the three persons (in singular and plural), and the existence of three genders (called 類 [class, kind]), but without examples.

Book 1 then begins with the first of fifty-eight lessons (some early lessons are very short — Lesson 1 is a single page). As the preface explains (Teufel 1906: iii-iv),[9] each lesson begins with the presentation of a paradigm, followed by words and phrases to be learned by heart. A German exercise then follows, which pupils are not merely to translate, but — 'and this cannot be sufficiently emphasized' — also to memorize. There follow questions for pupils to answer in German and, finally, a Chinese exercise to be translated. Lesson 1 begins by presenting the paradigm of the personal pronouns. Since the written distinction between the male, female, and neutral variants of the Chinese third-person pronoun *tā* (他,她,它) had not yet been established (see Huang 2009), this means that *er*, *sie*, and *es* are each rendered as 他; *sie*, listed three times as the plural in turn of *er*, *sie* and *es*, is translated three times as 他们. The first German exercise consists entirely of translating each pronoun from German to English; the Chinese exercise requires pupils to do the same in reverse. Lesson 2 then introduces the verb 'to be' (*sein*); and Lesson 3 introduces the 'simple naked sentence' by introducing predicate adjectives to accompany the personal pronouns and the copula. The paradigm uses *fleissig* [diligent] as its model (*ich bin fleissig, du bist fleissig*, etc.), but seven new adjectives are added, so that numerous (albeit repetitive) variations on this simple sentence can be practised in the exercises. Lesson 4 introduces question formation by inversion (*Bin ich fleissig? Bist du fleissig?* etc. (p. 4)), and the question words *was, wo, wer, wie* [what, where, who, how]. A handful of German male proper names are introduced. With the addition of a few set phrases (including *ja, zu Hause, in der Schule* [yes; at home; at school], the pupils now have a vocabulary of twelve non-function words in addition to pronouns, question-words and *sein* [to be] to produce numerous permutations of questions and answers in the exercises. Lesson 5 introduces *nein* and *kein*, so that it becomes possible to disagree with the proposed question.

The remainder of the first book follows this pattern, with new vocabulary being introduced slowly: numerals; school classroom vocabulary; talking about one's family, for which the comparative forms *ältere, jüngere* [older, younger] are introduced, in singular and plural. However, their formation is not analysed. Rather, *der ältere Bruder, die älteren Brüder* [the older brother(s)] corresponds to the Chinese single lexeme 哥哥, *die jüngere Schwester, die jüngeren Schwestern* [the older sister(s)] to 妹妹, etc. (Teufel 1906: 15), so accommodates to the Chinese conceptualization of family relationships, in which the age relationship is always explicit — an instance of 'localization' of content to the local teaching context. Despite the additional vocabulary, the exercises continue to feature 'diligent' pupils very prominently (in seven of the twenty-one sentences for translation into Chinese in Lesson 6, for example).

The explicit focus of each lesson is a grammatical point, so that by Lesson 12 (p. 27) pupils have been introduced to the demonstrative adjectives; possessive adjectives; numerals; adverbs of time, manner and place; and the preterite tense. This is a rapid progression, but the difficulty is reduced because Teufel deals only with simple sentences with the verb 'to be', so that the only case dealt with is the nominative; in Lesson 11, the preterite of the verb 'to be' only is taught: 'I was diligent' etc. Over these lessons, pupils have learned only another eleven nouns and four further adjectives. Comparatively early, at least relative to the sophistication of their vocabulary, pupils learn the unmarked sequence of adverbials (time–manner–place), illustrated in Lesson 10 with the step-by-step expansion of the sentence 'Die Schüler sind fleissig' [The pupils are diligent] by adding one adverb(ial) at a time (*heute, in der Schule, sehr*), culminating in the fifth sentence, 'Die Schüler sind heute in der Schule sehr fleissig' [The pupils are very diligent in school today] (Teufel 1906: 22). Throughout, the focus is on drilling the necessary manipulations of form and word order while minimizing the amount of vocabulary for the task.

Only in Lesson 13 do the first expressions for meeting and interacting with others occur: introductions, first encounters, saying where one comes from and talking about the weather. An unidiomatic 'Wie ist Ihr werter Name?' is a translation of the Chinese polite form of asking someone's name, 貴姓 [valuable name], presumably a deliberate accommodation to Chinese politeness norms. Finally, in Lesson 15 (p. 33) a second verb is introduced, *haben* [to have], along with the concepts of the nominative and accusative case (since the accusative case is required for the object of *haben*). However, the first exercises with the *subject–haben–object* structure do not yet require the pupil to manipulate the case endings, because the examples either use uncountable nouns (e.g. *Silber, Gold* [silver, gold]) or plurals, so that Teufel guides pupils step-by-step, first giving an opportunity for the underlying concept to be grasped, before the necessary grammatical forms are introduced (in Lesson 16). Once *haben* has been introduced, its preterite form is given in Lesson 17, as well as phrases requiring an accusative of definite time, e.g. *den ganzen Tag lang* [the whole day long] (although these are presented as set phrases, without explanation or definition).

The emphasis then shifts to vocabulary-building, with twelve lessons working on contexts in which numerals are needed. Lessons 18-20 introduce numerals from thirteen to a million; and vocabulary for talking about the population of Chinese regions, cities and of other parts of the world is introduced (Lessons 21-24). Lesson 25 introduces weights and measures; Lesson 26 currency; Lesson 27 time expressions; and Lesson 28 tackles simple addition, subtraction and multiplication in German. Lesson 29 introduces the ordinals and Lesson 30 the names of the months. (In Chinese, these are numbered, so that the theme of numerals is continued, in effect, e.g. February is 二月 [Month Two].)

After a dozen lessons with no new grammatical points, Lessons 31-33 introduce the formation of the superlative and comparative (with the model 'Ich bin am fleissigsten' [I am most diligent]; 'Ich bin der fleissigste' [I am the most diligent (of all)]; 'Ich bin fleissiger als du [I am more diligent than you], etc.). Lesson 34 (Teufel 1906: 85-87) returns to word order. Pupils are already very familiar by now with inversion in questions (introduced in Lesson 4, and used in virtually every lesson ever since, given the heavy reliance on question-and-answer exercises). Now the imperative with inversion is introduced (Studieren Sie fleissig! [Study diligently!]), as well as the expression of a wish (Wäre er doch fleissiger! [Were he only more diligent!]), though with no analysis of the subjunctive *wäre*. Lastly, topicalization of an element by fronting it is introduced (which, keeping the verb in second position, causes 'inversion' of subject and verb compared to the canonical SVO order): 'Fleissig ist jener Schüler'; dummy-*es* is also introduced, again requiring inversion: 'Es arbeiten die Leute (*versus* 'Die Leute arbeiten' [The people work]). The inversion rule for topicalization is thus introduced comparatively late, but again Teufel works step-by-step from the known — obligatory inversion for just one function, question formation, as used for the past thirty lessons — to the unknown, optional topicalization inversion. The next few lessons introduce the perfect and future tenses of *haben* and *sein*, which are then reviewed and combined in Lesson 39 with inversion rules presented in Lesson 34, so that pupils can now front elements in the perfect tense too: 'Fleissig ist dieser Schüler gewesen' [Diligent has this pupil been].

Lesson 40 introduces the subjunctive used for reported speech, in past, present, and future tenses. The same lesson also introduces subordinate clauses introduced by *man sagt/ hofft/ glaubt/ wünscht, dass* [One says/ hopes/ believes/ wishes that]. This lesson thus combines material that would more usually be distributed over several lessons, but again the cognitive burden is reduced by the fact that apart from the set phrases *man sagt* etc., pupils are still dealing with only two verbs, *haben* and *sein*, and only two basic sentences ('Man sagte, <u>ich sei fleissig</u>'; and 'Man wünschte, <u>wir hätten Bücher</u>' [[...] I am diligent; [...] we have books]).

It is not until Lessons 45, after all this complex nominal and verbal morphology, that verbs other than *haben*, *sein* and *werden* ('to become', but used to form the future tense) are introduced. On page 117, pupils finally encounter their first regular verb, *loben* [to praise]. The present, preterite, perfect and future tenses are all given in the same lesson. Given the focus thus far on the concept of being *fleissig*, we should not be surprised to discover that the favoured regular verb for practice is *lernen* [to learn], which occupies a full page of exercises on page 119. Subsequent lessons introduce various other verbal conjugations and reflexive verbs in swift succession, until Lessons 54 and 55 summarize the indicative and subjunctive conjugations side-by-side for comparison (as was done for *haben* and *sein* in Lesson 42).

Only in the last three lessons, having learnt all verbal morphology, does Teufel introduce anything beyond a simple clause. His step-by-step approach is evident as he starts in Lesson 56 with the straightforward case of sentences linked by the co-ordinating conjunction *und* [and], before turning to dependent clauses introduced by subordinating conjunctions (*als* [when]; and *weil* [because]), as in 'Weil dieser Schüler fleissig studiert, (deshalb) macht er Forschritte' [Because this pupils studies diligently, (therefore) he makes progress]. The optional, indeed unidiomatic, *deshalb* is inserted here to contrast the German structure with the Chinese pattern, where the causative 因為 *yīnwèi* [because] often co-occurs with a matching 所以 *suǒyǐ* [therefore] in the main clause. Lesson 58, the last in Volume I, introduces indirect questions in subordinate clauses, and 'if' clauses (with and without an explicit conjunction).

The vocabulary of all words and phrases used in Volume I, given at the back of the book, amounts to about seven to eight hundred entries, but many of them are verbs that were introduced only since Lesson 45. Teufel's main focus in this first volume is on manipulating basic sentence types, as well as practical skills in counting and measuring. The language that pupils encounter is thus a highly artificial, restricted range of sentences. Teufel's strategy offers an interesting contrast to other attempts to reduce the cognitive load on the learner by tightly controlling the vocabulary. For example, Thomas Prendergast's Mastery method also sought to reduce the cognitive load by working intensively with a small number of sentences (Atherton 2010). However, Prendergast's model sentences were long and complex, with shorter variations to be derived from them:

> Long sentences are selected upon a new principle, and shorter sentences, or Variations, are evolved from them by rearranging those words and excluding all others. Those Variations are all complete idiomatic sentences. The primary sentences are all divided into sections, each of which, with some of its Variations, forms a short lesson.
> The Variations are so devised that by mastering 100 words, the beginner obtains the free and habitual command of 100 complete sentences, with many more latent Variations in reserve. (Prendergast 1868: 3)

Rosenthal's *Meisterschafts-System* ([Mastery System], briefly discussed by Lorch (2016: 18), was inspired by Prendergast. Beginning with somewhat shorter sentences than Prendergast, Rosenthal's strategy was nevertheless to include numerous grammatical points in a single sentence. For example, the very first foundation sentence given in his German manual already exemplifies the use of all four cases; two tenses; main- and subordinating-clause word order; and negation: 'Mein Bruder hat Ihren Vater nicht gesehen, als er gestern in dem Laden des deutschen Kaufmanns war' [My brother did not see your father while he was in the store of the German merchant yesterday]; twenty-eight permutations of the seventeen-word sentence are then given, occasionally introducing additional vocabulary in the later permutations, as well as additional structures — such as questions — not used in the initial 'foundation' sentence (Rosenthal 1887: 28-34). Teufel, by contrast, keeps sentences maximally simple, and the vocabulary minimal. He reduces the burden by limiting himself to only two cases throughout Volume I, while covering a great many other grammatical concepts for both the verb and noun phrase.

Another striking example of Teufel's systematic grading occurs in the first two passages of the reader, presumably intended to serve as revision, perhaps at the beginning of a new school term or year. The first passage consists entirely of canonical word order (i.e. subject–verb–complement/object), except for one case of adverb-fronting in the very last sentence: 'Immer sagen sie dem Lehrer die Wahrheit' [Always they tell the teacher the truth] (Teufel 1908: 1). Pupils are thus (re-)introduced to reading a longer connected passage of German with minimal syntactical challenges. The second passage then equally deliberately features a wide variety of sentence types, albeit still in short sentences, including modal verbs, topicalization, passive, and an if-clause without *wenn* ('Haben sie ihre Aufgaben gemacht, so spielen sie oder helfen den Eltern bei der Arbeit' [[When] they have finished their exercises, they play or help their parents with their work]). This lesson, then, is carefully constructed to provide the teacher with material to revise all the syntactical structures that had been introduced gradually over the preceding two volumes.

Teufel's systematic approach is idiosyncratic, but is well summed up in one of his sentences for translation, 'Lerne das eine nach dem anderen' [Learn one thing after another] (Teufel 1907: 142). What is more, as I have demonstrated, Teufel's sequencing of material actually works. Just as vocabulary is built up very gradually, so each new structure in turn assumes and builds on knowledge of the preceding structures taught (and nothing more!).

Teufel's Grammar in the Context of Contemporary Pedagogical Currents

Idiosyncratic though Teufel's approach to teaching grammar is, his second and third books suggest an awareness of European pedagogical currents. Halfway through the first part of Volume II, after the introduction of all the relevant noun-phrase paradigms,[10] Teufel's focus shifts in Lessons 29–32 to the four seasons, beginning with autumn. Wall-pictures of the four seasons, first used in elementary school teaching, were a typical teaching aid in Reform Method language teaching from the 1890s onwards (see McLelland 2015b: 112–14 for German examples; the method is described by Rippmann 1899: 29–32). There is no reference in Teufel's book to the use of pictures, and the sequence is different, beginning with autumn rather than spring, but it seems likely that there is some connection, if not with Reform language teaching, then with elementary school teaching.

Teufel also uses object lessons (without using the term) in his reader, another pedagogical approach used in elementary school teaching and subsequently adopted by language teaching reformers (see McLelland 2015b: 112–13). Indeed, Teufel's first object lesson, describing a pupil's slate, is very similar to an equivalent lesson in an 1898 book of object lessons for teaching German to English-speaking pupils (Trotter 1898: 68–69): both lessons describe the board (Teufel specifies *Schiefer* [slate]), the wooden frame, and the stylus which needs to be sharpened. Other familiar objects chosen as the focus of lessons are an exercise book (also chosen by Trotter 1898), the blackboard, a pipe and a clock. Books and clocks are European objects that appear to have particularly fascinated Chinese people who first encountered them (Mühlhahn 2000: 337). A book is minutely described: its rectangular shape, its cover (of board, leather or linen), its binding, and thin pages of paper, each with two sides (Teufel 1908: 5–6). A clock, called a *großes Kunstwerk* [a great work of art], is described over the course of three lessons, with its face, hands, internal mechanism and pendulum (Teufel 1908: 50–54, Lessons 43–45).

Not all of Teufel's lessons in the reader take the form of object lessons. Some resort to techniques that have been used for centuries, verging on what Hüllen (1999: 79), referring to early medieval materials for language-learning in Europe, called contextualized word-lists. For example, a passage about a kitchen is little more than a context for a list of foodstuffs and objects (Teufel 1908: 56). Other passages on the baker, butcher and the cellar present vocabulary contextualized in a similar way. The words presented in the reading passage can also form the basis for associative vocabulary development in the list of 'new words' that follow the passage. For example, the word *versichern* [to assure, insure] in a passage sparks the phrase 'Ich gebe dir die Versicherung, dass ...' [I assure you that ...], but also *die Feuerversicherung* [fire insurance] (Teufel 1908: 90).

   Towards the end of his book, Teufel presents learners with model correspondence, personal and commercial. While not quite as ancient as the contextualized word-list, this, too, is a common feature of European language-learning materials from the seventeenth century onwards (some examples in textbooks of German for English learners are noted in McLelland 2015b: 53-55). The letters are very short and simple: a simple New Year's greeting to one's parents; a bill; a receipt; a reference; and, finally, a job application (Teufel 1908: 89-99). Unusual in the genre is the model letter to a *Wohltäter* [a charitable supporter], thanking him for his support and hoping to merit the trust placed in the writer (Teufel 1908: 90). Perhaps some pupils were required, or at least encouraged, to write such letters to sponsors of the missionary society back in Germany.

Conclusion

Teufel's grammar is the earliest known grammar for teaching German to Chinese learners, marking the beginnings of a counterpoint to the longer history of Europeans learning Chinese (see Chappell & Peyraube 2014). The analysis above has proved revealing in several ways. First, Teufel demonstrates at least a passing acquaintance with developments in elementary and/or Reformed foreign-language teaching, although it is difficult to be sure which, in his use of object lessons, for example. Second, while the decisions Teufel made in order to sequence his teaching of German grammar for his learners are unusual, they reflect an awareness of the cognitive burden of mastering new vocabulary *and* new structures at the same time, particularly for pupils learning a new writing system — a new challenge in German as a Foreign Language at the time. Third, teaching a foreign language is an opportunity to inculcate values and a particular view of one's own culture (see McLelland 2015b: 249-334 for the case of German in England); and we have seen that Teufel's grammar is one of the most explicitly moralizing attempts in German as a Foreign Language to exert soft power in this way. Finally, and in tension with this wielding of soft power, Teufel's pedagogy and its linguistic approach suggest a more complex and to some extent accommodating relationship with local culture and language. My analysis of this fascinating hybrid text is, like Teufel's own view of his grammar, a mere 'preliminary attempt on this as yet uncultivated territory' (*ein vorläufiger Versuch auf diesem noch unangebautem Gebiete* (Teufel 1906: iii)), but it illustrates the potential of such texts in the history of language teaching, the history of linguistics, and social and cultural history.

Bibliography

ATHERTON, MARK. 2010. '"The Globe of Language": Thomas Prendergast and Applied Linguistics in the 1870s', *Language & History*, 53: 15-26

CHAPPELL, HILARY, and ALAIN PEYRAUBE. 2014. 'The History of Chinese Grammars in Chinese and Western Scholarly Traditions', *Language & History*, 57: 107-36

GIANNINOTO, MARIAROSARIA. 2014A. 'Translation in Chinese Grammars: Bilingual Works by Western Missionaries, Diplomats and Academics in the 18th and 19th Centuries', in *Missionary Linguistics V / Lingüística Misionera V: Translation Theories and Practices. Selected papers from the Seventh International Conference on Missionary Linguistics, Bremen, 28 February – 2 March 2012*, ed. by O. Zwartjes, K. Zimmermann and M. Schrader-Kniffki (Amsterdam: Benjamins), pp. 231-50

——. 2014B. 'The Development of Chinese Grammars and the Classification of the Parts of Speech', *Language & History*, 57: 137-48

——. 2014C. 中文编写译著的拉丁文语法书:18 至 20 世纪初语言学研究的重要领域 [The Chinese Grammars of Latin: An Important Field of Nineteenth and Early Twentieth Century Linguistic Studies], *Latinitas Sinica. Journal of Latin Language and Culture*, 2014: 31-44

HUANG XINGTAO 黄兴涛. 2009. *A Cultural History of the Chinese Character 'Ta' (She): On the Invention and Identification of a New Female Pronoun* ("她"字的文化史 — 女性新代词的发明与认同研究") (Fuzhou: Fujian jiaoyu chubanshe)

HÜLLEN, WERNER. 1999. *English Dictionaries, 800–1700: The Topical Tradition* (Oxford: Clarendon)

KIM, CHUN-SHIK. 2004. *Deutscher Kulturimperialismus in China: Deutsches Kolonialschulwesen in Kiautschou (China) 1898–1914* (Stuttgart: Steiner)

LAPPER, GEORG. [1943]. *Singendes Lernen: Ich lerne singend Deutsch. Methode Lapper* ([n. p.]: Oldenbourg)

LEUTNER, MECHTHILD, and KLAUS MÜHLHAHN. 1997. *Musterkolonie Kiautschou: die Expansion des Deutschen Reiches in China: deutsch-chinesische Beziehungen 1897 bis 1914: eine Quellensammlung* (Berlin: Akademie)

LORCH, MARJORIE. 2016. 'A Late 19th-Century British Perspective on Modern Foreign Language Learning, Teaching and Reform: The Legacy of Prendergast's "Mastery System"', *Historiographia Linguistica*, 43: 175-208

MCLELLAND, NICOLA. 2011. *J. G. Schottelius's 'Ausführliche Arbeit von der Teutschen Haubtsprache' (1663) and its Place in Early Modern European Vernacular Language Study* (Oxford: Wiley-Blackwell)

——. 2012. 'Walter Rippmann and Otto Siepmann as Reform Movement Textbook Authors: A Contribution to the History of Teaching and Learning German in the United Kingdom', *Language & History*, 55: 125-45

——. 2015A. '"Teach Yourself Chinese" — How? The History of Chinese Self-instruction Manuals for English Speakers, 1900-2010', *Journal of the Chinese Language Teachers Association*, 50: 109-52

——. 2015B. *German through English Eyes: A History of Language Teaching and Learning in Britain, 1500–2000* (Wiesbaden: Harrassowitz)

——. 2016. 'German Global Soft Power, 1700-1920', in *Les Politiques linguistiques et culturelles extérieures des États européens (XVIIIème–XXème siècles)*, ed. by Marie-Christine Kok-Escalles et al. (Amsterdam: Amsterdam University Press), pp. 45-68

MÜHLHAHN, KLAUS. 2000. *Herrschaft und Widerstand in der 'Musterkolonie' Kiautschou: Interaktionen zwischen China und Deutschland, 1897–1914* (Munich: Oldenbourg)

MÜHLHÄUSLER, PETER. 2011. 'Deutsche schümpfen, chinese schümpfen, plenty sabbi: Die deutsche Sprache in Kiautschou', in *Kolonialzeitliche Sprachforschung: Die Beschreibung afrikanischer und ozeanischer Sprachen zur Zeit der deutschen Kolonialherrschaft*, ed. by T. Stolz, C. Vossmann and B. Dewein (Berlin: Akademie Verlag): 187-202

PASSY, PAUL, and ERNEST R. EDWARDS. 1904. *Aims and Principles of the International Phonetic Association* (Bourg-la-Reine, Seine: [Supplement to the *Maître Phonétique*]) (later edition 1914)

PRENDERGAST, THOMAS. 1868. *The Mastery Series. German*. 5th edn (London: Longmans, Green & Co.)

RAUCH, ANDREAS. 2015. 'La Chanson dans l'enseignement du français en Allemagne (1878-1930)', *Documents pour l'histoire du français langue étrangère ou seconde*, 54: 117-30

REES, D. J., and HENRY BAUMANN. 1910. *The Pictorial German Course (with pictures, descriptions, conversations and grammar)* (London: Modern Language Press)

REINBOTHE, ROSWITHA. 1992. *Kulturexport und Wirtschaftsmacht: Deutsche Schulen in China vor dem Ersten Weltkrieg* (Frankfurt am Main: Verlag für Interkulturelle Kommunikation)

RIPPMANN, WALTER. 1899. *Hints on Teaching German, with a Running Commentary to Dent's First German Book & Dent's German Reader* (London: Dent)

ROSENTHAL, RICHARD S. 1887. *The Meisterschaft System: A Short and Practical Method of Acquiring Complete Fluency of Speech in the German Language* (Boston: Meisterschaft Publishing) <https://catalog.hathitrust.org/Record/006537362>

TEUFEL, CARL. 1906–08. *Grammatik für Chinesen zur Erlernung der deutschen Sprache*, Vol. I 1906; Vol. II 1907; Vol. III 1908 (Jentschoufu (= Yanzhoufu): Druck und Verlag der katholischen Mission)

TROTTER, JAMES JEFFREY. 1898. *Object Lessons in German* (London-Edinburgh-New York: Thomas Nelson and Sons)

WARNKE, INGO H. (ed.). 2009. *Deutsche Sprache und Kolonialismus: Aspekte der nationalen Kommunikation, 1884–1919* (Berlin: de Gruyter)

Notes to Chapter 13

1. I gratefully acknowledge a British Academy Mid-Career Fellowship, during which this paper was researched and which also funded the digitization of the grammar discussed here. My thanks also to Mariarosaria Gianninoto for her advice on several points of detail.

2. On German attempts to exert soft power in China through German language teaching and wider educational policies in this colony, see Reinbothe (1992) and McLelland (2016).

3. For further examples and discussion, see McLelland (2016: 59-63).

4. Thanks to the online enquiry service of the SVD for these details. I know of three surviving copies of the grammar, held in the University of Basle Library, the National Library of Beijing, and the Library of Columbia University in New York; the SVD Library in Rome also holds a copy of the third part, the reader. I have consulted a digitized version of the Columbia University copy.

5. The three volumes are bound as a single volume in Columbia University Library. Volume I is the fourth edition, dated 1906; the second edition had been published in 1904; an earlier first edition was apparently quite different, covering in a single volume what became two separate volumes, I and II (see preface to the second edition (Teufel 1906: iii)). Volume II, Part 1, is the third edition, dated 1907, with only minor changes compared to the 1904 second edition (Teufel 1907: iii). Volume II, Part 2, seems to have appeared first in 1906; the second, unchanged edition, is dated 1908.

6. In the mid-1920s there were still about one thousand schools for Chinese children run by Evangelical or Catholic congregations from Germany, catering to some twenty-five thousand pupils (Werner 1988: 15). Another German who taught German in China and who is of some interest for the history of language teaching is Georg Lapper, who spent ten years teaching there, after first teaching as a primary school teacher in Germany. He is known for his 'singing method' of language learning (see Rauch 2015), apparently influenced by his time in China (Rauch, ibid.; see Lapper 1943 for this method applied to German).

7. The 'tongue-sounds' include plosives, fricatives, continuants and a nasal, but can be viewed as a large 'alveolar-postalveolar' group, made up of alveolar plosives (*d, t*), alveolar fricatives (*s, ss*), a postalveolar fricative (*sch*), and alveolar continuants (*l, n, r*). Indeed, Teufel's 'tongue-sounds' fit exactly into the 'tongue-point' group identified in one of the first official IPA charts of this period (Passy and Edwards 1904: 7). Thanks to Mike MacMahon for the reference and for

pointing out this correspondence. In the 1914 *Principles* by Passy and Edwards, the category was called 'Point and Blade', but the sounds that fit into it were the same as for 1904.

8. Gonçalves and many after him used *chū zuò* 初座 [first position] for 'nominative'; *di èr zuo* [second position] for 'genitive', etc.

9. 'Die einzelnen Kapitel schliessen sich an ein Paradigma an, dem jedesmal einige neue Wörter und Phrasen zum Auswendiglernen beigefügt sind. In dem darauf folgenden deutschen Übungsstück, das von den Schülern nicht blos übersetzt, sondern, was man nicht genug betonen kann, auswendig gelernt werden soll, sind die ersten Sätze in verschiedene Wendungen und Frageformen gebracht. Es dürfte ratsam sein, beim Unterricht auch die übrigen Sätze in ähnlicher Weise zu behandeln. Ausser diesen deutschen Übungssätzen finden sich in jedem Kapitel noch einige Fragen, welcher der Schüler selbst zu beantworten hat und endlich ein chinesisches Übungsstück zum Übersetzen' (Teufel 1906: III-IV).

10. Lessons 43 and 44 introduce adjective endings in nominative and accusative cases, first with no preceding determiner (Lesson 43), then with a definite article (Lesson 44).

CHAPTER 14

❖

Spanish as *Ersatz*: Advocacy for Spanish Language Education in the United States, 1914–1945

Jeff Bale

This chapter explores a specific period of advocacy on behalf of Spanish language education in the United States between 1914 and 1945. It details four central strategies that advocates used in their efforts to promote the language: (1) joining the chorus of anti-German chauvinism that had grown exceptionally loud as the First World War approached; (2) raising the prestige of Spanish by conflating it with Iberian and Iberian-American high culture, while simultaneously disregarding Spanish-speaking populations within the US; (3) casting Spanish language education as a patriotic act; and (4) framing Spanish in relation to US economic and political interests in Latin America. In this chapter, I demonstrate that by bolstering the same social and ideological forces that led to an overall decline in language education in American schools, opportunities to learn Spanish suffered a similar fate. The chapter begins by situating this specific case of Spanish language education advocacy within the context of Americanization and the rise of the US imperialism at the turn of the twentieth century. Second, it describes this advocacy as it occurred between 1914 and 1945, and includes discussion of the key actors and venues involved. It then turns to discuss the four advocacy strategies enumerated above. Finally, the chapter uses both empirical and interpretative analysis to assess these strategies on their own terms, that is, the extent to which they led to expanded Spanish language education in the United States between the two World Wars.[1]

Introduction

In the summer of 1915, Professor Frederick Bliss Luquiens wrote a paper for the *Yale Review* in which he advocated increased Spanish language education in the United States. To make his case, he started not with a discussion of that country, but rather with reference to Britain's declaration of war against Germany and the first complete crossing of the Panama Canal. Both had occurred the previous August. Luquiens contrasted the extensive newspaper coverage of the war with the scant attention paid to the Canal. For Luquiens, this contrast belied the Canal's obvious significance. He argued:

> having become used even to this world war, we may realize that the two events constitute one of the most striking coincidences in history, at least in the history of trade. The declaration of war meant the immediate diminution of South America's trade with Europe in general and Germany in particular. The opening of the canal at last put Ecuador, Peru, and Chile commercially within our reach. It seemed as if the hand of fate at one and the same moment were opening the door of South America to us and closing it upon Europe. (Luquiens 1915: 699)

As Luquiens himself conceded, however, 'not all opportunities that glitter [...] are golden' (Luquiens 1915: 701). He listed several factors impeding the USA's ability to walk through this open door. Many of his concerns touched on trade, given that the USA's banking and consular infrastructure lagged behind that of Great Britain and Germany. However, for Luquiens the most important factor was American public opinion towards its neighbours, which he claimed ranged between apathy and antipathy. He stated that public opinion 'is suffering from an insufficient supply of the two necessities of its life — knowledge of and sympathy with South America. And both these would come through the study of Spanish' (Luquiens 1915: 707).

Given such reasoning, one might assume that Luquiens was an economist, a political scientist, or otherwise an expert in international relations. In fact, he was a professor of Spanish and French. Luquiens himself acknowledged that 'it seems a far cry' (Luquiens 1915: 706) to link American economic interests in Latin America with Spanish language education. Nevertheless, he insisted on the centrality of the latter to the former in no uncertain terms, concluding:

> There is a familiar rhyme about an old woman whose pig wouldn't jump over the stile until water quenched fire, and fire burned stick, and stick beat dog, and dog bit pig — whereupon all turned out as it should. In like manner we may achieve success in our South American trade through a series of agencies. It will come through machinery [of trade], markets, and money, which will come through public opinion, which will come through Spanish, which will come through our educators and our teachers of Spanish. Upon them rests the ultimate responsibility. (Luquiens 1915: 711)

A defter or more direct argument that foreign language educators are on the front lines of realizing the USA's economic or geopolitical interests has rarely been made.

This chapter is part of a larger study of the history of advocacy for Spanish language education between 1914 and 1945 (see Bale 2011a). The purpose of the study was to interrogate assertions like that by Luquiens that Spanish language education was central to realizing the USA's economic and geopolitical interests in Latin America. The purpose of this chapter is to analyse more closely the content of the advocacy itself. The chapter identifies four central strategies that advocates used: (1) joining the chorus of anti-German chauvinism that had grown exceptionally loud as the First World War approached; (2) raising the prestige of Spanish by conflating it with Iberian and Iberian-American high culture, while simultaneously disregarding Spanish-speaking populations within the USA; (3) casting Spanish language education as a patriotic act; and (4) framing Spanish in relation to the USA's economic and political interests in Latin America. In the chapter, I concede that linking Spanish to the dominant discourses of chauvinism and nascent American imperialism may have been a pragmatic approach to realizing advocates' goals. However, this approach to advocacy bolstered the same social and ideological forces that led to a decline in language education in American schools. The irony, as I demonstrate in this chapter, is that opportunities to learn Spanish suffered a similar fate. In other words, this seemingly pragmatic approach to language education advocacy failed.

I begin by situating the specific case of Spanish language education advocacy within the context of Americanization and the rise of the USA as an imperial power at the turn of the twentieth century. Second, I describe this campaign for Spanish as it developed between 1914 and 1945, including key actors such as Lawrence A. Wilkins and John D. Fitz-Gerald and the publications (e.g. *Hispania*) and organizations (e.g. National Education Association) through which they pursued their advocacy. I then turn to discussing the four advocacy strategies enumerated above. Finally, I rely on both empirical and interpretative analysis to assess these strategies on their own terms, that is, the extent to which they led to expanded Spanish language education in the United States in this era.

Americanization and the Rise of US Imperialism

To understand better this moment of advocacy for Spanish language education, it is important to situate it in the context of Americanization and the rise of the United States as a world power at the turn of the twentieth century. The term *Americanization* operates in the literature in a somewhat imprecise way. For one, it refers to a specific federal programme after World War I that sponsored citizenship and English language classes for adult immigrants (see McClymer 1980). For another, it is a term used broadly to refer to education policies and practices that emerged around the turn of the twentieth century. As has been well documented, while some thirty-five million immigrants entered the country between 1815 and 1915, there was a clear shift after 1885 as immigration increased from Southern and Eastern Europe. Although the literature on Americanization tends to focus on European immigration to the East and Midwest, immigration to the western USA increased at this time as well, as people from Mexico and East Asia migrated in significant numbers (Johnson 2002).

Complicating the terminological imprecision is that interpretations of this era in educational historiography have changed dramatically over time. Mirel (2010: 3) notes that '[f]or most of the twentieth century these Americanization efforts, especially those of the public schools, were viewed as a welcome and positive contribution to the making of American society'. By the 1970s, this assessment had come under sharp critique from revisionist historians. They argued that Americanization was in fact a programme that forced immigrant children and the children of immigrants to sacrifice their home language and cultural practices as the price of admission into the American mainstream (e.g. Karier 1975; Olneck 1989; Weiss 1982). Carlson (1987: 12) characterized this process most sharply as 'cultural genocide'. However, what had been a revisionist perspective has since become the 'standard view of Americanization education' (Ramsey 2011: 491). More recent historiography has challenged the revisionists' reading. It has questioned how exclusively negative or oppressive the era was in all instances by highlighting immigrant agency in choosing which Anglo-American practices they adopted and which linguistic and cultural practices from their heritage they maintained (e.g. Mirel 2010; Ramsey 2010; Zimmerman 2002; see Spack 2002 for analysis regarding Native Americans and English-language practices).

It is beyond the scope of this chapter to evaluate these historiographical developments; however, it merits mention that most applied-linguistic research of language planning and policy continues to adopt the revisionist perspective (e.g. Bale 2011c; Herman 2002; Lomawaima and McCarty 2006; Ricento 2003; Wiley 1998, 2002, 2007). Indeed, there exist two dominant narratives of Americanization within applied-linguistic literature that describe the educational experiences of emergent bilingual children during this era. The first of these was originally told in Kloss's (1998 [1977]) seminal history of bilingual education and Heath's (1981) early work on comparative language-policy analysis. This narrative characterizes the USA's language policy until the 1880s as essentially *laissez-faire*. Few formal policies existed either to restrict or to promote non-English languages, and there was general tolerance of the practice of such languages. Of course, this narrative is accurate only insofar as it excludes (in)formal policies regarding the languages of enslaved Africans and their descendants (Weinberg 1977). Besides the obvious omission, if this general characterization is correct, then it must also account for the decidedly intolerant language-education policies imposed from 1880s onward.

The history of those policies has been reported elsewhere (e.g. Carlson 1987; Kliebard 2004; Mirel 2010; Ramsey 2010; Reese 2011; Salamone 2010; Weinberg 1977; Weiss 1982) but, to recall, it includes three primary features. First is the general attitude towards European immigrants in the East and Midwest. Supporters of Americanization viewed schools as a venue that could contribute to the solution of the putative social problems of ethnic, religious and linguistic diversity. Not only should schools produce workers equipped with the skills required by an industrial, urban economy. But also, they should provide a common curricular and cultural experience (i.e. Anglo-Saxon and English-speaking) to counter the ethnic, linguistic and religious diversity of immigrant children (Carlson 1987; Weiss 1982). Second, these restrictive policies impacted on Native youth primarily through the institution of the boarding school, the first of which opened in Carlisle, Pennsylvania in 1879. Children from various Native nations were intentionally schooled together to inhibit communication in their native languages and the maintenance of their cultures. As Crawford (1992) has documented, eradicating Native languages and supplanting them with English ranked among the primary aims of boarding schools. Typically of settler-colonial projects, federal policy documents and administrators portrayed the suppression of Native children's language and culture as a civilizing mission. Finally, Americanization practices in the West and Southwest mirrored more closely the institutionalized exclusion of Native students than it did 'melting pot' practices more common in the East and Midwest. A dual system of segregated schools was established that prepared some Anglo students for their future role as leaders and owners, while preparing most Mexican and Asian students for life as workers (Cohen 1974; González 1990). Even in conditions of complete segregation, the aim was to replace the native language with English.

The second dominant narrative describing this era focuses on the fate of German language education vis-à-vis the First World War. As the War approached, the political dynamics of Americanization shifted to equate learning English with loyalty. By contrast, diversity was taught as unpatriotic (Herman 2002). Wiley (1998) presented an extensive account of the hysteria surrounding German and German Americans during the War, which included purges of German-language titles from public libraries; dismissal of entire German-language university staff; public assaults, including tarring and feathering, of German Americans and German religious minorities such as the Mennonites; and support from the National Education Association for English-only medium-of-instruction policies. German-language instruction was formally criminalized in Nebraska, while other states used various means, ranging from legislation and executive orders to local school-board rulings, to remove German from schools. Parallel to the exclusion of German, the number of states with English-only medium-of-instruction policies doubled from seventeen in 1913 to thirty-four in 1923. No matter the debates within educational historiography mentioned above about the precise nature of Americanization, there is little dispute that this era marked the end of German as the most prominent non-English community language, as well as of the longstanding tradition of German-English bilingual schooling in many areas of the USA (Ramsey 2010; Wiley 1998).

Although the fate of German-language education is typically explained in terms of the First World War, I have argued elsewhere (Bale 2011c) that it is too simplistic to limit our analysis to the War and its impact. Rather, the shift from essentially *laissez-faire* language policies in the 1880s to a series of restrictive language polices — culminating in the criminalization of German — needs also to be seen in light of the broader process by which the USA took their place as a world power at the turn of the twentieth century.

This ascendancy was rooted in four dynamics. The first was the meteoric rise of the USA's economy, which already by 1900 was the largest and most productive in the world (Lens 2003 [1971]: 151–52). Second, the federal state consolidated its power by means of the Civil War. With the abolition of slavery came the dismantling of non-capitalist economic relations in the South and the imposition of political power rooted in an industrialized economy in the North. Both developments led to a more powerful and more stable federal state able to assert its control over the entire American polity (see Harman 1999: 345–54). Third, Manifest Destiny, the belief that it was natural, inevitable and ordained by God that Americans settle the west and expand the nation's reach from coast to coast, existed as an ideology from the republic's earliest days. However, this ideology would not be realized in fact until after the Civil War. Westward expansion was a twofold process that included extermination or marginalization of Native nations and formal war with Mexico to establish control over specific territories (Lens 2003 [1971]: 111–34). In this way, American territorial expansion mirrored the (settler-)colonial projects of its European counterparts (Callinicos 2009: 151ff). The fourth and final aspect was the projection of US power across the Western Hemisphere. As with westward expansion, formal declaration of the USA's right to police the region (known as the Monroe Doctrine) had occurred earlier in the nineteenth century. However, the United States was not in a position actually to enforce that doctrine until much later. This pretence of protecting the region from European incursion facilitated the rapid expansion of American capital investment throughout the hemisphere; and triggered repeated military interventions in Central America, the Caribbean and beyond. The Spanish-American War of 1898 was the most ambitious among them, through which the United States acquired still more territory and established a military presence on two fronts (Lens 2003 [1971]: 236–74). That presence would expand immensely after the First World War, a conflict that Lens (2003 [1971]: 236) characterized as the 'the big leap' in US imperialism.

To be clear, the rise of US imperialism unfolded in fits and starts, not as a linear ascension. Important struggles challenged the consolidation of US power, even if in the end they could not prevent it. These struggles ranged from Radical Reconstruction after the Civil War in the South and the anti-racist politics of the Wobblies[2] as they organized industrial workers across the West to the Philippine Insurrection (1899–1902) against US occupation and the one million votes cast in 1920 for a Socialist candidate who was in jail at the time for opposing the First World War. In other words, there was nothing automatic or pre-ordained about how US imperialism developed. Nevertheless, by expanding our understanding of imperialism from merely an engagement in this or that war to a much broader political-economic dynamic of competition among wealthy nations to (re-)distribute power among them over the rest of world, we are able to make sense not only of the *specific* hysteria over the German language during the First World War, but also of the *general* trend towards cultural and linguistic homogenization, a process imposed in no small part through schooling. Indeed, as *external* US power expanded (insofar as 'external' includes economic growth and conflicts with Native nations, Mexico, Spain and the Central Powers), the *internal* enforcement of a singular national identity — one expressed in English only — became ever stricter.

Overview of the Campaign for Spanish Language Education

It is within this socio-historical and political-economic context that advocates began to call for expanded Spanish language education in the United States. The campaign in fact comprised two dynamics. The first is perhaps more accurately described as a process of professionalization of Spanish language education. Before the advent of mass public education in the USA, reading in ancient languages had dominated foreign language study within formal educational contexts. That tradition continued as foreign-language education was codified in the public school curriculum. Until the First World War, German, French and Spanish were the most-studied languages (Watzke 2003). However, the infrastructure to support Spanish language education as a distinct professional or academic discipline did not emerge until the late 1910s.

The second dynamic is specific lobbying on behalf of Spanish language education. This advocacy established three goals: to expand access to Spanish in secondary and tertiary institutions nationwide; to develop more effective teachers; and, consequently, to ensure more advanced proficiency among students. My analysis of the strategies that advocates pursued in this campaign follows below; here I describe the primary actors and the venues in which the campaign unfolded. In so doing, I identify the various primary sources that informed this study.

The most active figure in this campaign was Lawrence A. Wilkins. Wilkins was a high-school Spanish teacher in New York City who by 1917 had become the director of the foreign language programme for the city's public school system. During his tenure, Wilkins initiated and edited the *Bulletin of High Points in the Teaching of Modern Languages in the High Schools of New York City* (*Bulletin* 1917a). As a primary source, the *Bulletin* straddles the two dynamics of the campaign for Spanish described above. On the one hand, it played a central role in professionalizing foreign-language education by compiling a list of 'high points' (or *best practices* in current educational parlance); sample curricula; articulated scope and sequences for each language; artefacts produced by student language clubs; and announcements of general interest to language teachers. On the other, each issue led with a brief article by Wilkins, which often argued the centrality of Spanish language education to US society and its schools. In the end, the *Bulletin* had an impact beyond modern-language study, insofar as its focus expanded after the first two volumes to include the entire school curriculum. This broader *Bulletin* has long served as one of the most important primary sources for historical studies of New York City's public schools, although its roots in modern-language education are rarely acknowledged. Furthermore, the *Bulletin* had an impact far beyond New York, inspiring school systems from Los Angeles to Chicago to Philadelphia to initiate similar circulars. In addition to his work on the *Bulletin*, Wilkins was also author of several textbooks on Spanish language teaching methods.

Wilkins was also the founding president of the American Association of Teachers of Spanish (AATS),[3] formed in 1917. Early volumes of the Association's journal, *Hispania*, included proceedings from annual conventions and transcripts of speeches held. These proceedings constitute another primary source offering insight into individual actors' perspectives on Spanish. In general, university professors were the most frequent contributors. Some, such as John D. Fitz-Gerald, were professors of Spanish; others, in particular Nicholas Murray Butler, then President of Columbia University, were not.

Other actors were less directly involved in this advocacy, but their position in society gives some indication as to the extent of the consensus that had developed about the uses of Spanish language education. On the one hand, advocates solicited the opinions of 'popular oracles' (Doyle 1929: 51) in support of Spanish, including American Presidents Wilson, Coolidge and Hoover; the presidents of the National City Bank (now CitiBank), the United Fruit Company, and the US Steel Corporation; and popular culture figures such as aviator Charles Lindbergh and vaudeville performer, actor and cowboy Will Rogers. These opinions were then published in both popular and professional venues. On the other hand, high-level politicians, including a Secretary of the Treasury and even President-Elect Herbert Hoover, were dispatched to a number of educational and diplomatic events at which to make the case for Spanish.

As a final word about sources, I should acknowledge that I did not include an extensive search in American newspapers from the era. The purpose of this study was to understand the campaign for Spanish language education from the perspective of those who were most active in it, not in terms of how their efforts were represented by others. Moreover, I was most interested in the relationship between these efforts to expand Spanish language education and public schools of the era. This focus has to do as much with the ten years I spent as a language educator in secondary schools in the United States as it does with the other kinds of research I conduct on language policy and language education. Consequently, while I include the perspective and voices of university-based Spanish educators, I focused in terms of both data collection and analysis on the fate of Spanish at school in this era. While these are limitations to this study, they also point the way for future work on what has been a relatively under-studied era in the history of language education in the United States.

In addition to clarifying the sources that this study drew on, I should also note that the historical record does not reflect anything like minutes of meetings in which one plan or the other to promote Spanish is debated or voted on. In that sense, it is perhaps disingenuous to label this moment of language-education advocacy a 'campaign'. However, the consistency of message across the multiple venues described above, and especially advocates' success in marshalling opinions about Spanish language education held by 'popular oracles', suggest that this moment of language-education advocacy was something more than serendipitous convergence of opinion. Indeed, that 'something more' reveals troublesome, if familiar, ideological and practical features of the campaign for Spanish, to which the discussion now turns.

Strategies for Spanish Language Education Advocacy

One implication of the previous discussion about Americanization and the rise of US imperialism is that any individual or organization intending to promote foreign language study in this era faced — at best — an unfavourable political climate in which to do so. Advocates for Spanish took this challenge head-on. Indeed, the first three strategies that I describe below can be interpreted as advocates' efforts to respond, either directly or indirectly, to the constraints that Americanization placed on their efforts to expand access to Spanish language education.

A Superior for an Inferior Object

On 6 October 1917 Wilkins addressed the Modern Language Section of the High School Teachers' Association for New York City's public schools. His address was published later that month as the lead article in the *Bulletin of High Points* (*Bulletin* 1917c). Perhaps because he was speaking to a live audience of peers in the school system, his comments about the relationship between the War and language education were relatively muted — at least in comparison to what he would write in the next few years. He stated:

> An up-to-date modern language teacher is one who is alert to the issues of the times in which he lives. [...] He must relate his work to the living, vital present. The overwhelming fact facing this nation and facing us as citizens of this nation and facing us as teachers of the languages of other nations, is that oppressive fact that we are at war. And we are at war with a nation whose language many of you have taught, whose language has been more widely taught in all our schools and colleges than any other modern foreign language. And in view of the almost complete divergence of ideals and modes of thought existing in that nation and in our own [...] the most fair-minded and deliberative person cannot but ask, did not the pendulum swing too far in favor of the teaching of that language in our institutions? Has there not, after all, existed, possibly unsuspected heretofore, a greater real community of ideas and ideals between our own Anglo-Saxon race and those that speak in tongues from that of the Romans, the Americans of other days? Personally, I believe German should by all means be continued in our schools but that absolutely equal opportunities should be given to study the other languages. But the fact is that the pendulum swings now the other way, to the sunny Latin side, if you will. That is the up-to-date situation or condition. The French, Spanish, Italian and Portuguese languages and civilizations seem now in many ways to make most appeal to us as Americans. We are allies of the French, the Italians, the Portuguese. Sixty million fellow-Americans who live in lands to the south of us speak Spanish. (*Bulletin* 1917c: 2–3)

Different from the argumentation Wilkins deployed in later speeches and writings, this address to his fellow teachers relied heavily on the pragmatic notion of responding to changes in the world outside of school as a reason to replace German with Spanish. Yet even here, Wilkins conceded that German language education should continue.

Later in the address, however, he made a more specific demand of his fellow German teachers. The context of this second comment was the precipitous decline in German-language enrolments in the school system and the potential for teachers to lose their jobs. In response, the school system (for which Wilkins was by then an administrator) allowed German teachers to re-tool as teachers of other languages. In broaching this controversial topic, Wilkins demanded that veteran German teachers either proclaim their loyalty to the United States as a condition of continuing to teach that language, or keep their 'chagrin' about having to re-tool to themselves

(*Bulletin* 1917c: 3). Either way, Wilkins explained that all German teachers should be ready to become teachers of other languages, of Spanish in particular, and high-quality ones at that. He conceded that German teachers deserved sympathy for the situation they faced. However, 'if they do not meet the standards they will not be permitted to teach Spanish classes. The children of our schools must not be compelled to receive poor instruction just to keep teachers employed' (*Bulletin* 1917c: 3).

Less than a year later, Wilkins (1918a) addressed the Modern Languages section of the National Education Association (NEA) at its annual meeting, held in Pittsburgh that year. The NEA is now one of the two main teachers' unions in the United States. At that time, however, it functioned as a professional organization whose membership was made up primarily of principals and other school administrators, and was almost exclusively male (Murphy 1992). Wilkins's stance towards German in this speech was markedly different, declaring: 'We have had too much teaching of German in our schools. It was fast becoming the second language of our nation. And I personally believe that it was taught chiefly for the purposes of furthering propaganda originating in Berlin' (Wilkins 1918a: 208). Indeed, where earlier Wilkins had been more sympathetic to German teachers re-tooling themselves as Spanish teachers, now he was suspicious. He described German teachers who were writing Spanish textbooks and re-training as Spanish teachers as engaging in 'peaceful penetration'. He continued: 'I say beware, if these teachers are of German birth or German sympathies' (Wilkins 1918a: 220). The solution for Wilkins was clear: to substitute Spanish for German in the school curriculum. He stated:

> When I accepted the invitation of Professor Fife to speak on the topic, 'Spanish as a Substitute for German for Training and Culture,' it seemed to me unfortunate that two of the words in the topic bore a certain flavor of ill-repute. I refer to 'substitute' and 'culture.' Then I reflected that if such be the case, it is not the fault of us American teachers. 'Substitute' in the form of 'Ersatz' and culture in the guise of 'Kultur,' had not their origin in our land or language. Substitutes and substitutes for substitutes are offered today in Germany. These substitutes, be they chopped straw for wheat flour, mendacity for truth, paper for cloth, militarism for national freedom, composition for leather, piracy and murder for international law, the 'good old German god' for the true God, are all the substitute of an inferior for a vastly superior article, quality or principle. It is in no such sense, I assure you, that I offer Spanish as a substitute for German in our educational scheme. I offer a superior for an inferior article to provide training and culture for American youth. (Wilkins 1918a: 205)

In addition to aligning his comments with the explicit anti-German chauvinism so common during the war, this address counted among the few in which Wilkins made direct reference to Americanization.[4] He endorsed a central tenet of this movement, namely removing all non-English language instruction from the primary grades. Wilkins argued:

> I believe no foreign language should be taught in the elementary schools. Americanism and the three R's,[5] if you will, should be the subjects taught thoroughly well in such schools. There is no room or time for teaching foreign languages. (Wilkins 1918a: 220)

As an administrator for modern language education in the country's largest school system, this was an interesting stance to take, at least.

Writing in the *Education Review* in summer 1919, finally, Wilkins (1919b) further sharpened his rhetoric with respect to Germans and German–language education in the United States. Now that the War was over, there had been some calls to restore the study of classical German literature and culture at the university level. In response, Wilkins quipped:

> The American people and most of the world managed to get along uncommonly well without much German *Kultur* of any kind during the war. And there are so many other types of foreign culture that the world may draw upon which are not soiled by the trail of the serpent of Prussianism and which on analysis do not reveal a mix of 20 per cent culture and 80 per cent propaganda. [...] This *Kultur*, prized though it be still by some professors in American universities, has no longer any attraction for the American citizen, even for him of the most inquisitive turn of mind or for him of the intellectual élite. President Guth of Goucher College said: 'Germany has so influenced our own scholars and given them such a twist mentally that they have been unable to see how favorable they have been to ideas and opinions purely German'. (Wilkins 1919b: 291–92)

Besides the specific use of a German word *Kultur* to stigmatize the people and the language, as well as the vivid imagery and claims of political bias, what makes this final example particularly important is the venue in which it was published. Unlike a bulletin internal to a single school system, albeit the largest in the USA, and unlike addressing a sub-section of a professional group, the *Education Review* was a periodical read more widely in the United States in the early part of the twentieth century. In other words, one of Wilkins's sharpest arguments was made precisely in the venue with the widest reach.

While it would be inappropriate to argue that Wilkins spoke for all advocates of Spanish language education, he certainly was a leader among them. It is thus particularly important that the chauvinism in his rhetoric not only sharpened over time — even after the War had ended — but that he moved from advocating the 'equal opportunity' to teach multiple modern languages to calling for Spanish to replace German outright. Indeed, it was by echoing and reinforcing anti-German chauvinism that Wilkins's call for substitution, rather than just addition, could make any sense at all.

High-Status Culture versus Low-Status Spanish Speakers

During Thanksgiving week of 1915 a number of Spanish language educators gathered in New York City to lay the groundwork for what became the AATS two years later. At that meeting, Wilkins (1917) prepared comments in which he acknowledged a niggling problem for the growth of their profession. He described how anti-German chauvinism had undermined the already precarious prestige of Spanish language education. Of course, the point he made here did not seem to prevent his own anti-German rhetoric from growing sharper in the coming years, as I detailed above. Nevertheless, Wilkins conceded, 'many are beginning to realize, though they may have been slow to do so, that we Anglo-Saxons may possibly, after all, have overestimated our "superiority" and underestimated the Iberian and Iberian-American nations' (Wilkins 1917: 6). Correcting this overestimation constituted a second strategy for advocacy on behalf of Spanish language education. Advocates asserted that 'Spanish American' — by which they meant citizens of countries to the south of the United States and not Spanish speakers of Hispanic heritage living on territories that now belonged to the USA — were essentially the same as (Anglo-)Americans.

First, advocates stressed the existence of a rich high culture, both in Spain itself and in Latin America. For example, Fitz-Gerald produced a thirty-page monograph compiling an extensive list of the literary contributions of Spanish and Latin American authors. In fact, he claimed that, 'after the Bible', *El Ingenioso Hidalgo Don Quijote de La Mancha* was the greatest book ever written (Fitz-Gerald 1918: 13). Part of this stress on the literary tradition in Spanish is tied to the state of foreign-language education in the USA in the early twentieth century, at which time learning to read high literature in the target language was considered the primary goal (Watzke 2003). In this sense, highlighting the four-hundred-year tradition of Spanish language high literature comprised a logical effort to establish a certain prestige in learning Spanish on a par with study of English literature or other foreign-language literatures.

Second, advocates for Spanish language education described the independence movements that created the United States and of the republics of Latin America as espousing the same socio-political values. Fitz-Gerald (1918: 21), in the monograph cited above, concluded his discussion of Spanish language literature thus:

> From the loins of this glorious Spain have come eighteen sovereign and independent nations. The story of the discovery and conquest of the territory they occupy is one of the most amazing tales in all history. Their long, uphill struggle for independence has much in common with our own Revolution, and will therefore prove to be of very great interest to us in North America. Our affection for Washington and other Revolutionary and pre-Revolutionary heroes should endear us to Bolívar, O'Higgins, San Martín, Sarmiento and others.

Later, in fact, Fitz-Gerald addressed a central contradiction in his argument (i.e. that Spain can be both 'glorious' and a power from which to engage in 'an uphill struggle for independence'). He cited a further similarity that both the US and its Latin American neighbours have maintained a 'cordial relationship with the [respective] mother-land'.

Third, assertions about the similarities among the peoples of the USA, Spain and Latin America employed the same social category of 'race' that was used to denounce Germans and German-Americans. In his speech to the NEA mentioned in the previous section, Wilkins argued that learning Spanish 'provides the key to an understanding of a great race, in Spain and in Spanish America, a race that has much to contribute of help to us and the world at large' (Wilkins 1918a: 217). He described that race in terms of 'genuine courtesy', 'marked love of democracy', and 'sobriety, industry and long patience' (Wilkins 1918a: 217). In fact, it is because this race 'has spread its civilization more widely, perhaps, than any other race except the Anglo-Saxon' (Wilkins 1918a: 219) that Spanish speakers were essentially just like (Anglo-)Americans, thus rendering their language worthy of study.

This move to establish socio-political, cultural and, indeed, racial parity between 'Spanish American' and 'American' populations seems consistent with the historical context of Americanization in which Spanish language education advocacy occurred. Against this backdrop, rationalizing Spanish language education in terms of perceived similarities between 'Spanish American' and 'American' people is both an expected and reasonable rhetorical move. It not only attempts to counter the negative consequences of Americanization by elevating the peoples who speak Spanish natively to the same level as Americans. This move also attempts to create ideological space safe enough in which to implement expanded Spanish language study.

However, this socio-political, cultural and racial parity did not apply to native Spanish speakers living under the US flag. Here, the most compelling evidence is the absence of evidence. That is, very few advocacy texts acknowledged these populations at all. Wilkins, for example, made brief mention of the roughly two hundred thousand native speakers of Spanish living in New York City at the time, insofar as their presence provided an integral motivation for students to learn the language (Taylor and Wilkins 1920). Moreover, the odd reference to the need for Spanish in order to conduct business in the Southwest appeared throughout advocacy texts (e.g. Butler, Cutter and Shepherd 1934). By contrast, the only text that extensively addressed native Spanish-speaking populations within the USA did so in terms of their desire to act and sound like Anglos. The text is a transcript of a speech that Fitz-Gerald (1921) gave at the fourth AATS meeting in Chicago in 1920. Referring to 'the bilingual, biracial problem of our border states' (Fitz-Gerald 1921: 182), he described native Spanish speakers as '[t]hroughout all these years [...] consistently and persistently desirous of learning English and becoming thoroughly Americanized' (Fitz-Gerald 1921: 177). He claimed that 'we' had failed to do so insofar as public schools in those regions were neither staffed with native English-speaking teachers nor bilingual teachers with sufficient English proficiency. Consequently, this strategy of Spanish language education advocacy did not invoke Hispanic populations living in the USA as the basis on which to assert that Spaniards, Latin and North Americans shared important cultural or socio-political values. If anything, such populations presented a problem to the United States.

A Patriotic Duty at All Times

Similarly to the first two strategies, the third — positioning Spanish language education as a patriotic act — responded directly to the context of Americanization. As discussed above, the First World War brought a new dimension to Americanization efforts, even before the USA formally engaged in it. Using English in place of the home language became an important way for immigrants, no matter their origin, to demonstrate loyalty to the United States. By contrast, using or learning German was specifically construed as an act of sedition. This association between language use and loyalty put advocates of Spanish in a tough spot. They worked their way out of it by turning this association on its head and rebranding the learning and teaching of Spanish as a patriotic act.

Part of this rebranding was to connect Spanish language instruction directly to American involvement in the war. For example, in May 1918 the *Bulletin* included the work of Mr. Luria, Spanish teacher at DeWitt Clinton High School in the Bronx, as one of its suggested high points. Luria had submitted two items to the circular: '(1) material used by him for posters on the bulletin boards in the class rooms of Spanish classes; and (2) a plan for the correlation of modern language teaching with the development of patriotism and Americanism. Both are excellent', the *Bulletin* explained (*Bulletin* 1918a: 9). The poster called on students to buy war stamps as part of the war effort: 'Have you bought your war stamps? WHY NOT?' (*Bulletin* 1918a: 10; my translation). In addition, Mr. Luria submitted a text that could be used for dictations, which included the statements 'hiding your money is dangerous and antipatriotic. Investing your money is safe and patriotic' (*Bulletin* 1918a: 10; my translation). He closed his submission with a general teaching plan that could be used in any language classroom with the aim of 'bring[ing] to the pupil's consciousness the essential element of the present war activities' (*Bulletin* 1918a: 11). The plan included translating patriotic American songs into the target language; developing posters like his war stamp example; cutting out newspaper articles from foreign-language newspapers about the War; and 'memory work' (*Bulletin* 1918a: 12). As themes, Luria suggested focusing on food conservation, war stamps and liberty bonds (savings bonds issued by the US government during the War), all of which allowed for practice of the subjunctive mood and idiomatic expressions.

Beyond this direct association with the war, advocates of Spanish language education invoked patriotism at a more general or idealistic level. In his second presidential address to the AATS, for example, Wilkins (1919a: 37–38) stated:

> For the teachers of Spanish comprehend clearly that theirs is in essence a patriotic duty at all times. Besides offering themselves for participation in war service, they feel, I am sure, that in teaching Spanish well and effectively they are contributing much to the welfare of the country. They look into the future and see, as do all true American citizens, a greater United States of America. They have also the vision to see, I believe, a greater collective America, an America dedicated unitedly to the high ideals of freedom and democracy, an America stretching from our own land to the utmost Spanish- and Portuguese-speaking peoples of twenty independent republics.

The pan-Americanism expressed in this speech is a topic I address in greater detail in Bale 2011a and is beyond the scope of the discussion here. However, Wilkins's speech that year gives a sense of a broader definition of patriotism, to which advocates linked the teaching and learning of Spanish.

This sentiment was echoed by educators who were not directly involved with Spanish or even with modern-language education. In the October 1917, at the same meeting of modern-language teachers in New York City described earlier, Wilkins used his address to enumerate the characteristics of the 'up-to-date modern language teacher' (*Bulletin* 1917c: 5). Of the fourteen qualities he mentioned,

'*Patriotism* — love of America of the genuine, wholehearted sort and unquestioning support of and service to our government' (*Bulletin* 1917c: 6) topped the list.

The 'Purchasing Power of Hispanic America'

The final strategy for advocating Spanish language education had less to do with the context of Americanization, but instead was rooted in claims about the language's usefulness to US economic interests in Latin America. Indeed, as we saw with Luquiens (1915), advocates were remarkably well versed in the facts and figures of US trade and economic interests across the hemisphere; and were equally insistent that Spanish language education was central to supporting such interests. For example, in his speech to the 1915 AATS planning meeting, Wilkins (1917) referred to the collective impact on US trade prospects of the Panama Canal: direct ocean liner routes between New York City and Valparaiso, Chile; and new branches of the National City Bank in the region. In the foreword to his textbook of teaching methods, furthermore, he extended this list by citing a 227% increase in South American imports of US goods versus a 107% increase of US imports of South American goods from 1900 to 1913 (Wilkins 1918b: 7). In the May 1917 issue of the *Bulletin*, Wilkins (*Bulletin* 1917b) added to his case the centrality of South American raw materials to the expanding US economy.

Wilkins also argued that post-war restoration of the German economy posed a significant threat to the United States. In the October 1918 issue of the *Bulletin*, he reprinted a news report from the *New York World* describing intentions of major German and Austrian banks to resume trade with Latin America. Immediately after the reprinted article, Wilkins insisted: 'Is this not indicative enough of a necessity, greater than ever before, of a knowledge of Spanish among the young folks of our own land, if we would have them cope with Germany in competition for South American trade?' (*Bulletin* 1918b: 13). Underscoring his belief that Spanish language proficiency was central to US competition over Latin American markets, Wilkins (1919b: 291) wrote: 'In commerce it is not the language of our competitors which we need to know so much as it is the languages of our clients'.

Speaking to the fifth AATS meeting in Washington, DC in 1921, J. P. Wickersham Crawford, Professor of Spanish at the University of Pennsylvania, remarked: 'We all know, and a few of us remember, that something happened to the study of Spanish shortly after the year 1898' (Crawford 1922: 346). The reference was to the start of the Spanish-American War. This conflict played out on two fronts, in the Caribbean and in the Pacific. In addition to US armed forces occupying the Philippines as that country struggled for independence from Spain, the USA acquired territory that they continue to hold, namely Guam, Puerto Rico, and Guantanamo Bay in Cuba. After three and a half years, $170 million, an unknown number of Filipino and four thousand American deaths, the USA had dealt the final blow to the Spanish Empire. Expanding on what he meant by 'something happened', Crawford explained:

> During the period of the Great War, there was a marked increase in our
> political, commercial and even intellectual relations with the republics to the

south. The Caribbean, in particular, came to be regarded to a large degree as an economic dependency of the United States, and American commerce in that region grew to such an extent that we successfully challenged the commercial supremacy that had been divided between Great Britain and Germany. [...] All these factors combined to support a claim, which could not possibly have been successfully debated twenty years before, that both for purposes of foreign trade and for good citizenship in the broadest sense, it was imperative that a large number of our young people in schools and colleges should have adequate training in Spanish. (Crawford 1922: 347)

Crawford is certainly correct that it would have been difficult to claim a need for Spanish language education in terms of US commercial interests before 1898. The empirical question is whether that claim was ever realized in practice. I return to this question in the final part of this chapter. For now, I present two more data excerpts from later in this period of advocacy for Spanish language education, specifically between 1934 and 1936. Insofar as each continues to argue that the USA need more citizens who are proficient in Spanish, we begin to acquire a sense that the claims that Wilkins, Crawford and their colleagues made in the late 1910s and early 1920s in fact had gone unheeded.

For example, in 1934 *Hispania* published an unsigned article titled 'The Importance of the Study of Spanish' (Butler, Cutler and Shepherd 1934: 371). The brief article opened by making the case again as to why 'Spanish should most certainly be given a place in the curriculum of high schools and colleges on a par with other modern languages'. That the journal had to make such a plea suggests that over fifteen years of explicit advocacy on behalf of the language had still not achieved the desired result. To substantiate its claim, the journal published quotations from university presidents, magazine editors and prominent businessmen in support of Spanish. The opinion of Victor Cutter, President of the United Fruit Company, stands out as particularly noteworthy, given his company's status as the world's leading producer of bananas. Since the 1920s it had dominated well over 70 per cent of world banana production and controlled vast amounts of otherwise sovereign territory across Central and South America for its plantations (Bucheli 2008). From that vantage point, Cutter (Butler, Cutler and Shepherd 1934: 372) argued:

> I regard instruction in Spanish as an absolute necessity in every public school and college in our country. We are the leading nation in the Western Hemisphere, but we must not overlook the fact that to do business and retain the friendship of our Latin-American neighbors we must read and write their language fluently and correctly.

Finally, as World War II approached, Henry Hein (1936: 10–11), teacher at James Monroe High School in the Bronx, followed his analysis of the impending war with an urgent plea to Spanish language teachers to redouble their efforts. Hein cited demographic figures of emerging world powers in Asia and Latin America as threats to US economic stability. He wrote:

> At the same time all these countries south of the Rio Grande are developing their manufactures and their production of raw materials. [...] These Latin-American countries are going to gain tremendously in man power and in

wealth. What then? [...] Shall we be able to survive, standing only on our own feet? Europe will be out of the picture. It is Latin America upon whom we shall have to depend. Will they be with us or will the bronze and the yellow races divide world power between themselves? Isn't it high time that we did something now?

The urgency in Hein's words not only underscores the importance of advocacy for Spanish language education in terms of its economic usefulness, but also that this campaign for Spanish was not perceived to have been successful.

On its Own Terms

Advocates for language education in the United States have long used the rationales of US economic and geopolitical security to make their case. Indeed, following the events of 11 September 2001, the government of the United States renewed its commitment to language education in the name of national security. This move touched off another round of academic debate about the consequences of understanding language as a resource in this way (see Bale 2014). One of the difficulties applied linguists have had in evaluating this strategy is that it takes time to assess how language-education programmes develop and/or decline, particularly because applied-linguistic interest — more often, fretting — about the relationship between American national security and language learning only seems to re-surface in the wake of the latest geopolitical crisis (e.g. Sputnik; the international oil crisis in 1973-74; the rise of the Japanese auto industry in the 1980s; the First Gulf War in 1991; the 'War on Terror' after 2001), that interest rarely lasts long enough to assess, empirically or otherwise, what actually happens to language-education policies and programmes. However, a key benefit of historicizing this association in the USA between language education and ideologies of economic and geopolitical security, as I have done here, is that it allows for something like an assessment of that association. Although the primary purpose of this chapter was to analyse the content of multiple strategies that advocates used between the two World Wars to support Spanish language education, it is worth offering that assessment, as well.

As mentioned above, one key goal of this advocacy was to expand access to Spanish language education at the secondary and tertiary levels. Therefore, one empirical approach to assessing these advocacy strategies is to consider Spanish language enrolments across the period in which this advocacy took place. Watzke (2003) remains the most comprehensive analysis of foreign-language enrolments at the secondary level in the USA. Table 1, below, reports a selection of enrolment figures from the extensive appendices compiled in that study.

In addition to the dramatic fall in German enrolments after World War I, three points about these figures are noteworthy. First, French and Spanish were equal beneficiaries, at least initially, of the collapse of German enrolments, each increasing by relatively similar percentages while those for Latin continued their decline. Second, beyond the initial bump in Spanish enrolments, they in fact declined slightly across the period in which the advocacy reported here occurred. By contrast, French enrolments rose over this period. Most important, the

Year	Language Enrolments as a % of total foreign-language enrolments				Total FL enrolments*
	Latin	French	German	Spanish	
1909	58.4	11.8	28.2	0.8	67.9
1914	50.8	12.0	33.2	3.7	64.5
1921	50.0	28.1	1.2	20.5	53.1
1924	48.1	28.4	2.8	20.5	44.3
1927	46.3	29.6	3.9	19.9	40.9
1933	44.8	30.3	6.6	17.4	28.7
1948	35.7	21.6	3.6	37.5	21.9
1962	22.7	32.2	6.8	36.8	31.3
1974	5.1	29.7	12.0	50.9	24.1

TABLE I. *Selected Secondary Foreign Language Enrolments, 1909–1974*
(adapted from Watzke 2003: 141–42)
*As a percentage of total high school enrolments

overall proportion of secondary students studying any foreign language declined precipitously from around 68% to 22% in the first half of the twentieth century (see the right-most column of Table I). To be clear, while part of the decline in overall foreign-language enrolments is related to the consequences of Americanization as described above, another part of it has to do with the place of foreign-language education in the secondary curriculum. As attendance at and completion of secondary school expanded dramatically in the early twentieth century,[6] foreign-language study was effectively restricted to academically oriented students preparing for university. Watzke (2003) recounts the heated debates from that era as to what kind of student should be allowed to study foreign languages. Clearly, those debates were informed by the ethos of Americanization that characterized the era, but they were also coloured by longstanding assumptions that foreign-language study was primarily a question of mental training and thus best suited for university-bound students. The gatekeeping function that foreign-language study plays in the USA has remained fundamentally unchanged since this this period.

However, even if we allow for these other dynamics impacting on foreign-language enrolments in this era, the fact still remains that advocacy for Spanish appears to have failed, indeed on two counts. Not only did enrolments in Spanish fall absolutely, but also they fell relative to an ever-declining number of pupils studying a foreign language at all. Indeed, this decline occurred at the height of this advocacy on behalf of Spanish, from which we can infer that the aspirations of Spanish language proficiency for most, if not all, of America's youth went fundamentally unfulfilled.

Advocates' own interpretations of the state of Spanish language education near the end of this period of advocacy confirm this conclusion. Insofar as advocates continued to call for more Spanish into the mid- and late-1930s — that is, some fifteen years into this advocacy — we can reasonably conclude that advocates themselves had some understanding that their efforts were not succeeding. In addition to the insights from Wilkins and Hein mentioned in the previous section, advocates also repeatedly expressed concern throughout the campaign about the status or prestige of Spanish language education. For example, in response to 'open opposition to the study and teaching of Spanish' (Wilkins 1922: 410), Wilkins solicited the opinion of a number of prominent Americans about Spanish language education. He received responses from then Secretary of Commerce, Herbert Hoover, the Secretaries of War, Navy and State, as well as leading financiers stating that Spanish language knowledge was essential to the USA. In closing, Wilkins urged: 'Is it not high time that educators grasped the importance of those things that are advocated by the men of ample vision as quoted above?' (Wilkins 1922: 414). In a speech to the AATS in Los Angeles a year later entitled 'Educating the Educators', Wilkins (1923: 27) concluded that hitherto-negative attitudes among other teachers towards Spanish had not changed. According to Wilkins, most teachers still believed that Spanish was only an appropriate language for 'slower' children to study. Henry Doyle (1929: 52), Professor of Spanish at George Washington University, registered a similar complaint that Spanish continued to receive no respect among educators and that enrolments continued to decline. Doyle contrasted this state of affairs with what he described as 'wide public interest in foreign languages generally'. Doyle responded similarly to Wilkins by compiling an extensive list of opinions about the language held by prominent Americans. He cited Hoover, by then President-Elect, who called for compulsory study of Spanish during his 'Good Neighbor' tour of Latin America in 1928. Despite these and other opinions about Spanish held by prominent Americans, Wilkins was still compelled to complain as late as 1936 that 'sheer prejudice against Spanish', both among the population at large and among teachers, continued to exist (Wilkins 1936: 34). Thus, advocates' own reflections suggest that using the logic of Americanization to lobby for Spanish language education and by connecting it to US economic interests failed to add prestige to the language.

Conclusion

The central purpose of this chapter was to analyse the content of advocacy on behalf of Spanish language education in the United State between the two World Wars. As the discussion has demonstrated, proponents aligned their advocacy with the dominant discourses at the time of Americanization and the rise of US imperial power across the Western hemisphere. The socio-historical and political-economic dynamics behind these discourses triggered a steep decline in the number of students (both absolute and relative) studying a foreign language at all. This decline applied to Spanish, as well. That is, despite the efforts of Spanish teachers and professors — and despite the remarkable level of support they received from high-level politicians and other figures from popular culture — this advocacy failed to achieve its objectives.

While I am an applied linguist, rather than a trained historian, I am aware of the cardinal sin of presentism and thus have attempted to consider this era of advocacy as much as possible on its own terms (i.e. within its historical context). Nevertheless, as I have already suggested in the latter sections of the chapter, it is not by coincidence that I chose to design a historical study of advocacy of Spanish as a foreign language. This period of advocacy for Spanish is sorely understudied. Herman (2002) is the only example in the literature of which I was aware before designing and carrying out this study; and even then her discussion of Wilkins and Spanish is not the main focus of her study. By contrast, there is a vast literature on Americanization broadly, and on the fate of German specifically during this era. Likewise, it is not a coincidence that this study focuses on lobbying efforts that connect language education to the 'national interest'. It is true that subsequent examples of framing foreign-language education in terms of the USA's geopolitical and economic interests (e.g. the National Defense Education Act of 1958) have received more attention, although still not enough by far (see Bale 2014). However, as I suggested in the previous section, applied linguists' interest in this ideological connection has typically only followed some geopolitical crisis, rather than constituting a research agenda of an individual scholar or group of scholars. The study reported here is thus intended to fill a gap in the historiography and also to open up a more empirically based discussion about the consequences of linking language education to the US 'national interest'.

The historical case of Spanish suggests that this approach to advocacy failed to meet the objectives it set out for itself. A century later, more or less, it is true that advocates for foreign-language education have long since left behind the 'race talk' that was so prevalent in the strategies I analysed here. However, American geopolitical and economic interests continue to function as a primary, if not *the* primary, reason to learn an additional language, in what I have referred to elsewhere as 'the refrain' (Bale 2011b), echoing across decades of language-policy advocacy in the United States. The implicit question raised by this historical study is: why? The historical evidence discussed in this chapter further documents that linking language education to the same socio-historical and political-economic forces that reinforce cultural and linguistic homogenization ultimately closes the ideological and implementational space (Hornberger 2006) to carry out that language education in the first place. Thus, it seems clear, to me at least, that it is time for language education advocates to finally change our tune.

Bibliography

Primary sources

Bulletin of High Points in the Teaching of Modern Languages in the High Schools of New York City: V.[1]–2, April 1917–Nov. 1918. 1917a. (New York: Board of Education) <www.hathitrust.org>

'Anent of the Study of Spanish', 1917b. *Bulletin of High Points in the Teaching of Modern Languages in the High Schools of New York City* (New York: Board of Education), 1 (2): 1–4 <www.hathitrust.org>

'Requirements of an Up-to-date Modern Language Teachers; from the Standpoint of the Inspector'. 1917c. *Bulletin of High Points in the Teaching of Modern Languages in the High Schools of New York City* (New York: Board of Education), 1 (4): 2–9 <www.hathitrust.org>

'High Points'. 1918a. *Bulletin of High Points in the Teaching of Modern Languages in the High Schools of New York City* (New York: Board of Education), 2 (5): 8–14 <www.hathitrust.org>

'Notes and announcements'. 1918b. *Bulletin of High Points in the Teaching of Modern Languages in the High Schools of New York City* (New York: Board of Education), 2 (10): 10–22 <www.hathitrust.org>

BUTLER, N. M., V. M. CUTTER and W. R. SHEPHERD. 1934. 'The Importance of the Study of Spanish', *Hispania*, 17: 370–72

CRAWFORD, J. P. W. 1922. 'Facilities for the Advanced Study of Spanish' *Hispania*, 5: 346–53

DOYLE, H. G. 1929. 'Things are not what they seem', *Hispania*, 12: 49–58

FITZ-GERALD, J. D. 1918. *Importance of Spanish to the American Citizen* (Chicago, IL: Sanborn) <http://books.google.com> [accessed 25 October 2010]

——. 1921. 'The Bilingual-Biracial Problem of our Border States', *Hispania*, 4: 175–86

HEIN, H. E. 1936. 'Spanish and the Millennium', *Hispania*, 19: 9–12

LUQUIENS, F. B. 1915. 'The National Need for Spanish', *Yale Review*, 4: 699–711

TAYLOR, R. L., and L. A. WILKINS. 1920. 'The Value and Future of Spanish', *Hispania*, 3: 316–17

WILKINS, L. A. 1917. 'On the Threshold', *Hispania*, 1 (Organizational Number): 1–10

——. 1918A. 'Spanish as a Substitute for German for Training and Culture', *Hispania*, 1: 205–21

——. 1918B. *Spanish in the High Schools: A Handbook of Methods* (Chicago, IL: Sanborn)

——. 1919A. 'The President's Address', *Hispania*, 2: 36–40

——. 1919B. 'The War and World Languages', *Educational Review*, 58: 289–302

——. 1922. 'Concerning the Study of Spanish in the U.S.', *Educational Review*, 64: 409–14

——. 1923. 'Educating the Educators', *Hispania*, 6: 23–30

——. 1936. 'Horizons', *Hispania*, 19: 33–36

Secondary sources

BALE, J. 2011A. 'The Campaign for Spanish Language Education in the "Colossus of the North" 1914-1945', *Language Policy*, 10: 137–57

——. 2011B. 'Language and Imperialism: The Case of Title VI and Arabic, 1958–1991', *Journal for Critical Education Policy Studies*, 9: 376–409

——. 2011C. 'Tongue-tied: Imperialism and Second Language Education in the United States', *Critical Education*, 2 (8): 1–25

——. 2014. 'Heritage Language Education Policy and the "national interest"', *Review of Research in Education*, 38: 166–88

BUCHELI, M. 2008. 'Multinational Corporations, Totalitarian Regimes and Economic Nationalism: United Fruit Company in Central America, 1899-1975', *Business History*, 50: 433–54

CALLINICOS, A. 2009. *Imperialism and Global Political Economy* (Cambridge: Polity)

CARLSON, R. A. 1987. *The Americanization Syndrome: A Quest for Conformity* (London: Croom Helm)

COHEN, S. 1974. *Education in the United States: A Documentary History*, 5 vols (New York: Random House), IV and V

CRAWFORD, J. 1992. *Language loyalties: A Source Book on the Official English Controversy* (Chicago, IL: University of Chicago Press)

GONZÁLEZ, G. G. 1990. *Chicano Education in the Era of Segregation* (Philadelphia, PA: The Balch Institute Press)

HARMAN, C. 1999. *A People's History of the World* (London: Bookmarks)

HEATH, S. B. 1981. 'English in our Language Heritage, in *Language in the U.S.A.*, ed. by C. A. Ferguson and S. B. Heath (Cambridge: Cambridge University Press), pp. 6-20

HERMAN, D. M. 2002. '"Our patriotic duty": Insights from Professional History, 1980–1920', in *The Future of Foreign Language Education in the United States*, ed. by T. Osborn (Westport, CT: Greenwood), pp. 1–29

HORNBERGER, N. H. 2006. 'Nichols to NCLB: Local and Global Perspectives on U.S. Language Education Policy', in *Imagining Multilingual Schools: Languages in Education and Glocalization*, ed. by O. Garcia, T. Skutnabb-Kangas and M. E. Torres-Guzmán (Clevedon: Multilingual Matters), pp. 223–37

JOHNSON, T. 2002. *Historical Documents in American Education* (Boston, MA: Allyn and Bacon)

KARIER, C. J. 1975. *Shaping the American Educational State, 1900 to the Present* (New York: Free Press)

KLIEBARD, H. M. 2004. *The Struggle for the American Curriculum, 1893–1958*, 3rd edn (New York: Routledge Falmer)

KLOSS, H. 1998 [1977]. *The American Bilingual Tradition* (Washington, DC, and McHenry, IL: Center for Applied Linguistics and Delta Systems)

LENS, S. 2003 [1971]. *The Forging of the American empire: From the Revolution to Vietnam: A History of U.S. Imperialism* (London: Pluto Press; Chicago, IL: Haymarket Books)

LOMAWAIMA, K. T., and T. L. MCCARTY. 2006. *To Remain an Indian: Lessons in Democracy from a Century of Native American Education* (New York: Teachers College Press)

MCCLYMER, J. F. 1980. *War and Welfare: Social Engineering in America, 1890–1925* (Westport, CT: Greenwood)

MIREL, J. E. 2010. *Patriotic Pluralism: Americanization Education and European Immigrants* (Cambridge, MA: Harvard University Press)

MURPHY, M. 1992. *Blackboard Unions: The AFT and the NEA, 1900–1980* (Ithaca, NY: Cornell University Press)

OLNECK, M. R. 1989. 'Americanization and the Education of Immigrants, 1900–1925: An Analysis of Symbolic Action', *American Journal of Education*, 97: 402–05

RAMSEY, P. J. 2010. *Bilingual Public Schooling in the United States: A History of America's "polyglot boardinghouse"* (New York: Palgrave Macmillan)

——. 2011. 'A review of "Patriotic pluralism: Americanization Education and European Immigrants"', *Educational Studies*, 47, 490–94

REESE, W. J. 2011. *America's Public Schools: From the Common School to 'No Child Left Behin'* (Baltimore, MD: Johns Hopkins University Press)

RICENTO, T. 2003. 'The Discursive Construction of Americanism', *Discourse & Society*, 14: 611–37

SALAMONE, R. 2010. *True American: Language, Identity, and the Education of Immigrant Children* (Cambridge, MA: Harvard University Press)

SPACK, R. 2002. *America's second tongue: American Indian education and the ownership of English, 1860–1900* (Lincoln, NE: University of Nebraska Press)

WATZKE, J. L. 2003. *Lasting Change in Foreign Language Education: A Historical Case for Change in National Policy* (Westport, CT: Praeger)

WEINBERG, M. 1977. *A Chance to Learn: The History of Race and Education in the United States* (Cambridge: Cambridge University Press)

WEISS, B. J. (ed.). 1982. *American Education and the European Immigrant: 1840–1940* (Urbana: University of Illinois Press)

WILEY, T. G. 1998. 'The Imposition of World War I-era English-only Policies and the Fate of German in North America', in *Language Policies in the United States and Canada: Myths and Realities*, ed. by T. Ricento and B. Burnaby (Philadelphia, PA: Earlbaum), pp. 211–41

——. 2002. 'Accessing Language Rights in Education: A Brief History of the U.S. Context', in *Language Policies in Education: Critical Issues*, ed. by J. W. Tollefson (Mahwah, NJ: Earlbaum), pp. 39–64

——. 2007. 'The Foreign Language "Crisis" in the U.S.: Are Heritage and Community Languages the Remedy?', *Critical Inquiry in Language Studies*, 4: 179–205

ZIMMERMAN, J. 2002. 'Ethnics against Ethnicity: European Immigrants and Foreign-language Instruction, 1890–1940', *The Journal of American History*, 88: 1383–1404

Notes to Chapter 14

1. Many thanks to Andrew League for assistance in identifying and collecting primary sources that informed this study.
2. Wobblies is a common nickname for the International Workers of the World, an anarcho-syndicalist labour organization that led important movements for workers' rights, especially in the western US.
3. Now known as the American Association of Teachers of Spanish and Portuguese.
4. The specific term 'Americanization' did not necessarily circulate during the era in question. As mentioned above, it was the term used for a formal federal programme targeting adult immigrants; and in this example Wilkins used the term 'Americanism'. Nevertheless, the intent of his comment is clear.
5. This is a common way of using the alliteration in reading, writing and arithmetic to describe the presumed core of the primary school curriculum.
6. 'In 1890, high schools enrolled approximately 7 percent of all 14- to 17-year-olds; this jumped to nearly 38 percent in 1920 and 65 percent by 1936' (Reese 2011: 182).

CHAPTER 15

❖

Regards sur l'histoire de l'enseignement/ apprentissage du français langue étrangère au Proche-Orient: cas de la Jordanie

Carine Zanchi and Akram Odeh

This chapter offers a retrospective look at the history of teaching and learning French in Jordan, from its introduction as language of instruction within missionary schools to a second period involving linguistic and cultural co-operation between France and Jordan. In fact, it was France which took the initiative to support French-language teaching after 1970 to enhance political and cultural relations between the two countries. This co-operation had socio-economic aspects since France is the third largest investor in Jordan. Other forms of co-operation also exist to reinforce Franco-Jordanian co-operation in the domain of public administration and in legal, university, scientific and military domains. Even if Jordan, unlike other countries in the region, is not Francophone to the extent of being, for example, a member of OIF (Organisation International de la Francophonie), French has nevertheless gained a significant role and is currently the second foreign language, being taught as an optional subject by 250 teachers in 170 schools, public and private, to around forty-three thousand pupils. Accordingly, one Jordanian in three has studied French. Aside from providing an account of the general evolution of the role of French in the Jordanian education system, which has not previously been researched and described, this chapter traces the evolution of course books and examinations. Finally, it explains the challenges facing the teaching and learning of French in Jordan today.

Introduction

Le français s'est diffusé hors du continent européen à partir du XVIIe siècle principalement par l'intermédiaire des conquêtes de territoires, colonisation/ mandats et action des missions religieuses. Dans l'Empire ottoman, le français était devenu à la fin du XIXe et au début du XXe siècle, la langue de l'élite. En effet, comme le rappelle El Fakhri (2004: 36), 'l'introduction de la langue française [...] aux pays du Mashrek elle le fut sur une base religieuse et culturelle pour se développer au niveau des écoles, des salons et des affaires par la suite'. Même si la francophonie a une présence ancienne et vivace au Proche-Orient (Liban, Syrie, Palestine, Egypte), il est intéressant de constater que jusque dans les années 1950, la Jordanie a toujours été tenue à l'écart. L'introduction du français coïncide avec la création officielle de la Jordanie en 1948. Depuis cette date, le français a le statut de langue étrangère enseignée comme matière optionnelle ou obligatoire dans le système scolaire et universitaire.

Dans ce chapitre, nous reviendrons sur les étapes de l'implantation du français comme discipline scolaire obligatoire ou facultative en Jordanie. Dans un premier temps, nous verrons le rôle joué par les écoles religieuses dans la diffusion du français langue étrangère (FLE). Ensuite, nous parlerons des accords de coopération entre la France et la Jordanie pour officialiser ce statut de deuxième langue étrangère dans toutes les écoles publiques jordaniennes et enfin, nous finirons par dresser un panorama actuel de l'enseignement/apprentissage du FLE.

Faute d'espace, cette contribution se limitera à l'implantation du français dans l'école jordanienne; elle n'abordera pas l'historique et l'état actuel de la langue et de la culture françaises dans les universités jordaniennes ou dans les organismes français basés dans le Royaume Hachémite comme, par exemple, l'Institut Français, et elle ne reviendra pas non plus sur la représentation de l'image de la France auprès du public jordanien. L'état actuel du français, son histoire en Jordanie, et les rapports culturels qui lient la Jordanie à la France continuent d'être un terrain peu exploré en comparaison avec la Syrie, le Liban ou la Palestine historique.

En effet, nos recherches en bibliothèques et en ligne ont révélé que l'histoire de l'introduction et du développement du français dans ce royaume n'a pas suffisamment été étudiée. Certes, ce que le chercheur pourrait trouver comme ressources scientifiques serait des courts passages dans des thèses soutenues en France par des Jordaniens portant davantage sur l'état actuel du français en milieu universitaire que sur son implantation dans l'enseignement scolaire (Abdel-Fattah 2006; Alrabadi 2007).

Les Premiers Contacts de la Jordanie avec la francophonie

Avec le démantèlement de l'Empire ottoman et le découpage du Moyen-Orient par les Français et Anglais dans le cadre des accords Sykes Picot, la Jordanie a fait partie du monde arabe non francophone. Historiquement, la Jordanie était un territoire semi-désertique peuplé de Bédouins appartenant à l'Empire ottoman[1] pour être ensuite sous mandat britannique de 1919 à 1946. Ce territoire sous mandat britannique est confié à la dynastie Hachémite originaire du Hidjaz en Arabie Saoudite et a pris le nom d'Emirat hachémite de Transjordanie. A son indépendance en 1946, il devient le Royaume hachémite de Jordanie. En 1950, la Jordanie comprenait les territoires de Transjordanie, de Jérusalem-Est et de Cisjordanie annexés.

Plusieurs facteurs expliquent la pénétration de la francophonie en Jordanie. La création de l'Etat israélien a poussé sur le chemin de l'exil des centaines de milliers de réfugiés palestiniens dont une bonne partie, notamment la bourgeoisie palestinienne, étaient issus d'une véritable tradition francophone comme le souligne les statistiques suivantes:

> A la fin du xixe siècle, la France compte en Palestine 58 institutions, et plus de 100 institutions protégées; ces établissements abritent d'une part 178 religieux français masculins en charge de 1 000 élèves, et d'autre part 300 religieuses françaises, s'occupant de 2 200 élèves et de 80 000 malades. (Trimbur 2007: 99)

En effet, la Palestine faisait partie de l'Empire ottoman qui était favorable au français et dont il adopte le modèle pour ses élites un peu partout au Levant. Les relations économiques et culturelles entre cet empire et l'Hexagone ont commencé au XVIIIe siècle pour des raisons politiques, militaires et religieuses et ne porteront leurs fruits qu'au XIXe siècle, lorsque l'on a songé à faire du français la langue de la 'nation ottomane' qu'on projette de créer (Aksoy 2007: 58). Certes au début du XIXe, on estimait le nombre d'Ottomans qui maitrisaient le français à plus de trois millions (Gümüş 2009: 109). La majorité d'entre eux constituait l'élite intellectuelle, politique et militaire. La Palestine ne fait guère exception: le français était perçu comme un instrument de culture jusque dans les premières années du mandat britannique sur la Palestine (1920–48).

Selon Sanchez-Summerer (2009: 95, 119-21), qui a retracé l'histoire du français en Terre Sainte, les écoles chrétiennes localisées à Jérusalem attirent, durant toute la période ottomane, les élites chrétiennes essentiellement pour être ensuite élargies au début du XXe siècle aux élèves juifs et musulmans. Ceci illustre que les représentations de la langue française en Terre Sainte différaient selon les confessions: 'Chez les non-Musulmans, le français est langue de protection et d'éducation, chez les Musulmans, le français est indispensable pour faire carrière à l'intérieur du système ottoman car c'est la deuxième langue d'administration de l'Empire' (Sanchez-Summerer 2009: 122). Dans ces écoles, le français avait le statut de langue de scolarisation puisque les religieux catholiques étaient des francophones, et ils expliquaient le catéchisme en français dont l'usage était courant dans certains établissements en Palestine.

En plus de son statut de langue d'enseignement, le français, qualifié de 'langue de cœur' selon le P. Dhorme, devient une langue de communication assez importante dans la mesure où:

> à Jérusalem, le voyageur pouvait descendre dans n'importe quel hôtel, pénétrer dans les magasins les plus disparates, il était sûr d'être compris. Le français était la langue officieuse que chacun devait posséder pour entrer dans la société et se mettre en contact avec les étrangers. (cité dans Sanchez-Summerer 2009: 119)

Ces représentations du français s'étaient diffusées dans toute la Palestine historique puisque nombreux étaient les Palestiniens à être scolarisés à Jérusalem.

En s'installant en Jordanie après 1948, ces réfugiés palestiniens ont apporté avec eux leurs représentations de la langue française, à savoir une langue de l'élite et de culture. Ces représentations du français se sont diffusées auprès de la minorité chrétienne jordanienne pour ensuite toucher toute la bourgeoisie d'Amman. Par ailleurs, les Jordaniens qui se destinaient à la carrière de prêtre devaient aller en séminaire à Jérusalem-Est ou en Cisjordanie où l'enseignement était en latin et en français.

Implantation du français langue étrangère en Jordanie

Les Ecoles religieuses

Dès le début de son règne en 1921, la dynastie Hachémite s'est attelée à mettre en place des bases étatiques et à créer un sentiment d'appartenance à une même communauté nationale grâce à l'éducation nationale. Des efforts coordonnés de lutte contre l'analphabétisme ont été entrepris en mettant en œuvre des mesures stratégiques de développement de l'éducation.

Les seules écoles en Jordanie existant avant sa création officielle étaient princi-palement des écoles religieuses implantées essentiellement dans des localités chrétiennes. Officiellement, ces écoles n'enseignaient pas le français. Dès les années 1950, en raison de la situation géopolitique, des écoles religieuses chrétiennes originaires soit de Palestine soit du Liban se sont implantées en Jordanie avec leur propre personnel enseignant et ont introduit *de facto* le français dans leur cursus scolaire, c'est-à-dire de la maternelle jusqu'au lycée.

Les écoles les plus connues sont:

> — L'école du Rosaire[2]
> — Les Sœurs de Nazareth
> — Les Franciscains
> — Les Frères de la Salle[3]
> — L'école Nationale Orthodoxe
> — L'école le Frère de la Salle
> — L'école de Terra Santa.

Devant la volonté affichée d'arabisation du nouvel état hachémite, ces écoles n'ont cependant pas pu reproduire le modèle d'enseignement qui prévalait dans leur pays d'origine et où le français était langue d'enseignement. Par conséquent, dans ces écoles chrétiennes jordaniennes, le français a un statut privilégié de deuxième langue étrangère et à laquelle la minorité chrétienne était attachée. Selon le Ministère jordanien de l'éducation (1970), cinq mille élèves suivaient des cours de français dans quinze écoles chrétiennes en 1969–70.

L'Introduction officielle du français dans le système d'enseignement public jordanien

Ibtisam Ayoub fait partie des responsables jordaniens les plus actifs ayant coopéré et largement contribué à l'implantation du français dans le Royaume, et elle est actuellement la responsable de l'enseignement du français au Ministère de l'éducation en Jordanie. Elle a consacré une bonne partie de son mémoire de Master (Ayoub 2012) à l'introduction et au développement du français dans l'éducation publique en Jordanie, et sa recherche constitue la référence la plus complète, fiable et récente en Jordanie. Ayoub (2012: 12) rappelle que les relations économiques et politiques entre la France et la Jordanie ont débuté tout de suite après la création du Royaume en 1946. Néanmoins, les coopérations entre ces deux pays en matière culturelle et scientifique n'ont débuté qu'en juin 1965 avec le premier accord signé entre les deux gouvernements. Cet accord, selon Ayoub (2012: 13) prévoyait entre autres que chaque partie s'engage à encourager l'enseignement de la langue et la culture de l'autre.

L'application du coté jordanien s'est officiellement concrétisée en 1970–71 quand les gouvernements jordanien et français ont signé un accord de coopération afin d'introduire le français dans deux lycées publiques d'Amman en tant que matière facultative extra-curriculaire (c'est-à-dire, la note de l'apprenant n'entrait pas dans sa moyenne générale). Quatre enseignants ont été nommés, et deux classes ont été sélectionnées, la 10e et 11e, c'est-à-dire à partir de l'âge de quinze ans. Deux lycées — un de filles et l'autre de garçons de la capitale Amman — ont été choisis pour enseigner le français pour débutants, et 550 élèves ont bénéficié à partir de 1971 de cette innovation linguistique. Ayoub (2012: 17) ajoute que la rentrée scolaire de 1979–80 a vu le statut du français se transformer en devenant un enseignement scolaire à part entière en termes de réussite et d'échec car la note obtenue entrait dans la moyenne générale scolaire.

En 1988, le Ministère de l'Education a décidé, écrit Ayoub, d'attribuer au français le même statut que les enseignements de l'informatique, de la gymnastique et de l'éducation artistique. Les élèves pouvaient suivre deux cours, deux fois par semaine pour les classes équivalentes à la seconde et 1ère en France. Cette mesure a été généralisée dans les trois principales villes du Royaume: Amman, Irbid au nord et Zarka à l'est.

En 1994–95, on a étendu, souligne Ayoub (2012: 17), l'enseignement du français aux classes équivalentes à la 8e jusqu'à la seconde dans quelques écoles dans les trois villes citées, et en 1995–96 le français fonctionnel est devenu matière obligatoire dans l'enseignement professionnel pour la branche de l'hôtellerie.

En 2004, l'enseignement du français est rendu obligatoire pour les élèves qui le choisissent en classe de 8e (4e française) pour une durée de trois ans, et en 2005 une commission technique mixte a été créée pour gérer l'ensemble des aspects de la coopération linguistique et éducative entre le Ministère de l'Education et l'Ambassade de France.

Ouverture de départements de français au niveau universitaire

Cette diffusion du français dans le système éducatif jordanien a nécessité l'ouverture de départements de français pour former le personnel enseignant. Le département de langue et de littérature françaises de l'université de Jordanie a été créée en 1987–88. Le diplôme nécessaire pour être professeur est le B. A. Quelques universités publiques offrent des formations de type Licence ou B. A. dans le cadre de programmes 'Langue et littérature françaises'. Les étudiants non francophones ont la possibilité de débuter leur apprentissage de la langue française à l'université et de se perfectionner en français tout au long de leurs années d'études pour passer ainsi des statuts de non francophone et francisant à celui de francophone partiel (Zanchi 2015). A la fin de leur cursus en licence, les étudiants futurs professeurs sont censés avoir le niveau B2 du Cadre Européen Commun de Référence pour les langues (CECR).

En Jordanie, la formation universitaire est donc locale avec des curricula conçus localement et approuvés par le ministère de l'enseignement supérieur et de la recherche dont le principal souci est d'aider les jeunes diplômés à trouver des débouchés professionnels. Cette formation universitaire tient compte du profil des étudiants. Même si le français est la langue d'enseignement, l'arabe est la langue d'accompagnement universitaire. Ces cours universitaires sont enseignés principalement par des professeurs arabophones titulaires de doctorats en Sciences du langage obtenus dans des universités soit françaises soit francophones.

Les Examens et les Manuels

Les Examens

Avant la création du DELF (le diplôme d'études de langue française) en 1985, les élèves jordaniens des écoles religieuses passaient le Certificat (le premier niveau) et le Brevet (2ᵉ niveau), tests de niveaux, calqués sur le modèle libanais et qui comprenait les épreuves suivantes:

— une dictée
— de la grammaire
— une rédaction
— de la compréhension écrite
— un examen oral portant sur la compréhension d'un texte.

Cet examen était organisé par l'ambassade et le centre de coopération linguistique et culturelle.[4] Comme il est mentionné dans la préface du manuel *Le Test de tous les jours: cahier de grammaire structurale* (Samaha 1982a), le brevet d'ambassade comportait une épreuve éliminatoire qui consistait en un test de niveau de langue se présentant sous la forme d'une cinquantaine de questions. Dans la première page de la préface de ce manuel (Samaha 1982a: 5), l'ex directeur du Centre Culturel de Tripoli, G. Mechain, rappelait que:

> L'épreuve éliminatoire du Brevet d'Ambassade a pris, depuis la session de juin 1964, une forme nouvelle. Elle ne consiste plus en une composition française ou en un commentaire de texte, mais en un texte de Niveau de LANGUE comportant une cinquantaine de questions, destiné à juger les candidats uniquement sur leur connaissance de la langue. Le bon emploi de la langue est certes l'aboutissement de tout l'enseignement du français au cours de la scolarité.

Il est de plus mentionné que le bachotage, en cette matière plus qu'en toute autre, est d'un bien mince profit. Seuls des élèves habitués dès la 6ᵉ à pratiquer régulièrement le français dans les divers enseignements sont assurés du succès sans préparation particulière. Cette épreuve, comme mentionnée dans la préface, requérait un minimum de connaissance et de grammaire et *de facto* de préparation. Ce niveau élevé en langue française existant dans les écoles religieuses jordaniennes pourrait expliquer pourquoi les anciens élèves de ces écoles ont conservé un excellent niveau en français même s'ils ne pratiquent plus le français depuis le lycée.

Les Premiers Manuels de FLE utilisés en Jordanie

Les premiers manuels de FLE utilisés dans les écoles religieuses jordaniennes étaient des manuels libanais. Ces manuels avaient la particularité d'être adaptés au système éducatif libanais et à son public d'apprenants. Ils se présentaient sous la forme de lectures, grammaire et de conjugaison. Pour les plus jeunes, un manuel d'initiation à l'écriture et à la lecture était utilisé; il s'appelait *Des contes et des lettres, méthode mixte de lecture* (Rouyer, Boumoussa et Martei 1960).

Il est intéressant de constater que ces manuels de français étaient préférés aux manuels de langue généralistes existant sur le marché éditorial du français langue étrangère (FLE) comme le montre la préface du *Français de tous les jours* (Samaha 1982b: 2), dans laquelle Eugène Leber du bureau pédagogique d'Amman appréciait sa contextualisation au monde arabe:

> Combien de méthodes ont été mises au point pour l'enseignement du français langue étrangère! Et pourtant, rien n'a encore été élaboré pour certains pays arabophones. Pour notre région, c'est aujourd'hui chose faite.
> Enfin un livre qui ne dépayse pas le jeune arabe: il ne doit pas faire d'efforts pour apprendre et prononcer les noms propres et les prénoms, ce sont ceux de ses parents, des ses camarades, de ses frères et de ses sœurs. Tout l'environnement lui est familier: c'est une aide appréciable pour le professeur lui évitant ainsi de se lancer dans des explications confuses! Et ce n'est pas là son moindre mérite.

Les Manuels de langue utilisés pour l'enseignement/apprentissage du FLE de 1950 à nos jours

Depuis son introduction en Jordanie, l'enseignement/apprentissage (E/A) du français s'est toujours fait avec des manuels importés. De 1950 à 1990, les manuels de langue utilisés dans les écoles religieuses étaient principalement des manuels libanais de langue seconde. Cette situation s'explique par le fait que l'E/A du FLE est limité aux écoles religieuses privées qui reproduisent le même système d'enseignement que les écoles sœurs du Liban.

Il est intéressant de constater que ces manuels de français libanais sont vantés par les personnels de coopération linguistique des ambassades de France faute de disposer d'autres ressources. C'est encore l'époque où le français est limité à une certaine élite sociale principalement chrétienne qui n'a aucun problème à utiliser les manuels du Liban. Il est important de rappeler que dans les années 1950, le système éducatif jordanien est encore à l'état de balbutiement. Les élèves jordaniens des écoles religieuses sont habitués à utiliser des manuels libanais durant leur scolarité. Il faut mentionner que dans certains établissements principalement religieux, ces manuels de FLE sont encore utilisés.

A partir de 1990, date de l'implantation officielle du français dans le système éducatif jordanien qui se traduit par une massification et une démocratisation du français, les manuels de FLE généralistes c'est-à-dire conçus par des auteurs français ont été utilisés pour répondre à la demande linguistique. Cela se traduit par une importation curriculaire assimilée par certains (Pochard 2011: 52) à de l'entrisme pédagogique. Cette importation s'explique également par l'absence de manuels de FLE élaborés par des Jordaniens (Odeh et Zanchi 2011: 139).

La situation actuelle: vers un changement de représentations de la langue

De nos jours, la plupart des établissements scolaires qui enseignent le français se trouvent dans la capitale Amman et le nombre actuel de ces établissements est de quatre-vingts avec environ 32 000 élèves. La plupart de ces établissements sont des établissements catholiques où l'enseignement du français est obligatoire. Néanmoins, l'enseignement non chrétien dans le secteur privé s'est considérablement développé.

D'après les dernières statistiques communiquées par le Ministère de l'Education pour l'année 2016, on estime le nombre d'élèves inscrits dans les établissements privés à 450000 élèves, soit trente pour cent du nombre d'apprenants scolarisés dans le Royaume (Ministère 2016: 8). La majorité de ces écoles, qui se trouvent dans les principales villes, ne sont plus des écoles chrétiennes où le français est une matière importante et omniprésente; mais il s'agit d'écoles internationales, comme The American School, New English School, Canadian School, ou régionales, comme The Turkish School, ou enfin locales. Dans ces établissements scolaires, le français ne jouit toujours pas de statut de deuxième langue étrangère car le chinois, le turc et l'espagnol soit remplacent le français, soit sont en concurrence avec le français.

La langue française est enseignée aussi bien dans l'enseignement public que dans l'enseignement privé. Dans le système public, l'apprentissage du français est introduit comme matière optionnelle à partir de la 8e. Les apprenants doivent ensuite poursuivre leur apprentissage pendant plus de quatre ans avec la possibilité de choisir cette matière au baccalauréat jordanien appelé *tawjihi*.

Il existe un curriculum jordanien pour l'enseignement/apprentissage du FLE dans l'enseignement public, appelé le 'Cadre général et les acquis généraux et spécifiques de la langue française', conçu par le Ministère jordanien de l'éducation en 2006. Cet outil a été calqué sur le Cadre Européen Commun de Référence pour les langues (CECR).[5] Les examens du DELF et DALF[6] sont des diplômes reconnus et valorisés en Jordanie.

Dans l'enseignement public, les manuels de langue utilisés sont de type généraliste c'est-à-dire conçus par des auteurs français pour un public d'apprenants universels. Il s'agit de *Pile ou face* (Vassal 1992) et de *Tandem* (Albero, Bergeron et Bidault 2003).

Avec la mondialisation éducative, de nombreuses écoles internationales se sont implantées en Jordanie qui se réfèrent aux curricula anglais, américain, canadien ou français et qui ont d'autres systèmes d'évaluation des apprentissages comme le IB,[7] le Cambridge O Level, le GCSE,[8] le AP Test[9] et le Baccalauréat français. Les manuels de FLE sont variés et l'on dénombre plus d'une trentaine de manuels de FLE utilisés dans l'enseignement privé. En fonction des établissements scolaires, c'est une matière soit obligatoire soit facultative qui peut être introduite précocement ou tardivement avec une durée hebdomadaire qui varie en fonction des établissements.

La massification et démocratisation de l'E/A du FLE mis en place dans le cadre des accords entre la France et la Jordanie a fait perdre au français son statut de langue d'élite et de culture. Par ailleurs, le français a la réputation d'être une langue difficile et qui n'apparaît pas porteuse d'avenir dans la contrairement à l'allemand et au chinois. Du fait de son statut de matière scolaire, l'E/A du français souffre de représentations négatives qui entravent le processus d'apprentissage. Les apprenants ne sont pas motivés pour apprendre cette langue. Le français est enseigné comme une matière scolaire qui en fonction des établissements scolaires peut avoir le statut de langue obligatoire ou facultative. En effet, l'apprentissage ne se produira pas ou peu si l'apprenant n'est pas au minimum motivé ou prêt à apprendre.

Actuellement, la bourgeoisie d'Amman très anglophone et anglophile n'accorde plus la même importance au français, qui n'est plus perçu comme la langue de l'élite et de la culture. Le même constat se fait chez les Jordaniens d'origine palestinienne.

Même si la Jordanie accueille de nombreux réfugiés sur son sol, principalement des Irakiens et des Syriens, ils ne sont pas attirés par le français. Plusieurs raisons expliquent ce phénomène, surtout l'anglophonie des Irakiens mais aussi des Syriens qui malgré le mandat français (1923–46) n'ont pas gardé le français comme langue seconde à l'indépendance du pays.

Conclusion

Jusque dans les années 1950, la Jordanie nouvellement créée est restée à l 'écart de la francophonie du fait de son appartenance à la sphère anglophone. Au lendemain de son indépendance et en raison de la situation géopolitique qui a bouleversé le Proche-Orient, la Jordanie a eu ses premiers contacts avec la francophonie avec la venue des réfugiés Palestiniens et de l'implantation des écoles chrétiennes sur sol. En l'espace d'un demi-siècle, le français a réussi à s'imposer comme la deuxième langue étrangère enseignée après l'anglais dans tout le Royaume hachémite.

Même si le français a longtemps été perçu comme une langue de culture réservée à l'élite jordano-palestinienne, de nos jours ces représentations sur la langue n'ont plus cours. En effet, le français s'est démocratisé et massifié sous l'action de la politique linguistique de la France menée en Jordanie. Le français est même diffusé dans les provinces les plus reculées de Jordanie où les conditions de vie sont très précaires.

Le français est devenu une matière scolaire 'secondaire' dans le système éducatif jordanien. A l'heure de la concurrence linguistique, un des problèmes posés au français en Jordanie est comment motiver les apprenants à apprendre cette langue. L'autre problème qui existe — quel est l'intérêt d'apprendre une nouvelle langue étrangère autre que l'anglais?

Bibliography

ABDEL-FATTAH, FRANÇOISE. 2006. 'Représentations interculturelles et identités de contact dans l'enseignement de la culture française en Jordanie: enquête auprès des étudiants de début de troisième année à l'Université Al Albayt de Mafraq — Jordanie' (unpublished doctoral thesis, University of Franche-Comté)

AKSOY, EKREM. 2007. 'La Francophonie en Turquie de l'Empire à nos jours', *Documents pour l'histoire du français langue étrangère ou seconde*, 38/39: 57–66 <http://dhfles.revues.org/138> [consulté le 17 janvier 2018]

ALBERO, MICHEL, CHRISTINE BERGERON and MURIELLE BIDAULT. 2003. *Tandem niveau 1, livre de l'élève* (Paris: Didier)

ALRABADI, ELIE. 2007. 'Le Français sur objectifs spécifiques: le cas de l'enseignement du français des affaires en Jordanie' (unpublished doctoral thesis, University of Rouen)

AYOUB, IBTISAM. 2012. 'Relation entre la formation initiale et continue des professeurs de français en Jordanie et leur enseignement' (unpublished Master's thesis, University of Nantes)

CHAIGNE-OUDIN, ANNE-LUCIE. 2010. 'Jordanie', *Les Clés du Moyen-Orient* <http://www.lesclesdumoyenorient.fr/Jordanie.html> [consulté le 25 janvier 2018]

EL FAKHRI, SONIA. 2004. 'Le Liban et un siècle de littérature francophone', *Cahiers de l'association internationale des études françaises*, 56.1: 35-48

GÜMÜŞ, HÜSEYIN. 2009. 'Le Français dans les territoires de l'Empire Ottoman', *Synergie Turquie*, 2: 107-11

MINISTÈRE DES AFFAIRES ETRANGÈRES DE FRANCE. 2000. 'Diffusion de la langue française dans les pays arabes', *Encyclopédie de la francophonie* <http://agora-2.org/francophonie.nsf/Documents/Arabofrancophonie--Diffusion_de_la_langue_francaise_dans_les_pays_arabes_par_Ministere_des_Affaires_etrangeres_de_France> [consulté le 15 mai 2018]

MINISTÈRE JORDANIEN DE L'EDUCATION. 1970. *Les Statistiques de l'année 1970* (document en arabe). Archive du Ministère de l'Education jordanien

———. 2006. *Le Cadre général et les acquis généraux et spécifiques de la langue française pour les cycles premier et secondaire* (Amman: Ministère de l'éducation)

———. 2016. *Le Rapport annuel*, Publication du Ministère de l'Education jordanien 1: 1-68

ODEH, AKRAM, and CARINE ZANCHI. 2011. 'Choix, adaptation et contextualisation du manuel de FLE pour les apprenants arabophones', *Revue de langue, littérature et études culturelles*, 4.1: 135-49

POCHARD, JEAN-CHARLES. 2011. 'Pratiques curriculaires associées à l'action linguistique française hors de France', *Recherches et applications*, 49: 49-62

ROUYER, H., P. BOUMOUSSA, and S. MARTEI. 1960. *Des contes et des lettres: méthode mixte de lecture* (Jounieh: Samir)

SAMAHA, JOSEPH. 1982A. *Le Test de tous les jours: cahier de grammaire structurale* (Jounieh: Samaha)

———. 1982B. *Le Français de tous les jours* (Jounieh: Samaha)

SANCHEZ-SUMMERER, KARÈNE. 2006. 'Langue(s) et religion(s) en Palestine mandataire au sein d'institutions éducatives catholiques: établissements des Frères des Ecoles chrétiennes et Sœurs de Saint Joseph de l'Apparition 1922–1940', *Documents pour l'histoire du français langue étrangère ou seconde*, 37: 93–132

———. 2009. 'Les Langues entre elles dans la Jérusalem ottomane (1880-1914) : les écoles missionnaires françaises', *Documents pour l'histoire du français langue étrangère ou seconde*, 43: 119–43

TRIMBUR, DOMINIQUE. 2007. 'Catholiques français et allemands en Palestine, XIXe-XXe siècles', *Bulletin du Centre de recherche français à Jérusalem*, 18: 92-106 <https://bcrfj.revues.org/115>

VASSAL, JEANNE. 1992. *Méthode de français: Pile ou face* (Paris: Clé International)

ZANCHI, CARINE. 2015. 'De francisant à enseignant de français: réflexion sur le parcours de formation des enseignants arabophones de français langue 3', *Revista Electrónica Matices en Lenguas Extranjeras*, 9: 135–51

Notes to Chapter 15

1. La Jordanie faisait partie du sandjak de Damas (1516–1917) (Chaigne-Oudin 2010).
2. Déjà dans les années 1880, des écoles du Rosaire furent créées en Jordanie.
3. <http://www.lasalle-po.org/index.php?page=hsects#section4> [consulté le 17 janvier 2015]. La première école fut ouverte en 1950 grâce à l'intervention de l'Ambassadeur de France de l'époque, Son Excellence Dumarcay.
4. Devenu L'Institut français.
5. <http://www.coe.int/t/dg4/linguistic/cadre1_fr.asp> [consulté le 7 avril 2015].
6. 'Le DELF (Diplôme d'Etudes en Langue Française) et le DALF (Diplôme Approfondi de Langue Française) sont les seuls diplômes de français langue étrangère délivrés par le Ministère français de l'Education Nationale. Ils sont valables à vie et bénéficient d'une reconnaissance internationale. Ils vous permettent de valider officiellement votre apprentissage de la langue française' <http://www.delfdalf.fr/> [consulté le 3 octobre 2014].
7. Baccalauréat international <http://www.ibo.org/> [consulté le 12 mars 2015].
8. C'est un examen britannique de fin d'études secondaires que passent tous les élèves au Royaume-Uni.
9. Les examens 'Advanced placement' existent dans les systèmes éducatifs américain et canadien et sont requis pour une acceptation à l'université <http://www.collegeboard.com/student/testing/ap/cal/cal2.html> [consulté le 10 décembre 2014].

CHAPTER 16

❖

Intentions for Teaching and Failures of Learning: Historical Roots of English-Language Education Policies in Post-Independence India

Krishna Dixit and Amol Padwad

Against the backdrop of a historical overview of policies concerning English-language education under British India, this chapter focuses on the period after India's Independence, comparing intentions and outcomes in relation to the learning of English. We argue that post-Independence policies carry a hangover of policies from the previous two centuries in their conceptualization of and assumptions about teachers of English, showing a continued neglect of teacher preparation, teacher identity and teacher autonomy. This neglect, we suggest, has been a key factor in the poor learning outcomes and overall dissatisfaction with English-language teaching in India throughout its history. We conclude with some implications for present-day teacher education policy.

English-language education is one of the core areas of the present Indian education system, with English a compulsory language across the curricula from primary to undergraduate levels, requiring a huge investment of financial and human resources. Since the formal inception of English in education in the latter half of the eighteenth century, various committees and commissions — from the General Committee of Public Instruction (1823) set up by the East India Company to the most recent National Knowledge Commission (2009) — have advocated a prominent place for English. Today, English is the second most widespread medium of instruction, and looks set to become the most widespread medium of instruction in the Indian education system (Mukherjee 2012). Ever since its inception, however, English-language education in India has been accompanied by a deep sense of dissatisfaction with learning outcomes, a dissatisfaction expressed both officially and by the public. In this chapter we attempt to explore this dissatisfaction with specific reference to the policies of teaching English in the post-Independence era in the formal state education sector. We aim to analyse the policies by linking them to their historical roots in the pre-Independence era and therefore begin the chapter with a brief overview of the history of English-language education in India, while the second section discusses some key educational policies since India's independence that have had a strong bearing on English-language education in contemporary India. Drawing on these policy intentions and prescriptions, we discuss in the third section some possible causes of failure in learning outcomes. The chapter concludes with some lessons from and implications of this analysis.

Historical Context

A range of studies aimed at describing, discussing and debating English in India (for example, Mahmood 1985; Vishwanathan 1989; Mehrotra 1998; Krishnaswamy and Krishnaswamy 2006) concur that it was Lord Macaulay's Minute of 2 February 1835, often called the 'Manifesto of English Education in India', that was responsible for the inauguration of an English-language-oriented education system. However, saying so amounts, metaphorically speaking, to giving the credit for the victory in a cricket match to the batsman who scores the winning run. A long list of persons and events contributed to the rising trajectory of English in India, culminating in Macaulay's Minute. Foundations for the introduction of English were laid by Sir Charles Grant, Chairman of the East India Company, in the 1790s. He prepared the first blueprint of education in English for Indians in 1792, bemoaning what he saw as the moral, social and intellectual decline of Indian civilization and hoping to reverse it through Western education via the English language (Mahmood 1895: 113–14). Grant is, therefore, often called 'the father of modern education in India'. He recommended:

- The introduction of English as the medium of instruction in a Western system of education that included literature, natural sciences and mechanical inventions in order to remove the superstitions prevalent among Indians;
- The adoption of English as the official language of the East India Company and its local administration for easy communication between the rulers and the ruled. (after Krishnaswamy and Krishnaswamy 2006: 12)

Other events that contributed to strengthening the role of English included the Charter Act renewal of 1813, which drew attention to a split in ideologies among the educational leadership of the time in India between Anglicists and Orientalists, the former supporting and the latter opposing English education in India. A crucial factor offering a clear rationale for the East India Company to intensify English education was the demand for English from several key Indians. The most often cited was Raja Ram Mohun Roy, who, in a letter to Lord Amherst in 1823, strongly advocated English education for Indians, claiming that a Western system of education would facilitate the modernization of India. A key development that really triggered the motivation of Indians to learn English was William Bentinck's decision in 1829 to offer employment in the East India Company only to English-speaking Indians. He remarked that the English language was 'the key to all improvements' of Indians (cited in Ghosh 2009: 34). Yet another factor that contributed to the strengthening of English was Charles Wood's Despatch [to Lord Dalhousie, then Governor-General of India] (1854), which created a new space in the Indian education sector, namely Higher Education, by recommending the establishment of universities. This space was, and still is, dominated by English as the primary language of teaching, learning and research.

Wood's Despatch of 1854 was followed by several commissions that deliberated on the place of English in Indian education. Perhaps the most crucial one among them was the Indian Universities Commission of 1902, which led to the Indian Universities Act of 1904. Bemoaning the very poor level of English of university entrants, the Commission fixed the responsibility for the dismal situation onto schools. Apart from this, there was a whole series of commissions and committees on the education of Indians, including the Indian Education Commission (1882), the Calcutta University Commission (1917), the Abbot-Wood Committee (1936–37) and the Zakir Hussain Committee (1937). A notable common point among them is that none of these committees opposed education in English language, although they advocated, to different degrees, teaching vernacular languages alongside English.

In summary, it can be observed that English-language education started in India with a moral imperative. English-language education appears to have been intended as a Humanist venture, combined with what William Bentinck (cited in Ghosh 2009: 35) said to the General Committee of Public Instruction on 26 June 1829:

> It is the wish and admitted policy of the British Government to render its own language gradually and eventually the language of public business throughout the country, and [...] it will omit no opportunity of giving every reasonable and practical degree of encouragement to the execution of this project.

Given this, it can be concluded that English entered Indian education within a discourse highlighting its potential contribution both to moral improvement and to the provision of modern knowledge, especially in science and technology, and of opportunity for a better future. This last point is particularly important because the imperative for effective teaching and learning of English occupies a central position in policies and public opinion nowadays due to the general perception that it is a passport to economic prosperity and social mobility. It would not be altogether wrong to suggest that Macaulay largely succeeded in realizing the aim of English-language education as a form of social reform initiated by Sir Charles Grant in 1792. Although Macaulay's policy of government funding for English-medium education was reversed after Independence, English-medium schools have emerged over the length and breadth of the country to such an extent as to make Krishnaswamy and Burde (1998: 11) remark that 'English teaching in India is the world's largest democratic enterprise of its kind'. However, as Masani (2012: 233) notes, 'Macaulay would have been appalled by the very poor standard of English taught in Indian schools and colleges'.

English after Independence: Policies and Realities

The debates and discussions around English in the early years of post-Independence India were largely centred on its place in education, alongside other issues like medium of instruction and projection of Hindi as the national language. The first Prime Minister of independent India, Jawaharlal Nehru, was a supporter of a greater role for English in education, and he frequently recommended English as a compulsory subject in schools. He always emphasized the development of Indian languages but also believed that English should not be discarded, since to do that would 'amount to closing a window on the world of technology' (Gokak 1964: 5). Opponents of English perceived it as a symbol of the continuation of colonial hegemony and demanded its removal. But its supporters insisted on retaining it in education, perceiving it as an avenue to modern knowledge, especially in science and technology. There was also strong political support for English from non-Hindi-speaking southern parts of India, which saw the opposition to English from the northern 'Hindi belt' as a ploy to impose Hindi on them. Against this backdrop several commissions and committees continued to deliberate over the issue of English language education. Indeed, Krishnaswamy and Sriraman (1995: 37) remark that 'the story of English teaching in independent India has been one of commissions and omissions!'. Table 1 summarizes the key policy milestones that shaped ELT during the post-Independence period.

The first of the post-Independence commissions was the University Education Commission (1948–49), chaired by Sarvapalli Radhakrishnan, which recommended the use of Indian languages for education but also expressed the desire that English should be studied so that people would not close themselves to developments around the world. This commission saw English as a vital link to the outside world (Ministry of Education 1962a [1950]: 316). The Commission noted:

> English [...] must continue to be studied. It is a language which is rich in literature — humanistic, scientific and technical. If under sentimental urges we should give up English we would cut ourselves off from the living stream of ever growing knowledge. [...] English is the only means of preventing our isolation from the world. (ibid.: 283–84)

The second commission that strongly supported English was the Secondary Education or Mudaliar Commission (1952–53). It observed that English was an international language (Ministry of Education 1962b [1953]: 47) and echoed the view of the previous commission that the English language brought knowledge of western thought and literature. The report notes:

> [T]he present position of India in the international sphere is partly due to the command that educated Indians have acquired over English. Many eminent educationists and scientists have, therefore, expressed the opinion that under no circumstances should we sacrifice the many advantages that we have gained by the study of English. (ibid.: 51)

Following this was the Official Languages Commission (1956–58). This attempted to replace English with Hindi but, facing strong opposition from non-Hindi

Name of the commission/ committee	Recommendations relating to English
University Education Commission (1948–49)	• English is a vital link to the world • English is a language of knowledge and literature • English is a link language in multilingual India
Secondary Education Commission or Mudaliar Commission (1951–53)	• English should be learnt, as the medium of Higher Education is English • English should be introduced from Class 5 • The right kind of methods should be implemented
Official Languages Commission (1956–58)	• Attempt to institute Hindi in place of English • Widespread protests against the move to make Hindi the national language • Government promise to continue the use of English and recommendation about the mandatory study of English in school
The Education Commission or Kothari Commission (1964–66)	• English is a 'library language' and should continue in education • Reasonable degree of proficiency in English is mandatory for the award of certification • Need for special units for teaching English as language as distinct from literature
National Policy on Education (1968), National Policy on Education (1986), and Acharya Ramamurti Commission (1990)	• English should continue in school curriculum • Central Hindi Institute, CIE and CIIL should work with CBSE, NCERT and state governments 'to spell out modalities of ensuring uniformity in the matters of English language acquisition'
National Curriculum Framework (2005)	• English is one of the languages of India • Varying scenarios of ELT • Need to promote uniformity in ELT across the country
National Knowledge Commission (2009)	• English should be introduced from Class I • Lack of English is one of the obstacles to accessing higher education • Adoption of new teaching methods and materials for teaching English
Twelfth Five Year Plan (2013)	• Ensure good quality education in Science, Maths and English • Implement common curricula and syllabi of nationally acceptable standards for Science, Maths and English in all schools in the country • Need for bridge courses in English • Need of English for employment

TABLE 1. Important Milestones in post-Independence ELT Policy

speaking areas, ended up recommending the use of English and also advocated the mandatory study of English in schools (Krishnaswamy and Krishnaswamy 2006). Another commission that thoroughly discussed the role and place of languages in education was the Kothari Commission (1964–66), which deliberated on several key issues like national integration, needs of advanced knowledge in science and technology and the mother-tongue-versus-English issue. It concluded that English was needed for both international and intra-national communication (National Council for Education, Research and Training 1970: 22), recommending that, for exposure to advanced knowledge, 'the teaching and study of English should continue to be promoted right from the school stage. [...] English will serve as a link language in higher education for academic work and intellectual inter-communication' (ibid.: 35).The Commission said:

> As English will, for a long time to come, continue to be needed as a 'library language' in the field of higher education, a strong foundation in the language will have to be laid at the school stage. We have recommended that its teaching may begin in class V, but we realize that for many pupils, particularly in the rural areas, the study will not commence before class VIII. (ibid.: 364)

Further developments that supported English language included the National Policy on Education of 1968, the National Policy on Education of 1986, and the Acharya Ramamurti Commission (1990). These also recommended English due to its role as a library language, international language and link language within India. They recommended that the Central Hindi Institute, the Central Institute of English (now: English and Foreign Languages University, Hyderabad) and the Central Institute of Indian Languages working with the Central Board of Secondary Education (CBSE), National Council for Education, Research and Training (NCERT), and state governments should spell out the 'modalities of ensuring uniformity in the matters of Indian and English language acquisition' (Krishnaswamy and Krishnaswamy 2006: 133).

With the liberalization of the economy in 1991, the demand for English increased tremendously and it became even more central in the public discourse on education. The National Curriculum Framework of 2005 responded to popular demand with these words:

> English in India is a global language in a multilingual country. A variety and range of English-teaching situations prevail here owing to the twin factors of teacher proficiency in English and pupils' exposure to English outside school. The level of introduction of English is now a matter of political response to people's aspirations rather than an academic or feasibility issue, and people's choices about the level of its introduction in the curriculum will have to be respected, with the proviso that we do not extend downwards the very system that has failed to deliver. (NCERT 2005: 38)

The National Knowledge Commission (NKC) (2006–09) was the first official body to argue unequivocally for a central place for English in education. This Commission proceeded from the premise that English is one of the languages of India and an essential asset for individual and national development. It also identified inadequate competence in English as one of the causes for India's underdevelopment. It found that 'school-leavers who are not adequately trained in English as a language are always at a handicap in the world of higher education' (NKC 2009: 27). Accordingly, it recommended that English should be introduced, along with the first language (either mother tongue or the regional language), starting from Class I. Further, the NKC also focused on the need to reform the pedagogy of English-language teaching and the use of all available media to supplement traditional teaching methods.

The latest policy document in the series has been the approach paper for the Twelfth Five-Year Plan prepared by the Planning Commission of India (2013), which argues that proficiency in English is as essential as mathematics and science and that everyone should receive quality education in these three subjects. One of the objectives of the Twelfth Plan is to 'implement common curricula and syllabi of nationally acceptable standards for Science, Maths and English in all schools in the country' (Ministry of Human Resource Development 2013: 72).

The above overview shows that the English language has always received strong support in post-Independence educational policies and a special role has always been found for it. Overall, the grounds for the existence and continuation of English-language education in India have been argued to be the following:

- English is needed for advanced knowledge, especially in the fields of science and technology;
- English is the language of knowledge;
- English contributes to national integration;
- English is looked upon as cultural capital;
- English is vital for individual and national progress.

To this list we may add a recent argument that English is a means to attain social equality and justice and economic welfare, as increasingly perceived by underprivileged classes and castes in India.

However, all through the history of English-language education in India there has existed a persistent sense of dissatisfaction with the ways and outcomes of the teaching and learning of English. As a representative sample, we reproduce here statements from three documents spread a century apart. The first one comes from the Indian Universities Commission Report of 1902. It says:

> Notwithstanding the prominent position given to English throughout the course, the results are most discouraging. Students, after Matriculation, are found to be unable to understand lectures in English [...] it appears to be the case that many students pass through the entire University course without acquiring any command of the language, and proceed to a degree without even learning to write a letter in English correctly and idiomatically. (Cited in Krishnaswamy and Krishnaswamy 2006: 67)

The second statement, about fifty years later, marks the first occurrence of publicly expressed Indian dissatisfaction in the post-Independence period and suggests that there has been no change in the situation:

> We are convinced that if a language is to be learnt, it should be studied so as

> to use it effectively and with correctness in written or spoken form. But that is not seen to be happening in case of English and other languages too. (Ministry of Education 1962b [1953]: 256)

The final statement, another sixty years later, is drawn from the Planning Commission of India's vision statement for the Twelfth Five Year Plan. It remarks that:

> Despite improvements in access and retention, the learning outcomes for a majority of children continue to be an area of serious concern. Several studies suggest that nearly half the children in grade 5 are unable to read a grade 2 text. (Planning Commission of India 2011: 96)

Thus, even though the long series of policy documents summarized above display common arguments and objectives for the continued presence of English in education, they also consistently indicate inadequate learning outcomes. The three policy documents cited, spread across a century, are representative of a common lament about the failure to develop English proficiency in Indian learners in spite of a long history of English education in India. In the following section we speculate on some causes of this failure, tracing their historical roots in the policy provisions themselves.

Understanding Failures of Learning

There are certain contextual factors like the size and complexity of the education sector in India and the continuingly ambiguous status of English which may partly explain why the learning outcomes in English have remained poor after Independence. India is a country with thirty official languages, over four hundred other languages and dialects and over one hundred major cultural-ethnic communities. The size of the education sector is massive, with 1.3 million schools, 227 million students, 7.2 million teachers, over 640 universities, and thirty-eight thousand higher education institutes (NCERT 2011).The position of English in India is also ambiguous in that it is neither an Indian language nor a completely foreign language; and is studied by almost every student but not widely used in general social life. English in India has, accordingly, been described variously as, for example, a 'national foreign language' (Gokak 1964), as 'auntie's tongue' (Dasgupta 1993), or as the 'unofficial national language' of India (Chaudhary 2002: 38).

However, the large size of the education sector and the ambiguity and complexity of the status of English in India are fairly recent phenomena, whereas poor learning outcomes have been a consistent concern during the last two centuries. These two factors, therefore, cannot adequately explain the failures in the learning of English in post-Independence India.

In the remainder of this chapter we argue that the post-Independence conceptualization and consequent treatment of the teacher is one probable cause behind the poor learning outcomes in English. It needs to be acknowledged that the Mudaliar Commission (1951–53) hinted at this reason in its report. We also wish to demonstrate that this conceptualization and treatment are basically a hangover of pre-Independence thinking regarding teachers of English. We discuss below two interconnected aspects of this neglect, that is, with regard to teacher preparation and to neglect of teacher identity and autonomy.

Neglect of Teacher Preparation

One common point across all policy documents seems to be the assumption that a ready force of teachers is available and present to translate the policy dictates into reality. All commissions and committees refer to the importance of teachers in enhancing learning outcomes, but recommendations seem limited to top-down training of teachers to deliver curricula or implement changes. The policy documents do not discuss the issue of how to prepare teachers for the mammoth task of teaching English in a complex, multilingual context like India. However, they all discuss the severe shortage of competent teachers and propose moulding teachers to achieve desired targets.

For example, the first education commission in post-Independence India, namely, the University Education Commission of 1948-49 laments the fact that teachers are not available in the required numbers. The report says: 'There is great disparity between what our country requires and what our education offers. We produce a large number of arts and law graduates, but not enough teachers, administrators, doctors, engineers, technicians, scientific researchers and the like' (39). People apparently became teachers without undergoing any preparation. Kumar (2014: 82) points out that somebody leaving school with a grade four pass could become a primary teacher, even decades after Independence. He found that in 1963 only 20% of teachers working at high school were matriculates (i.e. had completed pre-university school education) (ibid.). Nevertheless, the Commission report does not discuss how teachers may be prepared. It is difficult to see how these teachers would have adequate knowledge and skills to manage their teaching without professional preparation as a teacher.

Three years later, the Secondary Education or Mudaliar Commission (1951–53) took stock of several earlier policies such as Wood's Despatch (1854), the reports of the Hunter Commission (1882) and the Hartog Committee (1929) and observed that talent was still not attracted to the teaching profession due to 'unsatisfactory general conditions':

> It is interesting to note that the [Hartog] Committee reviewed the position of the training of teachers and the service conditions of secondary teachers and remarked 'that enough cannot be done in the short space of nine months which is all that is usually available, to uproot the old methods of teaching to which many of the students are accustomed.' The best pupils were not attracted to the teaching profession, the Committee held, because the best type of men cannot be attracted to the profession so long as the general conditions remain unsatisfactory and only too frequently the teachers have no heart in their work. (Ministry of Education 1962b [1953]: 11)

Reiterating the problem of the shortage of 'well-qualified and experienced teachers who can handle English classes in schools and colleges', the Commission remarked: 'We believe this is one of the important reasons for deterioration in the standard of English at the University stage' (ibid.: 55). However, the Commission did little more than recommending some specific qualifications for teaching English. For example, teachers for high schools teachers were expected to be graduates with a teacher training diploma.

Still later, the Achayara Ramamurti Commission (1990) found that teachers were not sensitive to the needs of the context and society. The report observed that teachers 'have little or no links with the concerns and situations of the community in which the school is placed and for the people, whose children they teach' (MHRD 1990: 23). It suggested that English Language Teaching Institutes should design in-service training for teachers, inspectors, and principals (ibid.).

The National Curriculum Framework (2005) recognized the need for adequately qualified and motivated teachers. Recommending a shift from a transmission mode to a constructivist mode of teaching it seemed implicitly to blame teachers, observing that, 'in the name of "objectivity", teachers sacrifice flexibility and creativity. Very often teachers, in government as well as private schools, insist that all children must give identical answers to questions' (NCERT 2005: 18). It found several faults with teachers:

> Teachers lack basic pedagogic skills (understanding where the learner is, explaining, asking appropriate questions) and an understanding of the processes of learning to read, which range from bottom-up processes such as syllable recognition and letter-sound matching to top-down processes of whole-word recognition and meaning making from texts. They also often lack class-management skills. They tend to focus on errors or hard spots rather than on imaginative input and articulation. (ibid.: 41)

Interestingly, while the National Curriculum Framework (NCERT 2005) seems to view both English-language proficiency and pedagogic knowledge and skills as essential for teachers of English, other policy documents toe a different line by privileging English-language proficiency over pedagogic competence. A recent and explicit example is the report of the National Knowledge Commission, which argues for 'defined but flexible norms for the minimum qualifications of teachers' (NKC 2009: 39). However, the 'flexible norms' seem reduced to English-language proficiency when it proposes hiring unprepared and under-qualified teachers:

> In order to meet the requirement for a large pool of English language teachers, graduates with high proficiency in English and good communication skills should be inducted without formal teacher training qualifications. They could be selected through an appropriate procedure developed by the National Testing Service and then given a short-term orientation. The nearly four million school teachers all over the country, regardless of their subject expertise, especially teachers at the primary level, should be trained to improve their proficiency in English through vacation training programs or other short-term courses. (ibid.: 28)

It is plausible to argue in this connection that a tradition of according priority to English proficiency can be traced back to the early history of teaching English in India. In those early years of English teaching the teachers were native English-speaking missionaries. Being a native speaker appeared to be a key and sufficient qualification to become an English teacher (Kumar 2014), a practice that continued through the nineteenth century, when English missionaries and wives of colonial British officers worked as teachers (Coppin 2010). Malabari (1876) laments the absence of 'proper' teachers of English but rejoices on having met Reverend William Dixon from Belfast. He claims that he gained native-like proficiency in English because of this native-speaker teacher. There are many other instances of native teachers following on from John Miller (who published *The Tutor*, possibly the first book meant for teaching English in India, in 1797 (Howatt with Widdowson 2004: 71). Their proficiency in English was seen to render any other requirement like pedagogic skills or educational knowledge redundant. This perception continued to influence English-language education policies in independent India, in which no particular attention has been paid to pre-service or in-service preparation of teachers of English. Not surprisingly, the reports of the various commissions and committees over the last two centuries seem more concerned about the English proficiency of teachers than their pedagogic competence, with the latest in the series — the NKC (2009) quoted above — formally taking a stance in favour of English proficiency at the cost of teaching competence.

The repercussions of the neglect of teacher preparation in policies continue even today. Barring a couple of exceptions, there is no English-specific pre-service teacher education programme to prepare teachers of English. A common, general, teacher-education programme, with a small subject-specific elective component, is offered to all kinds of teachers. The in-service training programmes are typically short-term, isolated events aimed at equipping teachers with sets of skills required, for example, to implement new curricula or assessment systems. Teacher preparation and continuous teacher professional development are still viewed from a very narrow and instrumental perspective, with little scope for teachers' needs and interests (Padwad and Dixit 2011 and 2014). The various English-language teaching institutes and state institutes of English set up in different parts of India after Independence have depended on overseas expertise and models for teacher education and training, thus neglecting local contexts. These are characterized by 'acquisition-poor' (Tickoo 1997) and resource-poor environments, with the following key challenges:

- low student motivation;
- lack of educational resources;
- large classes,
- rigid administration;
- focus on examination results;
- unrealistic expectations from teachers and students;
- low teacher motivation.

Prevalent teacher education and training programmes do not adequately address these practical challenges or equip teachers to deal with them. In short, education policies and practice seem to neglect not only teacher preparation and development, but also the contexts in which teachers work.

Neglect of Teacher Identity and Autonomy

The character of teaching in indigenous traditions was different from that initiated by the East India Company (see Kumar 2014 for more on this). In indigenous Indian academic traditions the teacher was conceived as someone with specialized knowledge who enjoyed full autonomy while educating children. The teacher had complete freedom in deciding the content, choosing approaches and setting the pace of teaching and learning as deemed appropriate for learners, while working in independent, autonomous academies. However, with the advent of state-run public education with prescribed curricula and textbooks this power of the teacher to decide what and how to teach was permanently lost. Kumar (ibid.: 5) observes that, following this:

> the teacher had no say in the selection of knowledge represented in the school curriculum. His low salary (ranging between INR 5 to 20 during 1951 to 1972) and status ensured that he would not exercise any professional autonomy or even have a professional identity.

If this 'new' form of teacher is contrasted with the indigenous teacher, one finds that in the pre-colonial period teachers were a part of the community, which supported their livelihood by giving them donations in cash and kind. The new teacher, by contrast, was an employee with a salary. However, the very low salary ensured that 'only the neediest, and among them the most helpless, would go for [teaching]' (Meston 1936, cited in Kumar 2014: 79).

Agnihotri and Khanna (1995: 18) note that 'teachers have little or no say in matters of text selection and preparation of course materials and evaluation systems. [...] unfortunately their voice does not receive any recognition'. They note that this neglect of teacher autonomy results in deskilling them. This trend, too, has a long history dating back to the introduction of Western education in India. Since the beginning of this educational venture, Kumar (ibid.: 4) observes, 'the job of deciding, selecting, shaping knowledge was performed by the "enlightened outsider". This was the role that the British officers and missionaries involved in developing an education system for India adopted'.

This trend led to the emergence of what Agnihotri and Khanna (1995) and Kumar (2014) call 'expert culture'. In an education system with 'expert culture' teachers are considered incapable of planning, choosing or deciding what and how to teach, and are expected merely to follow the plans and prescriptions prepared for them by capable and competent 'experts', who may not be teachers. To aggravate the matter, teaching is not recognized as an intellectual job. Teachers were and still are engaged in non-teaching work such as national-census implementation, election work, office administration, accounts-keeping and now cooking midday meals. What Kumar (2014: 70) states about teachers in early post-Independence decades holds true even today: 'The range of functions that a schoolteacher could be asked to perform was itself a testimony of his low status and the non-specialized image of his job. Obviously, the academic challenge involved in teaching children was not recognized'.

We see a vicious circle operating in the conceptualization and treatment of teachers throughout the history of English language education in India. The neglect of comprehensive and holistic teacher preparation, substituted with short-term, narrowly instrumental and delivery-oriented occasional training, brings unprepared and un(der)qualified teachers to English-language education. Such teachers lack the necessary knowledge and skills to work as competent and autonomous professionals. As a result an 'expert culture' evolves, which, instead of strengthening, further erodes teachers' competence and autonomy.

Conclusion and Implications

The overall conclusion suggested by our analysis is that, while English has continuously held a place of high importance in India since the late eighteenth century, learning outcomes have been poor and there has been a continuing lack of focus on effective teacher preparation. A continuing neglect of teacher autonomy and identity has contributed to the poor learning outcomes. This neglect appears to be a historical hangover from the earlier policies of English-language education in India, which typically assumed that teachers of English existed ready-made, which saw no need to deliberate on provisions for developing a cadre of teachers, and which perceived teachers as mechanical human resources incapable of autonomous professional work and requiring 'expert' help and guidance.

These findings need to be further corroborated through more in-depth and extensive studies of English-language education policies in India. However, some important implications already emerge for English-language teacher education in particular and education in India in general. It seems that the currently prevalent national concern regarding very low achievement levels in learning English has a long history, since this concern has kept on surfacing periodically during the last two hundred years. In order to address this concern, fundamental changes in teacher preparation and development appear to be a top priority. Although some past commissions and policy documents have acknowledged the teacher as the key factor influencing learning outcomes, the issue of how this key factor needs to be strengthened remains to be addressed adequately. Another important implication for teacher-education policies and programmes is that these need to be relevant to the contexts of teachers; to critically re-examine historically derived perspectives and perceptions about teachers; to show ways to get away from the 'expert culture' which still continues to dominate; and to propose more locally appropriate and effective models and mechanisms of teacher preparation.

Bibliography

AGNIHOTRI, R. K., and A. L. KHANNA. 1995. 'Introduction', in *English Language Teaching in India: Issues and Innovations*, ed. by R. Agnihotri and A. L. Khanna (New Delhi: Sage), pp. 12–28

CHAUDHARY, S. 2002. 'Sociolinguistic Context of English Language Teaching in India', in *Readings in English Language Teaching in India*, ed. by S. Kudchedkar (Hyderabad: Orient Longman), pp. 37–66

COPPIN, L. 2010. 'The British-Indian Experience: Flora Annie Steel as an Unconventional "MEMSAHIB"' (unpublished Master's thesis, University of Ghent) <http://lib.ugent.be/fulltxt/RUG01/001/457/922/RUG01-001457922_2011_0001_AC.pdf> [accessed 3 June 2015]

DASGUPTA, P. 1993. *The Otherness of English: India's Auntie Tongue Syndrome* (New Delhi: Sage)

GHOSH, S. C. 2009. *The History of Education in Modern India* (Hyderabad: Orient Blackswan)

GOKAK, V. K. 1964. *English in India* (Bombay: Asia Publishing House)

HOWATT, A. P. R., WITH H. G. WIDDOWSON. 2004 [1984]. *A History of English Language Teaching*, 2nd edn (Oxford: Oxford University Press)

KRISHNASWAMY, N., and T. SRIRAMAN. 1995. 'English Teaching in India: Past, Present and Future', in *English Language Teaching in India: Issues and Innovations*, ed. by R. Agnihotri and A. L. Khanna (New Delhi: Sage), pp. 1-41

——, and A. S. BURDE. 1998. *The Politics of India's English* (New Delhi: Oxford University Press)

——, and L. KRISHNASWAMY. 2006. *The Story of English in India* (New Delhi: Foundation)

KUMAR, K. 2014. *Politics of Education in Colonial India* (New Delhi: Routledge)

MAHMOOD, SYED. 1895. *A History of English Education in India* (Delhi: Idarah-I-Adbiyat-I)

MALABARI, B. M. 1876. *Indian Muse in English Garb* (Bombay: Reporter's Press)

MASANI, Z. 2012. *Macaulay: Pioneer of India's Modernization* (Noida: Random House)

MEHROTRA, R. 1998. *Indian English: Texts and Interpretation* (Amsterdam: Benjamins)

MESTON, W. 1936. *Indian Education Policy* (Madras: The Christian Literature Society)

MINISTRY OF EDUCATION. 1962A [1950]. *The Report of the University Education Commission* (New Delhi: Government of India)

——. 1962B [1953]. *Report of the Secondary Education Commission: Mudaliar Commission Report* (New Delhi: Government of India)

MINISTRY OF HUMAN RESOURCE DEVELOPMENT, INDIA.1990. *Report of the Committee for the Review of National Policy on Education* (New Delhi: Government of India)

——. 2013. *Faster, Sustainable and More Inclusive Growth: An Approach* (New Delhi: Planning Commission of India)

MUKHERJEE, A. 2012. 'Two Crore Indian Children Study in English-medium Schools', *The Times of India*, 2 March <http://timesofindia.indiatimes.com/india/2-crore-Indian-children-study-in-English-medium-schools/articleshow/12105621.cms> [accessed 26 January 2018]

NATIONAL COUNCIL FOR EDUCATIONAL RESEARCH and TRAINING. 1970. *Education and National Development: Report of the Education Commission, 1964–66* (New Delhi: National Council for Educational Research and Training)

——. 2005. *National Curriculum Framework* (New Delhi: National Council for Educational Research and Training)

——. 2011. *Eighth All India Survey of Education* (New Delhi: Ministry of Human Resources Development)

NATIONAL KNOWLEDGE COMMISSION. 2009. *National Knowledge Commission Report to the Nation, 2006–2009* (New Delhi: Government of India)

PADWAD, A., and K. DIXIT. 2011. 'ELE Policy and Pedagogy in India: A Study of the Curriculum Framework for Teacher Education', in *English Language Education in South Asia: From Policy to Pedagogy*, ed. by Lesley Farrell, Udaya Narayan Singh and Ram Ashish Giri (Delhi: Cambridge University Press India), pp. 245–57

——, and K. DIXIT. 2014. 'Continuing Professional Development Policy "Think Tank": An Innovative Experiment in India', in *Continuing Professional Development in English*

Language Teaching, ed. by D. Hayes (London: British Council), pp. 249–70

PLANNING COMMISSION OF INDIA. 2013. *Education and Literacy: Twelfth Five-Year Plan* (New Delhi: Government of India)

TICKOO, M. L. 1997. 'Towards an Alternative Curriculum for Acquisition-poor Environments', in *Second Language Acquisition: Socio-cultural and Linguistic Aspects of English in India*, ed. by R. Agnihotri and A. L. Khanna (New Delhi: Sage)

VISHWANATHAN, G. 1989. *Masks of Conquest* (New Delhi: Oxford University Press)

CHAPTER 17

❖

The 'Wave' of Japanese Language Education in Secondary Schools: The Case of Aotearoa/New Zealand

Sharon Harvey

Drawing on the metaphor of Hokusai's well-known woodblock print *The Great Wave off Kanagawa* [*Kanagawa okinami ura*], this chapter seeks to critically examine the 'wave' of Japanese-language education in secondary schools in New Zealand. The rising popularity of the Japanese language was somewhat contiguous with the expansion in Japan's post-World War II economy and New Zealand's increasing reliance on that economy for imports and exports and as a major source of tourism. Japanese constitutes one of only two languages (the other being French) for which the people who claim to speak the language in New Zealand have, at times, considerably outnumbered the diaspora living in the country. Consequently, New Zealand can count Japanese as a relatively successful subject language. However, as other languages have become popular and the fortunes of Japan on the world stage have waned, particularly in the face of the rising importance of China, Japanese-language education in New Zealand has experienced a slow but steady decline. This chapter looks at the diverse drivers that produced Japanese as a very successful language of education by the mid-1990s and then delivered the subsequent, seemingly relentless demise of the language through to the present. While this case is country-specific, it can prove instructive for considering how Japanese and perhaps additional Asian languages have fared in other English-dominant jurisdictions, for example Great Britain, Australia, Canada and the United States. Moreover, it raises questions about how decisions are made over which subject languages are taught in schools, as well as their long-term sustainability, particularly those that have been introduced for relatively instrumental or economic reasons.[1]

Introduction

The choice of subject languages we teach in schools and the reasons for which we teach them, as well as the connections of these to geopolitical contexts, are fields rarely explored in the education and/or language-learning literature. In this chapter

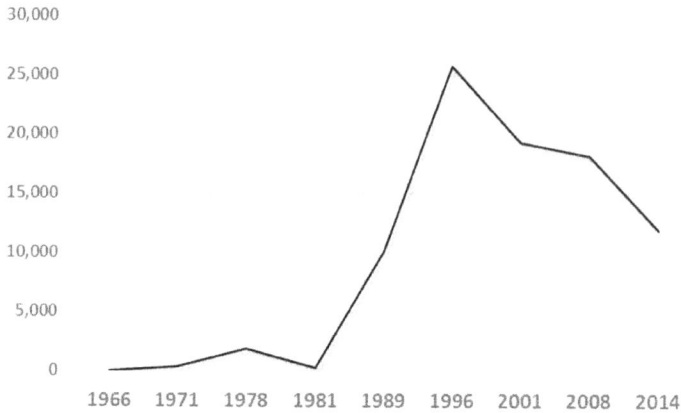

FIG. 17.1. Japanese Language Enrolments in New Zealand Secondary Schools
(Department of Education 1967: 32, 1972: 31, 1979: 40, 1983: 10, 23; Ministry of
Education 1990: 39, 2017: data file)

I seek to examine some of these associations as a way of historically accounting for
the rise in popularity of Japanese in New Zealand secondary schools and its more
recent decline, even in the face of Japan's continued importance to New Zealand.
Linking the image of Hokusai's *Wave off Kanagawa* (1830) to the rise and current
decline of Japanese language education in New Zealand seems apt for several
reasons. In terms of numbers of learners in schools the metaphorical wave began to
rise modestly in the late-1960s (see Figure 17.1).

The Japanese wave peaked in secondary schools in 1996 and has declined since
then. For several years in the late-1990s Japanese even surpassed French (see Table
1). The steepest decline occurred in 2009 to 2010, when numbers dropped by
nearly three thousand from 17,304 in 2009 to 14,506 in 2010 (Ministry of Education
2015).

Year / Language	1966	1971	1981	1989	1993	1996	1997	1998	1999	2004	2008	2014
French	43,678	46,200	35,456	31,275	26,057	22,040	20,500	20,990	22,906	25,689	28,245	20,478
Japanese	3	265	251	10,039	21,991	25,783	24,578	21,701	21,479	20,982	18,157	11,888

TABLE 1. Number of Secondary School Students Studying Japanese and
French in New Zealand (Department of Education 1967: 32, 1972: 31, 1983: 10, 23;
Ministry of Education 1990: 39, 1994: 54, 2017: data file)

Just as some have read Hokusai's rogue wave (*okinami*) as a sea mountain of inexor-
able impact, perhaps even dominance, from the West, washing up on Japan's shores
in the nineteenth century (Nigro [n.d.]), the rise of Japanese-language education
in New Zealand involved a recognition of the mounting economic and political
importance of Asia. It had been apparent since World War II and Britain's failures
in Dunkirk and Singapore that New Zealand's view of itself as a mini-version of

Britain in the South Pacific needed to change (King 2011: 488). Britain's further retreat on the world stage in the post-war period, along with its entry into the European Common Market in 1972, meant that New Zealand had to redirect its security relationships and trade aspirations towards the Asia-Pacific Region. In 1981 Japan was New Zealand's third biggest two-way trading partner; by 1984 it had jumped to number one and through the 1980s it oscillated between numbers one and two. However, as Japan's economy began to lose strength in the early 1990s, New Zealand's trade emphasis shifted to Australia and the United States, and more recently to China and South Korea. Still, Japan remains important to New Zealand. In 2014 it was New Zealand's fourth most important trading partner (Treasury 2014: 27) and the fifth-largest source of inbound tourists.

Japan has not just been significant to New Zealand: it was the most important non-Western world power in the second half of the twentieth century and has only recently been surpassed by China in this regard (Monahan 2011: 1). In the 1980s Japan was the second-largest economy behind the USA (Wade 1990: 3). Currently Japan is the third-largest economy in the world after the USA and China and is predicted still to hold fourth place behind India in 2030 (Smialek 2015). According to the *Encyclopædia Britannica* Japanese is the ninth most widely spoken language in the world (Crystal and Robins 2015). Clearly, Japan and the Japanese language remain important in geo-political terms and this effect is particularly pronounced in the Asia-Pacific region.

Because of its post-World War II global and regional significance, Japanese is a subject language within many national secondary curricula and at universities throughout the world. In Australia, Japanese has been the most popular subject language since the 1970s (de Kretser and Spence-Brown 2010: 10). A great deal of investment has gone into building Japanese teacher capacity, designing resources and writing curricula in many countries, and this is also the case for New Zealand. For a number of Western countries Japanese was the first Asian language ever taught as a subject language in schools and universities. From this perspective alone, country histories of Japanese-language education are an important means for understanding East–West relations. It is important to remember also that Japanese continues to be a significant additional language in many *Asian* countries (Japan Foundation 2012: 7) although it has been displaced by English as a second or foreign language in recent years (Yoshikawa 2013).

Subject Languages and New Zealand's Relationship with Japan

Japanese, introduced into the New Zealand education system in the early 1960s, was the first new subject language in New Zealand secondary schools for more than a century. Prior to this, the mix of subject languages had stayed more or less the same since European settlement. French was the most commonly taught foreign language, followed by Latin and then German. In many aspects of New Zealand's educational and wider societal life, New Zealand modelled itself on Britain. Subject languages in schools were no exception. In the early 1900s the new headmistress of

Auckland Girls Grammar School pointed out 'that New Zealand pupils lagged far behind their English counterparts in modern languages' (Northey 1988: 49). The answer was to employ a mistress from the United Kingdom: 'In March 1908 it was agreed that a language teacher should be recruited from Britain. [...] The position attracted thirty two applicants, and Miss Frances Grellet [...] from Cambridge [...] was appointed' (ibid.: 46).

New Zealand did not follow its pioneering neighbour Australia in this regard. Japanese was offered at The University of Sydney as well as in New South Wales state secondary schools from 1918, the reason stated being the growing trade between the two countries. The decision to offer Japanese was apparently 'the first decision of the kind reached by any European country [sic]' ('Japanese to be taught in schools' 1918: 7). From the time of Australia's first foray into Japanese-language teaching it was to be fifty more years before New Zealand began offering Japanese.

New Zealand, as part of the Allied Forces, had been at war with Japan in World War II and participated in the occupation of that country soon after. From the 1950s the mainstay of the relationship with Japan was growing trade. Full diplomatic representation between New Zealand and Japan was established in 1958, the same year in which a commerce agreement was signed. Full General Agreement on Tariffs and Trade (GATT) relations were inaugurated in 1962. Japan has always been more important to New Zealand than vice versa. However, as Japan sought to build its post-war profile in the Pacific, New Zealand could be a useful ally and broker when necessary. Despite serious tensions in the relationship in the 1960s and 1970s bilateral trade rose from just a few million New Zealand dollars at the beginning of the 1960s to NZ$500 million in 1972 (Larkin 1980: 191).

By the late 1980s New Zealand's economic interdependence with Japan was considerable. Japan fluctuated between being first or second most important trading partner; it was a significant source of tourist revenue; and the yen figured prominently in New Zealand's internal investment as well as in borrowing from abroad. The swift increase in trade and tourism highlighted New Zealand's cultural and linguistic unpreparedness for working with Japan. Writing in 1988, I observed 'it does appear that New Zealand has disadvantaged itself by not planning for the future and training its people in the kind of skills that would enable them to work innovatively and confidently with the Japanese' (Harvey 1988: 17). Until the late 1970s New Zealand had almost no diplomatic representatives who could speak Japanese. However, from this time the decision was taken for young career diplomats to be assigned to spend most of their career in Japan and they were sent on intensive two-year language-training courses there to prepare for their role (Harvey 1988: 26–27). Nevertheless, by the late-1980s Mr Rod Miller had still been the only New Zealand Ambassador to Japan (from 1976 to 1983) who had functional proficiency in Japanese (Harvey 1988: 27).

While trade was the mainstay of the bilateral relationship between Japan and New Zealand, a growing number of people-to-people contacts supported economic interests in the post-war period. Sister-city relationships grew over this time as did the New Zealand interest in martial arts. New Zealanders found further common interests in pottery and pursuits such as ikebana. The Japanese people, meanwhile, hosted many Māori performing-arts groups, especially in their domestic tourist hotels, and honed their rugby skills playing and training with New Zealand coaches and visiting players (Harvey 1988: 233, 238). Education, and especially Japanese-language education, has been an important part of the story of contact between New Zealand and Japan. The earliest efforts at teaching Japanese in New Zealand centred on the Japan Societies, particularly those in Wellington and the Waikato (Wells 1985). Japanese was also taught through adult-education classes in Wellington in the early 1960s, mainly to business people, school teachers, and employees of government departments and producer boards ('Speaking Japanese essential for trade matters' 1963: 10).

Japanese in New Zealand Secondary Schools: 1970s and 1980s

Because of the growing importance of the bilateral New Zealand–Japan relationship and New Zealand's understanding of its need to look to Asia for trade and diplomatic purposes, the teaching of Japanese in New Zealand secondary schools followed its introduction into the university system (Harvey 1988: 126; Oshima and Harvey 2017: 501–02). In 1970, the total number of students studying Japanese language at New Zealand secondary schools, including adults in evening classes, was 297. In 1971, Japanese was offered as a University Bursaries subject (Harvey 1988: 127).[2] From 1971 to 1973 there was a relatively small growth in the number of secondary students taking Japanese. By 1974, however, the total number of secondary students had jumped to 1086 and fourteen secondary schools were offering Japanese. This increase was partly due to a rise in third-to-fifth form students (now called Years 9 to 11) taking the language, who may have been attracted to the subject by the fact that internal assessment for School Certificate Japanese had begun in 1973.[3] Sixth-form (Year 12) intakes increased in 1974 due to the availability in that year of Japanese as a University Entrance subject[4] as well as an approved Sixth-Form Certificate course[5] (Harvey 1988: 128). In 1978, the total number of secondary schools offering Japanese had risen to thirty-eight while the number of students taking Japanese totalled 1901 (Department of Education 1979: 23). By 1980, however, numbers had decreased considerably. Only 1498 students took Japanese that year. Although total numbers had risen again to 1762 by 1983, the number of secondary schools offering the subject had dropped to twenty-nine. The South Auckland region, in particular, had seen a substantial and continuing decline in numbers since 1974. In 1974, 182 students in seven South Auckland schools were learning Japanese. In 1981, only twenty-five pupils in two secondary schools were taking the subject (Department of Education 1983: 10, 23).

A number of factors were identified as contributing to the decreasing popularity of Japanese in New Zealand secondary schools in the early 1980s. Personal communications in 1981 to 1982 from the Ministry of Foreign Affairs (MFA) (cited in Harvey 1988: 129) indicate that declining enrolments in Japanese reflected the continuation of a wider trend for New Zealand students to study non-language subjects. This decline was partly blamed on an administrative structure which tended to discriminate against all language teaching. In some cases languages were 'cut out' in order to simplify school timetables; or the popularity of languages subjects was reduced by scheduling them at inconvenient times. In addition, option systems in New Zealand secondary schools were competitive and Japanese was routinely set against subjects such as accounting, economic studies or a science at sixth- and seventh-form (Years 12 and 13) levels. As unemployment rates were rising during New Zealand's economic recession in the early 1980s, a growing number of students opted for subjects which would give them more readily employable skills. Even university graduates in Japanese and those who had spent some time in the country found Japan-related jobs difficult to secure.

Furthermore, Japanese had a variety of starting points within secondary schools; as a result, some examination candidates had been exposed to only one or two years study of Japanese. According to MFA personal communications (Harvey 1988: 130), this was reflected in poor examination performance and consequent disillusionment with the subject which saw the disappearance of Japanese in some schools. In response to the problem, a number of schools stopped allowing students to begin their study of Japanese at sixth-form level as early as 1978. Falling general rolls in secondary schools, with the departure of New Zealand's 'baby boom' generation by the late-1970s, meant that subjects like Japanese with small numbers contracted further, became uneconomical to staff, and had to be discarded. In schools with fewer than ten students taking Japanese and serviced by an itinerant teacher, the situation tended to be highly unstable anyway and would fluctuate from year to year.

Personal communications from the MFA also indicated that the supply and quality of teachers affected the decline in numbers at this time. Teachers of Japanese were not always available where there was a demand for Japanese. Often, when teachers moved away from a school they could not be replaced; in many cases the result was a decline in the interest in Japanese in the school. Compounding the problem of teacher supply in the early 1980s was the loss of a high proportion of student teachers of Japanese to other employment. The limited linguistic skill in Japanese of New Zealand teachers also hampered the early Japanese language situation, with the minimum requirement for teaching being only one year's part-time university study of Japanese. In addition, teachers of Japanese could also be teachers of other foreign languages, most often European languages, which require different learning and teaching skills (Scott 2014: 190). Being a skilled French teacher, for example, did not necessarily mean that a person would also be a good teacher of Japanese.

Despite these problems, the mid-1980s saw a considerable expansion in secondary school students taking Japanese at all levels. However, some thought the increase came too late (Harvey 1988: 132). Ideally, significant numbers of New Zealanders should have been learning Japanese prior to the mid-1970s' boom in political and economic contacts. It was also a concern that at the very time ties with Japan were becoming significant for New Zealand, in the late 1970s and early 1980s, the numbers of Japanese-language learners in New Zealand secondary schools actually dropped. This produced a shortage of Japanese speakers in the work force and universities in the years that followed. Moreover, the total number of secondary students taking Japanese in the mid-1980s still only amounted to around 1.7% of the total secondary school population (Levett and Adams 1987: section 5.6); and many of the problems associated with teaching Japanese in New Zealand, in terms of staffing, funding and resources, continued.

Building Teacher Capacity: New Zealand–Japan Teacher Exchanges

As Japan's significance to New Zealand became increasingly apparent, the effort to build Japanese skills came from a number of quarters. New Zealand MFA records indicate their role in coordinating a 'hands together' (Easton 1999: 54) approach to dealing with Japan. When Prime Minister Tanaka visited in October 1974 the Tanaka-Rowling Cultural Agreement was signed and this resulted in the establishment of the New Zealand Japan Exchange Programme (NZJEP), which instituted, along with the Japan Foundation and the Japanese Ministry of Education, reciprocal educational and cultural exchanges. These exchanges proved to be an important factor in the professional development of New Zealand teachers of Japanese as well as in providing models of native-speaker Japanese in New Zealand schools.

From the late 1970s, teacher exchanges took 50% and sometimes more of the annual NZJEP budget (Harvey 1988: 125).[6] New Zealand teachers on exchange in Japanese schools were able to improve their competence in the Japanese language, and to develop a more accurate and in-depth perception of the country and people. On a teacher's return to New Zealand, experiences and skills could be passed on to students. While in Japan the New Zealand teachers helped the Japanese school's English programme and considerably increased staff and student awareness of New Zealand.

An agreement for the direct exchange of secondary teachers between the New Zealand and Japanese educational authorities was in operation from 1979.[7] The Japanese Ministry of Education first sent a teacher to New Zealand under the programme in that year and sent replacements for a number of years. New Zealand was not able to reciprocate until 1983 (Department of Education 1984: 5), as the NZJEP found themselves financially overcommitted and could not afford to fund a New Zealand teacher in Japan for the first few years. When the money was available, finding teachers willing to take part in the exchange was a challenge.

There were also challenging situations with Japanese teachers sent to New Zealand under the exchange. The teachers attended a two-week course, prior to their departure for New Zealand, on 'Teaching Japanese as a Foreign Language'. However, they were given minimal briefings on what to expect in terms of culture shock, their range of teaching responsibilities and the differences between New Zealand and Japanese secondary schools. Because of a lack of money, the orientation period in New Zealand for the teachers was also inadequate.[8] The result was that Japanese teachers generally did not cope well in New Zealand classrooms. Particular problems included discipline in the classroom (not being able to control a class or being too strict); difficulties with proficiency in English; and differing expectations of teaching duties.[9] In some years the Japanese exchange teacher was expected to take over a full range of teaching responsibilities, including, sometimes, teaching technical subjects in English. As the Japanese Ministry of Education made clear to the New Zealand Education Department, it was not reasonable to expect the Japanese teacher to teach anything but Japanese language and culture.[10] In a few cases where Japanese teachers did not manage classes effectively, the number of Japanese language learners dropped off. It took the return of the New Zealand teacher to remedy the situation, thus demonstrating the need to build up the number of New Zealand teachers of Japanese.[11]

For its part, from 1979 the Japan Foundation sent four or five New Zealand teachers of Japanese to Tokyo annually to attend an intensive two-month language course (Harvey 1988: 152). The teachers were taught methods of language instruction; they were able to collect materials for the classroom; and they also learned how the Japanese education system worked. The visits were well-funded and helped the ongoing task of raising the level of Japanese-language teaching in New Zealand. The Foundation also held an annual training program in New Zealand for New Zealand teachers of Japanese. During the 1980s the Japan Foundation sent a considerable number of educational resources to New Zealand including videos, books and Japanese typewriters (Harvey 1988: 153). Throughout the 1980s New Zealand did comparatively well on a per capita basis from the Japan Foundation (established by the Japanese government in 1972), possibly receiving about four times the expenditure on Japanese language education (per head of population) compared to Australia (Harvey 1988: 92). Nevertheless, the Japanese worked in close cooperation with New Zealand educational authorities, particularly the Department of Education, in allocating available funds. At this time, the height of Japanese economic success, Japan was aware of the danger of being seen to 'overdo' things and laying themselves open to accusations of cultural imperialism (Harvey 1988: 92).

Further Developments

Through the late 1980s and early 1990s, and building on all the efforts that had been made in the preceding decades, the number of students taking Japanese increased steadily, peaking at 25,783 in 1996 (Ministry of Education 1997). At around the same time, more schools introduced Japanese as an optional language (Japan Foundation 2000: 6). The popularity of Japanese at the secondary level then declined after the mid-1990s but Japanese kept its place as New Zealand's second most (or, for a few years in the 1990s, most) popular subject language in secondary schools for nearly thirty years. In 2015, however, with Japanese numbers at 10,843 and Spanish numbers at 11,464, secondary learners of Spanish surpassed Japanese learners (although both were dropping) (Ministry of Education 2015). The decline in secondary learners has been attributed, at least to some extent, to a downturn in the Japanese economy (McLauchlan 2007: 39), along with the rising popularity of Chinese and Spanish (Ministry of Education 2015). The rise, and now steady decline, of Japanese in the New Zealand education system mirrors the path that Japanese has taken in Australia and other countries (de Kretser and Spence-Brown 2010: 11; Japan Foundation 2012: 5).

The wave of popularity Japanese has had in New Zealand education can be attributed to an increasing economic profile, Japan's status as a major global and Asian power, and a historical relationship which has been longer and more substantial than New Zealand's connections with other Asian countries. Also contributing to the rise, however, has been strong government encouragement from quarters not always associated with subject languages in schools. The records of the New Zealand MFA (Harvey 1988: 148–51) show how interested and active the Ministry was in supporting Japanese-language education in New Zealand and how officials worked in tandem with the New Zealand Department of Education and through the NZJEP to encourage Japanese in New Zealand schools. On the Japanese side, the role of government and quasi-governmental organizations, namely the Ministry of Education and the Japan Foundation, were important in promoting the relationship.

For all the effort, however, mistakes were made. Throughout the 1980s, the period Japanese language was being established in New Zealand secondary schools, the New Zealand political climate was undergoing major shifts towards what has been characterized as neo-liberal governance (Kelsey 1995: 293). A lack of overall coordination in New Zealand's somewhat deregulated 'Tomorrow's Schools' (Butterworth and Butterworth 1998: 117) meant that infrastructure, language-teacher professional development, language learning pathways and funding probably needed much more planning and management compared to what actually happened. The period therefore provides both positive and negative lessons for other jurisdictions looking to build national proficiency in one or more subject languages.

Recently, Oshima and Harvey (2017: 503–04) have observed that as Japanese-language education established its status in New Zealand, a variety of issues were raised and discussed. These included:

1. High student attrition rates at an early stage of learning, both at secondary and tertiary levels (e.g. Holt 2006: 87);
2. An inadequate level of proficiency reached by students in Japanese by the end of secondary school (Harvey 1988: 154–55);
3. A lack of curriculum continuity between secondary and tertiary institutions (East, Shackleford and Spence 2007: 23; Haugh 1997: 10), as well as between secondary schools (Haugh 1997) due to differences between course curricula at each school;
4. A lack of advanced Japanese teaching (Harvey 1988; Trotter 1985);
5. A shortage of suitably qualified secondary teachers (Guthrie 2005: 53–54; Haugh 1997: 10)
6. The presence of native Japanese speakers in senior Japanese classes at secondary level, which has made it difficult for other students to achieve high grades (Haugh 1997: 10; McLauchlan 2007: 39–41);
7. Combined classes for different levels of proficiency due to insufficient/uneconomical numbers of students at each level (McLauchlan 2007: 37).

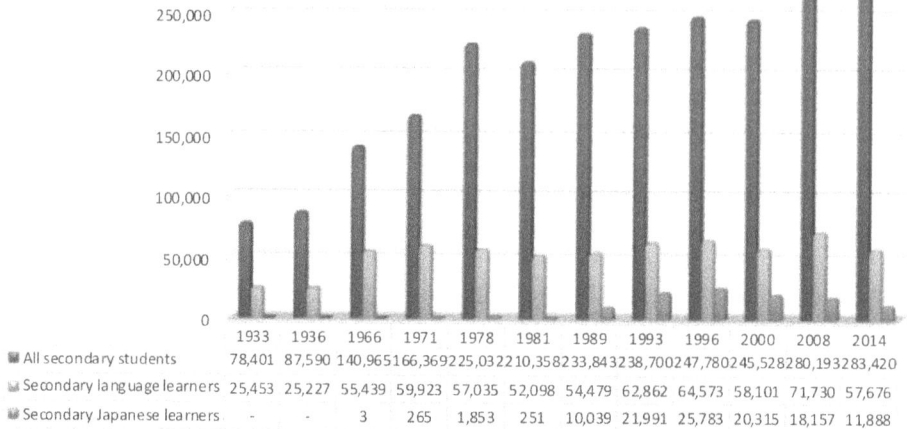

	1933	1936	1966	1971	1978	1981	1989	1993	1996	2000	2008	2014
All secondary students	78,401	87,590	140,965	166,369	225,032	210,358	233,843	238,700	247,780	245,528	280,193	283,420
Secondary language learners	25,453	25,227	55,439	59,923	57,035	52,098	54,479	62,862	64,573	58,101	71,730	57,676
Secondary Japanese learners	-	-	3	265	1,853	251	10,039	21,991	25,783	20,315	18,157	11,888

FIG. 17.2. Comparison of the Number of Secondary School Students, Secondary Language Learners and Secondary Learners of Japanese (Department of Education 1967: 32, 1972: 31, 1979: 40, 1983: 10, 23; Education: Primary and Post-primary Education, 1934: 34, 43; Education: Primary and Post-primary Education, 1937: 40, 49; Ministry of Education 1990: 39, 1994: 54, 2015: data file)

Many of these issues were identified more than three decades ago (Harvey 1988: 126–35), most are still unchanged and many are interrelated. The severe decrease in secondary students in New Zealand learning *all* subject languages over the last six years (Ministry of Education 2015) could be a testament to the fact that the issues above need to be attended to even more urgently than previously (see Figure 17.2).

What seems to have been missing in New Zealand's development of Japanese-language education over the long term is oversight and coordination from the Ministry of Education. The promotion of Japanese in many cases was left to schools themselves. Where there was enthusiasm and sufficient budget Japanese was able to thrive, but once this disappeared there were no underpinning educational or policy requirements to maintain Japanese (or any other subject language) in schools (Oshima 2012: 14). The array of problems with Japanese in secondary schools examined by Oshima and Harvey (2017: 509–13) are symptomatic of a lack of centralized responsibility for languages in New Zealand.

Conclusion

The wave of Japanese language learning in New Zealand secondary schools over the last fifty years is a story of boom and bust. Numbers grew through the 1970s, dropped momentarily in the early 1980s and then rose exponentially through the late 1980s to a peak of 25,783 secondary students in 1996. At this time Japanese surpassed French in secondary schools. However, numbers have declined markedly in the ensuing twenty years.

An examination of the history of Japanese in New Zealand secondary schools shows that it was introduced largely for instrumental reasons in the 1960s. The promise of a rising Japanese economy coupled with the imminent entry of Britain to the European Common Market saw New Zealand scanning the world for trading partners to replace the dominance of Britain as an export market for New Zealand agricultural goods. New Zealand had been at war with Japan only twenty years earlier but a growing recognition of Japan's economic and political role in the Pacific especially, along with a small but perhaps surprising array of people-to-people contacts in areas such as the martial arts, sports and fledgling sister-city relationships bolstered the arguments for Japanese in New Zealand schools. As the sources referred to in this chapter attest, the New Zealand Ministry of Foreign Affairs was an important player in building Japanese-language education. The Ministry linked itself deliberately to the Department of Education's work in developing Japanese, most notably (but not only) through the activities of the NZJEP. Alongside these efforts were the substantial contributions of Japanese organizations like the Ministry of Education and the Japan Foundation, both guided by a sensitive post-war Japanese foreign diplomacy.

As noted in the earlier part of this chapter, Japan is still an important country regionally and globally. Many young people are more interested in Japan for cultural reasons (Kawamura 2012: 1) than for economic reasons and so motivations for learning Japanese may be less instrumental than they once were. Moreover, the Japanese diaspora has risen quite swiftly in New Zealand and Japanese nationals now number 14,118 (Statistics New Zealand 2013), providing some demand for Japanese as a community language. After fifty years of secondary Japanese-language education in New Zealand and at a time when it would be beneficial to have at least one strongly embedded Asian language in New Zealand schools, it seems wasteful that numbers are decreasing so rapidly.

Some studies suggest that the status of English as a global language and an international lingua franca dissuades students in English-speaking countries from learning a subject language (Dörnyei and Ushioda 2011: 71–72). Ideas that 'English is enough' and that languages are more difficult than other subjects, particularly when in publicly monolingual societies languages do not seem to provide an employable skill even at the end of university study (Oshima 2012: 42), appear to be mitigating against language study. Japanese, then, may well have suffered also from this global turn to English.

This chapter serves as a tale of warning to other English-dominant countries tempted to leave the learning of languages to the schooling 'market place'. Languages, and perhaps especially Asian languages, given their relatively great 'language distance' from English (Elder and Davies 1998: 5), need long-term support from educational authorities. The 'hands together' (Easton 1999: 54) approach of the 1970s and 1980s, which saw a very interested foreign-affairs involvement in Japanese language-education in New Zealand, needed to be carried through to the heart of education planning. To avoid the wave of secondary Japanese-language education crashing on the shore, educational leadership and administration in languages should have — but unfortunately has not — stayed strong and interested in the fate of all languages in New Zealand secondary schools and in this case, particularly, Japanese.

Bibliography

BUTTERWORTH, G., and S. BUTTERWORTH. 1998. *Reforming Education: The New Zealand Experience, 1984–1996* (Palmerston North: Dunmore)

CRYSTAL, D., and R. H. ROBINS. 2015. 'Language', in *Encyclopædia Britannica* <http://www.britannica.com/EBchecked/topic/329791/language/292862/Most-widely-spoken-languages> [accessed 15 February 2018]

DEPARTMENT OF EDUCATION. 1967. *Education Statistics of New Zealand for 1966* (Wellington: Department of Education)

——. 1970. *Asian Language Teaching in New Zealand: 1970 and Predictions for 1971* (Wellington: Curriculum Development Unit)

——. 1972. *Education Statistics of New Zealand for 1971* (Wellington: Department of Education)

——. 1974. *Asian Language Teaching in New Zealand* (Wellington: Curriculum Development Unit)

——. 1979. *Education Statistics of New Zealand for 1978* (Wellington: Department of Education)

——. 1983. *Asian Language Survey in New Zealand School and Tertiary Institutions, as at August 1983* (Wellington: Department of Education)

——. 1984. *New Zealand — Japan Exchange Programme: New Zealand Report, 1983–1984* (Wellington: Department of Education)

DÖRNYEI, Z., and E. USHIODA. 2011 [2001]. *Teaching and Researching Motivation*, 2nd edn (Harlow: Pearson)

EAST, M., N. SHACKLEFORD, and G. SPENCE. 2007. 'Promoting a Multilingual Future for Aotearoa/New Zealand', *Journal of Asian Pacific Communication*, 17: 11-28

EASTON, B. 1999. 'Hands Together', *The New Zealand Listener*, February 27, p. 54

Education: Primary and Post-primary Education. 1934. *Appendix to the Journals of the House of Representatives* (Session I, E-02) <http://atojs.natlib.govt.nz/> [accessed 15 February 2018]

Education: Primary and Post-primary Education. 1937. *Appendix to the Journals of the House of Representatives* (Session I, E-02) <http://atojs.natlib.govt.nz/> [accessed 15 February 2018]

ELDER, C., and A. DAVIES. 1998. 'Performance on ESL Examinations: Is There a Language Distance Effect?', *Language and Education*, 12: 1-17

GUTHRIE, J. 2005. '"Have you got a Japanese teacher up your sleeve?" New Zealand Principals' Perceptions of Language Teacher Supply', *New Zealand Studies in Applied Linguistics*, 11 (2): 43-58

HARVEY, S. 1988. 'The Third Dimension: Cultural Relations between New Zealand and Japan in the Post-War Period' (unpublished Master's thesis, University of Auckland)

HAUGH, M. 1997. *The Teaching of Japanese in New Zealand: A National Profile* (Auckland: Institute of Language Teaching and Learning)

HOKUSAI, K. 1830. *Hokusai's Wave off Kanagawa* [Colour Woodblock] (New York Metropolitan Museum of Art) <https://www.metmuseum.org/art/collection/search/45434> [accessed 2 November 2017]

HOLT, R. F. 2006. 'Persistence Factors in Secondary School Additional Language Study', *Journal of Language and Learning*, 5: 86-97

'Japanese to be taught in schools'. 1918. *Evening Post* (Wellington), 2 April 1918, p. 7

JAPAN FOUNDATION. 2000. *Present Condition of Overseas Japanese-language Education: Survey Report on Japanese-language Education Abroad 1998 summary* <http://www.jpf.go.jp/j/japanese/survey/result/dl/e_gaiyou.pdf > [accessed 9 February 2018]

——. 2012. *Survey Report on Japanese Language Education Abroad* <http://www.jpf.go.jp/j/japanese/survey/result/dl/survey_2012/2012_s_excerpt_e.pdf> [accessed 9 February 2018]

KAWAMURA, Y. 2012. *Fashioning Japanese Subcultures* (London: Berg)

KELSEY, J. 1995. *The New Zealand Experiment: A World Model for Structural Adjustment* (Auckland: Auckland University Press; Bridget Williams Books)

KING, M. 2011. *The Penguin History of New Zealand* (Auckland: Penguin)

DE KRETSER, A. D., and R. SPENCE-BROWN. 2010. *The Current State of Japanese Language Education in Australian Schools* (Carlton South: Education Services Australia) <http://pandora.nla.gov.au/pan/121288/20100713–1124/www.deewr.gov.au/> [accessed 9 February 2018]

LEVETT, A., and A. ADAMS. 1987. *Catching up with our Future: The Demand for Japan Skills in New Zealand. A Report to the New Zealand Japan Foundation and the Department of Education* (Wellington: The Foundation)

MCLAUCHLAN, A. 2007. *The Negative L2 Climate: Understanding Attrition among Second Language Students* (Palmerston North: The Sasakawa Fellowship Fund for Japanese Language Education)

MINISTRY OF EDUCATION. 1990. *Education Statistics of New Zealand for 1989* (Wellington: Ministry of Education) <http://www.educationcounts.govt.nz/publications/series/2507/edstats_nz_04> [accessed 9 February 2018]

——. 1994. *Education Statistics of New Zealand for 1993* (Wellington: Ministry of Education) <http://www.educationcounts.govt.nz/publications/series/2507/edstats_nz_04> [accessed 9 February 2018]

——. 1997. *Education Statistics of New Zealand for 1996* (Wellington: Ministry of Education) <http://www.educationcounts.govt.nz/publications/tertiary_education/Education_Statistics_of_New_Zealand/edstats_nz_89–03> [accessed 9 February 2018]

——. 2015. *Secondary Subjects by Student Gender & Year Level, 1996–2014* (Wellington: Ministry of Education) <http://www.educationcounts.govt.nz/statistics/schooling/student-numbers/subject-enrolment> [accessed 9 February 2018]

MONAHAN, A. 2011. 'China Overtakes Japan as World's No. 2 Economy', *The Wall Street Journal*, February 14 <http://www.wsj.com/articles/SB10001424052748703361904576142832741439402> [accessed 15 February 2018]

NIGRO, P. [N.D.]. 'Off Kanagawa: Isolation, Identity, and Immortality in Hokusai's Great Wave', *ArtHistory.US* <http://arthistory.us/display.php?eid=31> [accessed 15 February 2018]

NORTHEY, H. 1988. *Auckland Girls' Grammar School: The First Hundred Years, 1888–1988* (Auckland: Auckland Grammar School Old Girls' Association)

OSHIMA, R. 2012. 'An investigation into the reasons of discontinuance of Japanese amongst first year tertiary students who have studied Japanese to Year 13 at Secondary School Study' (unpublished Master's thesis, Auckland University of technology) <http://hdl.handle.net/10292/4501> [accessed 15 February 2018]

——, and S. HARVEY. 2017. '"Japanese and the major are incompatible": Institutional Reasons for Dropping Japanese at the Transition from Secondary to Tertiary Education', *The Language Learning Journal*, 45.4: 499–517 <http://www.tandfonline.com/doi/abs/10.1080/09571736.2014.963643> [accessed 15 February 2018]

'Pioneering exchange programmes in Hokkaido'. 1981. *Daily Yomiuri*, 10 September

SCOTT, A. 2014. 'Teachers of Additional Languages in New Zealand Schools: A National Survey and Case Studies' (unpublished doctoral thesis, Massey University)

SMIALEK, R. 1990. *Governing the Market: Economic Theory and the Role of Government in East Asian Industrialization* (Princeton, NJ: Princeton University Press)

——. 2015. 'These Will Be the World's 20 Largest Economies in 2030', *Bloomberg Business* <http://www.bloomberg.com/news/articles/2015–04–10/the-world-s-20-largest-economies-in-2030> [accessed 15 February 2018]

'Speaking Japanese essential for trade matters'. 1963. *Dominion*, 16 April

STATISTICS NEW ZEALAND. 2013. *Statistics for Ethnic Group*. [Census ethnic groups profiles: Japanese]   <http://www.stats.govt.nz/Census/2013-census/profile-and-summary-reports/ethnic profiles.aspx?request_value=24753&parent_id=24726& tabname=#24753> [accessed 22 August 2016]

SWARBRICK, N. 2012. 'Primary and Secondary Education — Education from 1840 to 1918', *Te Ara — the Encyclopedia of New Zealand* <http://www.teara.govt.nz/en/primary-and-secondary-education/page-2> [accessed 15 February 2018]

TREASURY. 2014. *New Zealand Economic and Financial Overview 2014* <http://www.treasury.govt.nz/economy/overview/2014/18.htm> [accessed 15 February 2018]

TROTTER, A. 1985. 'Quest for Interdependence', *New Zealand International Affairs Review*, 10 (1): 8–11

WADE, R. 1990. *Governing the Market: Economic Theory and the Role of Government in East Asian Industrialisation* (Princeton, NJ: Princeton University Press)

WELLS, P. F. 1985. *Twenty First Anniversary of the Japan Society of Waikato Keynote Speech* (Wellington: Department of Education)

YOSHIKAWA, T. 2013. 'China becomes the world's top-ranking nation of Japanese-language learning', *Wochi Kochi Magazine*, 37 <http://www.wochikochi.jp/english/special/2013/12/china-becomes-the-worlds-top-ranking-nation-of-japanese-language-learning.php> [accessed 15 February 2018]

Notes to Chapter 17

1. I am grateful to Yulia Zelenkova, Kristie Elphick and Dr Moneeta Pal, who compiled the table and figures and helped with referencing and formatting for this chapter. In addition I would like to thank the anonymous reviewers, who have provided invaluable suggestions.

2. New Zealand University Bursary was the national qualification gained by seventh form/Year 13 students. It was replaced by the National Certificate in Educational Achievement (NCEA) Level 3 in 2004.

3. New Zealand School Certificate was the national qualification gained by fifth form/Year 11 students. It was replaced by NCEA Level 1 in 2002.

4. New Zealand University Entrance was the qualification gained by sixth form/Year 12 students and served as the minimum qualification for entering university. It was replaced by NCEA Level 2 in 2002.

5. New Zealand Sixth Form Certificate was an internally assessed qualification for sixth form (Year 12) students, enabling schools to provide a wider range of subjects beyond the academic subjects offered for University Entrance. It was replaced by NCEA Level 2 in 2002.

6. Interview with Ms N. Collins, International Division, Department of Education, 4 September 1986. During the years 1983 to 1987, Naomi Collins served as Secretary to the NZJEP within the International Division of the then Department of Education.

7. Personal communication from the MFA, 14 February 1979, cited in Harvey 1988: 149.

8. N. Collins, personal communication, 4 September 1986, cited in Harvey 1988: 150.

9. MFA, 26 June 1980, cited in Harvey 1988: 150.

10. MFA, personal communication, 3 December 1981, cited in Harvey 1988: 151.

11. N. Collins, personal communication, 4 September 1986, cited in Harvey 1988: 151.

INDEX

❖

This is a composite index to the three volumes of the History. References are to volume and page number: e.g., '3.116' refers to page 116 of volume 3. Where a locator refers to a chapter in French rather than English text, it is italicized.

www.ingramcontent.com/pod-product-compliance
Lightning Source LLC
Chambersburg PA
CBHW080541090426
42734CB00016B/3167